MW00389030

Orienting of Attention

Orienting of Attention

Richard D. Wright

Lawrence M. Ward

UNIVERSITY PRESS

2008

Oxford University Press, Inc., publishes works that further
Oxford University's objective of excellence
in research, scholarship, and education.

Oxford New York
Auckland Cape Town Dar es Salaam Hong Kong Karachi
Kuala Lumpur Madrid Melbourne Mexico City Nairobi
New Delhi Shanghai Taipei Toronto

With offices in
Argentina Austria Brazil Chile Czech Republic France Greece
Guatemala Hungary Italy Japan Poland Portugal Singapore
South Korea Switzerland Thailand Turkey Ukraine Vietnam

Published by Oxford University Press, Inc.
198 Madison Avenue, New York, New York 10016

www.oup.com

Library of Congress Cataloging-in-Publication Data

Wright, Richard D., 1956-
Orienting of attention/Richard D. Wright and Lawrence M. Ward.
p. cm.
Includes bibliographical references and index.
ISBN 978-0-19-513049-2
1. Attention. 2. Visual perception. I. Ward, Lawrence M. II. Title.
BF321.W75 2008
153.7'33—dc22
2007033087

9 8 7 6 5 4 3 2 1

Printed in the United States of America
on acid-free paper

In memory of G. Keith Humphrey
— scholar and wonderful friend

Foreword

Michael I. Posner
University of Oregon

In 1979, I was asked to give the 7th Sir Frederick Bartlett lecture to the Experimental Psychology Society meeting in Oxford (Posner, 1980). Because I had been greatly influenced by Bartlett's work and the previous lecturers in this series had been so prominent, I wanted to say something of importance. It was a fortunate time because for the last few years we had been studying orienting of attention to visual locations. I was particularly pleased with the finding that attention could be summoned to one location by a cue that informed the person that the target would come at a different location. For the first 100–200 ms the shift to the cue improved target reaction time (RT) at the cued location, but after 200 ms attention went to the most probable location and target detection RT improved there and became worse at the location of the cue. I thought we had trapped a covert reflexive attention shift to the cue and a voluntary shift to the probable target location, all without any shift of the eyes and in less than half a second. I had two hopes about this work. First, it would be possible to connect these purely cognitive studies to the cellular work of Vernon Mountcastle (1978) and of Robert Wurtz (Wurtz et al., 1980), suggesting an important role for parietal and collicular neurons in visual attention. Second was to use visual attention as a model for how attention in other domains might operate. Nearly 30 years later, this book tells the full story of what has been learned about and from the study of such shifts of visual attention.

Orienting of Attention represents an impressive, nearly encyclopaedic, survey of attention shifts, and their relation to the underlying brain anatomy and to the eye movement system. To me, what is most amazing about the story that unfolds in these pages is the close links between the observed behavior, such as either increased or decreased speed of target processing, and the underlying neural systems involved. A behavioral change in speed at the cued location occurs as the result of a set of specific changes in a largely agreed upon set of neural areas that serve as the sources of the attentional influence on targets (Corbetta & Shulman, 2002; Hillyard et al., 2004). The operation of this orienting network results in a shift in the baseline activity, as measured by cellular recording, EEG or fMRI, within the visual systems at the location indicated by the cue (Desimone & Duncan, 1995). These very specific neural changes that accompany the attention shift result in a priority, as indexed by reaction time, for the cued location. If at one time attention was a subjective concept explained by a vague inexplicable limited resource, at least within the domain of shifts of visual attention, that is no longer true.

This book also documents the important effort to model attention shifts. The models have progressed from crude metaphors of spotlights or zoom lens through explicit efforts to develop mathematical predictions (LaBerge, 1995). Explicit models not only summarize the data that exist, but also allow the user to make new and perhaps unanticipated findings.

The close anatomical relation between visual attention shifts and eye movements have led many to conclude that attention involves incipient eye movements that may or may not be expressed. This idea is behind Rizzolatti's popular premotor theory of attention shifts (Rizzolatti et al., 1987). The book gives careful coverage to all opinions on this issue and raises some critical points against too ready an acceptance of a purely premotor view.

It is somewhat ironic that modern work on attention was first summarized in detail in Broadbent's book *Perception and Communication* (Broadbent, 1958), which presented evidence for experiments involving separate messages to the two ears. Fifty years later this volume deals mostly with the visual system, but in one chapter it stresses the similarity of attention shifts in various sensory modalities, implying some commonalities in the attentional mechanisms regardless of the sensory system.

In the Bartlett lecture, I began with general issues about thinking as a skill which Bartlett had raised in his book entitled *Thinking* (Bartlett, 1958). I had hoped that the study of visual shifts would reveal common mechanisms that could be studied in the limited domain of orienting to sensory events but might transfer to attention as related to skilled performance and to our ability to keep a central program in the face of distraction. In this volume, these more general issues are only raised briefly in the epilogue. The final chapter discusses the use of social cues, the nature of volition, and the physiology of attention networks underlying alertness and executive control. I believe the methods and results so beautifully analyzed in this book can provide progress on understanding how attention develops, its significance in controlling thoughts and feelings, and how it illuminates pathology. If attention studies do transfer so widely, reading this volume may be useful to many who may only have a slight interest in visual shifts of attention, but hope that the integration of methods and the results obtained may be of use in other areas of attention and indeed in psychology as a whole (Posner & Rothbart, 2007).

References

Bartlett, F. C. (1958). *Thinking: An experimental and social study*. London: George Allen & Unwin.

Broadbent, D. E. (1958). *Perception and communication*. New York: Pergamon Press.

Corbetta, M., & Shulman, G. L. (2002). Control of goal-directed and stimulus-driven attention in the brain. *Nature Reviews Neuroscience, 3*, 215–229.

Desimone, R., & Duncan, J. (1995). Neural mechanisms of selective visual attention. *Annual Review of Neuroscience, 18*, 193–222.

Hillyard, S. A., Di Russo, F., & Martinez, A. (2004). The imaging of visual attention. In N. Kanwisher & J. Duncan (Eds.), *Attention and performance* (Vol. 20, pp. 381–390). New York: Oxford University Press.

LaBerge, D. (1995). *Attentional processing: The brain's art of mindfulness*. Cambridge, MA: Harvard University Press.

Mountcastle, V. M. (1978). The world around us: Neural command functions for selective attention. *Neuroscience Research Progress Bulletin, 14*(Suppl), 1–47.

Posner, M. I. (1980). Orienting of attention: The 7th Sir F. C. Bartlett Lecture. *Quarterly Journal of Experimental Psychology, 32*, 3–25.

Posner, M. I., & Rothbart, M. K. (2007). Research on attention networks as a model for the integration of psychological science. *Annual Review of Psychology, 58*, 1–23.

Rizzolatti, G., Riggio, L., Dascola, I., & Umiltà, C. (1987). Reorienting of attention across the horizontal and vertical meridians: Evidence in favor of a premotor theory of attention. *Neuropsychologia, 25*, 31–40.

Wurtz, R. H., Goldberg, M. E., & Robinson, D. L. (1980). Behavioral modulation of visual responses in the monkey. *Progress in Psychobiology & Physiological Psychology, 9*, 43–83.

Preface

Reading and learning about a rapidly growing area of science is challenging. Methodologies are constantly changing and, for readers of cognitive neuroscience, it is no longer enough to just keep up with refinements to data collection and analysis methods. New techniques are also being introduced on an increasingly regular basis for measuring brain activity and for interpreting those measurements. This is particularly true of the attention orienting literature. It may seem intimidating to those just starting to read it. And keeping up with this literature can also be a daunting task, even for those who actively contribute to it.

This book is for both the newcomers and the active contributors. Our goal has been to make covert orienting more accessible by describing it in terms of a framework that emphasizes methodology but also makes contact with the most up-to-date advances in our understanding of how the brain implements cognition. In some ways, the book is like a traveler's guide. We begin with an historical overview (which is important to both travelers and scientists). Much of the current literature on covert orienting has its roots in the 19th century, even though this often goes unsaid (and is perhaps underappreciated) by contemporary researchers. We also focus on areas of growth and rapid change, which is perhaps most interesting to those who are quite familiar with the literature (just as a travel guide is also tailored to those who visit a destination frequently). And in keeping with the travel guide analogy, we include lots of illustrations. You will find one wherever we felt that it could improve the clarity of the discussion.

What is not in this book? One aspect of attention we do not discuss in detail is visual search. We also do not spend much time in reviewing topics such as attentional blink, change blindness, automaticity, and divided attention. Instead, we focus almost exclusively on covert orienting. Other aspects of attention are brought into the discussion only to the extent that they are related to attention shifts. And even with regard to covert orienting, this is by necessity a selective review. Space constraints limited what we could discuss, and we had to exclude some research that, though important in other ways, did not contribute directly to the story we wished to tell.

Much of what is covered in this book grew from research and ideas developed by Michael Posner. He is perhaps the central figure and dominant influence in the field, and the title of the book, *Orienting of Attention*, is also the title of Posner's seminal 1980 article that was the catalyst for this field of research. We are grateful for his comprehensive review of an earlier draft of the book, and honored that he agreed to write the foreword.

We also thank the many others who helped us, and particularly Hermann Müller, David LaBerge, Zenon Pylyshyn, Peter McCormick, John McDonald, and Michael Silver; and we take sole responsibility for any errors of fact or interpretation that remain. In addition, we thank our editor, Catharine Carlin, for her patience and skill and encouragement. Perhaps most of all, we are grateful to Christian Richard. He designed and conducted several of the experiments discussed in chapter 4, created illustrations that served as templates for many of the figures in that chapter, and also played a major role in the development of a sensory activity distribution account of multiple location cueing effects. Finally, we thank our wives, Arlene Wright and Brigitte Renahte Ward, for their love, their support, and for enduring, usually with equanimity, the travails of living with academics who often were preoccupied by intellectual tasks.

Contents

Orienting of Attention

1

Introduction

People have known for millennia that, if we make the effort, we can shift our attention slightly to the side of where our eyes are pointing. Aristotle talked about it. It was also a common part of early introspective psychology (Wundt, 1912, p. 20). Lay terms for this are "using peripheral vision" and "looking out of the corner of the eye."

Hermann von Helmholtz was particularly interested in how we are able to concentrate attention on a portion of the visual field other than where our eyes are pointing. While known more generally for his work on human perceptual processing, Helmholtz was also a pioneer of attention research. During the period between 1842 and 1894, Helmholtz published more than 200 papers and books. He was a physician by training, a physicist, and a remarkable innovator. With the aid of his invention, the ophthalmoscope, Helmholtz was the first person to see inside the human eye. His ophthalmometer, the first device to allow precise measurements of lens curvature and reflected images in the eye, is still used today.

Helmholtz's Study of Attention Shifting

Helmholtz had a gift for improvisation when constructing models for optical work, and would sometimes use household materials such as his wife's thread spools, his children's building blocks, bits of string, and candle wax. It was this ingenuity that enabled him to conduct what is considered to be the first scientific investigation of our capacity to shift attention between different locations in the visual field.

The device Helmholtz constructed to study attention shifting was essentially a type of tachistoscope (a device for presenting visual stimuli for brief durations; see Wade, 2004; Wade & Heller, 1997). As described in his *Treatise on Physiological Optics* (1867/1925), he made a wooden box and painted the interior black. Holes in one side of the box were for the view point, and a hole in the opposite side allowed exterior light to pass through a small pinhole in the center of a stimulus display card (see Figure 1.1). The pinhole

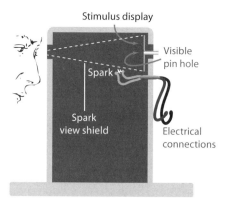

Figure 1.1 Depiction of the apparatus Helmholtz constructed to study our ability to shift attention independently of eye fixation. There were view holes in one side of the box and a hole on the opposite side for exterior light to pass through a pinhole in the stimulus display. Illumination of the display occurred when Helmholtz triggered a spark from an induction coil. Light from the spark was shielded from the observer's eyes by a strip of cardboard.

was the only visible light source inside the box. When Helmholtz wanted to fully illuminate the stimulus display, he triggered a spark produced by an induction coil connected to a Leyden jar (an electrical source commonly used in 19th-century experimentation). And, as seen in Figure 1.1, a strip of cardboard in the center of the box acted as a shield that prevented the spark's light from getting into the observer's eyes. This technique of limiting stimulus display duration with a brief period of illumination is sometimes called tachistoscopic presentation.

The stimulus display card had letters printed on it, as in Figure 1.2, and the illuminated pinhole in its center served as a fixation point for Helmholtz's eyes. When the display was darkened, the letter stimuli were imperceptible. When momentarily illuminated by the spark, however, portions of the display were visible and remained briefly in view in the form of a positive after-image. The period of illumination was so short that there was not enough time for him to make an eye movement while the display was visible. And any eye movements Helmholtz made after the illumination did not change the position of the after-image on his retinae. To our knowledge, this was the first technique devised to study the capacity to shift attention independently of ocular focus.

An important aspect of this demonstration was that Helmholtz continually fixed his eyes on the central pinhole and did not move them away from this location. Then, prior to triggering the spark, he decided which part of the darkened display he wanted to concentrate his attention on. During the brief period of illumination, those letters in the area where attention had been concentrated were most identifiable. In contrast, letters in the vicinity

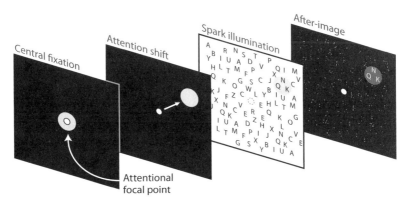

Figure 1.2 Depiction of the stimulus display Helmholtz used to study attention shifts. His attention was initially focused on the illuminated pinhole in the center of the darkened display. Then, prior to illuminating it with a spark, Helmholtz chose a peripheral part of the display to shift his attention to. He discovered that letters were most perceptible at the position attention had been shifted to.

of the ocular fixation point were difficult for him to identify. This was a particularly surprising result, given that stimuli are usually easiest to identify at the location that our eyes point to. What Helmholtz had demonstrated was that, when their locations do not coincide, visual analysis required for object identification appears to depend on attentional focus more than on ocular focus (see Figure 1.3).

Helmholtz concluded that we can voluntarily and selectively concentrate attention on a stimulus at a particular location without making eye movements (adjusting ocular focus) while at the same time excluding

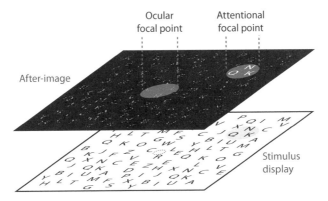

Figure 1.3 Helmholtz's demonstration of the independence of the attentional and ocular focal points. When these two focal points were not in alignment, he discovered that letters were more perceptible at the position he shifted attention to than at the position his eyes were directed toward.

attention from stimuli at other locations. He claimed, to paraphrase his words, that attention is free to direct itself by a conscious and voluntary effort upon any selected portion of the field of view; and that this results in an excited state of certain fibers within our nervous system that is preferentially transmitted to consciousness, independently of the motions of external moveable body parts such as the eye (Helmholtz, 1871; see also Warren & Warren, 1968, pp. 258–260). It is worth re-stating the result of this experiment. Helmholtz demonstrated in a systematic, scientific manner what had only been observed informally prior to his study that (a) we can shift attentional focus independently of ocular focus, and that (b) visual analysis depends more on where we are focusing attention than where our eyes are pointing. James emphasized in his *Principles of Psychology* (1890, p. 438) that this was "one of the most important observations for a future theory of attention."

While James noted the importance of this finding, he questioned one aspect of Helmholtz's interpretation of it. James felt that "looking out of the corner of the eye" is quite difficult, and that more of the unattended regions of a stimulus display (especially the ocular fixation point region) are processed than was implied by Helmholtz. Instead, James was sympathetic to a claim by Hering that both the peripheral stimulus object that attention is shifted toward and also the object that the eyes are pointed toward must be attended to (see James, 1890, p. 438). This occurs, according to Hering, because the attentional focal point expands in size to encompass both the peripheral stimulus and also the location associated with ocular focus (see Figure 1.4). This conflicts with Helmholtz's observations that letters in the vicinity of the fixation point were not identifiable when his attention was directed elsewhere. As will be evident later in the book (particularly in chapter 3), subsequent experimentation showed that Hering's attentional focal point proposal is incorrect. There is now little debate about Helmholtz's conclusion that the attentional focal point can be shifted independently of ocular fixation. The question that remains is how this is possible.

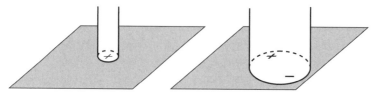

Figure 1.4 Hering proposed that when attention is shifted to a peripheral location in the visual scene while the eyes remain fixed at a central location, the attentional focal point expands so that the center of the display will continue to be attended to.

Ocular Fixation

The purpose of ocular fixation is usually to foveate an object of interest. We do this by moving our eyes to allow visual input to project onto a region in the center of the retina called the *fovea* (Figure 1.5). The fovea is a small depression, 0.2 mm in size, that contains photoreceptors that enable finely detailed visual input to be perceived clearly (Coren et al., 2004). Eye movements are necessary because our capacity for resolving fine details (visual acuity) declines progressively from the fovea to the retinal periphery. We overcome the limited resolving power of our retinae by moving our eyes to foveate objects so that we can perceive them most clearly.

While the central retina mediates high-acuity visual analysis, the peripheral retina is most sensitive to motion, brightness changes, and the sudden appearance of new objects. There is a progressive increase in sensitivity with increasing distance from the fovea to the retinal periphery (associated with a cortical magnification factor) that causes a trade-off between acuity and sensitivity (e.g., Carrasco & Frieder, 1997; Engel, 1971; Shulman et al., 1985; Van der Heijden et al., 1988). This retinal organization is efficient because it allows us to carry out high-acuity analysis of foveated stimuli while remaining vigilant and sensitive to stimulus events that may occur in the visual periphery.

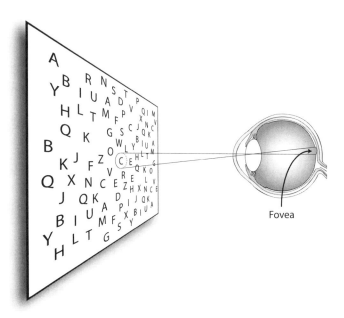

Figure 1.5 The foveal region is the central area of the retina that carries out the highest acuity visual processing. When looking directly at an object (e.g., the letter C in the figure), information about it is projected to the fovea.

From an acuity standpoint, an object can be perceived most clearly when the eyes point directly toward it to project its image to the foveae. What makes Helmholtz's discovery so intriguing is his suggestion that, when the attentional and ocular focal points are not in alignment, visual analysis is influenced more by attentional focus than by ocular focus. In other words, even though processing of the visual image occurs with the highest acuity where the eyes point to (the fovea), his finding suggests that visual processing may be most efficient at the location of attentional focus. While contemporary research indicates that the relationship between focused attention and eccentricity is more complex than originally suggested by Helmholtz (e.g., Carrasco & Yeshurun, 1998; Roggeveen & Ward, 2007a, 2007b, 2007c), visual processing does appear to be enhanced at attended locations.

Early Ideas About the Attentional Focal Point

By the early 1900s, there were several proposals about the nature of the attentional focal point. In his demonstration, Helmholtz was only able to focus on a single location at a time, which suggested that the focal point is unitary. This is consistent with a suggestion made centuries before by Hobbes (1655) that if the sense organs are occupied with one object, they cannot become simultaneously occupied by another object. One early description of variability in the spatial extent of the attentional focal point was the *Law of Two Levels* (Titchener, 1908). It held that observers can choose between two different states of attentional focus depending on the task at hand. If attention is focused on a specific object or a location, then it can be concentrated within a narrow focal point. But if attention is not focused on anything in particular, then its concentration can be distributed within a broad focal point that encompasses much of the visual field (see Figure 1.6). In the years that followed, researchers would refine this proposal by describing changes in attention's spatial extent in terms of metaphors such as a zoom lens (e.g., Eriksen & St. James, 1986).

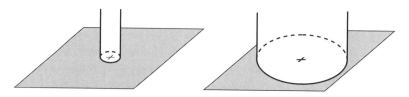

Figure 1.6 The *Law of Two Levels* holds that the spatial extent of attention is associated with one of two states. One is narrowly focused attention directed to an object or location of interest. The other is broadly distributed attention throughout the visual field.

Figure 1.7 James proposed that the distribution of attention in the visual scene could be volcano-like in shape, with the deepest concentration in the center and the shallowest concentration in the periphery.

James (1890) and Baldwin (1889) proposed that the concentration of attention within the focal point is conical in shape. As seen in Figure 1.7, they suggested that it has a "volcano-like" distribution with the highest level at the center and the lowest levels toward the periphery (which James called the fringe of consciousness). James thought that differences in the concentration of attention within the focal point would cause objects near the center of attentional focus to be perceived with the greatest clarity. Many years later, in an attempt to quantify attentional concentration, the term *attentional resource* would be coined (e.g., Kahneman, 1973). The notion of varying concentrations of attention within the visual field has since been conceptualized in terms of gradients of attentional resources (e.g., Downing & Pinker, 1985; Eriksen & Yeh, 1985; Palmer, 1990). The attentional gradient concept has also been incorporated into a proposal about the variability of attention's spatial extent (e.g., Eriksen & St. James, 1986).

Voluntary Orienting versus Attentional Capture

Long before Helmholtz demonstrated our capacity to shift attention independently of ocular fixation, many others speculated about the nature of these shifts. Hatfield (1998) noted in his comprehensive historical overview that attention focusing was alluded to in the writings of ancient Greek philosophers including Aristotle. Hatfield also pointed out that, even in the 4th century, writers such as Augustine of Hippo observed that attention can be involuntarily drawn, and particularly to objects of cognitive interest that "tug at" one's attention. In the 17th century, Descartes refined the observation that attention can be voluntarily fixated or involuntarily "captured" by objects. He attributed to the latter the emotion of wonder. For this reason, Descartes used the term "attention" to refer to voluntarily attending to an object; and the term "admiration" to refer to situations in which objects involuntarily attract attention. In keeping with this distinction, Braunschweiger (1899) summarized the attention literature in a 19th-century monograph by dividing it into intellectual (voluntary) and sensory (involuntary) dimensions.

Hatfield (1998) also pointed out that the nature of attention shifts was a topic covered in two 18th-century psychology textbooks, *Psychologia Emperica*

(1738) and *Psychologia Rationalis* (1740), published roughly 100 years before Helmholtz's demonstration of attention shifting. The author, Christian Wolff, discussed voluntary control of attentional processing, and the relationship between eye movements and shifts of attention. He also discussed ideas about an inverse relationship between the spatial extent of attention within the visual field and the intensity with which it can be directed to objects (see Figure 1.8). This pre-dated, by roughly 250 years, contemporary models of this relationship (e.g., the zoom lens metaphor) discussed in chapter 3. Wolff is rarely mentioned in the attention literature; presumably because his writings were published in German.

The early literature also includes ideas about our capacity to voluntarily maintain focused attention on an object or task. Descartes wrote that the ease of doing so seems to be inversely proportional to the intensity of distractions such as loud sounds and strikingly novel events. Helmholtz felt that maintaining focused attention at a particular location for any length of time was difficult because there is a natural tendency for attention to wander to new objects and then remain focused on them until their novelty subsides. James suggested that sustained focused attention on an object for more than a few seconds at a time is only possible if that object continually changes in some way. James, like Descartes, also felt that when interest in an object decreases, focused attention on that object will be particularly susceptible to capture by sounds, novel events, and other significant stimuli.

Like Braunschweiger (1899), James categorized attentional processing according to intellectual and sensory domains. Attentional processing in the sensory domain, in his terms, involved the accommodation or adjustment of sensory organs (James, 1890, p. 416). He referred to it as *passive attention* because he felt that it could be captured reflexively and effortlessly by an initially unattended stimulus if that stimulus was either very intense or sudden. Other writers of this time also noted that abrupt flashes in the visual periphery draw attention (e.g., Titchener, 1910). Attentional processing in the intellectual domain, according to James, involved voluntary, anticipatory preparation from within the cognitive centers concerned with the attended-to object. This proposal foreshadows one of the central themes

Figure 1.8 Wolff (1738, 1740) discussed the idea that when attention is narrowly focused, it is highly concentrated. On the other hand, when it is broadly focused, it is less concentrated at any given location.

in the contemporary literature—the distinction between goal-driven and stimulus-driven attentional processes.

Wundt and the introspective psychologists also distinguished between voluntary and involuntary attention, as did the Gestalt psychologists. Wertheimer (1923), for example, noted the difference between focused attention that results from voluntary concentration, and attention that is drawn to structural properties of perceptual figures in a stimulus-driven way. Koffka (1935, p. 395) talked about voluntarily focused attention in terms of a "force" going from the self to an object; and involuntary, captured attention in terms of a "force" going from an object to the self. Köhler (1947, p. 299) also recognized the flexible relationship between ocular and attentional focus. In his terms, attention "is experienced in its purest form when, while fixating a given point, we concentrate on one object after another in the periphery of the field." Thus, by the mid-20th century, it was well established that attention can be controlled in a voluntary manner, or captured by a sensory event.

Overt and Covert Orienting

Little research on attention was conducted during the behaviorist era that dominated North American and, to some extent, European psychology in the first half of the 20th century. There was interest, however, in studying the orienting response that animals make toward stimuli that capture their attention (e.g., Pavlov, 1927; Sokolov, 1960). Orienting is an adjustment of the animal's position relative to the stimulus in question. It usually involves a body, head, and/or eye movement. Russian neurophysiologist Ivan Pavlov called it the "investigating" or "what-is-it?" reaction. It has been traditionally studied by psychologists as a reflex-like response. When he entered his laboratory, for example, Pavlov observed that his dogs reflexively made an orienting response toward him. When orienting occurs, attention is also directed to the stimulus.

When animals are confronted with a novel stimulus, they usually show a strong orienting response toward it. But if the same stimulus is repeated continually, animals will habituate to it and their orienting responses will progressively weaken. This habituation reflects a gradual decrease in the extent to which an area in the brain stem called the reticular activating system (RAS) causes cortical arousal. As seen in Figure 1.9, the RAS arouses the cortex by a pathway that projects to the thalamus. In 1949, Moruzzi and Magoun discovered that electrical stimulation of the RAS of cats produced arousal and orienting responses. For that reason, many theorists in the mid-20th century believed that the RAS was the brain area that controlled attentional processing.

The term orienting has since been refined to distinguish between (a) shifts of attention that occur in synchrony with changes in body position and

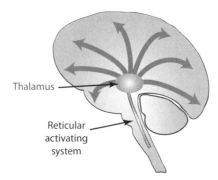

Figure 1.9 The reticular activating system (RAS) in the brain stem is responsible for arousal and is associated with orienting.

(b) shifts of attention that occur independently of body position. More specifically, *overt orienting* involves shifts of attention associated with detectable body movements, as described by Pavlov (1927). In contrast, *covert orienting* refers to shifts of attention not associated with any directly observable body movements (Posner, 1978). Covert orienting is the central topic of this book. One way to describe the Helmholtz demonstration outlined in the previous section would be to say that he covertly oriented his attention to locations within a stimulus display while overtly maintaining the position of his eyes and gaze toward the central fixation point. Figure 1.10 shows the relative positions of the ocular and attentional focal points during covert orienting.

Summary

Although it is often not acknowledged, the thinking of Helmholtz, James, and other theorists that preceded them has influenced, to a great degree, the contemporary study of attention shifts. Helmholtz's demonstration that attention can be shifted independently of ocular gaze, for example, is one of the foundational discoveries in the field. More recently, researchers have made significant progress in the identification of brain mechanisms

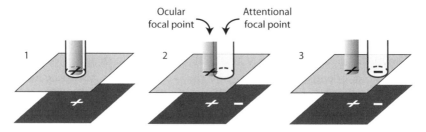

Figure 1.10 During covert orienting, the ocular focal point remains stationary while the attentional focal point is shifted to another location.

that mediate attention shifts and eye movements. We now know that there appears to be a common functional network of brain areas for both types of orienting (e.g., Corbetta et al., 1998). But many questions about attention shifts and eye movements remain. For instance, while an attention shift is not always followed by an eye movement, is the reverse true? And if eye movements are always accompanied by attention shifts, does the shift have to *precede* the eye movement to their common destination? Some researchers have argued that not only is this the case, but attention shifts also play a role in the programming of eye movements (e.g., Kowler et al., 1995). Another possibility is that, while attention shifts precede eye movements to their destination, eye-movement programming may be functionally independent of attention (e.g., Kingstone & Klein, 1993; Klein & Taylor, 1994). The relationship between attention shifts and eye movements is controversial, and investigations of it began with Helmholtz's demonstration some 150 years ago.

Another central topic of study in the contemporary attention literature is how attention shifts are controlled (e.g., Liu et al., 2003; Wright & Ward, 1998; Yantis, 1998). This work follows from a good deal of 19th-century writing about qualitative differences between attention that is *involuntarily* captured and attention that is *voluntarily* shifted. James (1890) described involuntary shifts in sensory terms and voluntary shifts in cognitive terms. With the development of empirical techniques like the location-cueing paradigm (e.g., Posner, 1978), researchers now study, in detail, many aspects of involuntary and voluntary attention shifts. And, as a demonstration of James' prescience, use of the location-cueing technique has allowed researchers to investigate the interplay between low-level sensory and high-level cognitive operations when the attentional focal point is shifted (e.g., Richard et al., 2003; Wright & Richard, 2003). Other 18th- and 19th-century writings dealt with the nature of the attentional focal point, how attention may be concentrated within it, and how it may vary in spatial extent. This laid the foundation for several lines of recent research about how attention is shifted, factors that influence the spatial extent of attentional focus, whether or not the focus can be split into multiple foci, and how specialized cortical areas may cause the focal point to disengage immediately prior to attention shifts (e.g., Posner et al., 1988).

Descartes (1649) suggested that voluntary orienting of attention to an object of interest is accomplished by "tilting" the pineal gland in the object's direction. Based on studies of the orienting response and arousal, mid-20th century theorists speculated that the brain area primarily responsible for mediating attention shifts is the RAS. This thinking has changed in recent years and it is now clear that no single brain area mediates attentional processing. As experimentation has become more sophisticated, it is evident that attentional processing is carried out in each of the brain areas associated with sensory processing, and in virtually every cortical area. And there is now strong evidence that a network of different brain areas mediates shifts of attention (e.g., Posner, 2004; Posner & Rothbart, 2007).

In the remainder of the book, we look at how the ideas of 19th-century thinkers and their predecessors (a) have been the subject of a number of debates about the nature of the attentional focal point; (b) have led to the development of new metaphors for attentional processing; (c) have led to a new appreciation of the interplay between sensory and attentional processing during covert orienting; (d) have been extended significantly because of advances in neurophysiological and functional brain imaging techniques; and (e) have led to proposals about the structure of the brain's attention networks and associated neurotransmitters that make the ability to pay attention possible.

2

Studying Attention Shifts
With Location Cueing

Helmholtz demonstrated that focused attention can be shifted voluntarily and independently of eye position. He also suggested that shifting focused attention to a particular region in the visual field can increase the efficiency of analysis of the items located there. With respect to the study of attention, the importance of this finding cannot be overstated.

One challenge facing researchers who systematically studied Helmholtz's finding was the need to develop a procedure that gave them some control over subjects' attention shifts. Keep in mind that in his demonstration, Helmholtz himself was the observer and he therefore had complete control over changes in his attentional state while performing the task. Unlike Helmholtz, experimental subjects are typically not as motivated to perform to the best of their ability. Thus, researchers needed a procedure that allowed them to know *where* subjects covertly shift their attention to, and *when* these shifts occur. Different methods for doing this have been developed, and they usually involve presenting some form of location cue about the impending target.

Few attempts were made to study covert orienting before the 1970s, and they produced little information about the nature of attention shifts (e.g., Grindley & Townsend, 1968; Mertens, 1956; Mowrer, 1941). The primary reason why it took more than 100 years since Helmholtz's pioneering work to develop a method for studying covert orienting was a general lack of interest in studying attention in the first half of the 20th century. In fact, researchers did not systematically investigate any aspect of attentional processing until the decline of the behaviorist era in the 1950s when experiments on auditory selection were conducted by Broadbent (1954, 1958) and Cherry (1953).

Another reason for the delay was that, prior to the 1970s, eye-movement monitoring technology was invasive, expensive, and not widely available.

Eye-movement monitors are necessary to verify that attention shifts occur independently of eye fixation. With the increasing availability of eye-movement monitors in recent years (see chapter 6), researchers have been able to study covert orienting without resorting to a time-limited display technique such as that used by Helmholtz.

Early Location-Cueing Experiments

One of the first experiments involving location cueing and attention shifting was published in 1960. The purpose was to study the storage capacity of very short-term (iconic) visual memory (Sperling, 1960). Subjects saw briefly presented stimulus displays containing, in some cases, three rows of four letters. After this brief presentation (50 ms in Figure 2.1), the letters disappeared and were replaced with a blank visual field. The duration of this blank field varied (100 ms in Figure 2.1). After the blank field, subjects were given a location cue (an auditory tone) about which row of letters they were to report. A high-pitched tone indicated the top row, a medium-pitched tone indicated the middle row, and a low-pitched tone indicated the bottom row of letters. Note that the tone did not sound until after the letters had physically disappeared, and subjects did not know beforehand which row would be cued. The main finding was that the cue allowed subjects to direct attention to a subset of the information stored in visual memory before it decayed. In addition to stimulating a great deal of follow-up research on iconic memory, this study contributed to the development of a location-cueing paradigm for studying shifts of attention.

Note that the location cues used in this experiment were auditory. While most of the research described in this book involved visual cues, auditory cues can also initiate attention shifts. We discuss the effects of auditory and cross-modal location cueing on attention shifts in chapter 8.

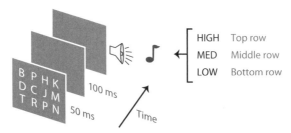

Figure 2.1 Display like that used by Sperling (1960) to study the storage capacity of iconic memory. After seeing a brief (50 ms) presentation of letter stimuli; a high-pitched, medium-pitched, or low-pitched tone was a signal to subjects about which row of letters they should report. Results indicated that location cueing could be used to direct subjects' attention to subsets of information still available in a visual memory store 100 ms after the letters disappeared.

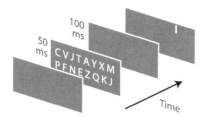

Figure 2.2 Display like that used by Averbach and Coriell (1961) to study the duration of information storage in iconic memory. When the location of a target letter was cued 100 ms after it had physically disappeared, subjects were still able to identify it. When the cue was presented 200 ms after the offset of the target, however, identification was significantly less accurate.

This study was soon replicated using visual location cueing. In one experiment, an array of letters was briefly presented and then followed by a blank field (Averbach & Coriell, 1961). After the array had physically disappeared, a cue (short vertical line) was presented above one of the locations previously occupied by a letter. Provided that the cue was presented within 100 ms of the letter's offset, as in Figure 2.2, the subjects were able to direct their attention to the cued location and identify the target letter. Identification accuracy declined to the chance level, however, when this delay was increased to 200 ms. The results support the claim that 200 ms is the maximum duration of information stored in visual memory.

In the early 1970s, it was shown that location cues could reduce target identification times by 30–40 ms relative to trials on which no cue was presented (e.g., Eriksen & Hoffman, 1972a). Figure 2.3 is an example of a stimulus display in which a cue (short vertical line) is presented near an impending target's location. This was one of the first indications that the facilitative effect of cueing on target identification may arise from subjects shifting their attention to expected locations of targets prior to their onsets.

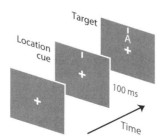

Figure 2.3 Example of the type of stimulus display used to study the effects of location cues on target identification response times.

Posner's Location-Cueing Paradigm

Posner and his colleagues are generally credited with developing and refining the location-cueing method that is commonly used to study covert orienting (e.g., Posner, 1978; Posner et al., 1978, 1980). While there are many variants, most location-cueing experiments have the following three aspects: (a) a central fixation point that subjects must continually direct their eyes toward throughout each experimental trial; (b) a target item to which subjects must respond (e.g., detect, identify); and (c) a location cue that is presented immediately before the target's appearance. The cue indicates, with a certain probability, the impending target's location. It can be used by the subject to begin the process of directing attention toward the expected target location prior to its onset.

Subjects participating in a location-cueing experiment usually see a sequence of stimulus presentations such as that in Figure 2.4. In this example, a fixation point is presented alone for 1000 ms, and then a location cue is presented to the left or right of it. There are a variety of ways to cue locations. In this case, the cue is a short horizontal line presented immediately below the expected target location. After the cue has been visible for 100 ms, the target appears (in this example, a small filled circle). The delay between cue and target presentation is the *cue-target onset asynchrony* (CTOA). Once they notice the target, subjects make a simple detection response (usually by pressing a button) as quickly as possible. There are variants of this as well. Instead of emphasizing response latency, for example, experimenters could require subjects to identify targets as accurately as possible.

Note that when CTOAs are less than 200 ms, subjects will not have enough time to make an eye movement to the cued location before the target appears because 220 ms is generally required to program and execute a regular saccade (e.g., Fischer & Weber, 1993; see chapter 6). Therefore, with CTOAs less

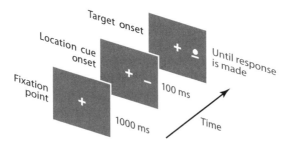

Figure 2.4 Experimental paradigm used by Posner and colleagues to study the effects of location cueing on target detection and identification responses. In this example, the cue (a horizontal bar) appears on the left or right side of the fixation point. After a short delay, a target (a circle) appears near the cued location, or on the opposite side of the display at an uncued location.

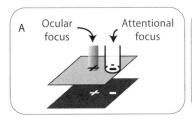
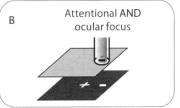

Figure 2.5 (A) In accordance with instructions, the subject's eyes remain directed toward the center of the display while attention is shifted. (B) In violation of instructions, the subject's eyes move with the attention shift and contaminate the data. Eye-movement monitoring enables experimenters to control for the latter.

than 200 ms, there would be little concern about eye movements (as opposed to attention shifts alone) being partially responsible for location-cueing effects (see Figure 2.5A). On the other hand, when CTOAs are greater than 220 ms, subjects have enough time to make a saccade to the cued location before target onset. This introduces the possibility that eye movements (overt orienting) might be responsible for any cueing effects that occur (Figure 2.5B). Thus, with longer CTOAs, a monitoring technique should be used to ensure that subjects' eyes remain stationary while they perform the task. By doing so, the experimenter can attribute any cueing effects to covert rather than overt orienting.

Cost/Benefit Analysis of Location-Cueing Effects

In one location-cueing experiment, subjects saw a stimulus display similar to that in Figure 2.4 and detected targets that appeared to the left or right of center (Posner et al., 1978, Experiment 3). On each trial, a location cue correctly indicated the target's location with a probability of 80%. In other words, on 80% of trials, the target appeared at the cued location. On the remaining 20% of trials, the target appeared elsewhere. When the target appeared at a cued location, the cue was *valid*. Conversely, when the target appeared at an uncued location, the cue was *invalid*. There also was a small number of trials on which a location cue was not presented. In its place, a *neutral cue* appeared immediately prior to the target's onset. Neutral cues are symbols that do not provide any information about target location and instead serve only as a temporal warning that the target is about to appear. The general result was that responses were *faster* on valid-cue trials than on invalid-cue trials. In a similar experiment, responses were *more accurate* on valid-cue trials than on invalid-cue trials (Posner et al., 1980).

Neutral-cue trials were included so that the experimenters could determine whether (a) valid location cues would facilitate responses and (b) invalid location cues would inhibit responses. To elaborate, the mean response time for detecting targets on neutral-cue trials provided a baseline measure to

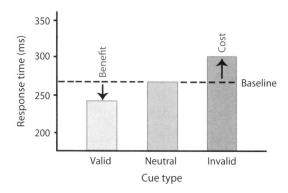

Figure 2.6 Cost/benefit analysis of the location-cueing effects on response times in Posner et al.'s (1978) Experiment 3. The difference between the mean invalid-cue response time and the mean neutral-cue response time indicates the *cost* of invalid cueing. The difference between the mean valid-cue response time and the mean neutral-cue response time indicates the *benefit* of valid cueing.

which the mean response times on valid-cue and invalid-cue trials could be compared. As seen in Figure 2.6, the difference between the mean invalid-cue trial and mean neutral-cue trial response times is the *cost* of invalid cueing on target detection responses. The difference between the mean valid-cue trial and the mean neutral-cue trial response times is the *benefit* of valid cueing on target detection responses. The cost/benefit analysis in Figure 2.6 indicates that the magnitudes of facilitative and inhibitory effects of location cueing on response times were 23 and 40 ms, respectively.

What do costs and benefits of location cueing in this type of experiment indicate about attentional analysis? Posner and colleagues (e.g., Posner, 1978, 1980; Posner et al., 1980) suggested that focused attention can be shifted to cued locations within a mental representation of the visual scene much like a moving spotlight, as shown in Figure 2.7. On valid-cue trials, they proposed that a shift of attention can be initiated to the expected target location before the target appears, thereby producing a response-time benefit. In this case, attentional analysis of the target would be getting a "head start" that was said to decrease target detection time. On invalid-cue trials, however, they proposed that a shift of attention would be initiated to a location on the opposite side of the display from the actual target location. This would produce a response-time cost because attention would need to be realigned with the correct target location after the target's appearance. In this case, attentional analysis of the target gets a "false start" at an incorrect location that was said to increase target detection time. As discussed in more detail in chapter 3, the moving spotlight metaphor stimulated a great deal of research and theorizing about the nature of shifts of focused attention.

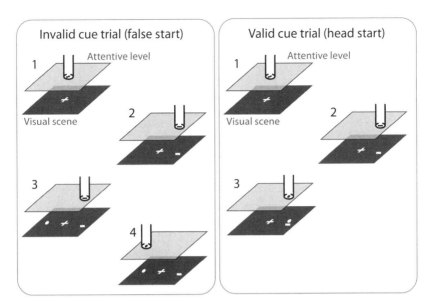

Figure 2.7 One account of the cost and benefit of location cueing is that, following cue presentation, the attentional focal point is shifted to the cued location. If the impending target also appears there a short time later, the subject gets a "head start" in responding to it. But if the target appears elsewhere, the subject suffers a "false start" and must re-direct attention from the opposite side of the display to the actual target location. The surface labeled "Attentive level" is a mental representation of the visual scene that attentional operations are said to be carried out within.

Goal-Driven and Stimulus-Driven Control

One of the central themes of early writing about attention is that it can be shifted voluntarily or it can be captured involuntarily by external sensory events. James (1890, p. 416) described voluntary shifts as part of the "intellectual domain" and involuntary shifts as part of the "sensory domain." Researchers can choose to study either voluntary or involuntary orienting, depending on whether they use symbolic or direct location cues. *Symbolic cues* are usually centrally presented arrows (as in Figure 2.8) or digits that subjects understand to indicate the expected target location. *Direct cues* are usually underlines, outline boxes, or bar markers that are presented in close proximity to the expected target location. Symbolic cues are sometimes referred to as central cues, push cues, or endogenous cues; and direct cues are sometimes referred to as peripheral cues, pull cues, or exogenous cues.

Symbolic location cues initiate attention shifts in a fundamentally different way than direct location cues. The former are meaningfully associated with a particular location and therefore must be interpreted by an observer in order to be used. For this reason, the initiation of an

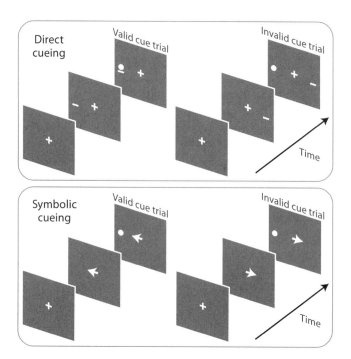

Figure 2.8 Examples of direct location cueing using a horizontal underline cue and symbolic location cueing using a centrally presented arrow. Cues are valid when the target appears at the cued location. Cues are invalid when the target appears at an uncued location.

attention shift by a symbolic cue is *goal-driven*. The observer processes the location information conveyed by the symbol and, on this basis, develops a computational goal for carrying out the task (which, presumably, would be to direct attention to the indicated location). Direct cues, on the other hand, produce their effect by virtue of being physically close to the target location. It appears that the facilitative effect of direct cues on target detection response times arises, in part, from some form of sensory activation that occurs at the cued location and enhances responding to a target that appears shortly afterward at the same location. No cognitive interpretation of direct-cue meaning is required and, instead, attention is captured by the onset of the cue. For this reason, the initiation of an attention shift by a direct cue is *stimulus-driven*. Shifts of attention initiated by symbolic versus direct cues have also been referred to as "intrinsic versus extrinsic" (Milner, 1974), "endogenous versus exogenous" (Posner, 1978), and "voluntary versus involuntary" (Jonides, 1981; Luria, 1973; Müller & Rabbitt, 1989). The distinction is important because different experimental results can occur depending on whether the researcher has used symbolic or direct cues.

Voluntary Cue Use

Cue validity is the percentage of trials on which the expected target will appear at a cued location. A low-validity cue (e.g., 20% accurate) is a poor indicator of the impending target's actual location and a high-validity cue (e.g., 80% accurate) is a good indicator of this location. Manipulations of cue validity have a greater effect on goal-driven attention shifts initiated by symbolic cues than they do on stimulus-driven attention shifts initiated by direct cues. As seen in Figure 2.9A, the effect of low-validity symbolic cues on responses to targets is usually smaller than that of high-validity symbolic cues (Jonides, 1981; Kröse & Julesz, 1989; Müller & Humphreys, 1991). The effect of low-validity direct cues, however, is *not* usually smaller than that of high-validity direct cues, despite the low probability that a target will appear at the locations indicated by the former (Jonides, 1981; Kröse & Julesz, 1989; Müller & Humphreys, 1991). Presumably, over the course of several trials of a location-cueing experiment, observers learn that low-validity cues are not useful for determining the impending target's location and, as a result, they do not *voluntarily* use these cues to direct their attention. Therefore, the attenuation of the facilitative effect of symbolic cues with validity decreases indicates that this effect is mediated by voluntary, goal-driven processes. In contrast, the continued facilitative effect of low-validity direct cues, even though subjects may have realized that they are not useful, indicates that this effect is mediated by reflexive, stimulus-driven processes.

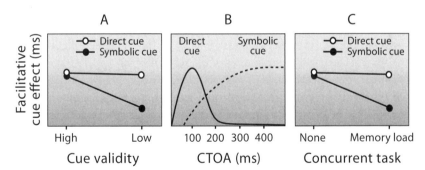

Figure 2.9 (A) General pattern of results of studies in which the validity of symbolic and direct cues was manipulated. Symbolic cueing has little effect on responses when cue validity is low. Direct cueing, on the other hand, continues to have an effect on responses even when cue validity is low. (B) General pattern of results of studies involving the manipulation of cue-target onset asynchrony (CTOA) with symbolic and direct cues. The effectiveness of direct cues on responses is maximal when the CTOA is 100 ms, and declines with further increases in CTOA. The effectiveness of symbolic cues builds more gradually until the CTOA reaches roughly 300 ms, and may be sustained at that level for a short time afterward. (C) General pattern of results of studies involving symbolic and direct cues and concurrent task performance. Whereas symbolic cues have less effect on responses when a concurrent (memory load) task is performed, direct cues are relatively unaffected by concurrent task performance.

Voluntary cue use was also studied more directly by giving subjects explicit instructions to ignore all location cues (e.g., Gottlob et al., 1999; Jonides, 1981; Lambert et al., 1987). These instructions virtually eliminated the effect of symbolic cues on responses to targets, but they did little to attenuate direct-cue effectiveness (Jonides, 1981). This indicates that while observers must voluntarily attend to symbolic cues to initiate attention shifts in a goal-driven manner, ignored direct cues will still trigger attention shifts in a stimulus-driven manner.

It should be noted that small but significant response-time benefits have been reported for targets appearing at locations of uninformative symbolic location cues (e.g., Sheperd et al., 1986). This finding was replicated in a subsequent study with the required eye-movement monitoring (Eimer, 1997) and also more recently (Ristic & Kingstone, 2006) without eye-movement monitoring (which, as pointed out in the previous section, is necessary when studying attention shifts to cued locations when using CTOAs greater than 200 ms). Eimer's (1997) electrophysiological study also showed that some cue-induced event-related potentials (ERPs) (e.g., occipital N1) occurred only on informative symbolic-cue trials and not on uninformative cue trials (see chapter 7 for a detailed description of electrophysiology and the ERP method). In chapter 9, we discuss a proposal that a small number of highly familiar symbols (e.g., arrows, schematic faces) may be associated with the development of an automatic tendency to orient attention in a cued direction.

Effect of Competing Attentional Demands

Another way to determine the extent to which goal-driven processing is involved in the performance of a task is to examine the effect of competing demands for attentional resources (cf., Schneider et al., 1984). In one experiment, the effectiveness of symbolic and direct cueing was compared when observers were required to identify targets at cued locations while at the same time performing a secondary, cognitive-load task (holding digits in memory; Jonides, 1981). Symbolic-cue effectiveness progressively diminished with increases in secondary cognitive load but direct-cue effectiveness did not change (see Figure 2.9C). This suggests that attention must be paid to the meaning of symbolic cues when initiating attention shifts to expected target locations. On the other hand, the independence of direct-cue effectiveness and concurrent task performance suggests that direct cues do not require attentional analysis for their onsets to facilitate responses to targets at cued locations.

Time Course of Cue Effectiveness

Studies of the time course of cue effectiveness also indicate that symbolic-cue effects are goal-driven and direct-cue effects are stimulus-driven. In one experiment, the effects of symbolic and direct cues on target detection response times were compared across a number of CTOAs ranging from 50 to 500 ms (Sheperd & Müller, 1989). Direct cues were most effective at the shortest CTOA, whereas symbolic cues were only fully effective at the longest CTOA. In a similar study, the effect of nonpredictive direct cues was maximal when the CTOA was 150 ms, and declined with further CTOA increases (Müller & Findlay, 1988; see also Adam et al., 2000; Nakayama & Mackeben, 1989). But the effect of symbolic cues was not maximal until the CTOA was increased to 300 ms, and it was sustained with further CTOA increases (perhaps it can be sustained for as long as 2 sec under certain conditions—see Posner et al., 1978). A similar experiment investigating symbolic- and direct-cue effects on response accuracy yielded the same pattern of results (Müller & Rabbitt, 1989). Thus, direct cues have their strongest effect on responses to targets at cued locations when the CTOA is 100 ms, but when the CTOA is increased from 100 to 200 ms, direct-cue effectiveness attenuates. This suggests that direct cues may facilitate responses to targets at cued locations on the basis of rapid sensory operations triggered by the sudden onsets of these cues. In contrast, symbolic cues require CTOAs of 300 ms or more to be maximally effective, which may reflect the time it takes to focus attention on the cue and interpret it. Figure 2.9B illustrates the typical time course of location-cue effectiveness as a function of the CTOA. Note that, at longer CTOAs (400 ms or more), there may be instances in which direct cues (a) continue to facilitate responses to targets (cf., Cheal & Lyon, 1991) or (b) inhibit responses to targets (Posner & Cohen, 1984). The latter effect is referred to as *inhibition of return*, and is discussed in detail in chapter 5.

   Why do facilitative direct location-cue effects dissipate after 200 ms? For a brief period of time, direct cues have the capacity to attract and capture attention, but somehow lose this capacity after 200 ms. One possible reason why direct-cue effects are transient is that the abrupt onset of a cue may cause sensory activation at that location in a representation of visual space. If a target should appear there shortly afterward and before the cue-triggered sensory activation has fully dissipated, then the observer could be more sensitive to its onset than would be the case if the target appeared elsewhere. In other words, direct-cue effects may dissipate after 200 ms because, like information stored briefly in visual memory, they are produced by transient, sensory activation.

Conscious Awareness of Cue Presentation
Another way by which goal-driven and stimulus-driven processing differ is the extent to which they are involved when location cues are presented below the subjective threshold of consciousness. In one study, a direct cue

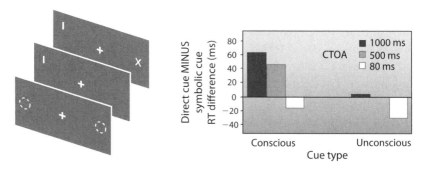

Figure 2.10 Example of display used by McCormick (1997, Experiment 3) to study the effect of subjectively unconscious location cueing on target identification responses. The circles (not visible during the experiment) indicate the two possible target locations. The direct cue symbolically indicated that the target would appear on the opposite side of the display on 85% of trials. On the trial shown in this figure, the target (X) appears at the symbolically cued location (as opposed to the direct cued location). Results showed that a symbolic cueing effect only occurred at the longer CTOAs (500 and 1000 ms), and only when subjects were consciously aware of the cue. When they were not aware of the cue, a direct cueing effect still occurred at the shorter CTOA (80 ms).

was presented at one of the locations to the left or right of central fixation (McCormick, 1997). The cue symbolically indicated that the target would appear at the location on the opposite side of the center on 85% of trials (and, because there were only two possible target locations, at the cue's physical location on the other 15% of trials; see Figure 2.10). Subjects were given explicit instructions about cue validity and clearly understood that the target had a high probability of appearing at the opposite location. The CTOA was 80, 500, or 1000 ms. In one condition, the luminance of the cue was systematically reduced until subjects were not consciously aware of its onset. As expected, symbolic cueing effects only occurred with the longer CTOAs (500 and 1000 ms). But, as seen in Figure 2.10, there was an interesting interaction between the CTOA and the degree to which subjects were consciously aware of cues. That is, when subjects were not aware of the cue, they were unable to shift their attention in a goal-driven manner to the symbolically indicated location. At the shorter CTOA, however, a direct cueing effect occurred when targets appeared at the physical location of the cue, even though subjects were unaware of cue presence. This indicates that, unlike goal-driven processes associated with symbolic cueing, stimulus-driven processes associated with direct cueing do not require conscious awareness to be initiated. In chapter 4, we describe an account of McCormick's 1997 finding that involves facilitation of responses by sensory processing. Table 2.1 is a summary of stimulus-driven and goal-driven control of attention shifts.

Stimulus-Driven Attentional Control	Goal-Driven Attentional Control
Associated with *direct cues* (a.k.a. peripheral or exogenous cues) that occur directly at or near a potential target location	Associated with *symbolic cues* (a.k.a. central or endogenous cues) that indirectly indicate a potential target location
Initiated by sensory events such as the abrupt onset of a direct cue or other transients	Initiated by cognitive operations, usually following interpretation of a symbolic cue's meaning
Is rapid and transient, and effectiveness peaks approximately 100 ms after triggering sensory event	Builds gradually, but effectiveness peaks and is sustained approximately 300 ms after the triggering event
Involuntary because it is minimally influenced by (a) instructions to ignore location cues and by (b) the predictability (validity) of cues	Voluntary because it is diminished by (a) instructions to ignore location cues and by (b) the predictability (validity) of cues

Table 2.1 Properties of Stimulus-Driven and Goal-Driven Control of Attention Shifts

nice summary

Attentional Capture by Abrupt-Onset Stimuli

When subjects perform target detection tasks, stimulus-driven shifts of attention to cued locations are sometimes referred to as *attentional capture*. Titchener (1908, p. 192) described it more than a century ago when he noted that any sudden change or movement has the potential to distract a person concentrating on a task. Other theorists suggested that capture may be mediated by an "early warning system" that directs attention to objects and locations of potential interest (Breitmeyer & Ganz, 1976, p. 31).

Yantis and colleagues are generally credited with conducting the first systematic studies of attentional capture (e.g., Yantis & Hillstrom, 1994; Yantis & Johnson, 1990; Yantis & Jones, 1991; Yantis & Jonides, 1984, 1990). Many of their experiments involved visual search for two types of targets. *Abrupt-onset targets* appeared suddenly within the visual search array after the distractor items were physically present. The time required to detect them was compared to that of *gradual-onset targets*. These were initially presented as stimuli with additional "irrelevant" lines serving as camouflage. As the trial proceeded, the camouflage would be removed to reveal the target. This technique was developed as a way to allow precise control of the timing of gradual stimulus onsets (Todd & Van Gelder, 1979). The display on the right in Figure 2.11 is an example of a trial with an abrupt-onset target (P). Nothing is physically present at its location prior to its appearance. The display on the left in Figure 2.11 is an example of a

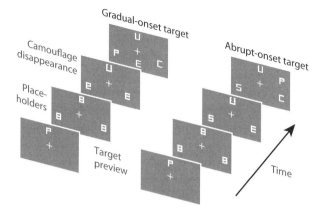

Figure 2.11 Example of the stimulus displays used by Yantis and Jonides (1984) to study the extent to which abrupt-onset and gradual-onset targets capture attention. A trial begins with a brief presentation of the target to be detected. This is followed by the presentation of placeholders that serve as camouflage for letter stimuli that are uncovered at these locations (i.e., gradual onset). On each trial, subjects determine whether or not the target is present or absent.

trial with a gradual-onset target (P) that appears when lines that comprise the figure-eight placeholders are removed to reveal it. It has been suggested that the placeholders may cause forward masking of gradual-onset targets, thereby delaying their detection (Gibson, 1996); however, the long temporal interval between placeholder and target presentation (1000 ms) appears to preclude this type of masking (Yantis & Jonides, 1996).

The general result of these experiments was that abrupt-onset targets were detected faster than gradual-onset targets. In particular, the flat display-size function for abrupt-onset targets in Figure 2.12 indicates that, regardless of set size, these targets were the first to be inspected during the search. The increasing slope of the display-size function for gradual-onset targets, however, indicates

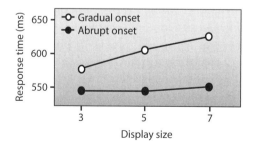

Figure 2.12 Results of an experiment by Jonides and Yantis (1988) showing that abrupt-onset targets capture attention more than gradual-onset targets. This is indicated by the minimal effect of search set size on abrupt-onset target detection.

that they were affected by search set size and therefore attended to serially. On this basis, the experimenters claimed that abrupt-onset targets capture attention (Yantis & Jonides, 1984). They also made a stronger claim that while targets with salient features such as brightness or color (i.e., singletons) can be used to efficiently guide visual search, only abrupt-onset stimuli capture attention in a purely stimulus-driven manner (Jonides & Yantis, 1988).

In the 1990s, it became clear that a more complex explanation of attentional capture was required. A number of researchers challenged Jonides and Yantis' (1988) claim that only abrupt onsets cause attentional capture (e.g., Folk et al., 1992; Theeuwes, 1991, 1992), and some argued that attention is simply attracted to stimuli with the highest relative salience (e.g., Braun, 1999; Lee et al., 1999). In addition, it was found that abrupt-onset stimuli do not always capture attention automatically if it happens to be actively engaged at another location (Lamy & Tsal, 1999; Theeuwes, 1991; Yantis & Jonides, 1990). In other words, ongoing goal-driven attentional processing can override stimulus-driven capture. This enhances the efficiency of visual analysis because, without the capacity to suppress attention shifts to stimuli that suddenly appear in our visual field, we would often be distracted by irrelevant visual events and it would be difficult to perform tasks requiring sustained attention and vigilance.

Other refinements appeared to be necessary when it was discovered that attention apparently can be captured by stimuli that are not associated with luminance changes. This led Yantis and Hillstrom (1994) to claim that it is not luminance changes associated with abrupt onsets that capture attention. They argued instead that it is the appearance of a new perceptual object that captures attention. In their terms, attention is captured when a new object (even one that is not accompanied by an abrupt luminance change) causes a new *object file* (Kahneman et al., 1992) to be opened. The rationale was that updating an existing object file should be slower and less efficient than opening a new one. Therefore, detecting a gradual-onset target that is associated with an existing object file should be slower than detecting a new object that has no existing object file. This claim is controversial. The results of some studies seem to support it (e.g., Folk & Remington, 1999; Oonk & Abrams, 1998). Theeuwes (1995), however, appeared to demonstrate that luminance changes are necessary for attentional capture. He also suggested that while Yantis and Hillstrom (1994) stated that their stimuli onsets were equiluminant, they were in fact associated with luminance changes within the computer display in the form of local pixel redistribution.

Perhaps the strongest indication that traditional views about attentional capture needed to be refined was a finding by Folk et al. (1992) that capture may be contingent upon the perceptual goal of the observer. These researchers found that when searching for a target defined by a unique color (e.g., red object in a background of green objects), abrupt-onset distractors did not appear to capture attention but distractors defined by color did. On the other hand, when searching for a target with an abrupt onset, distractors defined by color did not capture attention but abrupt-onset distractors did. On the basis of this finding, Folk et al. claimed that attentional capture is always under goal-driven control. It depends, they argued, on the type of task being performed.

This *contingent attentional capture* hypothesis holds that attentional capture is necessarily goal-driven. This is controversial and has been challenged by several researchers (e.g., Hickey et al., 2006; Theeuwes, 1991, 1992, 1994; Yantis & Egeth, 1999). There is, however, a growing acceptance of the weaker claim that attentional capture is, to some extent, modulated by goal-driven inputs. One indication that it is not completely under goal-driven control is a finding that abrupt-onset distractors captured attention even when they were always in nontarget locations, and when subjects had the strongest possible motivation to ignore them (Remington et al., 1992). Another indication is the finding that feature singletons that were targets but were presented only rarely did not capture attention, even though subjects' explicit goal was to detect them (Yantis & Egeth, 1999). Neither finding is consistent with Folk et al.'s (1992) contingent capture account. They suggest instead that attentional capture is not completely goal-driven, although it may be modulated by goal-driven input in certain circumstances (see also Ruz & Lupiáñez, 2002).

Methodological Issues

A great deal of research has been conducted on shifts of attention since the 1970s. While we now have a better understanding of covert orienting, several conflicting claims have been made about the nature of this phenomenon. In an earlier historical overview of this literature, we argued that part of the disagreement arises from variability in experimental methodology (Wright & Ward, 1994). As is the case with any maturing field of study, attention researchers continue to gain an understanding of how subtle methodological differences can lead to qualitatively different results. In this section, we describe some of the factors that can influence the results of location-cueing experiments. These methodological issues should be considered when attempting to evaluate the validity of opposing claims in the covert orienting literature.

CTOA and Cue Type

As mentioned in the previous section, direct and symbolic cues produce their strongest effects at different CTOAs. Direct cues are most effective when the CTOA is 100 ms. In most cases, however, these cues produce little or no facilitative effect on responses to targets when the CTOA is 200 ms or greater.

Symbolic cues, on the other hand, appear to have only a minimal effect when the CTOA is 100 ms. Instead, their effectiveness gradually increases as the CTOA is increased from 0 to 300 ms and longer (e.g., Müller & Findlay, 1988; Nakayama & Mackeben, 1989; Sheperd & Müller, 1989). There are several instances in the literature in which researchers did not appreciate this interaction between cue type and CTOA. The relative effectiveness of direct and symbolic cues has been compared, for example, only with short CTOAs (e.g., 50–115 ms in an experiment by Jonides, 1981) and only with long CTOAs (e.g., 1000 ms in an experiment by Posner et al., 1980). In fairness to these researchers, the development of the location-cueing paradigm was at its early stages when these experiments were conducted, and the interaction between cue type and CTOA was not studied systematically until the late 1980s. Occasionally, however, even contemporary researchers design experiments involving an inappropriate CTOA for the type of cue used because they have not taken the interaction of the two into consideration.

Trial Blocking

The order in which trials are presented in experiments is another potential concern. In particular, trials blocked by condition may yield less reliable data than trials presented in a completely randomized order because the former are more likely to be biased by condition-specific strategies than the latter (e.g., Sperling & Dosher, 1986). Some conflicting claims about attention shifting may be due to a failure to take this into account. For example, manipulation of cue/target separation had no systematic effect on responses in some experiments in which trials were blocked by condition (distance between invalid cues and targets) (e.g., Posner, 1978; Remington & Pierce, 1984). But other similar experiments with a randomized trial presentation order indicated that this manipulation did have a significant effect on responses (e.g., Downing & Pinker, 1985). The conflicting results may be attributable, in part, to the difference in trial presentation. When designing location-cueing experiments, this factor should be considered and, when possible (unless specifically interested in how subjects adjust to blocked presentations), trials should be in a completely randomized order rather than in blocks by condition.

Subject Expertise

Another factor that can potentially influence the outcome of location-cueing experiments is the expertise of the subjects. More specifically, experienced subjects may use attentional strategies that novice subjects have not developed. With several days of practice, for example, subjects in one study appeared to develop attentional focusing and de-focusing strategies (attentional disengagement) before target onset that novice subjects did not have at their disposal (Fischer & Breitmeyer, 1987; Fischer & Ramsperger, 1986). Differences in subject expertise may lead to conflicting claims. For instance, in one experiment with expert subjects (including the investigators themselves), a cueing effect in a particular condition did not occur (Hughes & Zimba, 1985). But in a replication experiment with novice subjects, there was a significant cueing effect in that condition (Rizzolatti et al., 1987). This difference may be attributable, in part, to subject expertise, and caution should be exercised when comparing the results of studies in which expertise varies.

Neutral Cueing

Cost/benefit analysis of location-cueing effects on responses to targets has played an important role in the study of attentional processes. As mentioned in the previous section, costs and benefits are determined by comparing mean responses on valid- and invalid-cue trials with the mean response on neutral-cue trials. Experimenters must take care to ensure, however, that (a) the neutral cue provides a warning signal about the target's impending onset that is equivalent in intensity to that provided by the valid and invalid cues and (b) the neutral cue provides no location-specific information that could be used to direct attention. If the neutral-cue warning signal intensity is not equivalent to that of the location cues or if the neutral cue is not purely location-nonspecific, then neutral-cue trials will not provide an accurate baseline measure for cost/benefit analysis. There has been a growing awareness of the limitations of neutral cueing in recent years, and these cues can be difficult to present in a location-nonspecific manner (see e.g., Jonides & Mack, 1984; Wright et al., 1995).

Jonides and Mack (1984) outlined a number of ways in which cost/benefit analyses can be misleading, and the assumption that neutral and location cues are similar in every way except for the target location information conveyed by the latter is easy to violate. For example, subjects may be more alert when responding to location cues than when responding to neutral cues. The possibility of this occurring is greater when the two types of cues are physically different, and also when they are presented in separate, homogenous blocks of trials (Sperling & Dosher, 1986). As a result, costs may be reduced and benefits may be inflated as in Figure 2.13. This is another reason why it is better to present trials in a completely randomized order and to avoid blocking trial presentation by condition. Neutral and location cues could also have different processing demands and, therefore, require different amounts of time to be encoded. Processing complexity of neutral and location cues must be highly similar in a given experimental situation to ensure that costs are not inflated by a relatively simple neutral cue and that benefits are not inflated by a relatively complex neutral cue. Jonides and Mack (1984) advised that neutral cues only be used when necessary, and then with caution. If they are used, neutral and location cues should be

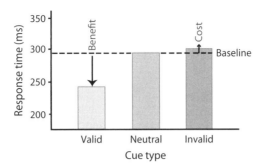

Figure 2.13 Neutral cues that are relatively more complex than the location cues in a particular experiment are more demanding to process than the other cues and, therefore, can produce inflated benefits and deflated costs.

as similar as possible in terms of physical appearance, the potential to alert observers, and the ease with which they can be encoded.

It is more difficult to select a direct neutral cue than a symbolic neutral cue. In particular, symbolic cues are usually presented in the center of stimulus displays prior to target onset and so they usually do not convey information about potential target locations on the basis of their physical position. Also, a symbolic neutral cue (e.g., plus sign) is similar, in terms of processing complexity, to a symbolic location cue (e.g., arrow). Choosing a direct neutral cue is more challenging because direct-cue onsets elicit visually triggered sensory activation and can potentially capture attention at their locations (e.g., Wright & Richard, 2003; Yantis & Jonides, 1984). One way that researchers have attempted to present direct neutral cues that we are particularly critical of is to simultaneously cue all possible target locations with multiple direct cues. The rationale is that if all locations are cued, then no useful information will be conveyed about the probable target location and, thus, attention (assumed, in this case, to have a unitary, indivisible focal point) will not be directed away from the center of the display. The multiple-cue neutral condition is based on the assumption that responses to targets are only influenced by attentional processing, and not at all by sensory activation associated with cue onsets. This assumption is incorrect. In chapter 4, we discuss in detail the proposal that the sensory effects of direct-cue onsets *can* facilitate responses to targets, and that multiple direct cue presentations should not be used for neutral cueing.

As seen in Figure 2.14, a better strategy for direct neutral cueing that minimizes the extent to which the cue is location-specific is to simply present a uniform flash of the entire display background (Mackeben & Nakayama, 1993). Note, however, that the relative strengths of the warning

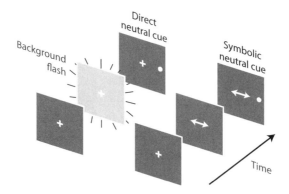

Figure 2.14 Direct and symbolic neutral cues. Caution must be exercised with direct neutral cues to ensure that they are location-nonspecific. One solution is to use a uniform flash of the display background as a temporal warning of the impending target's onset.

signals produced by the location cues and the background flash must be equivalent (cf., Ross & Ross, 1980). The experimenter must, therefore, pilot test to select an appropriate flash intensity before beginning the experiment. If location-cue/background-flash intensity differences are not equated, then cost/benefit analyses with a background-flash baseline are arbitrary at best. For a discussion of this method, see Wright et al. (1995).

Location-cue effects on target responses can also be assessed without a neutral-cue baseline measure simply by comparing mean responses on valid-cue and invalid-cue trials. This is not as informative as analyses that include a neutral baseline measure because it is unclear how much of the cue effect is due to costs of invalid location cueing versus benefits of valid cueing. It does, however, eliminate concerns about biases caused by inappropriate neutral cueing.

Summary

The location-cueing paradigm described in this chapter has been used extensively to study covert orienting. In an effort to preserve links with neuroscience research, Posner and colleagues (e.g., Posner, 1978; Posner et al., 1978, 1980) designed it to be simple enough to be performed by animals as well as humans. The task's simplicity also made it possible to study covert orienting in brain-injured patients and to trace the development of attention shifting in infants. The location-cueing paradigm is not the only technique that can be used to study covert orienting. As mentioned previously, some researchers studied attentional capture using variants of visual search tasks. And, as discussed in later chapters, attentional processing can also be studied with rapid serial visual presentation (RSVP) tasks. This involves presenting a stream of items at a single location; usually one every 80–100 ms. In one RSVP experiment, a cue (outline box around an item) was presented at some point during item presentation and subjects attempted to report the next four items in the stream (Weichselgartner & Sperling, 1987). The results indicated that items presented within 100 ms of cue onset were reported in an effortless manner whereas items presented 300–400 ms after cue onset required more effort and attention to report accurately. Thus, RSVP can be used to study attention and cueing effects.

Depending on the type of cue involved, the location-cueing paradigm can be used to study goal-driven or stimulus-driven control of attention shifts. Symbolic cues produce their effect in a goal-driven manner because they are meaningfully associated with a particular location and therefore must be interpreted by an observer in order to be used. Direct cues, on the other hand, produce their effect in a stimulus-driven manner by virtue of being physically close to the target location. Goal-driven shifts initiated by symbolic cues require attention, are voluntary, are disrupted by concurrent task performance, and require a relatively long CTOA (e.g., 300 ms). Stimulus-driven shifts initiated by direct cues occur independently of attention, are reflexive, are not disrupted by concurrent task performance, and occur only with a relatively short CTOA (100 ms). When the latter occur, some researchers say that attention is captured by the direct cue (e.g., Yantis & Jonides, 1984). While this is the generally accepted framework of attentional control, another framework was proposed in the early 1990s in which the initiation of stimulus-driven attention shifts was said to be cognitively penetrable (Folk et al., 1992). Advocates of this hypothesis suggested that all attention shifts are mediated by goal-driven processes. The more widely accepted view is that attention shifts initiated by direct cues are stimulus-driven, but occasionally they can be modulated to some extent in a goal-driven manner (e.g., to override attentional capture by an irrelevant stimulus). We discuss this issue in more detail in chapter 4.

The use of the location-cueing paradigm has led to a better understanding of covert orienting. But the occasional failure to appreciate the ramifications of subtle methodological differences has also been the cause of conflicting claims about attention shifts. Researchers must be aware of the interaction of CTOA and cue type, for example, when choosing the appropriate CTOAs for direct and symbolic location cueing. If a longer CTOA is chosen, then eye movements must also be monitored to ensure that the data reflect only covert orienting. In addition, if a neutral baseline condition is used to determine the costs and benefits of cueing, then care must be taken to select a location-nonspecific neutral cue that is similar in complexity to the location cues. Otherwise, the benefit of cueing could be inflated relative to the cost, or vice versa. A central theme of this chapter was that there are a number of methodological issues to which researchers must be sensitive when designing location-cueing experiments.

In the chapters that follow, we look at how variants of the location-cueing paradigm have been used to study the nature of the attentional focal point. A number of cleverly designed experiments have yielded proposals about (a) the extent to which attention remains engaged during covert orienting; (b) the potential divisibility of the attentional focal point when more than one cue is presented at the same time; and (c) an effect called inhibition of return that occurs when attention is shifted in response to sequentially presented cues. Each of these proposals has contributed to our understanding of how attention is shifted to objects and locations, and how these shifts may be physiologically instantiated by the brain's attention networks.

3

Properties of the Attentional Focal Point

Alcmaeon (450 BCE) is sometimes called the first neuroscientist. He is credited with developing the use of anatomical dissection as a tool of intellectual inquiry, and he is thought to be the first writer to champion the brain as the site of sensation and cognition (Gross, 1998). He also proposed an idea about vision that has since been adopted by contemporary theorists as a metaphor for the attentional focal point. In particular, when Alcmaeon first removed and dissected a human eye, he discovered that it contained water (i.e., aqueous and vitreous humors). While examining the optic nerves, he found that they come together behind the forehead. He reasoned that optic nerves function as light-bearing paths to the brain because, earlier in his life, he had received a physical blow to one of his own eyes that had caused him to see bright spots (phosphenes). On this basis, Alcmaeon concluded that the eye must contain light (fire), and that this light was necessary for vision (Figure 3.1). The idea of light in the eye was the basis for theories of vision that persisted beyond the Renaissance.

Although some prominent thinkers such as Aristotle rejected the idea that rays of light are emitted by the eyes like the beam of a lamp, it was a compelling metaphor to many at the time because lamp light can be directed toward discrete portions of the visual world of interest, just as our eyes can (Van der Heijden, 1992). The idea was so compelling, in fact, that it was not until the 18th century that it was finally discarded. One account of the refutation holds that Bidloo, a University of Leyden professor, locked himself inside a completely dark room together with a cat. He concluded that the theory could not be true because there was no detectable emission of light from the cat's eyes (Van Hoorn, 1972).

While the illumination metaphor was rejected as a description of vision, some theorists compared the attentional focal point to the spatially restricted beam emanating from an electric spotlight. Of course no one

Figure 3.1 Vision has not been compared to lamp light for hundreds of years, but the idea persists among some attention researchers who use the spotlight metaphor to describe shifts of the attentional focal point.

believes that "rays of attention" are emitted by the eyes when attending to an object of interest. But the metaphor is useful for describing selective attention to a discrete portion of visual space to the exclusion of surrounding areas. Hernández-Peón (1964) was among the first to compare attentional processing to a spotlight, and the metaphor has been used and refined by many others (e.g., Norman, 1968; Posner et al., 1980; Treisman & Gelade, 1980; see Figure 2.7).

The attractiveness of the spotlight metaphor is its simplicity. One can easily conceptualize the notion of focused attention and how it might be shifted sequentially to different locations in the visual field. In fact, it could be argued that adaptation of the spotlight metaphor inspired researchers to ask questions such as (a) at what speed can the attentional focal point be shifted from one location to another; (b) is the attentional focal point shifted in an analog or discrete manner; (c) is the size of the attentional focal point variable; and (d) can the attentional focal point be split into multiple foci?

Analog and Discrete Attention Shifts

Several models are based on the spotlight metaphor. One type assumes that attention shifts are carried out in an analog manner. An analog process shifts from one state to another by traversing the set of intermediate states (Shepard, 1975). For example, retrieving data from an electromagnetic tape is an analog process because, when two data points must be accessed from the beginning and from the end of the tape respectively, the tape reader's head must pass through all of the intermediate data points while the tape is wound ahead. Thus, if attention is shifted in an analog manner, it would move through space from one location to another by passing through the intermediate locations as it traverses the visual field (see Figure 3.2). Another model based on the spotlight metaphor assumes that attention shifts are carried out in a discrete manner. A discrete process shifts from one state to another *without* traversing intermediate states. For example, retrieving data using a computer's disk drive is a discrete process because, when two data

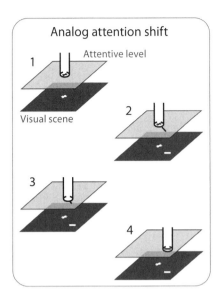
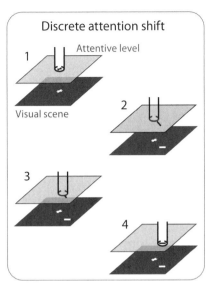

Figure 3.2 Use of the spotlight metaphor to describe two types of attention shifts. Analog shifts occur when attention remains engaged throughout the alignment. Discrete shifts occur when attention is disengaged at the origin, aligned with the destination, and then reengaged.

points must be accessed, the disk drive head does not pass through all of the intermediate points on the data disk. Thus, if attention is shifted in a discrete manner, it would move from its origin to its destination without passing through the intermediate locations and no attentional analysis would occur during the shift (see Figure 3.2). In terms of the spotlight metaphor, the beam remains on during an analog shift but is turned off during a discrete shift of attention.

One of the central themes of cognitive psychology, particularly in the 1960s and 1970s, was a renewed interest in the temporal properties and the stages of mental operations (e.g., Davidson et al., 1973; Posner & Boies, 1971; Shepard & Cooper, 1982; Sternberg, 1966, 1969). Posner's influential 1978 book, *Chronometric Explorations of Mind*, stimulated a growing interest in quantifying the time course of attention shifts. Some researchers tried to do so by determining whether costs and benefits of location cueing would vary with the distance between cues and targets. For example, would an increase in the distance between an invalid cue and target from 8° to 16° also increase the time required to shift attention from the cue to the target location? Their assumption was that if the attentional focal point is always shifted with a constant velocity and in an analog manner, then increasing this distance would affect response times. On the other hand, if the attentional focal point is shifted in a discrete manner, then increasing this distance may not affect response times because the time required to disengage attention at the origin and reengage it at the destination, presumably, is not a function of the distance between the two locations.

Some researchers found that increasing the distance between invalid cues and targets produced linear increases in response times (e.g., Shulman et al., 1979; Tsal, 1983). This suggested that the attentional focal point was shifted in an analog manner with a constant velocity. It also indicated that the speed of attention shifts may be quantifiable. Other researchers, however, found that changing the distance between invalid cues and targets did not affect response times (e.g., Kwak et al., 1991; Posner, 1978, p. 202; Sagi & Julesz, 1985; Skelton & Eriksen, 1976). And still other researchers found nonlinear increases in response times as a function of cue-target distance increases (e.g., Downing & Pinker, 1985; Remington & Pierce, 1984). The latter concluded that, if attention is shifted in an analog manner, shift velocity is proportional to shift distance (i.e., velocity increases with distance to be traversed).

As discussed in chapter 2, sometimes conflicting claims about attention shifts may be due to subtle methodological differences. Consider, for example, three studies that were conducted in the 1970s and 1980s to determine the velocity of shifts of the attentional focal point. In one of the studies, subjects detected targets that appeared at one of four locations in a horizontal array, 8° or 18° to the left or right of center (Shulman et al., 1979). Target locations were indicated by a symbolic location cue and the CTOA ranged from 50 to 500 ms (see Figure 3.3A). When the CTOA was 150 ms, response times were faster for targets at the 8° location on the cued side of the display than at the 18° location that was indicated by the symbolic cue. In addition, response times were the same for targets at the 18° cued location and at the 8° location on the uncued side of the display. When the CTOA was longer (350 and 500 ms), however, response times were faster for targets presented at either the 8° or the 18° location on the cued side than at either location on the uncued side. The experimenters concluded that attention was shifted in an analog manner from the center of the display toward the cued location at 18° eccentricity at a constant velocity, and passed through the location at 8° eccentricity when the CTOA was 150 ms (Shulman et al., 1979).

In another of these three studies, subjects identified a target presented at one of six locations 4°, 8°, or 12° to the left or right of a central fixation point (Tsal, 1983). Direct location cues were used with a CTOA ranging from 50 to 183 ms, and trials were blocked by target eccentricity (see Figure 3.3B). For targets at 4° eccentricity, responses were fastest when the CTOA was 83 ms and did not get faster with further CTOA increases. Similarly, for

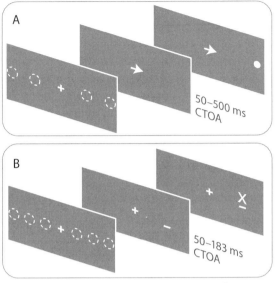

Circles (not visible during experiment) indicate
potential cue and target locations

Figure 3.3 (A) Example of the type of display used by Shulman et al. (1979) to
determine the nature and velocity of attention shifts to symbolically cued locations
at 8° and 18° eccentricity. (B) Example of the type of display used by Tsal (1983) to
determine the nature and velocity of attention shifts to direct-cued locations at
4°, 8°, and 12° eccentricity. In both studies, response times increased as the distance
between cue and target increased.

targets at 8°, responses were fastest when the CTOA was 116 ms. For targets
at 12°, responses were fastest when the CTOA was 150 ms. The experimenter
concluded that (a) the differences in these asymptote values reflected the
different times required to shift attention from the central fixation point
to the cued location and (b) the linear relationship between the CTOA
asymptote values and target eccentricity indicated that attention was shifted
with a constant velocity of 125°/sec (Tsal, 1983).

The results of the third study, however, were not consistent with the
claim about attention being shifted with a constant velocity (Remington &
Pierce, 1984). Subjects in this study detected targets at one of four locations,
2° and 10° to the left or right of a central fixation point. Symbolic location
cues were used with a CTOA ranging from 16 to 600 ms, and trials were
blocked by target eccentricity. Response times were faster for targets at 2°
eccentricity than for targets at 10° but, unlike the second study (Tsal, 1983),
a CTOA × target eccentricity interaction was not found. On this basis, the
experimenters concluded that the times required to shift attention by 2° and
by 10° were similar and, therefore, that the velocity of attention shifts is not

constant. Instead, they proposed that it is proportional to the distance that attention must travel (Remington & Pierce, 1984).

The conflicting results of these studies may be due, in part, to differences in methodology. In particular, two of the studies involved symbolic cueing (Remington & Pierce, 1984; Shulman et al., 1979) while the other involved direct cueing (Tsal, 1983). The studies that involved symbolic cueing used some CTOAs that have since been recognized as too short for this type of cue. A critical condition in one of the studies (Shulman et al., 1979) involved symbolic cueing with a 150-ms CTOA but, as mentioned in chapter 2, symbolic cues are not maximally effective with CTOAs less than 300 ms (see Figure 2.9B). In addition, while trials in one of the studies were presented in a randomized order (Shulman et al., 1979), trials in the other two studies were blocked by target eccentricity (Remington & Pierce, 1984; Tsal, 1983). The study with randomized trial presentation order (Shulman et al., 1979) led to the claim that attention shifts have a constant velocity whereas one of the studies with trials blocked by target eccentricity (Remington & Pierce, 1984) led to the claim that attention shifts do not have a constant velocity. Measurements of reaction-time performance tend to be more precise when the trials are randomized as opposed to those blocked by condition because the results obtained with the former are less likely to be biased by extraneous factors (e.g., subject alertness, response strategy). Therefore, differences in cue type, CTOA, and trial presentation may have affected the results of these studies.

It is also worth noting that the initial optimism about determining attentional velocity did not take into account the difficulty of measuring factors such as the attention shift termination point and the spatial extent of attentional focus throughout the shift. For manual movements, Fitts (1954) demonstrated that as target size decreased, movement time increased (Fitt's Law). Attention shifts also may be constrained by this relationship. When attention is shifted from one side of the visual field to the other, this may not require much time if the attentional focal point is broadly distributed, but could require significantly more time if the focal point has a smaller spatial extent. If so, then it would not be possible to measure attentional velocity precisely unless we also have the means to measure the spatial extent of the attentional focal point throughout the shift (which seems unlikely).

Occasionally, researchers use assumptions about maximum attentional velocity to account for their findings. Given the difficulty of determining this velocity and the lack of consensus about what it might be, any argument based primarily on such an assumption is not compelling and should be considered with caution.

In summary, the analog versus discrete attention shift debate was contentious in the 1980s, but less is said about this issue 20 years later. This arises, in part, from a realization that some of the experimental methodology was questionable (for detailed critiques, see Eriksen & Murphy, 1987; Yantis, 1988). Also, in the 1990s, the notion of disengaged attention became entrenched in the literature (Posner et al., 1988) and there is now considerable physiological evidence that attention is sometimes shifted discretely. On the other hand, there are also cases in which attention is clearly shifted in an analog manner, such as when we visually track moving targets (e.g., Holzman et al., 1973; Iacono & Lykken, 1979; see chapter 6). Therefore, perhaps the question we should be asking is not whether attention shifts are analog or discrete, but instead "when are shifts discrete and when are they analog?"

Attentional Disengagement

Posner et al. (1988) argued that in order to shift attention first it must be disengaged or "unlocked" from its current position. Brain activity in the parietal lobe is said to be heightened during this process (see Figure 3.4). Once disengagement has occurred, the location of the attention shift destination must be encoded and then the shift vector is calibrated. This operation is thought be carried out by a midbrain structure called the superior colliculus. When attention has been successfully directed to its destination, the final stage involves reengaging the attentional focal point at this location. The brain area responsible for engagement appears to be a part of the thalamus called the pulvinar. Once reengaged, attentive analysis can resume at the new location until the observer begins the sequence again. The physiological instantiation of attention shifting is discussed in more detail in chapter 7. We also describe a proposal about parietal cortical processes in an area called

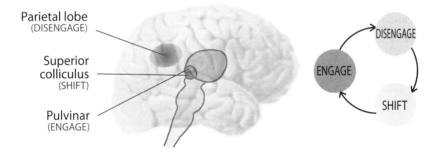

Figure 3.4 Sequence of operations proposed by Posner et al. (1988) when attention is shifted from one location to another. The sequence begins with the parietal lobe mediating attentional disengagement, followed by the superior colliculus mediating the attention shift while in a disengaged state, and finally the pulvinar mediating reengagement of attention at the shift destination.

the temporoparietal junction (TPJ) that are thought to be associated with attentional disengagement and that may play a "circuit breaker" role (Corbetta & Shulman, 2002). More specifically, the TPJ may send an interrupt signal to another part of the parietal cortex called the intraparietal sulcus (IPS) to pull focused attention away (disengage it) from performance of the current task so that it can be directed to a new and unexpected stimulus.

Figure 3.5 is an example of how this sequence of operations may be carried out when attention is shifted from the center of the visual field to the location of a new object. (a) Initially, attention is engaged on the central fixation cross. (b) When the circular object appears on the right side of the visual field, the sequence of operations begins with the disengagement of attention. (c) While attention is disengaged, midbrain collicular processes encode the location coordinates of the shift destination and prepare the channel of attention to be opened at this new position. (d) After the shift is complete, the attentional focal point is reengaged at the location of the new object and attentive analysis of its properties can begin. We are not saying that attention is always shifted in this manner (e.g., in many instances, attention presumably will not be actively engaged on a central fixation

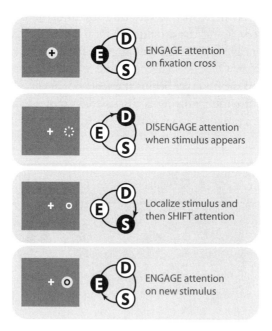

Figure 3.5 Simplified example of the sequence of operations that Posner et al. (1988) claimed occur when attention is shifted to the location of a new object. Initially, attention is engaged at the location of the central fixation point (denoted by white circle), but is disengaged when the object appears, and reengaged at the object's location after the attentional focal point is shifted there.

cross). The purpose of this example is to describe the disengage-shift-engage sequence in a clear and simple way.

Posner et al.'s (1988) attentional disengagement hypothesis is supported by the *fixation-offset effect*. In one study (Pratt & Nghiem, 2000), subjects identified targets that appeared in outline boxes on either side of the central fixation point (see Figure 3.6). Prior to target onset, one of the two potential target locations was cued by enlarging one of the boxes. In the No-Gap condition, the fixation point remained visible throughout the trial. In the Gap condition, the fixation point disappeared 200 ms before cue presentation (box enlargement). Response times were significantly faster in the Gap condition. The experimenters concluded that the disappearance of the fixation point caused attention to be disengaged prior to location-cue onset, thereby facilitating response times (Pratt & Nghiem, 2000; see also Mackeben & Nakayama, 1993).

This explanation is based on the assumption that stimulus offsets can trigger a state of attentional disengagement. In the Gap condition, attention could be shifted to the cued location sooner than would be the case in the No-Gap condition because the offset of the fixation cross caused attention to be "predisengaged" at the time of cue onset. Other researchers demonstrated that it was the disappearance of the fixation point and not a nonspecific warning that led to more rapid shifts of attention and, thus, to better performance (Mackeben & Nakayama, 1993). Similar results were obtained when the gap manipulation was used to study the latency of saccadic eye movements (e.g., Fischer & Breitmeyer, 1987; Fischer & Ramsperger, 1986;

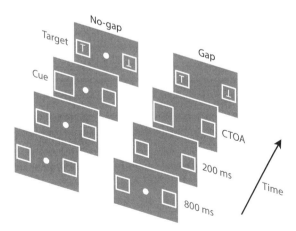

Figure 3.6 Example of the type of display used by Pratt and Nghiem (2000) to study the fixation-offset effect on attention shift latency. In the Gap condition, the central fixation point disappeared 200 ms before the location-cue onset. The CTOA in this experiment ranged from 16 to 200 ms.

discussed in chapter 6). Thus, the fixation-offset effect is robust and may indicate that attention is disengaged prior to being shifted.

Variable Spatial Extent of Attentional Focus

Attention shift models like those depicted in Figure 3.2 stimulated a great deal of research and theorizing, but it soon became apparent that they are limited. In particular, they lack a mechanism that can systematically vary the spatial extent of the attentional focal point. A more complete model would incorporate a mechanism for changing the location of the focal point and also its size.

One of the first attempts to measure the spatial extent of attentional focus required subjects to identify a target that was presented among an array of letters (Eriksen & Hoffman, 1972b). As seen in Figure 3.7, stimuli were positioned on an imaginary circle so that they were the same distance from the central fixation point, and the proximity of the target and distractors was systematically varied. The target-distractor stimulus-onset asynchrony (SOA) was also manipulated. More specifically, simultaneous presentation of a direct-cue bar marker and target was followed, a short time later (0–300 ms), by the distractors.

The result was an interesting interaction between SOA and target-distractor spacing. Distractors inhibited response times to a greater degree when they were within 1° of the target (Spacing 1), but only when the target-distractor SOA was 0 or 50 ms (see Figure 3.8). The effect of the cueing on responses was asymptotic by about 200 ms regardless of spacing. This suggests that at the longer SOAs, the attentional focal point was narrowed around the cue/target location prior to the onset of the distractors. On the basis of these results, the experimenters concluded that the spatial extent of focused attention can change in accordance with task demands (e.g., change from broadly encompassing both the target and the distractors to narrowly encompassing only the target).

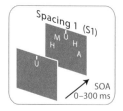 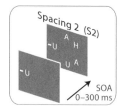

Figure 3.7 Examples of the type of stimulus displays in Eriksen and Hoffman's (1972b) experiment. With the S1 spacing, the distractor letters were adjacent to the target (U) indicated by the direct cue. With the S2 spacing, the distractor letters were farther away from the target.

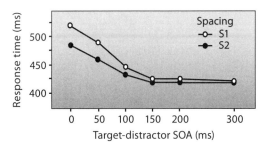

Figure 3.8 Some results of the Eriksen and Hoffman (1972b) experiment. At shorter target-distractor SOAs, the target was identified faster with the S2 spacing than with the S1 spacing. At longer SOAs, spacing had no effect on response times.

Another attempt to study variability of the spatial extent of attentional focus involved searching for a target letter within a circular array of eight letters (Jonides, 1980, 1983). When target locations were indicated by a symbolic cue, it was concluded that attention appeared to be distributed evenly among all eight letters. On the other hand, when target locations were indicated by a direct cue, it was concluded that the cued location appeared to have all available attention focused on it. Caution is advised when evaluating these results, however, because relatively short CTOAs were used with symbolic cues. Therefore, it should be expected that, at a CTOA of 75 ms, direct cues would be more effective than symbolic cues at eliciting the "focused mode" (as was the case in this study). Symbolic cues are not effective with a CTOA this short, and therefore the "diffuse attention mode" attributed to symbolic cueing may, in fact, be due to a CTOA that precludes symbolic-cue effectiveness. In fairness to the experimenter, however, the interaction between CTOA and cue type was not studied systematically until the late 1980s.

Another study conducted to examine task demands on variation of the spatial extent of focused attention required subjects to categorize one or all of a string of five letters (LaBerge, 1983). In one condition, subjects categorized the middle letter of the five-letter string and, in another condition, subjects categorized the entire letter string. It was hypothesized that subjects' attention would be narrowly focused on the middle letter in the letter-categorization condition, and more broadly focused on all five letters in the word-categorization condition. This was tested with a secondary task that involved occasionally presenting a probe digit at one of the five-letter positions after subjects made their letter or word-categorization response (see Figure 3.9).

The result of this secondary task was that, following a word-categorization response, probe digits were identified equally quickly when presented at any

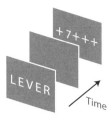

Figure 3.9 Example of the type of stimulus display used by LaBerge (1983) to study variability of the spatial extent of attention. A five-letter word was followed by a completely blank field and then, on some trials, a probe digit surrounded by plus signs in each of the original five-letter positions.

of the original five-letter positions (see Figure 3.10). On the other hand, following a middle-letter categorization response, probe digits were identified fastest when presented at the center position and slower when presented at the other positions. The experimenter concluded that while performing the middle-letter categorization task, subjects' attentional focus was narrowed to encompass primarily the area around the center position; and while performing the word-categorization task, their attentional focus was broadened to encompass the area around all five letters. In other words, the spatial extent of subjects' attentional focal point appeared to be adjusted in accordance with task demands from smaller (letter size) to larger (word size).

Studies of this type led to questions about the absolute minimum size to which the attention focal point can be narrowed. One attempt to answer this involved determining the minimum distance that an irrelevant stimulus could be to an attended stimulus and still have no disruptive effect on task

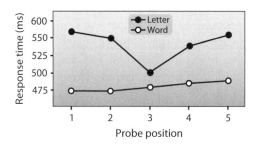

Figure 3.10 Results of LaBerge's (1983) experiment. The position of the probe digit had no significant effect on response times in the word condition. On the other hand, center location probe digits were associated with the fastest response times in the letter condition, and peripheral probe digits at original positions of the first or fifth letters were associated with the slowest response times. These results suggest that, in the letter condition, attention was narrowly focused on the middle letter prior to onset of the probe digit.

performance (Humphreys, 1981). The results indicated that the spatial extent of the attentional focal point is variable depending on where attention is focused relative to the fovea; its minimum size appears to be somewhere between 0.5° and 1° of visual angle.

Global/Local Processing

While some researchers studied the variability of attentional focus, others tried to determine whether or not there was a "default" setting for its spatial extent. In one study, subjects were shown bi-level stimuli that were large letters made up of smaller letters (Navon, 1977). The single large letter was referred to as being at the global level and an individual small letter was referred to as being at the local level (see Figure 3.11). When subjects were required to identify either global letters or local letters, the global letters were identified faster. It also took longer to identify local letters when they differed from the global letter they comprised (incongruent) than when they were the same (congruent). But it did not take longer to identify global letters when they differed from the local letters they were comprised of than when the global and local letters were the same. On the basis of this asymmetric pattern of interference and the overall faster identification of global letters, the experimenter concluded that the attentional focal point is, by default, set to a large (global level) spatial extent (Navon, 1977). The general implication of this conclusion is that the spatial extent of focused attention should be initially broadly distributed and should encompass the global shape of an object, but can be narrowed according to task demands.

The results of follow-up studies indicated that this proposal was overstated. For example, one series of experiments indicated that when subjects had just performed a task involving global-level visual analysis, the current spatial extent of their attentional focus would remain global, and this allowed them to perform a subsequent task involving global-level analysis faster than they could perform a subsequent task involving local-level analysis (Ward, 1982, 1983, 1985). Conversely, when subjects had just performed

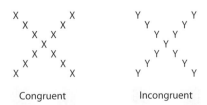

Congruent   Incongruent

Figure 3.11 Examples of the bi-level stimuli used by Navon (1977) to study global-local visual processing. Congruent bi-level stimuli consist of the same letter at the local and global levels. Incongruent bi-level stimuli consist of different letters at the local and global levels.

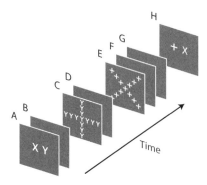

Figure 3.12 Example of the type of stimulus display used by Ward (1985) to study the level-readiness effect. Subjects saw a pair of targets to search for at the beginning of each trial. When they found a target, they pressed one response button if it was at the global level and another button if it was at the local level. The stimulus display sequence was (A) targets to be searched for on current trial; (B) blank screen for 500–1500 ms; (C) first bi-level stimulus visible for 100 ms; (D) blank screen until first response; (E) second bi-level stimulus visible for 100 ms; (F) blank screen until second response; (G) blank screen for 2000 ms at the end of trial; and (H) targets to be searched for on next trial.

a task involving local-level visual analysis, then the current spatial extent of their attentional focus would remain local, and this allowed them to perform a subsequent task involving local-level analysis faster than they could perform a subsequent task involving global-level analysis (see Figure 3.12). This *level-readiness effect* suggests that there is no default setting for the spatial extent of attentional focus, and that it may remain at its current setting (narrow or broad) until an adjustment is required to perform a new analysis (Ward, 1985).

Zoom Lens Metaphor

James (1890) suggested that as the area encompassed by focal attention grows larger, our capacity to attend to events within it should diminish as though attention is "spread thinner" over larger areas (a similar idea was discussed by Wolff, 1738, 1740; see Figure 1.7). One attempt to test this hypothesis involved presenting cues simultaneously at more than one location to determine whether or not changing the overall size of the cued area would affect the spatial extent of attentional focus (Eriksen & St. James, 1986; Eriksen & Yeh, 1985). In these experiments, cues, targets, and distractors were presented in a circular array. The researchers concluded that increasing the size of the cued area by presenting more cues led to a decrease in the concentration of attentional resources (i.e., they were spread progressively thinner; Eriksen & St. James, 1986).

Another multiple-cue experiment involved the presentation of a direct cue at one of four locations in a circular array of letter stimuli (3, 6, 9, and

12 o'clock positions) with a 150-ms CTOA (Eriksen & Yeh, 1985). On some trials, the direct cue served as a double cue (see Figure 3.13) because subjects were told that it cued both the location at which it appeared, and also the location diametrically opposite to it within the display. In other words, on some trials, the cue served as both a direct and a symbolic cue. A similar symbolic cueing manipulation was discussed in chapter 2 (McCormick, 1997; Figure 2.10). Targets were detected faster when they appeared at the primary (direct-cued) location as opposed to the alternate (symbolically cued) location. The experimenters concluded that responses to targets appearing at the symbolically cued location were slower because, on these trials, the spatial extent of attention must have been increased to encompass both the primary and alternate locations which, in turn, caused the concentration of attentional resources to decrease. Note, however, that symbolic location cues are not fully effective with CTOAs as short as 150 ms (see Figure 2.9B). This could explain why the direct location-cue effects were more pronounced than the symbolic location-cue effects, and we suggest that this be taken into account when evaluating the experimenters' account of these results.

Eriksen and colleagues (Eriksen & St. James, 1986; Eriksen & Yeh, 1985) refined the idea that the concentration of attention decreases as its spatial extent increases by describing this reciprocal relationship in terms of the resolving power of a camera's zoom lens. They suggested that both the attentional focal point and the zoom lens are adjustable from a low-resolution state encompassing a broad area to a high-resolution state encompassing just a narrow area of the visual field but with great resolving power. At lower resolutions, attentional resources were said to be spread more thinly across a larger area whereas, at higher resolutions, attentional resources were said to be concentrated within a smaller area (see Figure 3.14A). If true, then a target appearing within a

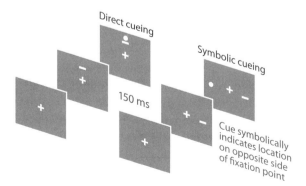

Figure 3.13 Example of the type of stimulus display used by Eriksen and Yeh (1985) to study the effect of direct location cues that, on some trials, also served as symbolic cues indicating the location on the opposite side of the display field.

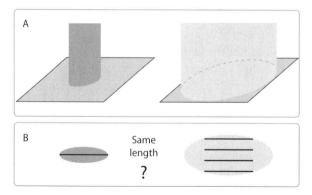

Figure 3.14 (A) Use of the zoom lens metaphor to describe the reciprocal relationship between the spatial extent of the attentional focal point and the concentration of attention within it. The smaller, darker attentional focal point denotes a greater concentration of attention. (B) In Palmer's (1990) experiment, comparisons of the lengths of a pair of single lines were more accurate than comparisons of the length of a single line to those of a group of four lines. Presumably the attentional focal point could stay the same size when comparing the former, but would have to increase in size and decrease in attentional concentration when comparing a single line to the larger group of four lines.

narrower focal point should be detected faster and more accurately than a target appearing within a broader focal point because, in the former case, a higher concentration of attention would be allocated to the target.

In one experiment, subjects saw one, two, or four horizontal lines for 100 ms (the study lines), followed by a 2000-ms blank field and then a single horizontal test line in the same location as the study stimuli (Palmer, 1990). Their task was to determine whether the test line was longer than the study lines. Accuracy in detecting differences between the length of the study and test lines was affected by set size. That is, the detectable difference in length between a single study line and the test line was half the detectable difference between a group of four study lines and the test line. In other words, subjects made more accurate judgments when comparisons involved a single study line as opposed to a group of four study lines. One account of this finding is that when a group of four lines was presented, the attentional focal point was enlarged to encompass them (see Figure 3.14B). And the resulting decrease in visual sensitivity caused by this enlargement therefore decreased the accuracy of line-length comparisons. This is consistent with the claim that the resolving power of the attentional focal point grows weaker as its spatial extent increases.

In an attempt to describe covert orienting of an attentional focal point that also varies in spatial extent, Eriksen (1990) suggested that when the focal point is shifted, it is de-focused at its original location and then refocused at its destination. Figure 3.15 is an example of how attention could be shifted between

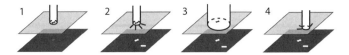

Figure 3.15 Shifting the attentional focal point from one location to another by expanding it to encompass both the origin and the shift destination, and then contracting it so that it is aligned only with the destination.

locations in the visual field if it occurs in an analog manner that traverses intermediate states of focus (i.e., narrow to broader to broadest at the original location and then broadest to less broad to narrow at the new location). To the best of our knowledge, most descriptions of focusing models in the literature imply that they are analog in the sense that the attention remains engaged while focusing occurs. Some researchers have suggested that adjustments of the focal point's spatial extent are discrete (e.g., Sheperd & Müller, 1989, p. 152), but there is nothing inherent about the nature of shifting by this method that favors analog as opposed to discrete focusing.

Can Attention Be Divided Into Multiple Foci?

Until the 1990s, it was generally assumed that the attentional focal point is unitary and indivisible. More recently, however, new types of attention tasks have produced data suggesting that, in some cases, attention may be divisible between objects. Some experimental results purporting to be evidence of focal point divisibility have been challenged and now seem questionable. But others appear to be valid. This is particularly true for feature-based attention tasks that are performed by focusing on items of one color versus another (e.g., Bichot et al., 1999; Gobell et al., 2004; see Figure 3.16), as opposed to space-based attention tasks involving location cues.

The idea that attention can be split into two or more attentional foci is controversial. And it may seem counterintuitive because it is difficult to imagine directing attention to several different locations in the visual field without attending to the areas between them. In addition, if we really could voluntarily divide attention in this way, why don't we do it whenever we need to perform difficult tasks involving serial analysis (e.g., searching for targets)? Presumably, if the strong claim about divisibility is valid, we should be able to divide attention into multiple foci as in Figure 3.17 and eliminate any need for effortful serial search by deploying attentional foci in parallel to many regions of the stimulus array. The answer appears to be that many claims about the divisibility of the attentional focal point are overstated, and supporting evidence is often based on the results of subtle experimental manipulations.

The focal point divisibility claim has been tested by presenting targets in each visual hemifield. In one study, subjects attended to an outline box in

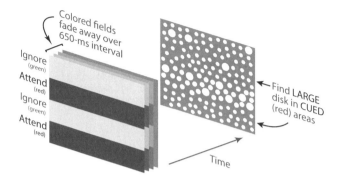

Figure 3.16 Example of the type of display used by Gobell et al. (2004) to study division of attention between colored regions during visual search. Prior to the onset of the search set containing small and large white disks, portions of the display were shown in red (darker background in the 1st panel of the figure) and green (lighter background in the 1st panel of the figure). Color served as a cue about which portions of the display were to be attended to and which were to be ignored. In this figure, for example, subjects would be required to attend to and search for targets only in the red areas while ignoring the green areas. Shortly before search set onset, the red and green color information was extinguished over the course of 650 ms and then subjects searched for the target (larger white disk) in the cued areas. The results indicated that attention can be divided between discrete locations when performing feature-based attention tasks.

each hemifield and detected targets that appeared within them (Castiello & Umiltà, 1992). The experimenters concluded that subjects were able to attend to two discrete locations at the same time because there was an inverse relationship between outline box size and response times. In a similar study with a more precise measure of attentional distribution, however, there was no significant difference in response times for probe items presented at cued locations and other locations directly between them (McCormick et al., 1998). In other words, while the first study purported to show that attention was divided into two foci, the replication indicated that a single attentional focal point appeared to encompass both cued locations as well as the intervening region.

The focal point divisibility claim has also been studied using electrophysiological measures. In one experiment, P1 amplitude modulation was measured while subjects monitored two of four locations for the presentation of

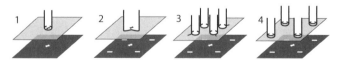

Figure 3.17 The multiple attentional focal point hypothesis holds that attention can be split into many discrete foci that can be simultaneously directed to several locations in the visual field to mediate spatially parallel attentional analysis.

matching symbols (Heinze et al., 1994a). They also performed a secondary task involving the detection of a probe stimulus either at a symbol location or directly between the two symbol locations (see Figure 3.18). The results of the secondary task indicated that P1 modulation occurred when probes appeared at symbol locations and also directly between symbol locations, but not elsewhere in the display. This suggests that a single attentional focal point encompassed both symbol locations and the intervening location between them (see chapter 7 for more information about electrophysiology and the ERP method).

Follow-up experiments involved a similar procedure, but also incorporated a feature-based manipulation (Malinowski et al., 2007; Müller et al., 2003). In particular, stimuli at the four locations were distinct by virtue of a unique flicker frequency (15.2, 8.7, 20.3, and 12.2 Hz). Like Gobell et al. (2004; Figure 3.16), the experimenters demonstrated that attention can be divided between subsets of items with a unique feature, but in this study the feature was flicker frequency rather than color.

Early attempts to determine whether or not the attentional focal point would divide in response to simultaneous multiple location cueing usually involved symbolic cues (see Figure 3.19). A number of studies were conducted and none indicated that attention was split into multiple foci (e.g., Kiefer & Siple, 1987; Klein & McCormick, 1989; McCormick & Klein, 1990; Posner

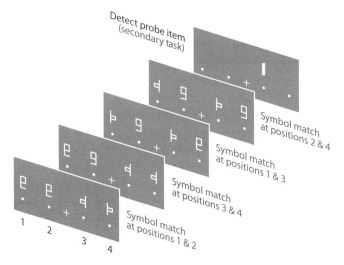

Figure 3.18 Example of the type of stimulus displays that Heinze et al. (1994a) used to study the potential divisibility of the attentional focal point. Successive displays were presented at 250–350 ms intervals. Each display could contain adjacent matching items or separated matching items that subjects attended and responded to. Occasionally, a probe item (rectangle) appeared at one of these four locations. P1 modulation occurred when the probe appeared at or between the locations of the previously presented matching items, but not elsewhere.

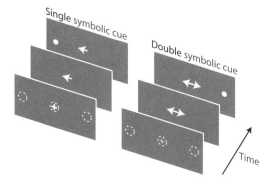

Figure 3.19 Single and double symbolic location-cueing displays. Subjects do not seem to be able to voluntarily split the attentional focal point into multiple foci in response to double symbolic-cue presentation. Circles (not visible during experiment) denote possible target locations.

et al., 1980). Instead, subjects seemed unable to direct their attention to multiple symbolically cued locations at the same time in anticipation of the impending target.

Another finding that is often mentioned as evidence for splitting of the attentional focal point is our ability to perform multiple-object tracking (MOT) tasks (e.g., Pylyshyn, 2007). The currently favored account of MOT, however, is that tracking is mediated by (nonattentional) spatial index tags and not by multiple attentional foci. This is discussed in more detail in chapter 5.

The study that is perhaps most frequently cited as evidence that the attentional focal point can be split into multiple foci was conducted by Kramer and Hahn (1995). Their experiment was based on the assumption that when comparing the identities of two target letters, response interference caused by distractor letters positioned between the targets would be evidence that a single attentional focal point encompassed both the targets and the distractors. On the other hand, if the intervening distractors do not cause response interference, then this would be evidence that the attentional focal point was split into two foci that were directed to the targets but not the distractors. The experimenters claimed that their data supported the second scenario (see Figure 3.20). They also replicated their finding in follow-up experiments involving the same type of stimulus display (Hahn & Kramer, 1998).

It has been suggested, however, that a critical assumption of the study was violated because the distractor letters were never *directly* between the target letters (Pye, 2003). As seen in Figure 3.21A, targets were positioned on an imaginary circle at the 10:30 and 1:30 clock positions on some trials, or the 7:30 and 4:30 clock positions on other trials. The distractor letters were also positioned along the circle between target pairs above the 10:30 and 1:30

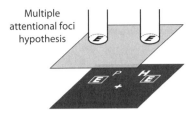

Figure 3.20 On the basis of their (1995) experiment, Kramer and Hahn claimed that the attentional focal point was split into two discrete foci that were directed to the target locations (letter Es inside cue boxes in this example).

positions or below the 7:30 and 4:30 positions. When stimuli were presented in a horizontal array so that the distractors were directly between the targets in a procedurally identical replication experiment, the results raised the possibility that distractors might interfere with target comparisons (Pye, 2003; see Figure 3.21B). When distractors are positioned above or below a pair of targets rather than directly between them, a single attentional focal point could be shifted from one target location to the other and not pass through the distractor locations (see Figure 3.22). A second possibility is that a larger but narrowed focal point could encompass both target locations without encompassing the distractors in the Kramer and Hahn (1995) experiment. In chapter 4, we propose another account of the Kramer and Hahn finding that is based on sensory facilitation of responses.

Other purported evidence of multiple attentional foci was obtained in a RSVP experiment (McMains & Somers, 2004). As seen in Figure 3.23, on

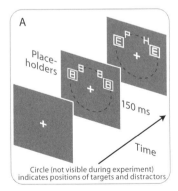
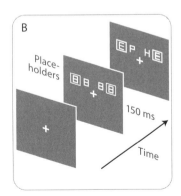

Figure 3.21 (A) Example of the type of stimulus display used by Kramer and Hahn (1995). Note that the distractor letters (P & H in this example) were not positioned directly between the target letters (Es in this example) and did not interfere with target responses. (B) Example of the type of stimulus display used by Pye (2003). Distractor letters (P & H in this example) were positioned directly between the target letters (Es in this example).

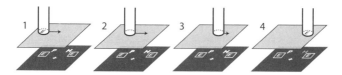

Figure 3.22 A single attentional focal point that is shifted from one target location to the other in Kramer and Hahn's (1995) stimulus display would not pass over the distractors, which were located above (in this figure) or below the targets.

some trials, subjects divided their attention between two RSVP streams on opposite sides of the display (while ignoring a stream in the center). They responded whenever currently visible items in the two attended streams were the same. On other trials, subjects monitored only the central stream and made memory-based matching responses (i.e., when the currently visible item matched a target previewed at the beginning of the trial). Note that the difference in response types across conditions is a potential design concern. In addition, subjects performed one version of the task (involving slower RSVP presentation rates) while in a functional magnetic resonance imaging (fMRI) scanner, and the results were compared to those obtained in a non-fMRI session (involving faster presentation rates). The researchers concluded that, in the two-stream condition, processing necessarily involved two discrete attentional foci. In particular, they stated that when subjects performed the two-stream task, the fMRI data showed activation of two discrete locations in the visual cortex corresponding to the two RSVP

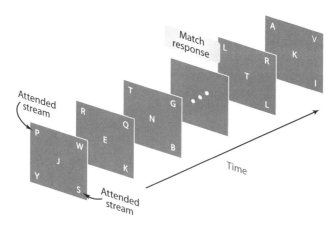

Figure 3.23 Example of the type of rapid serial visual presentation (RSVP) display used in the McMains and Somers (2004) experiment. As shown in this figure, subjects in two-stream condition attended to both the upper-left and the lower-right RSVP streams while ignoring the central stream. They responded whenever the currently visible items in the two attended streams matched.

streams, but not activation of an intermediate location corresponding to the unattended central stream. While acknowledging that hemodynamically based fMRI signals lack the temporal precision required to indicate whether or not the attentional focal point can be divided, they also argued that, when taken together, the fMRI session and non-fMRI session results supported their claim about multiple attentional foci (see also, McMains & Somers, 2005; Somers & McMains, 2005).

This claim may be overstated, however. One concern is that the timing parameters in the fMRI and non-fMRI sessions were not identical. Therefore, the nature of attentional processing may have differed across sessions. For example, because of the slower presentation rate, serial alternation of focused attention at two RSVP stream locations may have been more likely in the fMRI session (which could account for the pattern of fMRI data). In chapter 7, we discuss the limitations of fMRI and the need to use electrophysiological techniques to study attentional processing with greater temporal precision. Perhaps a replication of this experiment involving ERP measures would be more informative.

Also, the researchers' claim about multiple attentional foci hinges completely on what may be an incorrect assumption about the time course of attention shifts. More specifically, they argued that the "generally accepted" minimum time required to redeploy attention from one location to another is 200 ms (McMains & Somers, 2004, p. 683). This is about as slow as saccadic eye movement latency (see chapter 6). If true, then a single attentional focal point could not be shifted back and forth between two RSVP streams rapidly enough to perform the task when, in the non-fMRI session, the presentation rate was faster than 200 ms/item. The only other possibility, they reasoned, is the deployment of multiple attentional foci. Note, however, that it is not generally accepted that at least 200 ms is required to shift attention from location to another. Recent electrophysiological research has clearly ruled out claims that attention cannot be shifted from one item to another within 100 ms (Woodman & Luck, 2003), and the results of many visual search experiments show that far less time than 200 ms is required—perhaps only 25 ms (e.g., Wolfe, 1994, 1998; Woodman & Luck, 1999). If attention can be shifted between locations in as little as 25 ms, then dividing it into multiple foci would not be required to perform the two-stream RSVP task with a 173-ms presentation rate (used in the fMRI session of the experiment). There is currently no definitive estimate of the time course of attention shifts, in part, because estimates differ greatly depending on the experimental paradigm being used (see e.g., Luck et al., 2000, p. 434). Thus, while the fMRI data indicating separate activation sites in the visual cortex are intriguing, design concerns and a questionable assumption about

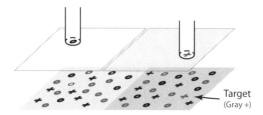

Figure 3.24 When visually searching a display to find a target, split-brain patients appear to have a separate attentional focal point for each hemifield (Luck et al., 1994a). The target in this figure is the gray plus sign.

maximum attentional shift speed weaken the argument that attention was split into multiple foci in this experiment.

In summary, there is evidence that attention can be divided across noncontiguous locations, but only in certain circumstances (e.g., Vogel & Luck, 2002), and perhaps not in response to multiple location cues. In a study of comissurotomized (split-brain) patients, it was found that when performing a visual search task, the transected corpus callosum (connects the cortical hemispheres) allowed each hemisphere to scan its visual hemifield independently with its own attentional focal point (Luck et al., 1994a; see Figure 3.24). This indicates that an intact corpus callosum unifies attentional analysis across the two cortical hemispheres and is involved in the maintenance of a single attentional focal point. Another experiment involving split-brain patients and multiple location cueing indicated that patients were unable to divide attention into two foci in response to symbolic cues (Holtzman et al., 1981). Taking this into account, Luck et al. (1989) suggested that, while they have independently functioning attentional systems available for visual search, even split-brain patients orient attention to symbolically cued locations with a unitary focal point.

LaBergian Activity Distribution Model

In the 1980s and 1990s, David LaBerge and colleagues developed a model of attentional analysis that involved parallel processing of visual stimuli at several locations at a time (e.g., LaBerge, 1995a, 1998; LaBerge & Brown, 1989). It was not, however, based on the notion that multiple attentional focal points were shifted to these locations. Instead, LaBerge proposed that stimuli trigger sensory operations that cause the formation of activity distributions within mental representations of the visual field (Figure 3.25). In other words, analysis of multiple stimulus onsets is said to be carried out initially by sensory processes rather than by attentional processes (i.e., multiple attentional foci). According to LaBerge, a single channel of focused attention can then be directed to the location of one of the activity distributions in either a stimulus-driven manner (attentional capture) or voluntarily in a goal-driven manner.

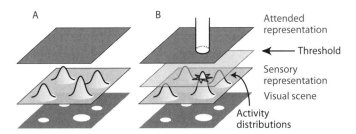

Figure 3.25 (A) Multiple stimulus onsets trigger the formation of LaBergian activity distributions in a sensory representation of the visual field. The most intense stimulus will produce the activity distribution with the greatest magnitude. (B) When the magnitude of an activity distribution exceeds a criterion threshold, this can lead to a channel of attention being opened at the corresponding location within a higher-level representation of the visual field.

Although they are similar in appearance, an activity distribution is not an attentional gradient. Instead, it is an accumulation of neural activity produced by sensory operations. Activity distributions can form at more than one location because, unlike what many researchers believe about attentional analysis, sensory activity is not constrained to a single location at a time and can change dynamically and in parallel at several locations within a representation of visual space. The magnitude of an activity distribution triggered by a high-intensity stimulus will also be greater than that triggered by a low-intensity stimulus. When this magnitude exceeds a threshold value, it can initiate the opening of a channel of focused attention at its corresponding location within a higher-level representation of the scene, as seen in Figure 3.25B.

There is a difference in the way attentional alignments are said to be carried out in an analog manner and the way they would be carried out as a result of activity distribution formation. The former involve movement. Attentional alignments mediated by activity distributions, however, are discrete. Neural activity that exceeds the criterion threshold will cause an attention channel to open at one location. This channel will then close and reopen elsewhere when attention is drawn in a stimulus-driven manner to a different location where neural activity has exceeded the criterion threshold. In a location-cueing experiment, the formation of an activity distribution will be triggered by the onset of each new stimulus (e.g., fixation point, cue, target). In Figure 3.26, the onset of a direct cue causes an activity distribution to form at its location. The magnitude of this distribution may be sufficient to begin the process of opening a channel of attention there before the onset of the target, thereby facilitating response times in a stimulus-driven manner. In contrast, the onset of a symbolic cue also causes an activity distribution to form, but at its physical location rather than at the location to which the cue symbolically refers. In this case, if an attention channel opens at the cued

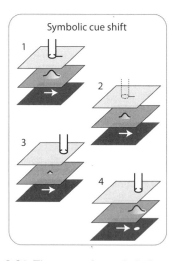 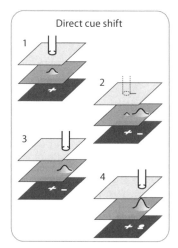

Figure 3.26 The onset of a symbolic location cue produces an activity distribution at the cue's physical location but *not* at the location symbolically indicated by the cue. Therefore, a goal-driven attention shift initiated by a symbolic cue cannot be facilitated by stimulus-triggered sensory activation. In contrast, the onset of a direct location cue produces an activity distribution at the cue's physical location (also the location indicated by the cue). Therefore, a stimulus-driven shift initiated by a direct cue can be facilitated by stimulus-triggered sensory activation.

location prior to target onset, this is the result of goal-driven input rather than stimulus-driven activity triggered by stimulus onsets.

While metaphors used to describe properties of the attentional focal point (e.g., spotlight, zoom lens) are sometimes referred to as models, they are not in a formal sense. The LaBergian activity distribution model, however, is one of the first to formally describe stimulus-driven and goal-driven control of covert orienting. More specifically, when a channel of attention is opened in a stimulus-driven manner, this is the result of sensory operations associated with activity distribution formation. When a channel of attention is opened in a goal-driven manner, this is the result of higher-level operations associated with the perceiver's beliefs, expectations, and general knowledge of the task being performed. In chapter 4, we discuss how this type of framework can be used to conceptualize the relative contributions of sensory and attentional analysis to location-cue effects.

Summary

The attentional focal point is often compared to a spotlight because it can be directed to discrete portions of the visual field. Many researchers have used this metaphor to conceptualize and develop hypotheses about covert orienting. In the 1980s, for example, a good deal of research was conducted to determine the velocity of attention shifts. This produced a number of conflicting claims and a contentious debate about whether the attentional focal point is shifted in an analog or a discrete manner. Over time, however, it became clear that both types of attention shifts may occur. Posner et al.'s (1988) hypothesis about attentional disengagement and discrete attention shifts is well supported by neurophysiological and behavioral data. And attention is clearly shifted in an analog manner when we visually track moving targets. Thus, a more appropriate question may be "when are shifts discrete and when are they analog?" Also in the 1980s, researchers refined the spotlight metaphor to account for variability of the attentional focal point's spatial extent. The results of several studies supported a suggestion by James (1890) and his predecessors that as the area encompassed by focal attention increases, the concentration of attention decreases. On this basis, Eriksen and colleagues (Eriksen & St. James, 1986; Eriksen & Yeh, 1985) described this reciprocal relationship by comparing the attentional focal point to the zoom lens of a camera. Although the limitations of the spotlight metaphor are now apparent, it could be argued that it was its simplicity that made the notion of covert orienting accessible and stimulated so much research.

Attentional focus is, by definition, selective and some researchers have suggested that its primary purpose is to reduce information (Tsotsos et al., 2005). For this reason, many ideas about (and models of) attention are based on the assumption that there is a single attentional focal point. In the 1990s, however, researchers began to find evidence of spatially parallel processing at discrete locations in visual space that seemed to indicate that attention can be divided into multiple foci. The issue is controversial; some results that initially appeared to support the multiple attentional foci hypothesis have been successfully challenged, and in some cases the claim appears to be overstated. But other results appear to demonstrate unequivocally that attention can be divided in this way. Therefore, rather than debating the absolute indivisibility of attentional focus, perhaps it will be more fruitful to ask when attention appears to be divisible and when it does not. Based on research conducted to date, it appears that attention is more likely to be divisible when performing feature-based attention tasks (e.g., dividing attention between regions on the basis of a unique feature like color) as opposed to space-based attention tasks involving location cues.

In the next chapter, we examine in detail a number of multiple location-cue experiments and, in doing so, consider whether or not the results implicate multiple attentional foci. We also look at how a version of the LaBerge (1995a, 1998) model might account for the results. Both types of explanations involve spatially parallel processing of multiple stimuli, but LaBerge's model holds that this parallel processing occurs at a sensory rather than an attentional level. In addition, we show how LaBerge's framework may provide valuable clues about the relationship between sensory and attentional processing when attention is covertly oriented.

4

Sensory and Attentional Mediation of Covert Orienting

When a new object appears in our visual field, different types of analysis are carried out as we orient toward, inspect, and identify it. The initial stages of this analysis are sensory. Retinal signals about the object's presence and approximate location are sent via the optic nerves to the midbrain collicular area and to the occipital lobe for further processing. Only then does attentional analysis of the object occur. Unlike sensory analysis, however, attentional analysis is not mandatory. As Yantis and Jonides (1990) demonstrated, when attention is actively engaged at another location, it will not always be captured by the appearance of a new object. But the object will trigger sensory operations that provide crude shape and location information to higher level processes.

When a direct location cue appears in our visual field, the initial stages of analysis are also sensory. The luminance change associated with the cue's onset triggers sensory processes that alert subsequent attentional processes that a cue has appeared. According to LaBerge and Brown (1989, p. 119), the neural activation associated with cue-triggered sensory analysis may lead to the formation of an activity distribution within a sensory representation of visual space. This, in turn, can trigger attentional analysis at the corresponding location within a higher level representation (see Figure 3.24). Regardless of the explanatory framework one adopts to account for cue effects, some degree of sensory processing of direct cues must precede attentional analysis.

Initial sensory analysis of a direct cue appears to serve two functions: it provides an alerting signal about the cue's presence; and it encodes, in at least a crude manner, the cue's location. This location information can then be utilized by subsequent operations that determine where to shift the attentional focal point. In Figure 4.1, the LaBergian activity distribution framework is used to describe this process.

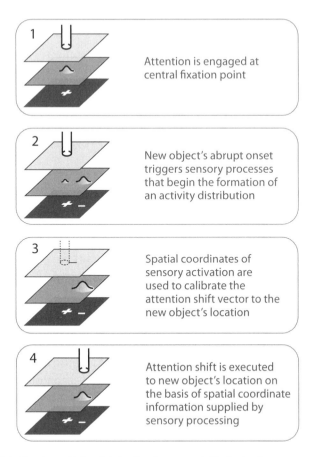

1   Attention is engaged at central fixation point

2   New object's abrupt onset triggers sensory processes that begin the formation of an activity distribution

3   Spatial coordinates of sensory activation are used to calibrate the attention shift vector to the new object's location

4   Attention shift is executed to new object's location on the basis of spatial coordinate information supplied by sensory processing

Figure 4.1 LaBergian activity distribution framework illustrates how sensory processing of a direct cue provides spatial coordinates used to calibrate an attention shift vector to the cued location.

The counterargument that sensory processes cannot be involved in the calibration of attention shifts is questionable for the following reason: for attention to be shifted to a direct-cue location, the spatial coordinates of the shift destination that are required to calibrate the attention shift vector *must* be provided by a nonattentional mechanism. That is, attentional analysis cannot supply location information required for its own initiation at a new location. Thus, when a direct location cue appears at a peripheral location, some of the visual analysis of the cue is nonattentional and it provides spatial coordinates required for subsequent attentional analysis to be initiated at that location.

Sensory Analysis and Location-Cueing Effects
Given that at least the initial stages of analysis of direct-cue onsets are necessarily sensory, it stands to reason that sensory processes associated with

direct cueing might affect responses to targets appearing at cued locations. Note that when a target appearing at a cued location is responded to faster and more accurately, this response facilitation has traditionally been attributed to attentional processing. But when the cues in question are direct cues, could it also be possible that *sensory* processing of cue and target onsets contributes to the response facilitation?

This question has been tested in a variety of ways. Psychophysical and electrophysiological procedures have been used, for example, to demonstrate that location cueing increases perceptual sensitivity to targets (e.g., Bonnel et al., 1987; Doallo et al., 2004; Downing, 1988; Fu et al., 2005; Müller, 1994; Müller & Humphreys, 1991; Possamai & Bonnel, 1991). Direct cues also appear to have a greater sensory effect on target responses than do symbolic cues (Müller, 1994).

In this chapter, we extend LaBerge's activity distribution framework to account for a number of experimental results indicating that sensory processing contributes to response facilitation. One critical assumption of the model is that activity distributions can form in parallel at several locations in a stimulus-driven manner (LaBerge & Brown, 1989, p. 109). A second assumption is that, after being triggered by a sensory event, an activity distribution will increase in size over time until, about 100 ms after the triggering event, it reaches a peak magnitude. Then it will begin to decrease in size until, about 200 ms after the triggering event, most of the activity has dissipated and the distribution has all but disappeared. This time course mirrors that of the effectiveness of direct location cues.

Another assumption of the model is that sensory processing of direct-cue and target onsets contributes to response facilitation in the following manner: if two stimuli appear briefly at or near the same location in rapid succession, the activity distribution triggered by the first stimulus may still be present when the second stimulus appears there. As seen in Figure 4.2, when this occurs, the first stimulus's residual activity combines with the activity triggered at or near the same location by the second stimulus to momentarily produce a higher level of sensory activation than the second stimulus could produce alone. This type of spatio-temporal summation of sensory distributions is thought to occur with successively presented sinusoidal gratings (see e.g., Sachs et al., 1971; Watson & Nachmias, 1980). In a direct location cue experiment, when the target appears at the cued location 100 ms after the cue, residual cue-triggered activation combines with target-triggered activation to produce an activity distribution of greater magnitude than would be case if the target appeared at an uncued location. This, in turn, causes a channel of attention to be opened up at this location more rapidly than it would at locations of activity distributions of lesser magnitude.

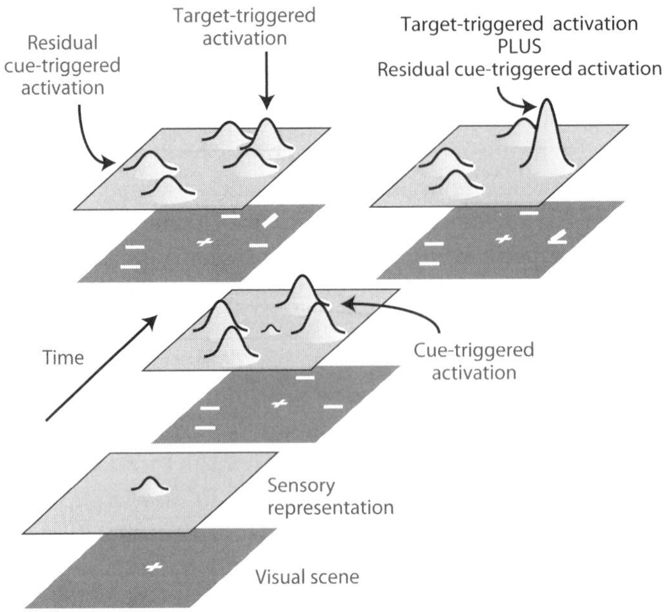

Figure 4.2 One assumption of the activity distribution proposal is that residual cue-triggered activation can combine with target-triggered activation to produce an activity distribution of greater magnitude than could be produced by a target appearing at an uncued location. This, in turn, causes an attention channel to open there more quickly than would be the case if the activity distribution was of lesser magnitude. In this way, sensory processing contributes to facilitation of responses to targets by direct cues.

Multiple Location Cueing

When targets are detected faster at cued locations than at uncued locations, this response facilitation is usually called a cue effect. Distinguishing between sensory and attentional contributions to cue effects is a nontrivial problem. As of the late 1990s, there was little agreement among researchers about how sensory and attentional processing might interact when cue effects occur. The multiple location cue paradigm, however, may be a promising way to study this interaction. With this goal in mind, we conducted a number of target-detection experiments that involved simultaneous multiple location cueing (Richard et al., 2003; Wright & Richard, 2003). Each trial usually began with the presentation of one or more direct cues at randomly selected locations. Then, following a delay that was usually 100 ms, a target appeared and remained visible until the subject detected and responded to it. Given that direct-cue effects occur even with low-validity cues (see Figure 2.9A), cues in these experiments were usually not informative about target location. In the example depicted in Figure 4.3, there are eight possible cue/target positions arranged in a circle around the central fixation cross. The cues are

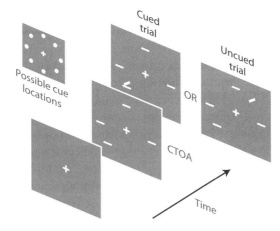

Figure 4.3 Example of a multiple simultaneous direct location cue display. In this figure, the direct cues are horizontal lines immediately below possible target locations, and the target is a diagonal line. Cue-target onset asynchrony (CTOA) is usually 100 ms in this type of experiment because this is the temporal interval at which direct cues are most effective.

horizontal lines located immediately below possible target positions and the target is a tilted line. The purpose of these experiments was to determine whether or not targets would be detected faster if they appeared at cued locations than at uncued locations.

The multiple location-cueing paradigm can be used to test several questions. In one experiment, for example, we varied the number of simultaneously presented cues to determine whether target-detection responses would be affected by this cue number manipulation. Cues were not informative about target location. Several different predictions can be made about the results. They vary in accordance with assumptions one makes about (a) the extent to which attentional focus will be divided into multiple foci in response to the onset of multiple direct cues and (b) the extent to which sensory processes contribute to cue effects.

Purely Attentional Account. Some researchers might assume that when a multiple direct-cue task is performed: (a) the attentional focal point is unitary and indivisible and (b) any cue effects that result are entirely due to attentional processing and not at all to sensory processing. On this basis, they might make the following prediction: when a single cue is presented on a given trial, then undivided attentional analysis of it may be possible. But if two cues are presented simultaneously, then a unitary and indivisible attentional focal point can be directed to just one of the two cued locations. Averaged over a number of two-cue trials, a cued location would be attended to only 50% of the time. As a result, the expected cue effect on response times on two-cue trials would be just 50% of that on single-cue trials because the mean response time would be based on the 50% of trials that yielded an attention-based cue effect plus the 50% of trials that yielded no cue effect (see Figure 4.4A). Similarly, when averaged over a number of three-cue trials, the expected cue effect on response times would be just 33.3% of that on single-cue trials because, on average, a cued location would be attended to only 33.3% of the time. And, when averaged over a number of four-cue trials, the expected cue effect on response times would be just 25% of that on single-cue trials because, on average, a cued location would be attended to only 25% of the time. The result is a pattern of cue effect magnitudes that diminish with increases in cue number.

For the sake of argument, one might propose that a purely attentional explanation of direct-cueing effects can be modified to account for a finding that cue effect magnitude is independent of cue number. For example, it could be argued that, while the attentional focal point is unitary, it can also assume a variety of irregular shapes to encompass all cued locations but none of the uncued locations between them. In Figure 4.5, the focal point assumes a banana-like shape to wrap around two cued locations without encompassing the location between them. This is an example of an argument about how cue effect magnitude might be independent of cue number if it also can be assumed that the shape of the attentional focal point is systematically distorted prior to target onset. It is not compelling, however, because there is no reported evidence that this is possible; and it is unclear

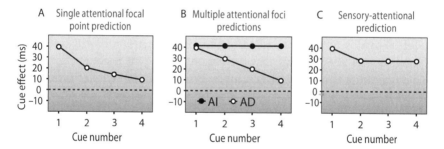

Figure 4.4 (A) A purely attentional account predicts that when multiple direct location cues are presented, cue effect magnitude at any given cued location should decrease as a function of cue number increases. (B) There are two multiple attentional foci proposals. The first holds that the concentration of attention within each focus is independent of foci number (AI proposal) and predicts that cue effect magnitude should also be independent of the number of cues presented. The second proposal holds that the concentration of attention within each focus is a negative function of foci number (AD proposal) and predicts that cue effect magnitude should decrease with cue number increases. (C) A sensory-attentional account predicts that cue effect magnitude should be independent of the number of cues presented because sensory processing occurs in parallel at all cued locations; but that, on single-cue trials, cue effect magnitude should be even greater because both sensory and attentional processes may contribute to facilitation of target-detection response times at the single cued location.

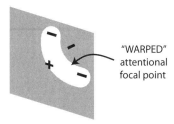

"WARPED"
attentional
focal point

Figure 4.5 An example of the irregular distortions of attentional focal point shape that would be required to account for multiple direct-cueing effects purely in terms of attentional processing with a unitary focal point.

why such a strategy would be adopted when performing a task in which the impending target's location on a given trial was not related to the cue locations. More specifically, given that targets were equally likely to appear at cued and uncued locations, a more efficient strategy for maximizing target detection would be to attend to all locations equally.

One might also argue that a unitary attentional focal point could simply expand to encompass more than one cued location. But, as seen in Figure 4.6, as cue number increases, the probability that a target will appear outside the attended area decreases (i.e., increasing focal point size increases the likelihood that both cued and uncued locations are attended to). Also, if it is assumed that there is a reciprocal relationship between the spatial extent of attention and the concentration of attention (see Figure 3.14), then increases in the size of the attentional focal point as a function of cue number should decrease the concentration of attention at any cued location. This, in turn, should cause cue effect magnitudes to decrease as a function of cue number increases. Thus, the purely attentional account of the results of this type of multiple location-cueing experiment is most consistent with a pattern of cue effect magnitudes that diminish with increases in cue number as in Figure 4.4A.

Figure 4.6 Effect of cue number on the size of the attentional focal point and the concentration of attention within it. The larger, darker attentional focal points denote a decrease in attentional concentration.

Multiple Attentional Foci Account. Some researchers might assume that when a multiple direct-cue task is performed: (a) the attentional focal point is divided into multiple foci that are directed to each cued location and (b) any cue effects that result are entirely due to attentional processing and not at all to sensory processing. On this basis, they might make one of the following predictions, depending on what they assume about the relationship between the number of attentional foci and the relative concentration of attention within each focus. Those who assume that there is a reciprocal relationship between the spatial extent of attention and the concentration of attention (see Figure 3.14) would presumably argue that as the number of foci increase, the concentration of attention within each focus decreases. We call this the attention-dependent (AD) proposal (Figure 4.7B). On the other hand, those who do not make this assumption would presumably argue that increasing the number of foci has no effect on the concentration of attention within each focus. We call this the attention-independent (AI) proposal (Figure 4.7A). Advocates of the AD proposal would predict that cue effect magnitude should diminish with increases in cue number (function labeled AD in Figure 4.4B). Advocates of the AI proposal would predict that cue effect magnitude should be unaffected by increases in cue number (function labeled AI in Figure 4.4B). In both cases, the effect of cue number on cue effect magnitude is predicted to be linear.

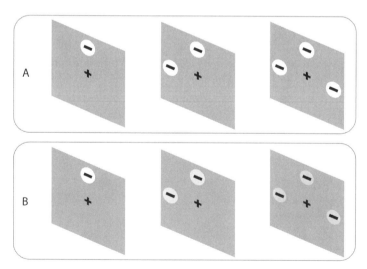

Figure 4.7 (A) The attention-independent (AI) proposal holds that increasing the number of foci has no effect on the concentration of attention within each focus. (B) The attention-dependent (AD) proposal holds that as the number of attentional foci increase, the concentration of attention within each focus decreases. The darker attentional foci denote a decrease in attentional concentration.

Sensory-Attentional Account. Some researchers might assume that when a multiple direct-cue task is performed: (a) the attentional focal point is unitary and indivisible and (b) any cue effects that result may be due to sensory processing as well as attentional processing. On this basis, they might make the following prediction: on single-cue trials, the cue should capture attention because it is only one vying for it. On multiple-cue trials, however, none of the cued locations should *initially* be attended to because it is assumed that attention cannot be divided between multiple locations. As outlined in Figure 4.2, however, sensory activity triggered by each cue's onset should cause the channel of attention to open faster when the target appears at a cued location as opposed to an uncued location. Therefore, on multiple-cue trials, sensory processes should contribute to cue effects; and the magnitude of these effects should be the same on two-cue, three-cue, and four-cue trials because sensory activation occurs in parallel across the visual scene. On single-cue trials, this sensory contribution to the cue effect should also occur; but attentional processing should contribute to the effect as well, because attention should be immediately captured by the cue. Therefore, on single-cue trials, the magnitude of the cue effect should be greater than that on multiple-cue trials because it is mediated by a *combination* of sensory and attentional processing. The predicted nonlinear function is depicted in Figure 4.4C.

A Systematic Investigation of Multiple Location Cue Effects

In this section, we review a number of target-detection experiments involving multiple location cueing that we conducted in collaboration with Christian Richard (Richard et al., 2003; Wright & Richard, 2003). The design of most of these experiments was similar to the description in the previous section, and usually the cue-target configuration was similar to that in Figure 4.3. Our goal was to systematically manipulate variables such as cue number, CTOA, cue luminance, and so on, to determine the relative contributions of sensory and attentional processing to cue effects.

Manipulating Cue Number

When one to four multiple simultaneous direct cues were presented, response-time benefits were associated with more than one location (Wright & Richard, 2003). On multiple-cue trials, significant cue effects occurred in all conditions and, although smaller than the cue effect on single-cue trials, they did not vary in magnitude as a function of cue number (see Figure 4.8A). This result is not consistent with either the purely attentional or the multiple attentional foci accounts outlined in the previous section (Figure 4.4). It is, however, consistent with the sensory-attentional account. The equivalence of cue effect magnitude on two-cue, three-cue, and four-cue trials indicates

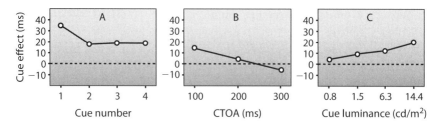

Figure 4.8 (A) Results of Wright and Richard's (2003) experiment involving manipulation of cue number. Cue effects occurred on trials involving 2, 3, and 4 simultaneously presented cues, and the effect was even more pronounced on one-cue trials. (B) Results of their experiment involving manipulation of cue-target onset asynchrony (CTOA). A cue effect occurred with a 100-ms CTOA, but not with longer CTOAs. (C) Results of their experiment involving manipulation of cue luminance. Cue effect magnitude was a positive function of luminance magnitude.

that cue effects were due, in part, to sensory analysis as outlined in Figure 4.2. It may even be possible for sensory processes to produce a direct-cueing effect independently of attentional processes (e.g., McCormick, 1997, Experiment 3; see Figure 2.10).

The larger cue effect on single-cue trials as opposed to multiple-cue trials suggests that, on single-cue trials, both sensory and attentional processing contributed to the cue effect. More specifically, the cost of invalid cueing was greater on single-cue trials than on multiple-cue trials, which could indicate that single cues captured attention but multiple cues did not. Assuming that a response-time cost is associated with attentional disengagement, directing attention to a single-cue location could (relative to multiple-cue trials) increase the time required to respond to a target that subsequently appeared elsewhere at an uncued location. That is, additional time may be required to disengage attention at the invalid-cue location and reengage it at the target location. On multiple-cue trials, no such cost would be incurred because the observer presumably would not direct attention to just one of the cued locations.

One might be tempted to suggest (although it is a weak argument) that, given that the cues provided no information about target location, multiple-cue presentation could have produced the results merely by decreasing the uncertainty about where the target would appear within the array of eight possible cue/target locations. The equality of response times on two-cue, three-cue, and four-cue trials demonstrates that this was not the case. Instead, cue effect magnitude was independent of cue number, and the effects were not due to changes in target location uncertainty.

Some additional tests and analyses were conducted to verify the validity of the multiple location-cueing procedure. In particular, while the appearance of the (tilted line) target at a cued location produced an "arrow head" configuration (see Figure 4.3), control experiments (e.g., target shape was changed to a small outline square) indicated that the results were not biased by potentially greater target salience attributable to this configuration (Richard et al., 2003). Also, responses to targets between cued locations were compared to those for targets that were clearly not between cued locations, and the results of this analysis indicated that cue effects were confined to cued locations and did not spread to intervening uncued locations (Wright & Richard, 2003, p. 931).

Manipulating CTOA

If cue effects produced by simultaneous multiple direct cueing arise, in part, from sensory activation, then their magnitude should be greatest at short CTOAs (100 ms) and decline with further CTOA increases (cf., Sheperd & Müller, 1989; see Figure 2.9B). On the other hand, if cue effects produced by simultaneous multiple cueing are caused primarily by sustained attentional processes, then they should still occur even when the CTOA is several hundred milliseconds (cf., Hughes, 1984). We tested this by presenting four simultaneous direct cues on each trial while varying the CTOA (100, 200, or 300 ms) (Wright & Richard, 2003). A significant cue effect occurred only when the CTOA was 100 ms (see Figure 4.8B). Given that the contribution of attentional processing to cueing effects appears to increase gradually as the CTOA is increased from 0 to 300 ms and beyond (e.g, Müller & Findlay, 1988; Sheperd & Müller, 1989), it is unlikely that the cue effect in the 100 ms CTOA condition was caused by attentional analysis (otherwise, cue effects should have occurred in the longer CTOA conditions as well). The results suggest, instead, that the cue effect was mediated, in part, by sensory processing.

Manipulating Multiple-Cue Luminance

If cue effects produced by simultaneous multiple location cueing arise, in part, from sensory activation, then they should change as a function of cue luminance because the magnitude of sensory activation is directly related to the magnitude of stimulus intensity. We tested this by presenting four simultaneous cues on each trial with a CTOA of 100 ms while varying the luminance of the cues (Wright & Richard, 2003). Significant cue effects only occurred when cue luminance was greater than or equal to 6.3 cd/m^2 (see Figure 4.8C). Note that the relationship between cue luminance and sensory activation magnitude appears to be different from the relationship between cue luminance and attention-based cue effects. The results of a previous study, for example, indicated that when the luminance of high-validity cues was manipulated at CTOAs longer than 100 ms (sufficient time for sensory activation triggered by cue onsets to attenuate and for attention to become actively focused at the cued location), luminance increases did not influence cue effect magnitude (Hughes, 1984). In the current experiment, however, the potential involvement of attentional analysis in processing cue information was minimal because noninformative (low validity) cues were presented with a short (100 ms) CTOA. The results indicate that the processes mediating the cue effects were closely associated with sensory activation.

Manipulating Cue Validity

In the experiments described so far, it was unlikely that subjects attended to any one particular cue on multiple-cue trials because the target was equally likely to appear at any of the possible cued or uncued locations. Therefore, there was no strategic advantage to shifting attention to a particular cued location prior to the target's onset. If subjects did, however, have an incentive to attend to one of the cues, the cue effect it produced may arise more from attentional processing than from sensory processing. We tested this by presenting four simultaneous cues on each trial with a CTOA of 100 ms, but we changed the color of one of the cues and made it highly predictive of the target location (Richard et al., 2003). Subjects would, therefore, have an incentive to attend strategically to the high-validity (unique) cue and ignore the other three (standard) cues that were not predictive of target location (see Figure 4.9). Cue colors were counterbalanced across conditions. We reasoned that if subjects attended strategically to the unique cue, then the cue effect it produced should be significantly larger than those produced by

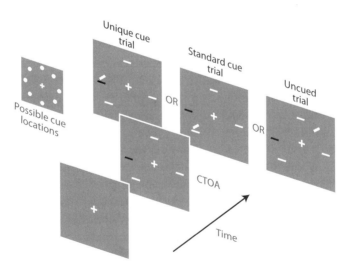

Figure 4.9 Multiple location cue presentation with one high-validity unique cue (red) and three noninformative standard cues (gray).

standard cues. But the latter should still produce smaller cue effects mediated by sensory processes.

While cue effects occurred at all cued locations, they were significantly greater at the unique-cue location. This suggests that sensory processing contributed to cue effects at all cued locations. Note that response facilitation mediated by goal-driven shifts of attention (e.g., like those initiated by a symbolic location cue) is typically minimal when the CTOA is as short as the 100-ms delay used in the current experiment (e.g., Müller & Findlay, 1988). Therefore, it is unlikely that the cue effect at unique-cue locations was caused entirely by goal-driven attentional processes. Instead, it appeared to be associated with two different components: (a) an attentional component that can be modulated by goal-driven factors and (b) a sensory component that can occur in parallel at multiple cued locations and is minimally affected by the same goal-driven factors. We refer to the combination of sensory and attentional mediation of the cue effect at the unique-cue location as the *unique-cue advantage*.

Additional experiments involving manipulations of the relative brightness of unique and standard cues had no effect on the pattern of response times or the occurrence of the unique-cue advantage, and the same pattern of response times and the unique-cue advantage also occurred when subjects were required to identify the target (Richard et al., 2003). This indicated that the processes mediating the multiple-cue effect and the unique-cue advantage are common to the performance of both detection and identification tasks; and they were not the result of a bias stemming from display-specific properties.

Manipulating Cue Onset

If standard-cue effects arise, in part, from stimulus-driven sensory activation, then they should not occur when cues have a gradual onset. As Yantis and colleagues have demonstrated (e.g., Yantis & Jonides, 1984; see Figure 2.11), gradual onset stimuli do not capture attention. Conversely, if unique-cue effects are due primarily to goal-driven attentional processing, then attention should still be directed to the unique cues regardless of the nature of their onsets. We tested this by presenting four simultaneous cues (one unique cue and three standard cues) on each trial with a 100-ms CTOA, but also presenting a placeholder at all possible cue locations for 1.5–2 sec prior to cue presentation (Richard et al., 2003). As seen in Figure 4.10, cues had gradual onsets by virtue of being at locations that were previously occupied by the placeholders. As a result of this gradual cue onset manipulation, cue effects occurred only at unique-cue locations and not at standard-cue locations. Moreover, the magnitude of the unique-cue effect was reduced relative to those in other experiments that involved abrupt-onset unique cues. The

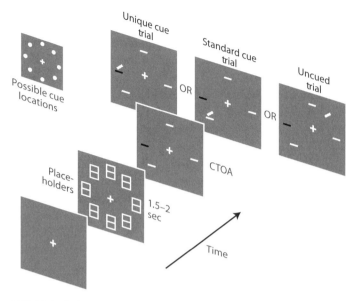

Figure 4.10 Multiple location cue presentation with gradual onsets. Cues appeared by virtue of removal of components of "Figure 8" placeholders.

elimination of standard-cue effects when cues had a gradual onset is another indication that sensory activation is associated with multiple-cue effects. The preservation of unique-cue effects, on the other hand, is another indication that goal-driven attentional processing contributes to their occurrence.

Manipulating Unique-Cue Validity

If unique cues produce greater cue effects than standard cues because their unique color captures attention in a stimulus-driven manner (cf., Wolfe, 1994), then reducing their validity to the chance level should not affect the magnitude of unique-cue effects. We tested this by presenting four simultaneous cues (one unique cue and three standard cues) on each trial with a 100-ms CTOA, but targets were no more likely to appear at unique-cue locations than at standard-cue locations (Richard et al., 2003). Cue effects of equal magnitude occurred at standard and unique-cue locations, and the unique-cue advantage disappeared. Therefore, the unique-cue advantage in other experiments was not the result of attention being captured by an object with a unique color. Instead, it was the result of a goal-driven response strategy based on the knowledge that unique cues had a high validity and therefore the target had a high probability of appearing at their locations. The preservation of standard-cue effects indicates that, even without goal-driven attentional processing, multiple-cue effects still occur.

Manipulating Unique-Cue CTOA

If standard-cue effects produced by simultaneous multiple cueing are due, in part, to sensory activation, then their magnitude should be greatest at short CTOAs (100 ms) and decline with further CTOA increases (cf., Sheperd & Müller, 1989; see Figure 2.9B). And if unique-cue effects are due primarily to sustained attentional processes, then these effects should still occur even when the CTOA is 300 ms or more. We tested this by presenting four simultaneous cues (one unique cue and three standard cues) on each trial while varying the CTOA (100, 200, 300, or 400 ms; Richard et al., 2003). The 100-ms CTOA is optimal for stimulus-driven effects and the 400-ms CTOA is optimal for goal-driven effects. Both unique- and standard-cue effects occurred with a 100-ms CTOA. But with a 400-ms CTOA, cue effects only occurred at high-validity unique-cue locations and not at standard-cue locations. This indicates that unique-cue and standard-cue effects are mediated by separate attentional and sensory processes that operate differently over time. Attentional processing occurs when observers have some incentive to attend to a particular location. Sensory processing occurs in parallel at multiple cued locations, even in the absence of an incentive to attend to a particular location within the display. Table 4.1 summarizes the multiple location-cueing effects described in this section.

Multiple Location Direct Cueing Effects
Cue effects occur at all cued locations when number of simultaneously presented direct cues per trial is 1, 2, 3, or 4
Cue effects occur at all cued locations when CTOA is 100 ms, but not when CTOA is increased to 200 ms or more (if all cues uninformative)
Cue effects occur at all locations of cues with luminance of 6.3 cd/m^2 or greater, but not at locations of cues with luminance of 1.5 cd/m^2 or less
Cue effects occur at all four cued locations, but with even greater magnitude at location of a high-validity, unique-color cue (i.e., unique-cue advantage)
Cue effect occurs only at location of the high-validity, unique-color cue when multiple location cues have gradual onsets
Cue effects occur at all four cued locations when CTOA is 100 ms, but only at location of the high-validity, unique-color cue when CTOA is 400 ms
Cue effects of equal magnitude occur at all four locations (i.e., no unique-cue advantage) when the unique color is uninformative (low validity) like the other three cues

Table 4.1 Summary of Wright and Richard's (2003) and Richard et al.'s (2003) Multiple Location Cue Experiment Findings

Activity Distribution Account of Multiple Location Cue Effects

When we began our investigation of multiple-cue effects, we made the following assumptions: (a) activity distributions are triggered by sensory events, are transient, and grow in magnitude as a positive function of stimulus intensity (LaBerge, 1995a, p. 85). (b) Stimuli that appear in rapid succession (e.g., within 100 ms of each other) at approximately the same location produce activity distributions that may combine into a single larger distribution (as in Figure 4.2). (c) When the magnitude of an activity distribution exceeds a particular criterion threshold, attention can be captured at that location in a stimulus-driven manner (LaBerge & Brown, 1989, p. 106). Each of these assumptions was supported by our findings.

The most detailed description of the activity distribution model is in LaBerge and Brown's (1989) article. The model was originally developed to describe the complex operations involved in shape identification. And the notion of an activity gradient seems to have been inspired by the need for a mechanism to account for the changing size of the attention channel. LaBerge and Brown (1989, p. 118) did, however, outline some assumptions about how the model could be used to describe shifts of attention to cued locations. We adapted this explanatory framework to account for the results of our multiple-cueing experiments (Richard et al., 2003; Wright & Richard, 2003).

A version of the LaBerge model is outlined in Figure 4.11. The flow of visual information begins with input to a representation of the visual field called the feature register. This is a low-level, sensory representation that receives only stimulus-driven input. Information about the locations of objects in this representation is then sent to the filter mechanism. This

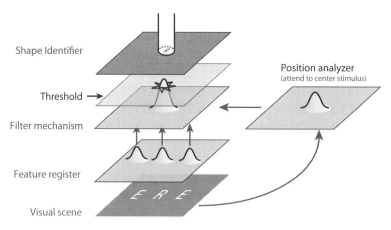

Figure 4.11 A version of LaBerge and Brown's (1989) shape identification model.

component of the model combines stimulus-driven input from the feature register with goal-driven input from higher order processing to determine the location at which a channel of attention should be opened. Goal-driven input is provided by a mechanism called the position analyzer. To elaborate, on the basis of the input it receives about the observer's beliefs, expectations, and perceptual goals, the position analyzer can guide the filter mechanism to the location of an object of interest or, in the case of symbolic location cueing, the expected location of the impending target. As a result of operations carried out by the filter mechanism, a single channel of attention is opened in a high-level representation of the visual field associated with the shape identifier.

Since the publication of LaBerge and Brown's article in 1989, there has been some confusion in the literature about whether the existence of multiple activity distributions implies that there are multiple attentional foci. The authors clearly state that this is *not* a property of the model. In their words, "the number of apertures or channels in the filter must be restricted to one. The opening of more than one filter channel would result in presenting more than one item to the shape identifier domain at one time, and unless the ensemble of items constituted a familiar shape, the shape identifier should fail to produce an identification response" (LaBerge & Brown, 1989, p. 103). Our adaptation of the activity distribution model is based on the same assumption that there is a single attentional focal point.

In the previous chapter, we noted that while the stimulus-driven activity associated with the onset of a symbolic cue causes an activity distribution to form at its physical location, it does not cause an activity distribution to form at the location to which the cue symbolically refers (Figure 3.25). Therefore, goal-driven input is required to direct attention to the symbolically cued location prior to target onset. According to LaBerge and Brown (1989), this is the role of the position analyzer. In particular, once the meaning of the cue has been analyzed by higher order processes, this information is received by the position analyzer if the observer is motivated to use it. As noted in chapter 2, this is a voluntary decision. The position analyzer, in turn, provides input to the filter mechanism that causes a channel of attention to open at the symbolically cued location. Figure 4.12 shows how this process would occur with our modified version of LaBerge and Brown's (1989) model. Our version is functionally equivalent but, to preserve the distinction between stimulus-driven and goal-driven influences, we separated the filter map into two levels of representation. The lower level, sensory representation contains stimulus-driven activity distributions (e.g., the activity distribution that forms at the cue's physical location) and the intermediate-level representation contains activity distributions that can be modulated by goal-driven input.

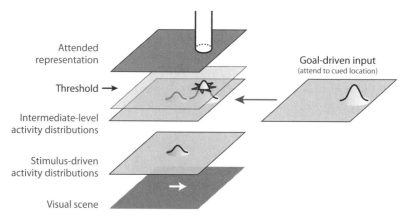

Figure 4.12 The onset of a symbolic location cue triggers the formation of an activity distribution at its physical location. Also, through the coordinated actions of higher order processes and a mechanism like LaBerge and Brown's (1989) position analyzer, it causes an activity distribution to open in a goal-driven manner at the cued location.

A modified activity distribution model can also account for the results of the multiple-cue experiments described in the previous section. More specifically, some of the experiments involved uninformative multiple cues that did not produce a cue effect when the CTOA was greater than 100 ms. This finding is consistent with the following assumptions about activity distribution formation and summation: when the temporal interval between cue and target onsets is optimal, the magnitude of the activity distribution produced by their combined onsets will be maximal. The experiments suggest that this optimal temporal interval is 100 ms. More specifically, when the CTOA is 100 ms, the combination of maximal cue-triggered activation plus target-triggered activation would produce an activity distribution that is larger than a distribution triggered by the target onset alone (see Figure 4.2). This, in turn, would facilitate the opening of the attention channel at that location. Presumably, at longer CTOAs, this does not occur because cue-triggered activity distributions have begun to dissipate (see Figure 4.13).

Another experiment indicated that multiple cues did not produce a cue effect unless their luminance was at least 6.3 cd/m². This finding is consistent with the assumption that activity distribution magnitude is a positive function of stimulus intensity. Figure 4.14 is a depiction of activity distributions that may be triggered by onsets of stimuli with the same intensities as the cues in the experiment. At the two lowest intensities (0.80 and 1.52 cd/m²), cue-triggered activation may not have been sufficient to produce a significant cue effect when targets were presented at these locations.

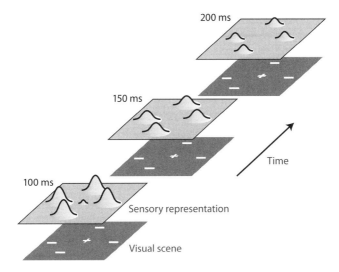

Figure 4.13 The results of the experiments suggest that activity distribution magnitude peaks after 100 ms and then dissipates rapidly. According to the model, if a target is presented at a cued location 100 ms after the cue, residual cue-triggered activation will be maximal and a significant cue effect can occur. If a target is presented at a cued location 200 ms after the cue, however, residual cue-triggered activation will not be sufficient to produce a cue effect.

In other experiments described in the previous section, a unique-cue advantage occurred when one of the multiple cues had a higher validity than the others. This can be accounted for by an additional assumption that cue validity also guides the opening of an attention channel at the unique-cue location in a goal-driven manner. This occurs in addition to the facilitative effect of having residual activation from the cue still there for 100 ms or so. The framework of the model can be modified to accommodate goal-driven input by positing that activity distributions can form in both an early sensory representation of the visual field and an intermediate-level representation

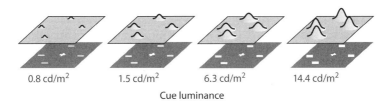

Figure 4.14 The magnitude of activity distributions triggered by abrupt-onset stimuli (e.g., direct cues) is a positive function of their luminance. The results of Wright and Richard's (2003) experiment indicate that low luminance direct cues do not trigger activity distributions of sufficient magnitude to produce significant cueing effects.

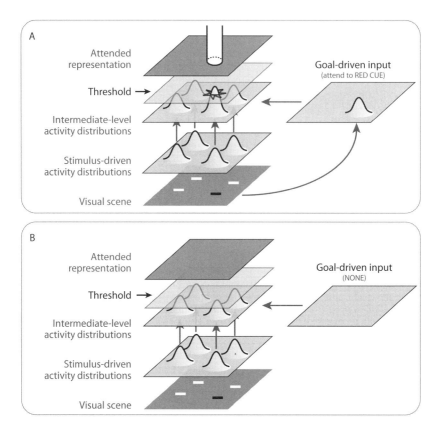

Figure 4.15 (A) When the observer is motivated to attend to the unique (red) cue, goal-driven input leads to an increase in the magnitude of the activity distribution at that cue's location in the intermediate-level representation. This, in turn, causes the channel of attention to open there first. The resulting cue effect is therefore due, in part, to goal-driven attentional processing. (B) When the observer is not motivated to attend to the unique (red) cue, goal-driven input does not modulate the magnitudes of the activity distributions.

(see Figure 4.15A). While the formation of activity distributions in the sensory representation is stimulus-driven, activity distributions in the intermediate-level representation can be influenced in a goal-driven manner in accordance with the task being carried out by the observer. As a result, cue effects can be produced by stimulus-driven processes associated with activity distributions triggered by multiple-cue onsets. And they can be produced by goal-driven processes associated with shifting attention to the unique-cue location. When the incentive to attend to the unique-cue location was removed by making it a poor predictor of the impending target's location, however, these cues (despite their unique color) were no more effective than other multiple cues. In this case, the model holds that subjects no longer open a channel of attention at the unique-cue location in a goal-driven manner independently of patterns of sensory activation triggered by cue onsets (see Figure 4.15B).

The persistence of a cue effect at the unique-cue location at a longer CTOA (400 ms) indicated that goal-driven processes could cause the attention channel to remain open in anticipation of the target, even after the sensory activation produced by the cue's onset had dissipated. That is, goal-driven input could sustain the activity distribution in the intermediate-level representation that was associated with the unique cue (see Figure 4.16). The same may be true of cue effects that occurred at the unique-cue location with gradual onset cues. The activity distributions that formed with the appearance of the placeholders 1.5–2 sec earlier would have dissipated when camouflage was removed and the cues were revealed. But goal-driven processes could cause the attention channel to remain open by sustaining the activity distribution associated with the unique cue.

In summary, these results confirmed several assumptions about the activity distribution framework. Activity distributions appear to be triggered by abrupt onsets of location cues but not by gradual onsets; they appear to be transient with a peak magnitude 100 ms after beginning to form and significant dissipation 200 ms after being triggered; and their magnitude appears to be a positive function of cue luminance. In addition, we found a dissociation between stimulus-driven contributions to cue effects and goal-driven contributions that is consistent with the model's assumption that both types of input guide the opening of a single channel of attention.

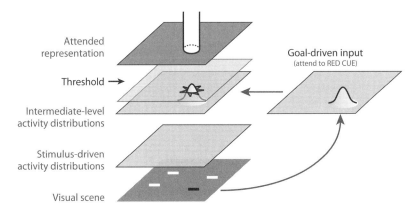

Figure 4.16 When cues have been visible for 400 ms, activity distributions triggered by their onsets have completely dissipated. Similarly, when cues have a gradual onset, activity distributions at their locations that were initially triggered by the onsets of placeholders have completely dissipated. When the observer is motivated to attend to the unique (red) cue, however, goal-driven input can sustain an activity distribution at that cue's location in a higher level representation.

Activity Distribution Account of Other Cue Effects

In chapter 2, we expressed our concern about one type of neutral-cue condition that has been used on occasion in direct-cue experiments. This involves simultaneously cueing all possible target locations with direct cues. The rationale for doing so is that, averaged over trials, attention will not be consistently captured by any one particular cue. Implicit in this reasoning is that responses will only be systematically influenced by attentional processing, and not at all by the sensory activation associated with cue onsets. On the basis of the research discussed in this chapter, we argue that this is not the case.

Consider, for example, a scenario in which the experimenter presents direct cues at both possible locations in a typical location-cueing experiment. This double cueing may trigger activity distributions that can combine with target-triggered activation to open an attention channel faster if the target appeared at either cued location than if the target appeared at an uncued location (Figure 4.17). In other words, double cueing facilitates responses to targets presented at either location and therefore is not a valid neutral baseline measure of cueing effects (see also Wright et al., 1995). If a cost/benefit analysis of location-cueing effects was conducted with the

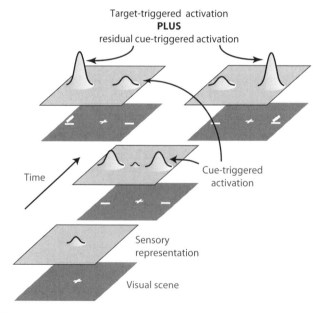

Figure 4.17 Simultaneous cueing at two locations can lead to sensory facilitation of cue effects. Therefore, use of multiple direct cueing as a neutral-cue condition can bias cost/benefit analyses and is not advisable.

mean double-cue response time as the baseline measure, then costs would be inflated and benefits would be deflated (see Figure 2.13 for an example of how a neutral baseline measure can bias cost/benefit analysis). This, in turn, could lead the experimenter to erroneously conclude that location cueing produced costs but no benefits.

Sensory facilitation at multiple-cue locations is a possibility whenever targets are presented there shortly after direct cues. This may have affected responses, for example, in the experiment by Kramer and Hahn (1995) described in the previous chapter. In this case, 150 ms before the onset of targets and distractors, two direct cues (outline boxes) and four placeholders were presented. Two of the placeholders were at cued locations (inside the outline boxes) and two were at uncued locations. As seen in Figure 4.18, the abrupt onsets of the cue boxes and placeholders at the cued

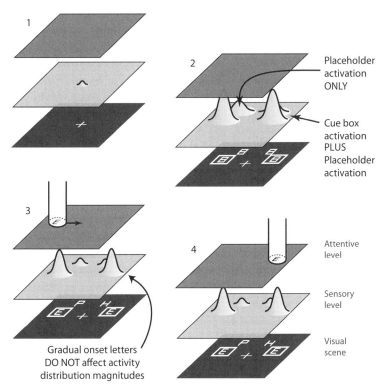

Figure 4.18 A sensory facilitation account of the results of Kramer and Hahn's (1995) experiment. Activity distributions triggered by two outline box cues combine with activity distributions triggered by the onset of placeholder. Their summation produces two larger and two smaller activity distributions. A channel of attention is opened in sequence by the larger distributions (the target locations) but not by the smaller distributions (the distractor locations).

locations could produce two larger activity distributions, and the onsets of only the placeholders at the uncued locations could produce two smaller activity distributions. The channel of attention is more likely to open at the location(s) of the activity distribution with the greatest magnitude (which, in this experiment, were the cued locations). Thus, while the experimenters concluded that two separate attentional foci must have been directed to the targets at the two cued locations because distractors at uncued locations between the targets did not interfere with responses, the scenario in Figure 4.18 suggests another explanation of the data. That is, sensory facilitation of items at cued locations (the targets) but not at uncued locations (the distractors) could also produce a pattern of response times suggestive of attentional processing at cued locations but not at intervening locations. More specifically, the two larger activity distributions at the cued locations may have caused a channel of attention to be opened there in sequence, but not at the locations of the two smaller activity distributions.

Sensory facilitation could also account for the results of an experiment discussed in chapter 2 (McCormick, 1997, Experiment 3). It is described here again briefly. There were two possible cue/target locations (on either side of center). The direct cue on each trial symbolically indicated with a probability of 85% that the target would appear at the opposite location (see Figure 2.10). In addition, the subjective threshold of the cue was lowered so that sometimes subjects were not aware of its onset. The critical finding was that when subjects were not aware of the cue, they did not appear to shift their attention in a goal-driven manner to the symbolically indicated location. At the shortest CTOA (80 ms), however, a direct-cueing effect occurred when targets appeared at the physical locations of cues, even when subjects were unaware of cue presence. This indicates that, unlike goal-driven processes associated with symbolic cueing, stimulus-driven processes associated with direct cueing do not require conscious awareness to be initiated.

One explanation of this finding is that the onset of a direct cue triggered the formation of an activity distribution at its physical location (see Figure 4.19). When a target was presented at this location 80 ms later, residual cue-triggered activation would combine with activation triggered by the target onset to produce a larger activity distribution than would be produced by a target presented at the other location. This, in turn, would cause the channel of attention to be opened faster when the target appeared at the physical location of the cue than at the other location, even when subjects were not aware of the cue's presence. One indication that this was the case is the additional finding that the direct-cue effect did not occur with longer CTOAs (500 and 1000 ms). Presumably, cue-triggered activation at the cue's physical location would have completely dissipated before target

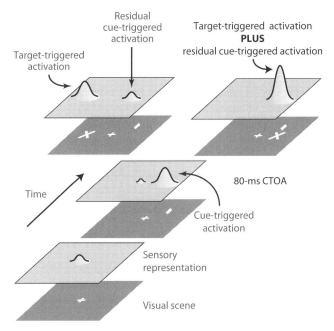

Figure 4.19 A sensory facilitation account of McCormick's experiment (1997, Experiment 3). When the target appeared near the direct cue within 80 ms, a cue-triggered activity distribution combined with the activity distribution triggered by the target. Their summation produced a larger activity distribution at this location than activity produced by the target when it appeared on the opposite side of the display from the cue. As result, the channel of attention would open faster when the target appeared at the physical location of the cue than when it appeared on the opposite side.

onset with the longer CTOAs, but summation of their activity distributions could occur when the CTOA was just 80 ms.

It should be pointed out that this study included three experiments. The first two showed that direct cues also produced the same effect at longer CTOAs, which is not consistent with this type of sensory facilitation explanation. The experiment we described, however, was more rigorous than the other two experiments in several ways. Eye movements were controlled for, more subjects participated, and a more precise measure of subjective awareness of the cue was adopted. Therefore, the results of McCormick's (1997) third experiment appear to be more robust than the other two. If so, then the unconscious attentional capture that occurred at a short CTOA may have been caused by sensory facilitation as outlined in Figure 4.19.

Summary

When a new object appears in our visual field, the initial stages of the visual analysis it triggers are necessarily sensory. Retinal and midbrain collicular processes associated with this sensory analysis provide an alerting signal about the object's presence and encode, in at least a crude manner, the object's location. This information is then available to higher order processing and could lead to attentional analysis of the object. Thus, sensory analysis provides spatial coordinates required to calibrate an attention shift vector to the object's location. One theory holds that this is accomplished by the formation of a neural activity distribution at the object's location within a sensory representation of visual space (LaBerge, 1995a, 1998; LaBerge & Brown, 1989). When the new object in question is a direct cue that will be followed a short time later by a target of interest at the same location, the initial sensory stages of visual analysis also appear to contribute to the cue's facilitative effect on target-detection response times. According to LaBerge's explanatory framework, neural activity triggered by the cue will still be present at its location within the sensory representation when the target appears there, and facilitation of target detection is due to summation of cue-triggered and target-triggered activation. In other words, the resulting cue effect is caused, in part, by sensory operations.

The simultaneous multiple-cueing paradigm appears to be a promising way to distinguish between sensory and attentional contributions to cue effects. In particular, the occurrence of cue effects at multiple locations at the same time requires an explanatory framework that includes a sensory mechanism for mediating the cue's facilitative effect on target-detection response times. This is because the occurrence of cue effects at multiple locations is difficult to account for solely in terms of attentional processing. To elaborate, if one assumes that attention is characterized by a single, indivisible focal point, then attending to multiple cued locations while at the same time excluding intervening uncued locations must be a serial process. The results of the multiple-cueing experiments described in this chapter indicate that cued locations were not attended to serially. If one assumes that attention can be divided into multiple foci that can be simultaneously directed to several locations, then attending to multiple cued locations while at the same time excluding intervening uncued locations is a parallel process. On this basis, one would expect a linear relationship between cue effect magnitudes and the number of cues presented on a given trial. The results of the multiple-cueing experiments described in this chapter were not consistent with this explanation either. Instead, there was a nonlinear relationship between cue effect magnitudes and cue number indicating that cue effects were mediated by a combination of sensory and attentional processing.

The results also indicated that stimulus-driven sensory contributions to cue effects can be distinguished from goal-driven attentional contributions. The cue effects indicative of sensory involvement occurred in parallel at multiple locations at the same time regardless of cue validity, but only when the

CTOA was short (100 ms) and only when cue luminance was greater than or equal to 6.3 cd/m². The cue effects indicative of goal-driven attentional mediation occurred at a single location when the CTOA was short or long (e.g., 400 ms), and when the cue had either an abrupt or gradual onset; but only when the cue was a useful predictor of probable target location (i.e., only when it was a high-validity cue). These results are consistent with the activity distribution account of multiple cueing. That is, stimulus-driven sensory processes produce activity distributions in response to abrupt stimulus onsets but not gradual onsets, the distributions reach their peak magnitude within 100 ms and dissipate soon after, and this magnitude is a positive function of stimulus intensity. Additional goal-driven incentive to attend to a particular stimulus (e.g., a high-validity location cue) would cause the channel of attention to remain open at its corresponding location in a higher level representation, even after stimulus-driven activity distributions within a sensory representation had dissipated and could no longer affect responses. In other words, both sensory and attentional processes can guide the opening of a single channel of attention and, in doing so, both can contribute to location-cueing effects on target-detection response times.

Regardless of the explanatory framework one adopts, it seems clear that some degree of sensory processing of direct cues precedes attentional analysis, and that there are dissociable sensory and attentional contributions to direct-cue effects. We suggest that the LaBergian activity distribution model can potentially provide alternate explanations of a number of findings in the covert orienting literature. In the chapters that follow, we examine (a) variants of the location-cueing paradigm (e.g., presentation of sequential cues and moving cues) indicating that covert orienting processes are, to some extent, object-based; (b) possible neuroanatomical correlates of the activity distribution framework and the brain's attentional orienting network; and (c) modifications of this framework to account for crossmodal covert orienting.

5

Sequential Attention Shifts

Attending to a visual scene to gather information about objects of interest involves dynamic, rapidly changing processes. The attention shifts mediated by these processes occur quickly and frequently just like eye movements. Whereas we have learned a good deal about covert orienting since the 1980s, most research conducted to date and discussed in earlier chapters is based on the detailed study of *single* shifts of attention from a fixation point to a cue or target. Our real-world experience, however, is characterized by continuous *sequences* of attention shifts. Thus, most laboratory experiments on covert orienting tell us only part of the story about how shifts are executed.

Sequences of attention shifts that we make outside the laboratory are usually associated with a particular perceptual goal. Although we occasionally execute shifts in a stimulus-driven manner, most sequences of attention shifts are not random orienting to abrupt-onset stimuli. Like eye movements, they tend to be strategic in nature. In this chapter, we examine ideas that have been proposed about multiple attention shifts.

Shifting Attention to Multiple Abrupt-Onset Stimuli

If a stimulus appears abruptly in a visual scene, it will, in some cases, trigger an attention shift to its location (e.g., Jonides & Yantis, 1988; Yantis & Jonides, 1984). Much of the evidence for this proposal is based on results of visual search experiments in which targets are found faster if their onsets are abrupt as opposed to gradual (e.g., Yantis & Jonides, 1984; see Figure 2.11). A sensory facilitation account of Yantis and colleagues' finding holds that activity distributions triggered by abrupt onsets of placeholder elements will dissipate during the 1000-ms interval prior to camouflage being removed to reveal gradual-onset targets (see Figure 5.1). In other words, unlike an abrupt-onset target, the appearance of a gradual-onset target is *not* associated with the formation of an activity distribution that could, in turn, cause an attention channel to open at its location.

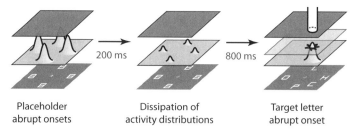

| Placeholder abrupt onsets | Dissipation of activity distributions | Target letter abrupt onset |

Figure 5.1 A sensory facilitation account of Yantis and colleagues' finding that abrupt-onset items capture attention more than gradual-onset items. In this example, when the four placeholders initially appear, they trigger the formation of four activity distributions. While not shown in the figure, an attention channel could open at one of these locations if the observer decided to focus on one of the placeholders in a goal-driven manner. After 200 ms, the activity distributions triggered by the placeholders will have dissipated. After 1000 ms, the removal of placeholder elements to reveal the gradual-onset items will not trigger the formation of activity distributions at their locations. However, the formation of a new activity distribution will be triggered at the location of the abrupt-onset letter (C in this example). This, in turn, causes a channel of attention to open at its location.

When this type of experiment is conducted, targets are no more likely to be abrupt-onset items than gradual-onset items. Therefore, subjects have no a priori incentive to attend strategically to abrupt-onset items to maximize the probability that they are focusing at a target location. Also, when attention is actively focused or engaged at a particular location, an abrupt onset of a new stimulus elsewhere will not "distract" the observer and will not disengage attention so that it can be captured by the new stimulus (Yantis & Jonides, 1990).

This override of attentional capture by abrupt-onset stimuli can be depicted with the activity-distribution framework. Figure 5.2 shows how, when an observer is motivated to attend to a particular stimulus (in this case, the red object), goal-driven input will cause a channel of attention to open at its location. While attention is actively engaged in this manner, however, the abrupt onset of the new object and its corresponding activity distribution will not cause the attention channel to close at the red object's location and be reopened at the new object's location. In other words, goal-driven input that causes attention to remain actively engaged at a particular location will override the effects of competing activity distributions triggered by sensory events (e.g., abrupt onsets of new objects) and prevent a channel of attention from being opened elsewhere.

In another series of experiments, subjects searched for a target letter positioned among multiple distractor letters (Yantis & Johnson, 1990). Half of the stimuli had abrupt onsets and half had gradual onsets (Figure 5.3). Subjects responded to abrupt-onset targets faster than to gradual-onset targets, which indicates that attention was directed to abrupt-onset stimuli

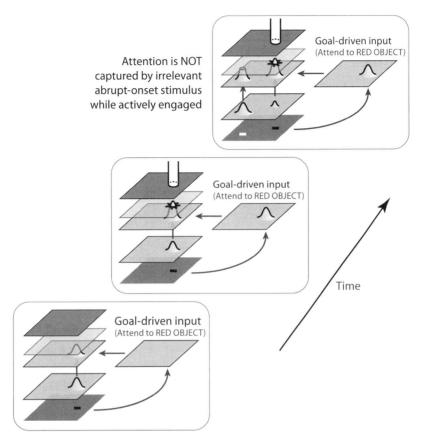

Figure 5.2 An account of Yantis and Jonides' (1990) finding that the attention capturing effect of an abrupt-onset stimulus can be overridden by top-down attentional allocation. Goal-driven input causes an activity distribution to form at the location of the red object that the observer is motivated to attend to. This, in turn, causes an attention channel to open at that location, and to remain open there despite the abrupt onset of a new object a short time later.

before being directed to gradual-onset stimuli. To use the researchers' terms, the abrupt-onset stimuli had a higher *attentional priority* (cf., Shomstein & Yantis, 2002). This was the case even when as many as four abrupt-onset stimuli were presented on a trial. The researchers concluded that, when presented simultaneously, approximately four abrupt-onset stimuli can be attended to with a higher priority than any of the gradual-onset stimuli.

On this basis, Yantis and colleagues developed a formal model of attentional priority (Yantis & Johnson, 1990; Yantis & Jones, 1991). One of its properties is that a limited number of elements can be assigned a high priority, and will be processed first or most rapidly. Then the remaining items in the display will be processed in a random order. Moreover, even if attention

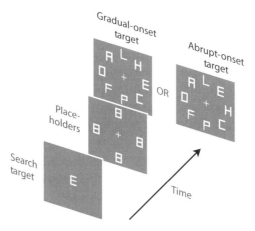

Figure 5.3 Example of the type of stimulus display used by Yantis and Johnson (1990) to study the attentional priority of abrupt-onset stimuli.

is actively engaged, attentional priority is preserved for a brief period of time. This allows high-priority items to remain temporarily indexed while attentional analysis is carried out elsewhere. Thus, when performing a visual search task, attention is said to be directed to different locations in a sequence determined by the order of the strongest priority signals (see Müller & Humphreys, 1991, for a related proposal).

Yantis and Jones (1991) refined this idea with their proposal that the limited number of items that can be prioritized (i.e., 3–5) could be accounted for by *temporally modulated tagging*. They based this on the results of experiments indicating that the number of items receiving attentional priority is not fixed and depends on the nature of the search task. In particular, when a visual search display is presented as in Figure 5.3, all items are tagged but, for purposes of illustration, those with high priority have initially greater tag strengths. In Figure 5.4, tag strength is denoted by the size of the tag. Items with higher tag strengths have attentional priority and are processed before items with lower tag strengths. With the passage of time, however, the strength of tags allocated to high-priority items decays to the same level as that of tags allocated to low-priority items. In other words, unless they are refreshed, the strength of these tags decays over time, thereby limiting the number of high-priority items that can be processed.

Yantis and colleagues proposed that the allocation of spatial index tags is associated with response facilitation and the *attraction* of attention. Sequential location-cueing experiments, however, often produce a pattern of results known as *inhibition of return* (IOR; e.g., Posner & Cohen, 1984). One explanation of this effect is that spatial index tags allocated to location

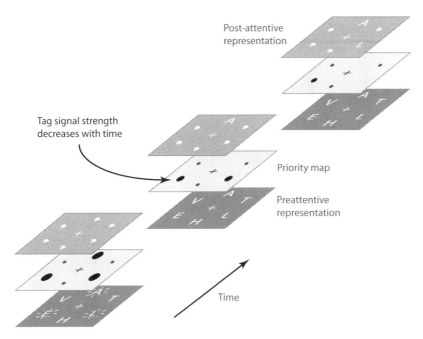

Post-attentive
representation

Tag signal strength
decreases with time

Priority map

Preattentive
representation

Time

Figure 5.4 Attentional priority of abrupt-onset stimuli as described by Yantis and Jones (1991). The Priority Map contains tags at locations corresponding to each item in the search display (the Preattentive Representation). Tag strength (denoted by tag size) is initially greatest at the locations of the three abrupt-onset items (A, E, and L). The strength of the tags decays over time, but still allows the observer to first attend to the A, and then attend to the L before their attentional priority dissipates completely.

cues are associated with response inhibition and the *repulsion* of attention. If the same type of tag is involved in both situations, then this suggests that tags themselves are neither facilitative nor inhibitory. They function only as markers for other higher level processes that place either a high or a low priority on directing attention to tagged locations.

It has been suggested that spatial index tagging is carried out at an intermediate stage of visual processing (e.g., Ullman, 1984, 1996). One way to distinguish between different stages of visual analysis is to consider the extent to which they are stimulus-driven versus goal-driven. The initial stage, as shown in Figure 5.5, is often referred to as low-level vision, and is characterized by parallel processes that are triggered in a stimulus-driven manner. These processes are not consciously available to the perceiver and seem immediate and effortless. In contrast, high-level visual processes are usually serial and under goal-driven control. The perceiver is also usually aware of their execution (e.g., when visually searching for a target among a collection of objects). Between low- and high-level vision there appears to be an *intermediate* stage that involves rapid but sometimes serial operations. Like low-level processes,

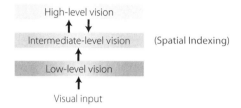

Figure 5.5 Flow of information between three levels of visual processing. Low-level vision receives input only from visual transducers. Intermediate-level vision, on the other hand, receives stimulus-driven input from low-level processing and goal-driven input from high-level vision. The concept of intermediate-level vision allows theorists to account for visual processing that is fast and somewhat reflexive like low-level processes, but also, in an indirect way, is under goal-driven control.

they seem immediate and effortless while, at the same time, being under some degree of goal-driven control. If this framework is valid, then perhaps tags used by intermediate-level processes, while initially neutral, may be designated by high-level processes as either facilitative or inhibitory, depending on the task being performed. More specifically, perhaps it is the goal-driven influence of spatial index allocation that allows these tags to be associated with facilitation in some situations (e.g., mediation of attentional priority of abrupt-onset items during visual search) and inhibition in other situations (e.g., IOR).

One way that the activity-distribution explanatory framework can be modified to incorporate tagging of abrupt-onset stimuli is shown in Figure 5.6. The simultaneous abrupt onsets of four stimuli trigger the formation of four activity distributions (unlike the gradual-onset items, which do not trigger activity distributions; see Figure 5.1). Each of the activity distributions is tagged by a spatial index in an intermediate-level representation of the visual field. The tagged activity distributions then trigger the formation of other activity distributions at their corresponding locations in another intermediate-level representation. These are the locations of the items with the highest attentional priority. A channel of attention is opened at one of these locations to determine whether the item there is the target. If not, it is closed and then opened at another tagged location. When this occurs, the properties of the tag at the first location change to denote that this item has already been attended to (tag changes from white to black in Figure 5.6 to denote this). This sequence continues at each of the high-priority, tagged locations, and then at the untagged locations. Temporal modulation of tags could also occur, as proposed by Yantis and Jones (1991), if it is assumed for example that the tags disappear once activity distributions dissipate to a certain level. In other situations, perhaps as a result of goal-driven processing, tags could remain allocated to locations if they made visual analysis more efficient (e.g., during visual search).

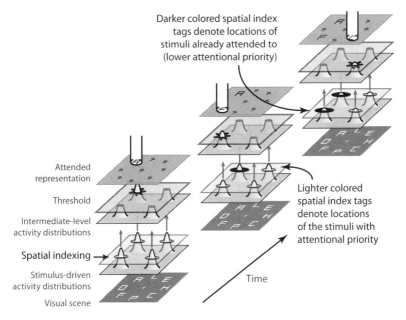

Figure 5.6 A modified version of the activity-distribution explanatory framework that incorporates spatial index tags. In this example, a visual search display is presented with four abrupt-onset stimuli and four gradual-onset stimuli. Tags are allocated to the activity distributions triggered by the four abrupt-onset items. The tags mark the items with a high attentional priority. A channel of attention is then opened in sequence at tagged locations before it is opened at the locations of the other items. Tags at already-inspected locations are mentally labeled (a darker color in the figure) so that they can be kept distinct from those at locations that remain to be inspected.

Spatial Indexing

Spatial index tagging has been studied in a number of ways and perhaps most compelling is the study of our ability to visually track multiple moving objects (Pylyshyn & Storm, 1988). This is known as the multiple-object tracking (MOT) task. In the original experiment, observers were shown a number of identical objects (e.g., 10) and asked to keep track of a subset of them (see Figure 5.7). As the objects moved randomly and independently, observers could track at least four or five with nearly the same efficiency as tracking one. Given that the speed of object movement exceeded even the most liberal estimate of the metaphorical spotlight velocity (250°/sec) in the attention literature, the experimenters concluded that a serial "scanning and encoding" procedure involving alignments of a single attentional focal point was not sufficient for keeping track of four targets at the same time. Instead, they claimed that tracking appears to involve some form of parallel processing that dynamically maintains the locations of as many as four or five objects simultaneously. MOT is a robust phenomenon and has been replicated several times

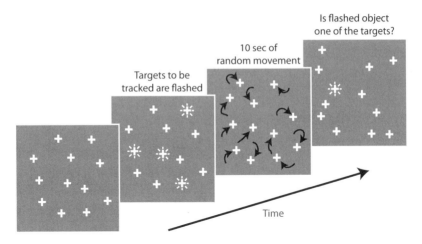

Is flashed object
one of the targets?

10 sec of
random movement

Targets to be
tracked are flashed

Time

Figure 5.7 Example of the type of stimulus display used by Pylyshyn and Storm (1988) to study multiple-object tracking (MOT). On this trial, 4 of the 10 "+" signs flash briefly to denote their target status. Then, after 10 sec of random movement during which the subject attempts to keep track of all the targets, the "+" signs stop and one of them flashes. The subject must decide if it was one of the targets or not.

(e.g., Alvarez et al., 2005; Jovicich et al., 2001; Liu et al., 2005; Oksama & Hyönä, 2004; Pylyshyn, 2004; Scholl & Pylyshyn, 1999; Sears & Pylyshyn, 2000; Viswanathan & Mingolla, 2002).

Pylyshyn (1989, 1998, 2003, 2007) accounted for MOT in terms of spatial indexing. In particular, he proposed that a limited number of indexes (approximately 4) are allocated to objects, and the allocation can be maintained independently of attention as the objects move. When performing a MOT task, the primary role of indexes is simply to stay "glued" to the objects (see Figure 5.8). If, at some point, observers must verify that a particular object is a target, they can respond on the basis of whether the object is indexed or not. Pylyshyn called these indexes *FINSTs* (an acronym for Fingers of INSTantiation). Note that, like Pylyshyn, Yantis, and colleagues (Yantis & Johnson, 1990; Yantis & Jones, 1991) also proposed that the number of index tags is limited to four or five.

When an observer is asked to visually track a subset of moving objects, attention is clearly required. On the other hand, Pylyshyn and Storm's (1988) data indicate that tracking several moving objects in parallel is unlikely to be the result of rapid shifts of a single attentional focal point. Therefore, it is tempting to conclude that the focal point may be divisible into multiple attentional foci during the performance of this task (e.g., Cavanagh & Alvarez, 2005). As pointed out in chapter 3, however, some studies commonly thought to demonstrate that the attentional focal point is divisible in this way (e.g., Castiello & Umiltá, 1992; Kramer &

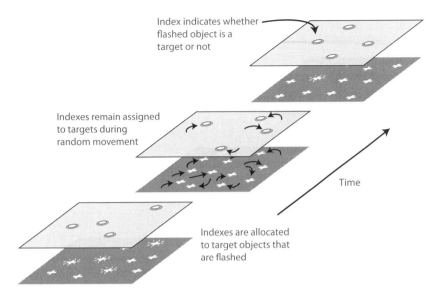

Index indicates whether flashed object is a target or not

Indexes remain assigned to targets during random movement

Time

Indexes are allocated to target objects that are flashed

Figure 5.8 FINST spatial indexes are assigned to the four targets that are flashed. During the movement of the "+" signs, the indexes remain dynamically assigned to the subset that were denoted as targets. Then, after movement stops, if the flashed "+" sign has an index allocated to it, the observer will know it is a target.

Hahn, 1995) have been challenged; and other studies suggest that, while performing certain visual tasks, the attentional focal point is unitary (e.g., Heinze et al., 1994a; McCormick & Klein, 1990; Woodman & Luck, 2003). At this time, the evidence supporting the claim that multiple attentional foci mediate MOT is equivocal (Pylyshyn, 2007). Rather than concluding that tracking is mediated by multiple foci, Pylyshyn argued that, while observers must pay attention when performing a tracking task, the maintenance of individual target identities is not entirely due to alignments of focused attention. In other words, while attention is required to control the operation of an intermediate-level tracking procedure, and the initiation of these processes and selection of the subset of objects to be tracked are said to be under the observer's control, the maintenance of this identity information while the objects are in motion is said to be preattentively mediated by spatial indexes.

MOT is another example of a task that might involve facilitative tagging. Pylyshyn and Storm (1988) argued that performance breaks down when tracking six or more targets at the same time because only four or five indexes are available. In terms of the model we described in chapter 4, many activity distributions can form in response to sensory events, but perhaps only four or five of these distributions can be spatially indexed (see

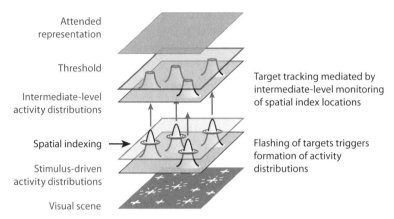

Attended representation

Threshold

Intermediate-level activity distributions

Spatial indexing

Stimulus-driven activity distributions

Visual scene

Target tracking mediated by intermediate-level monitoring of spatial index locations

Flashing of targets triggers formation of activity distributions

Figure 5.9 Modification of the activity-distribution framework to incorporate spatial indexing hypothesized by Pylyshyn and Storm (1988) when performing a multiple-object tracking task. Four of the 10 objects are flashed to denote their status as the targets to be tracked. The increase in stimulus intensity associated with flashing triggers the formation of four activity distributions at target locations within a sensory representation of the visual field, and the allocation of four spatial indexes at these locations within an intermediate-level representation. When the objects begin to move, the spatial indexes remain dynamically bound to the targets and tracking can be mediated by intermediate-level monitoring of index position. This obviates the need for a tracking scheme involving the alignments of multiple attentional foci.

Figure 5.9). Note that when an abrupt-onset target captures attention, indexing may be stimulus-driven (such as in Figure 5.6); but when an observer makes a decision about which objects to attend to when performing the MOT task, indexing may be goal-driven (Annan & Pylyshyn, 2002; Pylyshyn, 2003, p. 229). This is consistent with an assumption of the FINST hypothesis that spatial index allocation can be stimulus-driven or goal-driven, depending on the task to be performed.

Yantis (1992) suggested a different explanation of MOT that does not involve multiple spatial indexes. Instead, he proposed that observers may track multiple targets by imagining that they are vertices of a deforming polygon and then tracking the polygon as a whole. This suggestion is consistent with findings that MOT performance improved (a) when subjects were told about the "virtual polygon" strategy and (b) when object trajectories were constrained so that the virtual polygon could never collapse upon itself (Yantis, 1992). Pylyshyn's (2001, p. 143; 2004) counter-argument was that the polygon strategy does not change the logical requirements of the MOT task because each target object still has to be tracked independently to determine the moment-to-moment locations of the vertices of the polygon. Another indication that MOT is not mediated by a single attentional focal point directed to a virtual polygon is a finding that luminance increments were detected faster at locations of tracked targets than at other locations of untracked targets within a polygon area bounded by the targets (Sears & Pylyshyn, 2000).

Note that the results of another type of experiment based on the *preview-search task* indicated that under some conditions more than four or five locations might be marked at one time (e.g., Watson & Humphreys, 1997, 1998, 2000). These experiments typically involved the sequential presentation of a portion of a visual search set in one color (e.g., green) followed by a brief delay (1000 ms) and then the presentation of the remaining search-set items plus the target in a different color (e.g., blue). The critical finding was that only the second set of items had a significant effect on target-related responses. In other words, the first set was effectively eliminated from the set of items that subjects serially inspected to find the target. While it has been suggested that each item in the first set was eliminated by visually marking it with an inhibitory tag (Watson & Humphreys, 1997), Pylyshyn (2004, p. 820) argued that there is a critical difference between the MOT task and the preview-search task. In the latter, the inhibited items are always grouped, either temporally or by motion, whereas in MOT studies the only common property that nontargets have is that they are the items that are not being tracked. And when this is the case, Pylyshyn proposed that performance is mediated by a limited-capacity spatial indexing mechanism.

Inhibition of Return

As mentioned previously, most covert orienting research is based on the detailed study of single attention shifts from a fixation point to a cue or target. In the mid-1980s, however, Posner and colleagues began their study of sequential attention shifts to asynchronously presented location cues (e.g., Posner & Cohen, 1984). This experimentation led to the discovery of a fascinating effect called inhibition of return (IOR). In simple terms, IOR is the inhibition of responses to objects appearing at recently cued or recently attended locations.

The IOR effect typically occurs when two stimuli are presented in succession prior to a target's onset. In a sequential cueing experiment, the first cue is usually presented at a peripheral location and is followed, 200 ms later, by a second cue at the central location. Then, a short time later (usually 200 ms), a target is either presented at the first cued location, the second cued location, or an uncued location (see Figure 5.10). Detection response times are significantly slower for targets presented at the first cued location than for those presented at the second cued location, and even the uncued location (Posner & Cohen, 1984). IOR is typically measured by comparing response times for targets appearing at previously cued/fixated locations with response times for targets appearing at uncued locations. It is a robust effect and has been replicated using many different paradigms.

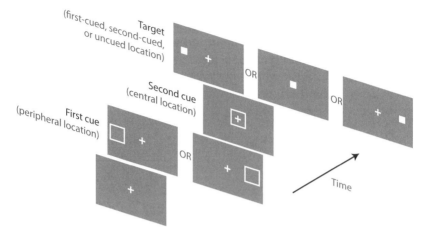

Figure 5.10 Example of the stimulus display used in a typical inhibition of return (IOR) experiment. In this figure, the first cue (an outline box) is presented at a peripheral location, the second cue is presented at the central location, and then the target appears at either of these locations or at the uncued location. The IOR effect is indicated by slower responses to targets appearing at the first cued location than at the uncued location.

As mentioned in chapter 2 (see Figure 2.9B), direct location-cue effects on responses to targets are greatest when the CTOA is roughly 100 ms, and begin to dissipate when the CTOA is increased to 200 ms (e.g., Müller & Findlay, 1988; Nakayama & Mackeben, 1989; Sheperd & Müller, 1989; Weichselgartner & Sperling, 1987). When the CTOA is increased beyond 200 ms, direct cue effects can diminish completely or, in the case of the experiments described in this section, can be associated with inhibition of responses to targets as in Figure 5.11 (e.g., Maylor, 1985; Maylor & Hockey, 1987; Posner & Cohen, 1984; Possamai, 1985; Wright & Richard, 1998, 2000). This inhibition appears to last as long as 3 sec after cue onsets (Clohessy et al., 1991; Samuel & Kat, 2003; Tassinari et al., 1989; but see also Tipper et al., 2003). It has been suggested that this duration corresponds to the time required to make at least two or three saccadic eye movements (Posner & Cohen, 1984). This is intriguing, given that there is a close relationship between IOR and saccadic programming (also discussed in chapter 6).

One proposal about the biphasic effect of direct cueing is that a stimulus onset triggers the simultaneous buildup of activation of facilitative and inhibitory components (Posner & Cohen, 1984). This is sometimes called the *opponent-process* account of IOR (Francis & Milliken, 2003). Following the cue onset, the facilitative component is initially dominant and has a positive effect on target-detection responses (see Figure 5.12). The activation of this facilitative component is transient, however, and it dissipates within about

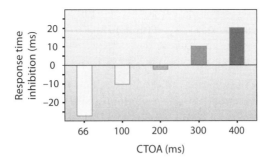

Figure 5.11 Wright and Richard's (2000) finding that the magnitude of the inhibition of return (IOR) effect changes as a function of the temporal delay between cue and target onsets. Two cues were presented in succession, followed by the target. When the delay between the first cue and the target was short (e.g., 66 ms), the cue had a facilitative effect on responses to targets. When this delay was longer (e.g., 400 ms), the cue had an inhibitory effect. CTOA refers to delay between onset of first cue and target.

200 ms. The inhibitory component then becomes dominant roughly 300 ms after the cue onset until perhaps 3000 ms or more. In other words, both components are said to be triggered by the cue onset, but at short CTOAs (e.g., 100 ms), the inhibitory component's effect is masked by the stronger activation of the facilitative component. At longer CTOAs, the inhibitory component is dominant because it is no longer masked by the transient activation of the facilitative component. Thus, the opponent-process account holds that the onset of a direct cue facilitates detection of targets presented at cued locations 100 ms after cue onsets, but inhibits detection of targets presented at cued locations from 300 ms to perhaps 3000 ms after cue onsets.

In the years following the first report of the IOR, many other experiments on the effect were conducted. Some of the questions addressed were: the extent to which IOR occurs with discrimination versus detection responses

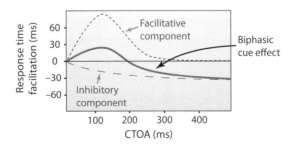

Figure 5.12 The opponent-process proposal about the biphasic effect of direct location cueing on responses in inhibition of return (IOR) experiments occurring as a result of the combined actions of an initially dominant but transient facilitative component and a slower acting but sustained inhibitory component. CTOA refers to delay between onset of first cue and target.

(e.g., Cheal et al., 1998; Lupiáñez et al., 1997; Pratt & Abrams, 1999; Pratt & Fischer, 2002; Pratt et al., 1997; Prime et al., 2006); the relationship between IOR and eye movements (e.g., Abrams & Dobkin, 1994; Godijn & Theeuwes, 2002, 2004; Hunt & Kingstone, 2003; Kingstone & Pratt, 1999; Taylor & Klein, 2000); and the extent to which the magnitude of the IOR effect diminishes smoothly as a function of distance from cued locations (e.g., Bennett & Pratt, 2001; Maylor & Hockey, 1985; Pratt et al., 1998, 1999; Samuel & Weiner, 2001; Snyder et al., 2001; Spalek & Hammad, 2004). Because of space constraints, we cannot describe this rapidly growing literature in detail. Instead, we focus on studies related to possible mechanisms for marking the locations of sequential attention shifts.

Inhibition of Return and Spatial Indexing

When someone examines many items in a visual scene, the efficiency of this serial analysis can be improved if a mechanism is available to mark items that have already been examined to keep them separate from the remaining items. Doing so would reduce the frequency of rechecking previously inspected items and, instead, guide analysis more efficiently toward uninspected items. On this basis, Posner and colleagues proposed that the IOR effect is associated with a mechanism that biases visual search toward novel items (e.g., Clohessy et al., 1991; Harman et al., 1994; Posner & Cohen, 1984; Posner et al., 1985). Using their terms, processing is "inhibited from returning" to previously inspected objects.

The following is a simple example of strategic marking. When counting items in a visual scene, responses might be rapid and seem effortless. To accomplish this, however, marking may be involved. For instance, the count could begin in the upper-left region of the scene and move across to the right side. Figure 5.13 shows how this could involve marking with four spatial indexes to keep track of items once they have been inspected. Without the capacity to keep counted and uncounted items distinct, this type of task would be difficult to perform efficiently and accurately.

Note that when tasks associated with IOR are performed, some form of marking operation is a logical requirement. More specifically, when IOR

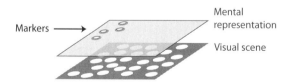

Figure 5.13 While counting objects, an observer might adopt a strategy that involves moving a set of markers within a mental representation of the visual scene in order to keep track of the ones that have already been tallied.

occurs, attention is presumably directed to the first cued location and then elsewhere before the target onset (the "return" of attention associated with the effect's name implies that focused attention was directed elsewhere). Therefore, this first cued location must be marked in some way while attention is directed away from it. Moreover, the maintenance of that location information is *necessarily* nonattentional. A growing body of evidence indicates that nonattentional maintenance of location information during visual analysis could be mediated by spatial indexing.

One indication that indexing is associated with the IOR effect is the discovery that IOR can be *object-based*. In particular, a number of experiments were conducted in which the first cue was moved to a new location soon after it was presented (Tipper et al., 1991, 1994). Figure 5.14 shows a simplified example of a trial in a typical experiment of this type. In one study, IOR occurred at the new location of the cue after its movement was complete (Tipper et al., 1994). In other words, IOR was associated with object-based processing. In addition, IOR also occurred at the original location of the cue. Thus, cue movement produced object-based and *location-based* IOR (see also, Jordan & Tipper, 1998; Leek et al., 2003).

If the IOR effect is mediated by the same type of spatial indexing mechanism proposed by Pylyshyn, and an indexed object moves during

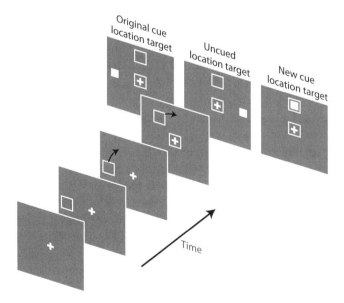

Figure 5.14 Simplified example of the type of display used to study object-based inhibition of return (IOR). After the first cue is presented, it begins to move. During the first cue's movement, a second cue is presented at the central location. Object-based IOR occurs at the moving cue's destination and location-based IOR occurs at the cue's original position.

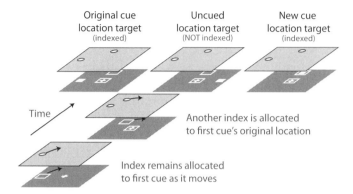

Original cue
location target
(indexed)

Uncued
location target
(NOT indexed)

New cue
location target
(indexed)

Time

Another index is allocated
to first cue's original location

Index remains allocated
to first cue as it moves

Figure 5.15 Allocation of spatial indexes to the moving cue's original position and to its destination. As a result, the target would appear at an indexed location on "Original Cue Location" target trials and on "New Cue Location" target trials. But the target would *not* appear at an indexed location on "Uncued Location" target trials.

the course of an experimental trial, then the inhibition associated with that object should move along with it, as in Figure 5.15. More specifically, the object-based IOR that occurred in Tipper et al.'s (1994) experiment could have been mediated by a spatial index (like those thought to mediate MOT) remaining dynamically bound to the cue. And location-based IOR could have been mediated by a second index remaining assigned to the cue's original location.

Pylyshyn and Storm (1988) hypothesized that there are four or five spatial indexes available. This is consistent with the discovery that IOR can occur at more than one location at the same time. One example is the simultaneous occurrence of object-based and location-based IOR at two different locations (e.g., Tipper et al., 1994). Posner and Cohen (1984) also found an IOR effect at two locations simultaneously. They conducted an experiment in which, in the single-cue condition, a direct cue was presented at a peripheral location to the left or right of center and then, 200 ms later, a distractor stimulus was presented in the center of the display (see Figure 5.10). This is typical of experiments on the IOR effect. In the double-cue condition, direct cues were presented simultaneously at two peripheral locations and then, 200 ms later, a distractor stimulus was presented in the center of the display (see Figure 5.16A). In this condition, IOR occurred when a target was presented at either peripherally cued location. And, more important, the magnitude of IOR on double-cue trials was not significantly different from that on single-cue trials. On this basis, Posner and Cohen (1984, p. 539) suggested that multiple-location IOR may not be explainable purely in terms of attentional processing and, instead, attributed it to "the energy change present at the cued positions."

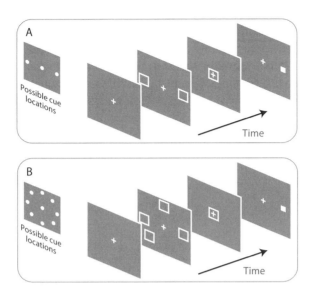

Figure 5.16 (A) An example of a double-cue trial in Posner and Cohen's (1984) experiment on multiple-location inhibition of return (IOR). (B) An example of a four-cue trial in Wright and Richard's (1996) experiment on multiple-location IOR.

Inspired by Posner and Cohen's (1984) finding that IOR can occur at multiple locations, we conducted a replication experiment in the early 1990s to determine whether the effect could be obtained at as many as four locations simultaneously (Wright & Richard, 1996). One to four cues were presented at the same time, followed by a centrally located cue, and then the target (see Figure 5.16B). Like Posner and Cohen, we found that IOR occurred at multiple locations simultaneously (in this case, as many as four locations) with roughly equal magnitude (see Figure 5.17). And, like Posner and Cohen (1984, p. 539), we concluded that multiple-location IOR may not be explainable purely in terms of attentional processing. We suggested instead that cued locations may be initially encoded by spatial indexes, and

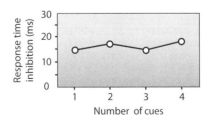

Figure 5.17 Results of Wright and Richard's (1996) experiment on multiple-location inhibition of return (IOR). The IOR effect occurred with roughly equal magnitude at each cued location on trials involving simultaneous single, double, triple, and quadruple cues.

that this marking operation contributed to the multiple-location IOR effect that was obtained. Multiple-location IOR has since been found by several other researchers (e.g., Danziger et al., 1998; Dodd et al., 2003; Paul & Tipper, 2003; Snyder & Kingstone, 2001; Tipper et al., 1996).

In summary, Pylyshyn's (1989, 1998, 2003, 2007) spatial index hypothesis holds that there is a limited pool of four to five indexes that can remain dynamically bound to objects as they move. If these spatial indexes are involved in the processing that mediates IOR, then two predictions yielded by the hypothesis are: (a) IOR should be object-based (i.e., dynamically bound to moving objects) as well as location-based and (b) it should occur at as many as four or five locations. Both these predictions have been confirmed.

In a previous section, the activity-distribution framework was modified to incorporate tagging of abrupt-onset stimuli (Figure 5.6). Figure 5.18 depicts a similar modification with one possible account of tagging operations when IOR occurs. That is, stimuli that trigger the formation of activity distributions may be tagged by a spatial index at their corresponding locations in another

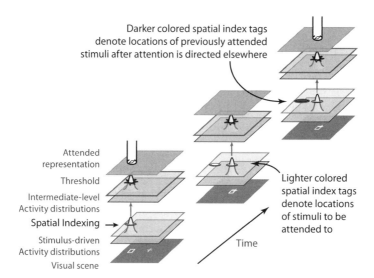

Figure 5.18 A modified version of the activity-distribution explanatory framework that also incorporates spatial index tags to convey the marking operations that may produce the inhibition of return (IOR) effect. In this example, a direct location cue is presented on the left side of the display. A tag is allocated to the location of the activity distribution triggered by the cue's onset, and a channel of attention is opened at that location. Then another direct cue is presented in the center of the display. A second tag is allocated to the location of the activity distribution triggered by this cue's onset, and a channel of attention is then opened at the central location. Once this occurs, properties of the tag at the already-inspected location on the left side of the display change (a darker color in the figure) so that this location can be kept distinct from other locations that remain to be inspected. If a target should subsequently appear at a location designated by this type of tag, responses to it would be inhibited.

intermediate-level representation. Index allocation is stimulus-driven as a result of the same abrupt onsets that trigger activity-distribution formation. A channel of attention would then be opened in sequence at the indexed locations and, after attention had been directed elsewhere, the properties of the index tag at the location that had just been attended to would change to denote that the item had already been inspected (shown in Figure 5.18 by a change in tag color from white to black). In other words, the tag becomes inhibitory after attention is moved away to a different location. This framework is speculative and more direct evidence is needed before we could claim that this is what happens. But a tagging algorithm of this type could make serial visual analysis more efficient.

Inhibitory Tagging During Serial Search

Posner and Cohen (1984) speculated that some form of marking operation associated with IOR helps us to search the environment more efficiently. This idea was tested with a visual search experiment that involved a secondary task requiring detection of a probe stimulus (Klein, 1988). In one condition, search for the target positioned among distractor items was effortless because the target popped out by virtue of possessing a unique feature (e.g., a bisecting line) not shared with the distractors (see Figure 5.19). In the other condition, search was serial and effortful because the target did not possess a unique feature and did not pop out (cf., Treisman & Souther, 1985). As is usually the case with experiments of this type, when the target popped out, subjects' target

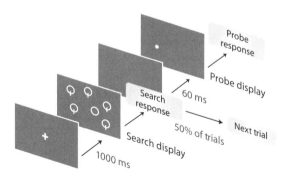

Figure 5.19 Example of the type of display used in Klein's (1988) experiment on the role of marking during serial visual search. On the trial illustrated in this figure, the target was a circle without a bisecting line positioned among distractors (circles with bisecting lines). Serial search was required to make a target present/absent response. On half of trials in the experiment, the search task was followed by a probe-dot detection task. The dot appeared at one of the locations previously occupied by a search-set distractor, at the location previously occupied by the search target, or at a location that was previously unoccupied by a search-set item. Probe-dot detection responses were slowest on serial search trials when the dot appeared at search-set distractor locations. This suggests that, during serial search, the locations of distractor items may be temporarily inhibited in the same manner that locations are inhibited when inhibition of return (IOR) occurs (i.e., inhibitory spatial tagging).

present/target absent response times were rapid and virtually independent of search-set size. On the other hand, when the target did not pop out, response times were slower and increased as a function of search-set size. This replicated the typical visual search finding that target items are searched for serially if they do not possess a unique feature (e.g., Treisman & Gelade, 1980).

The secondary task is what made this experiment unique. On a randomly selected half of the trials, after subjects made a target present/target absent response and the search stimuli were removed, a small probe dot was presented somewhere within the visual display and the subjects were required to make a speeded detection response to it. The probe dot sometimes appeared at a position previously occupied by a distractor item, the position previously occupied by the target, or a position that was not occupied by any of the search-set items on that trial (i.e., an "empty" location). The result was an interesting interaction between the type of search that was conducted on that trial and the location of the probe dot when the secondary task was performed. When the trial involved a unique-feature target that popped out, probe-dot detection times did not vary as a function of dot location. But when the trial involved a target that did not possess a unique feature and therefore had to be searched for serially, probe-dot detection times depended on dot location. More specifically, when the dot appeared at one of the locations previously occupied by a distractor item, it took longer to detect than when it appeared at an "empty" location that was not previously occupied on that trial. The experimenter concluded that the slower responses to probe dots at distractor locations relative to empty locations indicated that the former were "tagged" during the serial search that preceded the secondary task, and that, despite the removal of the search stimuli, these tags remained allocated to locations previously occupied by distractors when the probe-detection task was performed. This is consistent with the claim that the IOR effect is mediated by a marking operation.

Note that the *inhibitory tagging* effect is subtle and can be difficult to replicate. We were able to do so only after conducting several pilot experiments while carefully adjusting temporal and spatial display parameters so that the difficulty of the search task was in the "sweet spot" required to yield the effect. This may be why, in the years since the result was first reported, other researchers published papers describing their failure to find the effect (e.g., Hooge et al., 2005; Klein & Taylor, 1994; Wolfe & Pokorny, 1990). The inhibitory tagging effect has also been replicated several times, however (e.g., Klein & MacInnes, 1999; Müller & von Mühlenen, 2000; Ogawa et al., 2002; Takeda & Yagi, 2000), and there are some indications that location indexing thought to be associated with inhibitory tagging may be mediated, in part, by a cortical area called the intraparietal sulcus (e.g., Sapir et al., 2004; see chapter 7).

As stated previously, object-based IOR was found in experiments involving moving location cues (e.g., Tipper et al., 1994). It has since been demonstrated that the inhibitory tagging effect will still occur even when visual search sets are composed of moving items (Ogawa et al., 2002). This is another indication that spatial indexes with the capacity to remain dynamically bound to moving objects mediate serial search for a target among distractors.

We conducted a related experiment with Christian Richard to determine whether the number of markers available to "tag" distractor locations during serial search is limited to four or five (as would be predicted by the FINST hypothesis). Visual search displays consisted of either 6 or 30 items. The results replicated the findings of previous experiments involving this paradigm. Following serial search, when the probe dot appeared at one of the locations previously occupied by a distractor item, it took longer to detect than when it appeared at an "empty" location that was not previously occupied on that trial. Of note, however, was an interaction with search-set size. In particular, statistically significant inhibition of response times for probe dots at distractor locations (relative to those at empty locations) occurred only with 6-item search sets (17.8 ms) and not with 30-item search sets (4.5 ms). Thus, when associated with larger visual search sets (e.g., 30 items), the probe-detection task may not be a sensitive measure of the inhibitory tagging effect. More specifically, if only a limited set of distractors can be marked at any given time (e.g., 4 or 5), then a probe dot would be more likely to appear at one of the marked locations in a 6-item condition than in a 30-item condition (see Figure 5.20). This is consistent with the idea that serial search is mediated by a strategic allocation of a limited set of spatial indexes.

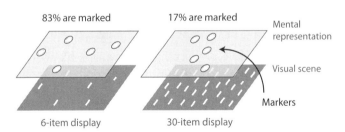

Figure 5.20 If only a limited number of spatial indexes are available during serial visual search, the relative proportion of indexed locations to unindexed locations will decrease as set size increases. On the assumption that five indexes are available, the relative proportion of indexed locations in a 6-item display is 83% and the relative proportion in a 30-item display is only 17%. Therefore, if a probe dot appears at random at one of the item locations, there is a significantly greater chance that it will be at an *indexed* location if the search-set size is smaller (e.g., 6 items). The greater likelihood of an inhibitory tagging effect with smaller search sets may indicate that tagging is mediated by a limited number of indexes (perhaps only four or five).

Two extreme types of serial analysis are memory-less random search and perfect-memory systematic search. Under memory-less random search, every object has an equal probability of being inspected at any time during search and, as there is no memory of past inspections, objects may be visited more than once (cf., Horowitz & Wolfe, 1998). Under perfect-memory search, however, object inspections are remembered and objects are never reinspected. The serial search described in this section is somewhere between these two extremes. One reason why may be because it is mediated by a systematic search mechanism, but that mechanism is constrained by the limited number of spatial indexes available for marking inspected objects.

A study of the relationship between working memory load and the IOR effect also indicated that a limited number of spatial indexes may be involved (Castel et al., 2003). Subjects performed target-detection tasks known to elicit IOR. In addition, they performed variants of a secondary task that taxed working memory. Given that the inhibition of multiple objects at different locations over a relatively long period of time requires some form of working memory, the experimenters hypothesized that this secondary task performance, if spatial in nature, could eliminate IOR. The results indicated that nonspatial working memory tasks (e.g., counting odd numbers) had no effect on IOR but that *spatial* working memory tasks (i.e., encoding the directions of arrows; encoding the relative positions of probe items) disrupted it. The experimenters concluded that the performance of a spatial task eliminated IOR because the same mechanism was involved in preserving the inhibited location and in performing the secondary spatial task. In their words, "the inhibited location is held in a form of visual spatial working memory, such that intervening tasks involving the same working memory processes disrupt the trace of the inhibited location" (Castel et al., 2003, p. 979). In terms of the mechanism involved, perhaps task performance was mediated by spatial indexes, but their limited number (e.g., 4 or 5) necessitated their removal from objects associated with inhibition while performing the primary (IOR) task so that they could be reallocated while performing the secondary (spatial working memory) task.

Inhibition of Return Is Not Reflexive

Direct location cueing can have a biphasic effect on target-detection responses as a function of CTOA (i.e., initially facilitative at CTOAs less than 200 ms, and then inhibitory at longer CTOAs). As mentioned previously, the opponent-process account of IOR holds that direct cue onsets trigger the simultaneous activation of facilitative and inhibitory components. As seen in Figure 5.11, the facilitative component is said to be dominant during the first 200 ms but, after its transient effect subsides, the inhibitory component is no longer masked and is dominant at longer CTOAs. But to what extent are activation of facilitative and inhibitory components mandatory? A growing body of evidence indicates that, while the facilitative effects of direct cueing are stimulus-driven and reflexive, the same does not appear to be true of the inhibitory effects of cueing (e.g., Schendel et al., 2001).

In chapter 2, it was noted that direct location-cue effects on responses to targets are stimulus-driven and reflexive whereas symbolic-cue effects are goal-driven and strategic. Some of the studies supporting this conclusion involved manipulations of cue validity and CTOA (see Figure 2.9). We conducted an experiment to determine the extent to which IOR would be affected by cue validity and CTOA manipulations (Wright & Richard, 2000). One result was a telling interaction between these two variables. In particular, at shorter CTOAs (66 and 100 ms) and regardless of cue validity, the first of two successive direct cues had a facilitative effect on detection times for targets appearing at their locations. At a longer CTOA (400 ms), however, the first cue had an inhibitory effect on detection times, but only when the cue was uninformative (see Figure 5.21). When high-validity cues were used, IOR did not occur. This suggests that, unlike the facilitative effects of location cueing, the inhibitory effects (IOR) are less reflexive and more cognitively mediated like goal-driven processes.

This finding indicates that the IOR effect occurs only when there is some degree of uncertainty about where the target will appear. Over trials, subjects may realize that targets are very likely to appear at high-validity cue locations, and the attenuation of IOR in this case improves search efficiency. Similarly, subjects may realize that targets are very *unlikely* to appear at low-validity cue locations. The attenuation of IOR on such trials also improves search efficiency. Perhaps, with low-validity cues, this is because

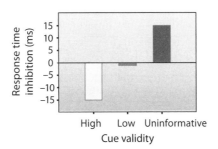

Figure 5.21 Results of Wright and Richard's (2000) experiment. This figure shows the effect of cue validity on inhibition of return (IOR) when the CTOA was 400 ms. Cues produced IOR only when they were uninformative. In contrast, no IOR occurred when cues had a low validity (when targets rarely appeared there). In addition, a facilitative effect of cueing occurred instead of IOR when cues had a high validity. These findings show that IOR is influenced in a goal-driven manner by cue validity.

there is little need to spatially index these locations. From an efficiency standpoint, limited processing resources (indexes) are unlikely to be used to keep track of locations where it is apparent that the target very probably will *not* occur. Instead, these locations may be eliminated entirely from the search set or at least not given special (inhibitory) treatment (cf., Treisman, 1998; Treisman & Sato, 1990).

The attenuation of IOR as target predictability increases has also been studied by presenting targets at the same location on successive trials (Maylor & Hockey, 1987). The magnitude of the effect decreased slightly after three trials on which the target was presented at the same location, and it continued to decrease as a function of the number of consecutive trials with target location repetition. On this basis, the experimenters concluded that IOR is more likely to occur if, over trials, target location is randomized, and that attenuation of IOR can be attributed to subjects' subjective expectancies about target location (Maylor & Hockey, 1987, p. 53; see also, Posner et al., 1984a; cf., Taylor & Donnelly, 2002). This is another indication that the occurrence of IOR is, to some extent, under the observer's control.

A more direct test of the goal-driven nature of IOR would be to create a scenario in which the occurrence of the effect would depend on the observer's beliefs about objects in the visual scene. This is sometimes referred to as *cognitive penetrability* (Fodor, 1983; Pylyshyn, 1984, 1999). One intriguing finding is that IOR occurred at a cued location, even when the cue in question was not visible and "appeared" to be occluded by an illusory Kanisza square (Yi et al., 2003). This result was replicated in an experiment involving cues that moved across the stimulus display and seemed to disappear behind a similar type of square composed of illusory contours (Jefferies et al., 2005). More specifically, on some trials, a cue moved across the screen and then disappeared as though it were moving behind an illusory square (as in Figure 5.22). On other trials, a cue moved across the screen and, while this was occurring, the objects at each corner of the illusory square moved outward to degrade the illusion. It was clear, on the latter trials, that the cue had simply disappeared and was not occluded. The results indicated that when subjects *believed* that the cue was still present but occluded by the square, IOR occurred when a target was subsequently presented at that location (which supports Yi et al.'s finding). On the other hand, when subjects believed that the cue had simply disappeared (in the condition in which the illusory square was degraded), IOR did not occur when a target was presented there. This is strong evidence that IOR is not purely a stimulus-driven effect, and that it can be influenced in a goal-driven manner as well. In Pylyshyn's terms, IOR is cognitively penetrable.

Note that MOT is also possible despite the presence of occluding objects. In particular, if a tracked object disappears behind an occluder and reappears

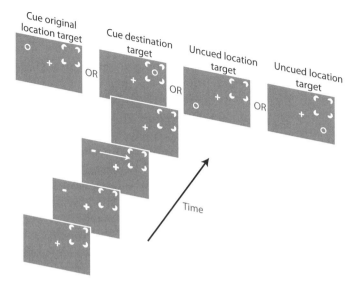

Figure 5.22 An example of the stimulus display in Jefferies et al.'s (2005) study. Trials began with the movement of a cue (horizontal line) across the display toward an illusory square as though it was moving behind it. This was followed by the onset of a target (unfilled circle) at the original location of the cue, the perceived destination of the cue, or one of two movement-independent locations above or below the cue movement vector (the uncued locations in the figure). When subjects *believed* that a moving cue was occluded by a square composed of illusory contours, inhibition of return (IOR) occurred when a target was presented there. When subjects believed the moving cue had simply disappeared, IOR did not occur. This shows that IOR is cognitively penetrable.

in a way that is consistent with a persisting object, tracking performance is unaffected by occlusion (Scholl & Pylyshyn, 1999; see Figure 5.23). Perhaps, in this case, a spatial index remains dynamically bound to the object, even when it appears to pass momentarily behind an occluding surface and then reappear again. If, however, its disappearance and reappearance is not consistent with a persisting object, the binding of an index to this object will be terminated (cf., Mitroff et al., 2004). This may also be the case in the experiment outlined in Figure 5.22 (Jefferies et al., 2005). When subjects believed that the cue moved and still persisted behind an occluding figure, a spatial index might remain bound to the cue and, as a result, IOR would occur at that location. On the other hand, when they believed that the cue was removed (as opposed to being occluded), a spatial index that might have been bound to it during the movement may have been removed and IOR would not occur at that location.

The findings discussed in this section imply that there is a *strategic* aspect to IOR. This may seem counterintuitive, given that the effect appears to be mediated by lower level processes. And it is not entirely consistent with

Figure 5.23 Example of a stimulus display like those used by Scholl and Pylyshyn (1999) in which multiple moving objects seem to disappear behind an occluding vertical bar and then reappear in a manner indicative of persisting objects. When this is the case, multiple object tracking performance is not disrupted by occlusion.

the opponent-process account of IOR, which holds that activation of the inhibitory component is a mandatory effect of direct cueing (see Figure 5.11). It is, however, consistent with the fact that serial visual search is, by nature, strategic and improves with practice (cf., Lee & Quessy, 2003). A number of studies have shown, for example, that over the first 10 years of life, the efficiency of search continually improves (e.g., Enns & Cameron, 1987). We speculate that this practice effect could be due, in part, to refinement of strategies for reallocating a limited number of indexes to different items during the course of a search.

IOR is also affected by practice (e.g., Lupiáñez et al., 2001; Müller & Von Mühlenen, 1996). For example, an IOR practice effect appears to be associated with the direction in which people first learn to read (Spalek & Hammad, 2005). Reading skills, of course, develop only with extensive practice. Subjects who learned to read from left to right (e.g., English) showed a left–right IOR bias, whereas those who learned to read from right to left (e.g., Arabic) showed a right–left IOR bias. Indications that IOR is associated with learned rather than reflexive processes are consistent with Wright and Richard's (1998) claim that IOR is similar, in some ways, to an automatized visual routine that appears to be reflexive, but can be influenced in a goal-driven manner (cf., Cavanagh, 2004). In chapter 9, we discuss the results of a study in which IOR was produced by merely *observing* another subject performing an experimental trial (Welsh et al., 2005).

Research on the IOR effect has contributed in several ways to what we know about processes mediating sequential attention shifts. The evidence indicates, for example, that a marking operation may guide sequences of attention shifts by labeling locations that attention should *not* be shifted to. In other words, markers may constrain the set of potential shift destinations. Also, this marking operation appears to be mediated both by object-based and by location-based processes. As thought to be the case with MOT, it appears that more than one object or location can be marked at any given time, and that perhaps marking is mediated by a limited number (e.g., 4 or 5) of spatial indexes. In addition, while commonly assumed to be the result of stimulus-driven processes, it appears that IOR is also, to some extent, under goal-driven control. This is consistent with the idea that marking associated with the guidance of sequential attention shifts is carried out at an intermediate level of visual processing.

Summary

Most of the covert orienting experiments conducted to date and discussed in previous chapters tend to focus on the detailed study of *single* shifts of attention. On the other hand, most visual search experiments, while concerned with serial shifts of attention, tend *not* to focus on the mechanisms involved in programming these shifts. The studies described in this chapter, however, provide some insight about operations involved in the execution of sequential attention shifts. An emerging theme of this research is that some form of spatial indexing appears to mediate covert orienting. In some situations, indexing appears to guide a shift of attention to its destination (e.g., Yantis & Johnson, 1990; Yantis & Jones, 1991); while in other situations involving serial inspection of a visual scene (e.g., Posner & Cohen, 1984), indexing appears to guide attention away from locations that it has already addressed. More specifically, spatial indexing appears to be associated with response facilitation and the *attraction* of attention (e.g., Yantis & Johnson, 1990; Yantis & Jones, 1991), and also with response inhibition and the *repulsion* of attention (e.g., Posner & Cohen, 1984).

Why might this be the case? We suggest that the allocation of indexes (or tags) to objects is not inherently facilitative or inhibitory (Wright & Richard, 1998). Instead, indexes may serve as marker tokens that can be used by higher level processes in accordance with the task being performed (cf., Cavanagh, 2004; Pylyshyn, 2003, 2007; Ullman, 1984, 1996). During serial visual search, for example, a visual routine could mark previously inspected objects in an inhibitory manner to improve search efficiency. On the other hand, when performing a task such as MOT, another visual routine could use the same set of indexes, but in a facilitative manner. Using Yantis and Johnson's (1990) terminology, indexes may serve to designate locations that have either a high or low attentional priority, depending on the observer's current goal.

To account for our ability to track multiple moving objects, Pylyshyn and Storm (1988) developed the FINST hypothesis. That is, maintenance of individual target locations is not due to alignments of focused attention, but is instead preattentively mediated by four or five spatial indexes. Four or five is also the number of abrupt-onset objects that Yantis and Johnson

(1990) suggested can be tagged as having high attentional priority. Another assumption of the FINST hypothesis is that spatial index allocation can be stimulus-driven or goal-driven, depending on the task to be performed. Index allocation is also said to be dynamic in the sense that indexes can remain assigned to objects, even as they move within the visual field, and even when these objects are occluded from view. If true, then perhaps spatial indexes mediate some types of object-based attentional processing.

Inhibition of return is the inhibition of responses to objects appearing at recently cued or recently attended locations. It has been suggested that response inhibition may be associated with a mechanism that "inhibits processing from returning" to previously inspected objects. When a location cue moves after it is presented, object-based IOR can occur at its new location and location-based IOR can occur at its original location. Object-based IOR may be due to a spatial index remaining dynamically bound to the cue as it moves, and location-based IOR may be due to a second index being assigned to the cue's original location. While IOR is often thought to be mandatory and reflexive, it can be influenced by cue validity manipulations, practice, left-to-right reading bias, and beliefs about cue occlusion by illusory objects. This indicates that IOR is flexible and, to some extent, goal-driven. Thus, when a sequence of attention shifts is executed, inhibition of responses to targets appearing at previously attended locations (other than the most recent one) could be due to inhibitory tagging with some form of spatial index. In sum, although there is no consensus about the operations mediating sequences of attention shifts, there are indications that some form of marking operation is involved.

In the chapters that follow, we consider the possibility that there is a link between mechanisms that mediate sequences of attention shifts and those that mediate sequences of eye movements. We know, for example, that the duration of the IOR effect corresponds to the time required to make at least two or three eye saccadic movements (Posner & Cohen, 1984; Samuel & Katt, 2003). This raises questions about the extent to which common mechanisms could mediate the guidance of eye movements and attention shifts. We also examine studies indicating that IOR occurs following the presentation of auditory and cross-modal stimuli, and discuss research conducted to determine the physiological instantiation of IOR mechanisms.

6

Eye Movements and Attention Shifts

Eye movements and attention shifts usually occur together. Some of the first studies of eye movements and visual perception were based on the assumption that, at any given time, the center of fixation of the eyes is the center of attention (e.g., Buswell, 1935). By extension, tracking someone's eye movements was thought to reveal that person's "path of attention." Helmholz's demonstration, however, indicated that ocular fixation and attention can be oriented independently (described in chapter 1; see Figure 1.3). For this reason, although most contemporary eye tracking researchers tacitly assume that attention is linked to foveal gaze, they also acknowledge that this may not always be so (Duchowski, 2003, p. 14).

The relationship between eye movements and attention is controversial. It has been argued, for example, that the concept of covert orienting is overemphasized by contemporary vision researchers and that when observers are free to move their eyes, covert attentional scanning rarely occurs (Findlay & Gilchrist, 2003; but cf., Pollatsek & Rayner's, 1999, counter-argument). The goal of this chapter, however, is not to debate the relative importance of covert and overt orienting to visual analysis, but rather to examine the relationship between attention and eye movements when covert orienting occurs.

Much of the research we have discussed up to this point involved shifts of attentional focus while ocular focus remained stationary. But what happens when ocular focus does not remain stationary? And what role does attention play in making eye movements? In this chapter, we examine the relationship between these two types of orienting.

Oculomotor System

When we point our eyes toward objects of interest while inspecting a visual scene, we align retinal images of these objects with a central region of the retina called the *fovea*. This is a small depression, 0.2 mm in size, in the center of the retina (Coren et al., 2004). Photoreceptors within the fovea enable finely detailed visual input to be perceived clearly (Hirsch & Curcio, 1989). The retinal region outside the fovea contains photoreceptors that initiate visual analysis at a much lower resolution. The limited spatial extent of the foveal region means that much of the visual field is nonfoveal. Tasks requiring analysis of fine details of a visual scene (e.g., reading small print) are performed more efficiently if the visual input is received primarily by foveal receptors. Therefore, inspection of the visual field usually involves a number of eye movements that foveate objects of interest.

The human retina is structured so that there is a trade-off between our capacity for resolving fine details and our sensitivity to changes in the visual scene. Visual acuity is greatest within 1° of the center of the fovea, and drops off sharply after 5° (outside the parafovea; De Valois & De Valois, 1988; see Figure 6.1). The greater acuity provided by foveal receptors (as opposed to peripheral retinal receptors) comes at the cost of decreased sensitivity to changes in light intensity and positions of objects. The neural architecture that enables foveal optic nerve fibers to have small receptive fields, and therefore high acuity, also limits the number of photoreceptors that provide input to these nerve fibers. This results in a decrease in their overall sensitivity to stimulus onsets and to motion. Conversely, because optic nerve fibers originating in the retinal periphery have much larger receptive fields, many more photoreceptors contribute to their activation. As a result, retinal periphery nerve fibers are significantly more sensitive to stimulus onsets and to motion than are foveal nerve fibers (e.g., Shulman et al., 1985; Van der Heijden et al., 1988). This is why, as astronomers have long known, it is easier to detect a faint visual stimulus when looking "sideways out of the corner of the eye." The Little Dipper, for example, is a constellation of stars that can be found more easily when looking "off the fovea." This retinal organization is efficient because it allows us to carry out high-acuity analysis of foveated stimuli while remaining vigilant and sensitive to stimulus events that may occur in the visual periphery.

In some cases, when large movements are required, overt orienting involves more than just eye movements. When orienting across distances

Foveal (2°)
Parafoveal (10°)

Figure 6.1 Visual acuity is greatest within the foveal visual field, and drops off sharply outside the parafoveal field.

greater than about 20°, a combination of head and eye movements normally occurs; and, when orienting across extremely large distances, trunk and body movements also take place (Sanders, 1963). There are also instances in which *only* overt orienting occurs. Some animals (e.g., great horned owls) have a limited ability to move their eyes, and are able to orient with head and body movements only. Gilchrist et al. (1997) also described a case of a woman (AI) who, since birth, could not move her eyes, and compensated for this with head and body movements.

Types of Eye Movements

We make a variety of eye movements including vestibulo-ocular reflex movements, vergence movements, and microsaccades. Most research on the relationship between attention and eye movements, however, focuses on either *saccades* or *smooth pursuit movements*. Saccades are the movements we make most frequently. As seen in Figure 6.2, they are characterized by rapid, "jump-and-rest" foveations of objects that occur when we scan a scene or read. There are a number of accounts of the origin of the term saccade (e.g., Gregory, 1990). According to Tatler and Wade (2003, p. 177), it is derived from the French words *saquer* or *sachier* meaning "to pull." In between each saccade, there is a fixation period during which the eyes are relatively still (but not completely still; cf., Martinez-Conde et al., 2004) while visual analysis of the foveated object is carried out, and the trajectory of the next saccade is calibrated. The speed of saccades makes them an efficient way to search and explore the visual field in a rapid manner.

We also make pursuit movements frequently to maintain foveation of moving objects. Unlike saccades, pursuits are characterized by a smooth motion without abrupt starts and stops. When tracking a moving object, our eyes move in correspondence with it to maintain, as accurately as possible, the position of the object's retinal image within the foveal region.

Figure 6.2 Example of the type of "jump-and-rest" scan path that occurs when we make saccades.

Saccades. Although fast eye movements were mentioned in the 1800s by several vision researchers (e.g., Helmholtz, Hering, Mach), recognition of the jump-and-rest pattern of saccades is generally credited to Javal (1878, 1879) and other 19th century French ophthalmologists. Some readers may be familiar with the term "goal-directed" saccade (e.g., Fischer & Breitmeyer, 1987; Fischer & Weber, 1993). This is sometimes used in the eye-movement literature to convey that the observer "allows" a saccade to be made to a particular location corresponding to a sensory event. In this book, however, we use the same naming convention for the control of saccades that we used in previous chapters for the control of attention shifts. That is, saccades initiated by sensory events such as abrupt-onset stimuli are referred to as stimulus-driven. Saccades initiated on the basis of an observer's goals and intentions (e.g., a voluntary eye movement to a symbolically cued location) are referred to as goal-driven.

Whereas saccade programming occurs well below the level of conscious awareness, these eye movements are generally under voluntary control and can be suppressed when we choose to do so. It has also been shown, however, that saccades can be captured in a stimulus-driven manner once observers decide to make an eye movement (Theeuwes et al., 1998, 1999). In one experiment, subjects searched for and made a saccade to a target of a particular color, and stimulus-driven oculomotor capture occurred if another item sometimes appeared abruptly in the visual field at the instant when they were about to move their eyes. As shown in Figure 6.3 (distractor condition), saccades that should have been made to the target location were sometimes made in error to the irrelevant item with the abrupt onset. This demonstrates that saccade programming sometimes can be stimulus-driven (see also, Ludwig & Gilchrist, 2002).

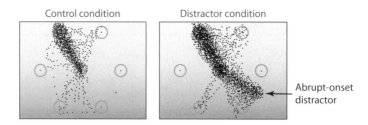

Figure 6.3 An approximation of the results of Theeuwes et al. (1999) experiment indicates that some saccades can be captured by irrelevant abrupt-onset stimuli. Saccade data in the left panel are from the control condition (no abrupt-onset distractors appeared). They show that saccades usually were made from the center of the display to the target in the upper left quadrant. Data in the right panel are from the abrupt-onset distractor condition. They show that saccades frequently were made to the distractor in the lower right quadrant as well as to the target. Saccades made in error to abrupt-onset distractors are evidence of stimulus-driven oculomotor capture.

Adults can make saccades as large as 40° but, when performing everyday tasks, typical saccade magnitude is 18°–20° (Land et al., 1999). Estimates of the maximum saccade velocity range from 600°/sec to 1000°/sec. Saccade velocity is not constant, however. At the beginning of a saccade, the eyes accelerate at a rate that can reach 40,000°/sec². As they near their destination, they have a comparable rate of deceleration. A typical long saccade made by adults will align the fovea with the intended destination with an error of only 5%–10% of the distance moved. Thus, saccades are fast and impressively accurate.

The speed and accuracy of saccades comes at a temporal cost, however. Before each saccade, there is a fixational pause called the saccadic refractory period that usually lasts about 150–600 ms, and about 90% of viewing time is devoted to fixations (Irwin, 1992). During this time, the direction and magnitude of the next saccade's trajectory from origin to destination is calibrated, and an oculomotor program is prepared. When the saccade is initiated, a signal is sent to the oculomotor muscles and the eyes are in motion for about 10–100 ms (Shebilske & Fisher, 1983). This is about 10% of the total viewing time of a typical fixation. On average, the time required to calibrate and execute a saccade is roughly 220 ms. Thus, we can usually make no more than four saccades per second. Compared to the speed of other aspects of visual analysis, the programming stage of saccadic eye movements is relatively slow.

Saccades are *ballistic* movements. Once a particular trajectory has been calibrated and the saccade begins, the eyes can be moved without further programming (although cf., Zee et al., 1976). For this reason, saccades have been compared to firing a projectile with a cannon because, once the vector between the origin and the destination is calibrated and the initiation signal is sent, the projectile moves without further guidance (Zingale & Kowler, 1987). In addition, once initiated, new information cannot modify ballistic movements. In the case of saccades, the cutoff point for modifying the movement appears to be about 70 ms prior to the start of the movement (Findlay & Gilchrist, 2003, p. 28). One disadvantage of this ballistic aspect of saccades is that, during programming, they require precise information about their destination. Presumably, this contributes to the time required for calibration. But the advantage of ballistic movements is that, once initiated, they are extremely rapid and require no additional feedback to be guided to their destinations.

Pursuits. Pursuit movements are considerably slower and less accurate than saccades. Pursuits have a peak velocity of about 30°/sec, and their velocity depends on the velocity of the object that is being tracked. The same is true of pursuit accuracy. Pursuits can match slowly moving objects almost perfectly, but there is a tendency to under-pursue rapidly moving objects.

When under-pursuit occurs, the position of the object's image on the retina slips out of the foveal region rather than remaining in a constant position, and the object begins to appear and smeared (Murphy, 1978).

Unlike saccades, pursuit movements are not ballistic. Instead, because moving objects change position from one moment to the next, tracking is only possible if signals are continuously sent to the eye muscles to provide constant updates about object location. This feedback loop is thought to code both current object position and also perceptual and cognitive expectations about object motion (Kowler, 1989). This enables us to alter the speed and direction of pursuit movements whenever needed to maintain tracking accuracy.

The accuracy of pursuit movements improves with practice and pursuit is a learned skill. While infants have the ability to make small saccades at birth, they are unable to make pursuit movements (Maurer & Lewis, 1998). Instead, they follow moving objects with their eyes by making a series of small movements called *hypometric saccades* (Aslin & Salapatek, 1975; cf., Hainline, 1998; see Figure 6.4). It is not until infants are 10–12 weeks old that they first develop the capacity to make pursuit movements (Aslin, 1981). The pursuit movements made by preschool children, 4 and 5 years of age, are also less accurate than those made by adults; perhaps because children at this age are less able than adults to anticipate changes in the motion (Kowler & Martins, 1982). Thus, making accurate pursuit eye movements is a skill that appears to be acquired gradually with practice and experience.

Attentional Engagement During Pursuits and Saccades. While the purpose of pursuit movements is to maintain visual analysis while the eyes are in motion, the same is not true of saccadic eye movements. Saccades are much faster than pursuits but, to prevent a blurring effect that can occur even with the much slower pursuit movements, visual analysis is suppressed during the 10–100 ms period in which the eye is in motion (Breitmeyer, 1980; Burr et al., 1994). As a result, information about the visual scene is not updated until the saccade is completed. And, even for a brief period of time after the saccade is completed (as well as just before the saccade is

Figure 6.4 While adults are able to make single long saccades (30° or more), infants in the first 2–3 months of life make a series of smaller hypometric saccades to cover the same distance. They also make hypometric saccades when learning to make pursuit eye movements.

initiated), the threshold for detecting targets increases (Matin, 1972). Thus, the observer is effectively blind during saccades, and visual analysis during the course of a series of these eye movements is actually a composite based on several different fixations. But our experience is a "seamless comprehension" of the visual world with no awareness of the visual suppression.

The extent to which visual processing can be suppressed during a saccade was demonstrated in a compelling study in which visual scenes were changed while observers' eyes were in motion (Grimes, 1996). Subjects in this study were told that their memory for the images would be tested, and were also told that they could expect occasional scene changes to occur. An eye tracking and image manipulation procedure was used to present color photographs of natural scenes and, while subjects' eyes were in motion during saccades, some scene details were altered. Even though they were aware that this could occur, subjects missed surprisingly large changes. For example, as seen in Figure 6.5, after subjects viewed one image of a room containing furniture and other items, it was replaced with a modified image (flower pot in a different location) while their eyes were in motion during a saccade. A significant number of subjects fail to detect changes of this type. On another trial, they viewed an image portraying a bridegroom wearing a formal gray coat with a matching gray silk hat standing beside his new father-in-law who was wearing a black tuxedo with matching top hat. While subjects' eyes were in motion during a saccade, the hats of the two men were switched but none of the subjects detected this event. And on still another trial, subjects viewed an image in which four people were standing on a beach. Only 50% of them noticed a change in one of the swimsuits from bright pink to bright green. Thus, large changes to a visual scene are very likely to go unnoticed if they occur during saccades because visual analysis is suppressed during that time (cf., Simons & Rensink, 2005).

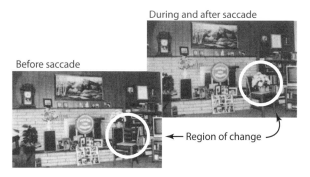

Figure 6.5 Example of stimulus pair used in Grimes' (1996) experiment. When the change in the flower pot's position occurred while subjects' eyes were in motion during a saccade, most were unable to detect it.

This finding is consistent with results of other experiments on the integration of information across saccades (e.g., Henderson, 1997; Irwin, 1991; Rayner & Pollatsek, 1983). As researchers developed techniques for studying it without the need for precise eye tracking and saccade-yoked scene alterations (e.g., Rensink et al., 1997), the effect came to be known as *change blindness* (see also, Mack & Rock, 1998). One robust finding is that changes to attended objects are more detectable than are changes to unattended objects (O'Regan et al., 2000). Saccade preparation, however, appears to have the opposite effect on change blindness. The results of one study indicated that changes were more apparent at locations to which a saccade was about to be made, than at saccade launch points (Henderson & Hollingworth, 1999). Thus, while observers performing this type of task frequently fail to detect substantial scene modifications unless they are explicitly attending to them, they appear to be sensitive to modifications at saccade destinations. Many other experiments on change blindness have been conducted since the effect was first reported but, because of space constraints, we cannot describe this literature in detail and instead direct the interested reader to some examples and reviews of this research (Beck et al., 2001, 2006; Cavanaugh & Wurtz, 2004; Huettel et al., 2001; Reddy et al., 2006; Simons & Ambinder, 2005; Simons & Rensink, 2005; Tse et al., 2006).

Unlike during saccades, attention remains engaged during pursuit movements, and can even facilitate them. Subjects in a series of studies were able to perform pursuit movement tracking tasks more accurately when they focused their attention on a moving target to read changing letters or numbers (Shagass et al., 1976), notice a target color change (Levin et al., 1981), or when they were required to press a button whenever the center of a moving target filled (Iacono & Lykken, 1979; see Figure 6.6). Moreover, deficits

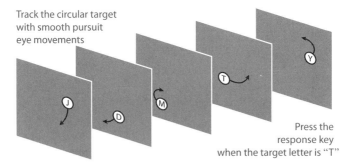

Figure 6.6 Example of an experimental trial on which subjects track a moving circle with smooth pursuit eye movements while monitoring the identity of the letter inside. When the letter changes to the target "T," a response is required. Tracking of the circle's movement is more accurate in this type of condition than in a control condition in which letter identity is not monitored.

Saccades	Pursuits
Peak velocity of 600°/sec to 1000°/sec and acceleration can reach 40,000°/sec²	Peak velocity of 30°/sec and acceleration much slower than saccades
Movement is ballistic	Movement requires feedback
Target foveation is very accurate, but latency of about 220 ms associated with calibration usually occurs	Target foveation is less accurate, and depends on observer's skill level for tracking moving objects
Smaller saccades (less than 6°) executed by newborns	Long learning period required to execute with peak efficiency
Similar to *discrete* attention shifts because attention is disengaged during movement	Similar to *analog* attention shifts because attention remains engaged during movement

Table 6.1 Properties of Saccadic and Smooth Pursuit Eye Movements

in tracking ability that are common in schizophrenic patients (Holzman, 1985; Holzman et al., 1973) were attenuated in another experiment when these patients were required to attend to and analyze the target for some type of detail as it moved (Van Gelder et al., 1990). This indicates that engaged attention facilitates pursuit movement tracking accuracy, and that pursuit movement deficits may be related to an inability to maintain focused attention on moving objects.

With regard to the discussion of analog and discrete attention shifts in chapter 3, saccades could be considered discrete because, in a sense, attentional focus is "turned off" while the eyes are in motion. On the other hand, pursuits could be considered analog because they occur, as much as possible, while attention remains actively engaged. Both types of eye movements serve to foveate targets, but saccades are high-speed foveations of a sequence of discrete locations in a visual scene, whereas pursuits are a lower-speed "analog" analysis of an object as it moves within a scene. Table 6.1 is a summary of the properties of saccadic and pursuit movements.

Eye-Movement Programming
Several cortical and subcortical brain areas are active when we make eye movements, but the role of the superior colliculus in saccade programming is critical. The superior colliculus contributes to eye-movement target selection for both saccades and smooth pursuit movements (in concert with the frontal and parietal cortex). This visual information is then converted to motor signals that the superior colliculus sends to the midbrain and brainstem oculomotor generating centers that control the eye muscles via the cranial nerves.

The superior colliculus has multiple layers that are stacked like the pages of a book. The superficial (upper) layers receive direct inputs from the retina, and the intermediate and deep (lower) layers receive inputs from cortical visual areas and send inputs to the saccade generation centers (Sparks & Mays, 1990). Each layer contains maps of visual and oculomotor space, and some neurons in these layers have both visual and oculomotor responsiveness (Robinson, 1972; Schiller & Koerner, 1971). The results of one study, for example, indicated that certain neurons in monkeys became active in response to a direct location cue, even when the response was either a saccade or some other manual movement (e.g., button press) without a saccade (Kustov & Robinson, 1996). This is consistent with findings that monkey superficial layer neuron activity can occur as a result of attending to a stimulus without making a saccade to its location (Goldberg & Wurtz, 1972; Mohler & Wurtz, 1976). Thus, as will be discussed in chapter 7, the superior colliculus plays a role in mediating both attention shifts and eye movements.

Several different types of neurons have been identified in the superior colliculus (Fuchs et al., 1985). *Build-up cells* have a firing rate that begins to increase well before the movement, and their activity reaches a peak as the saccade is initiated. *Pause cells* (or omnipause cells) normally have a steady, uniform firing rate but, 5–15 ms prior to a saccade, there is a brief pause in their activity (irrespective of saccade direction and amplitude). *Burst cells* are active for a brief period of time immediately preceding saccade initiation. Their receptive fields are laid out topographically within the intermediate and deep layers, and they only become active when saccade destinations correlate with their locations within an oculomotor map (i.e., when saccades are made in a certain direction and with a certain amplitude). Electrical stimulation of a burst cell can also trigger a saccade, and its destination in visual space will correlate with the cell's location within an oculomotor map (Sparks & Mays, 1983). It has been suggested that pause cells may be part of a "when" component of saccadic control and burst cells part of a "where" component (Van Gisbergen et al., 1981).

The extent to which oculomotor programming is cortical appears to depend on the nature of the saccade involved. A meta-analysis of neuroimaging studies conducted by Grosbras et al. (2005) indicated that goal-driven saccades are associated with more cortical activity than are stimulus-driven saccades. The physiology of eye movements and attention shifts is discussed in more detail in chapter 7.

Eye Tracking Methodology

Techniques for measuring eye movements have existed in various forms for many years (Wade & Tatler, 2005). The first attempt to record eye movements using *corneal reflection*, for example, was reported in 1901 (Robinson,

1968). Photographic methods were introduced by Dodge (1907) and others in the early 20th century (Wade et al., 2003). Eye-movement recordings were also attempted as early as 1898 using a plaster of Paris ring attached directly to the cornea and to mechanical linkages to recording pens (Young & Sheena, 1975). This technique was refined in the 1950s using a contact lens attached to a reference object (e.g., coil of wire that produces a voltage when it moves in a magnetic field; or a small mirror that reflects a light source). The modern *scleral contact lens* method is one of the most precise ways to measure even the smallest eye movements, but it is extremely invasive.

Some of the early published work on eye tracking includes Buswell's (1935) use of photographic eye-movement monitoring to determine where people directed their gaze when they viewed art. In the years that followed, Yarbus (1967) used the scleral contact lens method (with an attached mirror to reflect a light source) to produce one of the first clear depictions of eye movements. Noton and Stark (1971) conducted a similar study and coined the term *scanpath* to describe the sequence of eye movements made when viewing a visual scene (Figure 6.2).

In covert orienting experiments, subjects are usually required to keep their eyes fixated at the center of the display throughout a trial. One method is to simply instruct subjects to do so (without using any additional eye tracking measures). This is not recommended, however, because a good deal of data indicates that subjects (particularly naive ones) have difficulty obeying such an instruction (e.g., Colegate et al., 1973). Another method is to film subjects' eyes throughout the course of an experiment and, after the data have been collected, review the film to determine which trials were contaminated by eye movements and should therefore be excluded from data analysis. The disadvantages of the film analysis method are that scoring films is time consuming, tedious, and prone to error. Moreover, if a large enough number of data trials are discarded, the experiment's statistical power can be significantly reduced. These limitations can be overcome by using a real-time eye-monitoring technique. This enables experimenters to detect eye movements during the course of data collection and to eliminate trials contaminated by eye movements when they occur, having subjects repeat such trials later in the experiment.

Two categories of real-time eye-movement monitoring techniques are (a) those that measure the position of the eyes relative to the head and (b) those that measure the orientation of the eyes in visual space. The latter execute *point-of-regard* measurements. Some techniques are only suitable for measuring point of regard if the observer's head is stabilized. The EOG (electro-oculography) method, for example, is generally not suited for point-of-regard measurements; but if the observer's head is stabilized, it can be used in covert orienting experiments to ensure that the eyes remain stationary.

Measurement of EOGs was the most widely used method of eye tracking in the 1970s (Young & Sheena, 1975). When electrodes are placed near the eyes, it is possible to detect fluctuations in the permanent potential voltage (approximately 1 mV) between the cornea and the fundus when the oculomotor muscles contract. The disadvantages of this method are that it does not produce reliable measures of medium and large saccades and, even when no eye movement has been made, the signal can change (e.g., the signal is affected by the observer's state of dark adaptation). The EOG method is, however, an inexpensive and relatively easy way to detect the presence or absence of eye movements.

The advent of the modern digital computer and fast image processing hardware facilitated the development of real-time, video-based, corneal-reflection eye trackers. These systems work by measuring changes in the amount of infrared light that is reflected off the cornea as the eyes change position. Infrared light is used because it is "invisible" to the eye and, therefore, does not distract the subject. In addition, infrared detectors are not influenced to any great extent by other light sources and so the ambient lighting level does not affect measurements. The spatial resolution (size of the smallest eye movement that can be detected) of video-based corneal-reflection trackers is fairly high (to about 1° of visual angle over a 30° viewing range), and this method is relatively noninvasive. It is now said to be the most widely used technique for measuring point of regard (Duchowski, 2003), and it is a good choice for attention research.

Most corneal-reflection eye trackers use a video camera to provide input to a computer about the current positions of the subject's pupil and iris/scleral boundary (see Figure 6.7). On the basis of these two points of reference, the computer is able to disambiguate head movement from eye movement and determine point of regard. Head stabilization does not need to be stringent with this type of system because the positional difference between the pupil center and corneal reflection will change with pure eye movement,

Figure 6.7 Pupil and iris/scleral boundary corneal reflection produced by infrared illumination can be used to compute an observer's point of regard.

but will remain relatively constant with minor head movements. Some corneal-reflection systems, however, do not measure point of regard without head stabilization. For example, some systems track the iris/scleral boundary using photodiodes (mounted within goggles) and infrared illumination, and they measure eye movements relative to head position. One advantage these systems have over video-based systems is that their relatively high sampling frequency (e.g., 600 Hz) allows for precise measurement of eye movements. By comparison, the sampling frequency of video-based systems is typically limited to a 60 Hz video frame rate, which means that the maximum sampling rate is once every 16 ms (usually even longer because the tracker may need additional time to process each video frame).

Corneal reflections are also known as *Purkinje images* (Crane, 1994), and video-based eye trackers typically locate the first Purkinje image. Another type of system called the dual Purkinje tracker typically measures the first and fourth Purkinje images (the first image is the reflection off the cornea, and the fourth image is the reflection off the rear surface of the lens). This system is quite precise and can separate translational and rotational eye movements, but head stabilization may be required.

Using an eye tracking system can be a challenge and, until recently, little published information was available to assist researchers with this endeavor. There is some helpful information, however, in a chapter by Collewijn (1998). And researchers considering setting up a video-based, corneal-reflection system for the first time may find Duchowski's (2003) *Eye Tracking Methodology* useful.

Disengaged Attention and Saccades

Attention is clearly disengaged during saccades, as indicated by saccadic suppression. Given that attentional disengagement is required for saccade execution, is it also part of the saccade preparation process? In chapter 3, we described an experiment that was conducted to test Posner et al.'s (1988) hypothesis that attentional disengagement occurs prior to attention shifts (Pratt & Nghiem, 2000). Subjects performing a target-identification task saw stimulus displays that, in some cases, involved the disappearance of the central fixation point followed by a 200 ms blank field just before the cue and target were presented (see Figure 3.6). Relative to a control condition in which the fixation point remained visible throughout the trial, response times were significantly faster in the fixation-offset condition. The results suggested that the disappearance of the fixation point triggered a state of attentional disengagement that, in turn, facilitated responses (also found by Mackeben & Nakayama, 1993). The occurrence of the *fixation-offset effect* on attention shifts when stimulus presentation involves a 200 ms gap between fixation point offset and cue-target onset raises the possibility that it may also affect saccades.

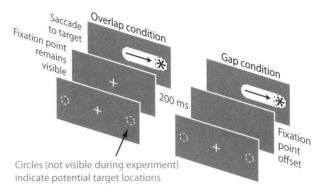

Figure 6.8 Example of the type of display in Saslow's (1967) experiment on the effect of a blank field on saccade latency. In the overlap condition, the fixation cross remains visible throughout the trial. In the gap condition, the fixation cross disappears and the display is empty prior to saccade target onset.

Saslow (1967) conducted one of the first experiments to test this question. Using a stimulus display similar to that in Figure 6.8, he found that the saccade latency was roughly 220 ms when the central fixation point remained visible, but only 150 ms when the fixation point disappeared shortly before target onset. Saslow is generally credited with naming this the *gap effect*. During the time between fixation point offset and target onset, there was nothing in the blank visual field to attend to and this was thought to initiate some preparatory process that shortened saccade latency. Fischer and others (e.g., Fischer, 1998; Fischer & Breitmeyer, 1987; Fischer & Ramsperger, 1984, 1986) replicated Saslow's finding using a similar stimulus-presentation paradigm, and discovered a class of saccades with even shorter latencies than those found by Saslow (i.e., roughly 100-ms latency as opposed to the 220-ms latency of regular saccades; see Figure 6.9). They named these eye movements *express saccades* because their preparation requires less time than that for regular saccades.

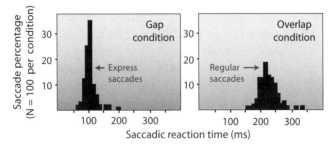

Figure 6.9 Data from Fischer's (1998) report of express saccades. In the gap condition, the modal saccade latency was approximately 100 ms (express saccades). In the overlap condition, the modal saccade latency was approximately 220 ms (regular saccades).

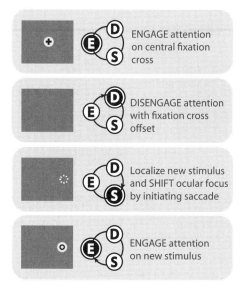

Figure 6.10 Fischer's attentional predisengagement explanation of express saccades based on Posner et al.'s (1988) proposal. Initially, attention is engaged on the central fixation point, but is then disengaged with fixation point offset. The disengagement process is completed during the 200-ms blank interval and, when the target appears, the saccade can be executed immediately. Attention is then engaged on the target.

Fischer and colleagues proposed that the shorter latency of express saccades is the result of attentional disengagement occurring prior to the saccade preparation process (e.g., Fischer & Breitmeyer, 1987; Fischer & Ramsperger, 1984). This argument was based, in part, on the finding that express saccades do not occur if attention is actively engaged at a particular location (including the saccade destination; Mayfrank et al., 1986) prior to saccade preparation. On the other hand, if attention is not actively engaged when an eye-movement target is presented, express saccades can occur. On this basis, Fischer argued that attentional disengagement is a precursor to saccade execution. When disengagement has already occurred prior to preparation of a saccade to the impending target (e.g., as a result of fixation point offset), the result is a short latency, express saccade (see Figure 6.10).

The *anti-saccade* task involves waiting for a saccade target to be presented somewhere within a stimulus display and then, when the target appears, making an eye movement to the mirror-image location on the opposite side of the display (Figure 6.11). If the target appears in the left hemifield, for example, an anti-saccade would be a saccade in the opposite direction to a position at the same eccentricity in the right hemifield. In this context, saccades made directly to target locations are called pro-saccades. Several studies have shown that while express saccades will occur when performing

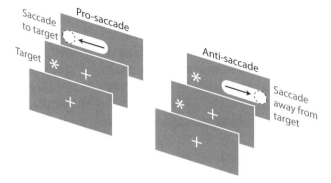

Figure 6.11 The anti-saccade task involves making a saccade to the mirror-image location on opposite side of the display from where a target appears. A pro-saccade is an eye movement to the target location. Express saccades occur in the pro-saccade condition, but not in the anti-saccade condition.

a pro-saccade task, they do not occur when performing an anti-saccade task (e.g., Fischer & Weber, 1992; Reuter-Lorenz et al., 1991). Fischer and Weber (1992) argued that subjects cannot make express anti-saccades because performance of this task requires that attention be engaged on the target to begin preparing a saccade in the opposite direction (i.e., the target serves as a symbolic cue about the location coordinates of the saccade's destination on the opposite side of the display). The inability to make express anti-saccades was considered a further indication that express saccades occur only when attention is disengaged prior to saccade preparation.

The superior colliculus plays a critical role in the mediation of express saccades. Several studies indicate that when saccades occur, intermediate layer collicular neurons are activated in the following sequence: (a) build-up cells whose receptive fields correspond with the eye movement's destination gradually begin to increase their activity; (b) just before the saccade, there is a decrease in the activity of visual fixation neurons whose receptive fields correspond with the currently fixated location; and then (c) burst cells begin to fire as the saccade is executed. Normally, fixation neurons are active when the eyes are stationary and inactive when the eyes are in motion during a saccade. When express saccades occur, however, fixation neurons are *not* active during the gap period in which the fixation point is removed and the field is blank for 200 ms (Dorris & Munoz, 1995, 1998; Everling et al., 1998). In other words, even though fixation neurons are normally active when the eyes are stationary, they are deactivated by a gap field of this type. Also, when express saccades occur, movement neurons (i.e., build-up and burst cells) increase their activity during the gap period even though they are not normally active this far in advance of a movement (Dorris et al., 1997; Dorris & Munoz, 1998; Edelman & Keller, 1996; Everling et al., 1999).

Thus, when the saccade target is presented after the gap period, fixation neurons have already been deactivated and movement neurons have already increased in activation. The result is a shorter latency, express saccade to the target location.

Damage to the superior colliculus can reduce or eliminate the occurrence of express saccades. For example, ablation of one monkey superior colliculus (the superior colliculus is composed of two colliculi; see chapter 7) eliminated express saccades to the contralesional visual field (the area represented by that colliculus prior to its removal), but express saccades could still be made to the contralateral field of the intact colliculus (Schiller, 1998; Schiller et al., 1987). Impaired express saccades were also reported in a case study involving a patient (SR) with midbrain/collicular dysfunction related to a dietary thiamine deficiency (Sereno et al., 2006). Prior to thiamine treatment, the patient was unable to make express saccades normally elicited by a gap period involving fixation point offset. After treatment, however, the patient recovered the capacity to make these rapid saccades.

It should be noted that express saccades were the subject of debate among attention and eye-movement researchers in the early 1990s (see e.g., Fischer & Weber, 1993, for peer review commentaries about this proposal). An initial concern was that only a few laboratories were able to consistently replicate the finding. This subsided with a growing number of replications, but another concern reflected the controversial nature of the relationship between attention and eye movements. In particular, while many researchers now accept that there is a separate class of short-latency saccades that occur as a result of fixation offsets, some have questioned Fischer's proposal that attentional disengagement is a precursor to saccade preparation. Others have attempted to argue that while disengagement does occur prior to saccade preparation, it is a type of oculomotor disengagement rather than attentional disengagement (e.g., Kingstone & Klein, 1993; Klein & Taylor, 1994). Researchers' opinions about Fischer's attentional predisengagement proposal seem to vary in accordance with their beliefs about the functional relationship between attention shifting and eye movements. The latter is discussed in the next section.

Relationship Between Attention and Eye Movements

Wright and Ward (1998, pp. 158–160) described three possible forms that the functional relationship between covert orienting and eye-movement mechanisms could take: (a) the *independent systems proposal* holds that saccade and attention shift mechanisms are entirely different, and part of separate systems. A prediction of this proposal is that locations of attention shift and saccade destinations can be simultaneously encoded, even when they are in opposite directions. (b) The *common system proposal* holds that saccades and attention shifts are mediated by the same mechanism. Some authors sympathetic to this view and wanting to emphasize their commonality refer to saccades simply as overt shifts of attention (e.g., Beauchamp et al., 2001). If a common mechanism mediates both types of orienting, then the destinations of attention shifts should be encoded in terms of the same direction/amplitude coordinates used to encode saccade destinations. (c) The *interdependent systems proposal* holds that saccade and attention shift mechanisms are not mediated by a common system but do share resources or computations at some stage. For example, both mechanisms may receive input from the same sensory representations (e.g., sensory activity distributions) when encoding orienting destinations. If so, then performance of both systems will be optimal when encoding the same destination, and impaired when encoding different destinations.

Posner (1980) also described possible relationships between covert orienting and eye-movement mechanisms, but in terms of a continuum between a common system and two independent systems. In between these two states, he suggested that a functional, learned connection between systems can produce a relationship that is similar, in some ways, to the interdependent systems proposal described in this section.

Independent Systems Proposal

The notion that covert orienting can occur independently of overt orienting is now entrenched in the attention literature. An extension of this idea was speculation by some researchers that covert and overt orienting could be mediated by functionally independent mechanisms (e.g., Hunt & Kingstone, 2003; Klein, 1980; Klein & Pontefract, 1994; Remington, 1980). More specifically, it was suggested that attention shifts and saccades are not causally linked, and that both may be drawn concurrently to peripheral events, but by different mechanisms.

Note that this proposal addresses *functional* independence rather than physiological independence. Recent research indicates that the latter is unlikely. The results of several neuroimaging studies, for example, show that there is significant overlap in the neural structures mediating saccades and attention shifts (e.g., Beauchamp et al., 2001; Corbetta et al., 1998; Perry & Zeki, 2000). Figure 6.12 is an approximate reproduction of the results for a single subject in an event-related fMRI experiment involving stimulus-driven attention shifts and saccades (Beauchamp et al., 2001). It shows activation increases in several of the same cortical areas [particularly the intraparietal sulcus (IPS) of the parietal lobe and the frontal eye fields (FEFs) of the frontal lobe] when either type of orienting occurs.

The overlap of neural structures mediating saccades and attention shifts was also shown in a comprehensive literature review (Corbetta, 1998), and

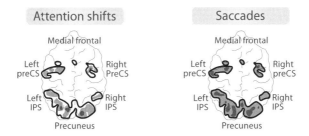

Figure 6.12 Approximate reproduction of data from Beauchamp et al.'s (2001) functional magnetic resonance imaging (fMRI) study of stimulus-driven attention shifts and saccades. The outlined regions show the common areas of activation for both types of orienting. Labeled areas are the intraparietal sulcus (IPS) in the parietal cortex and precentral sulcus (preCS) area of the frontal cortex near the frontal eye fields.

a more recent meta-analysis of several neuroimaging studies (Grosbras et al., 2005). These studies indicated that, for both stimulus-driven and goal-driven orienting, the attention shifting and saccade mechanisms are clearly not physiologically independent. Figure 6.13 is an approximate reproduction of surface-based representations of functional brain activity when attention was shifted with or without concurrent saccades (Corbetta, 1998). Flat maps of this type provide more precise information about the locations of heightened activity because they allow visualization of activity buried in sulci while preserving the exact topological relationship between points. The results indicate that the saccade and attention shift mechanisms share a number of the same functional anatomical areas in the human brain

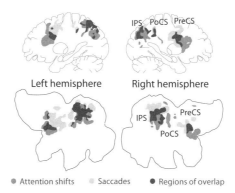

Figure 6.13 Approximate reproduction of Corbetta's (1998) analysis of studies of brain activation during attention shifts and saccadic eye movements. The figure shows two-dimensional flattened surfaces of the brain. The high degree of overlap of attention shift and saccade areas indicates that the attention shift and saccadic systems share neural substrates and perhaps common functional mechanisms. Labeled areas are the intraparietal sulcus (IPS) and the postcentral sulcus (PoCS) in the parietal cortex, and the precentral sulcus (PreCS) in the frontal cortex near the frontal eye fields.

(particularly in the frontoparietal cortical areas) and that they appear to be tightly linked.

The neuroimaging data on the overlap of neural structures mediating attention shifts and eye movements are also consistent with single-cell studies and with lesion studies. Experiments involving monkeys, for example, showed that several cortical and subcortical areas respond when either saccades or attention shifts occur. These include the FEF, dorsolateral prefrontal cortex, posterior parietal cortex, superior colliculus, and pulvinar nucleus of the thalamus (e.g., Andersen et al., 1985; Bushnell et al., 1981; Mountcastle, 1978; Petersen et al., 1987; Robinson et al., 1978; Wurtz et al., 1980). In addition, damage to cortical areas in humans and monkeys can produce deficits in both saccades and attention shifting (e.g., DeRenzi, 1982; Mesulam, 1981; Posner et al., 1984b). Thus, the single-cell and lesion data provide additional evidence that some brain areas mediate both saccades and attention shifts. This is not consistent with the independent systems proposal.

Common System Proposal

Given the overlap of neural structures mediating attention shifts and eye movements, it may be tempting to speculate that both types of orienting are mediated by a single system. This tight integration is favored by several researchers. Some have argued that "without a good explanation for the purpose of an independent attentional mechanism, it seems more probable that covert attention reflects the actions of a system closely tied to the overt saccade system, in a manner similar to that proposed by the premotor theory of attention" (Findlay & Gilchrist, 2003, p. 48).

According to premotor theory, covert orienting is mediated by the motor system responsible for generating saccades, although the actual eye movement is withheld in this case (Rizzolatti et al., 1987). In other words, rather than being the result of a separate attention shifting mechanism, covert orienting is a by-product of the oculomotor system. The theory arose, in part, from the results of a target-detection experiment (see Figure 6.14). On some trials, the target was presented in the same visual hemifield as an invalid cue. On other trials, the target and an invalid cue were presented in opposite hemifields. The critical finding was that, even though the distance between cue and target was the same in both cases, target-detection response times were slower when they were presented in opposite hemifields than when they were presented in the same hemifield. This was called the *meridian effect* because it resulted from responses to cues and targets presented either on the same side or on opposite sides of the (unseen) vertical meridian that divides the left and right hemifields.

The premotor account of the meridian effect is based on the assumption that there is a temporal cost of direction recalibration when making successive

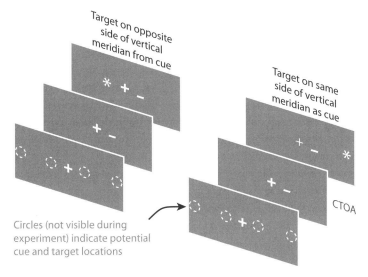

Target on opposite side of vertical meridian from cue

Target on same side of vertical meridian as cue

CTOA

Circles (not visible during experiment) indicate potential cue and target locations

Figure 6.14 Example of a display used to study the meridian effect. Following the presentation of an invalid cue, a target appears on the same side of the vertical meridian dividing the display but at an even greater eccentricity than the cue; or an equal distance away from the cue but on the opposite side of the vertical meridian. Despite the equivalence of cue-target distance in both cases, response times are longer when the target and invalid cue are on opposite sides of the meridian.

saccades. To elaborate, when two saccades are made in the same direction, there is no need to recalibrate (which takes time) the direction component of the second saccade's vector. As a result, the latency of the second saccade is shorter than would be the case if the two saccades were made in different directions. Rizzolatti et al. (1987) reasoned that this temporal cost of direction recalibration could also explain why there appears to be a meridian effect on attention shifts. That is, when the target appeared in the same hemifield as the cue, but at an even greater distance from the center, attention shifts to the cue and then to the target were in the same direction. On the other hand, when the target appeared in the opposite hemifield from the cue, attention shifts to the cue and then to the target were in opposite directions. According to Rizzolatti et al., target detection was slower in the latter case because the direction component of the second shift had to be recalibrated. In other words, they proposed that the same calibration procedure that appears to be involved in programming saccades is also involved in programming attention shifts. On this basis, they concluded that covert orienting is a product of the oculomotor system.

The idea that attention shifts are planned-but-not-executed saccades has been challenged by several researchers (e.g., Crawford & Müller, 1993). Also, while a number of studies indicate that there is overlap of neural structures mediating attention shifts and eye movements, it is not great enough to conclude that the two types of orienting involve exactly the same brain regions. Instead, some areas of the parietal and frontal cortex are uniquely active when either attention shifts or saccades occur (Corbetta & Shulman, 1998, p. 1357). And, where there appears to be physiological overlap, it is possible that separate sub-populations of neurons can be driven by different signals within the same cortical region and, therefore, attention shift and saccade processes may be using entirely different neuronal mechanisms within the same area (Corbetta et al., 1998, p. 768).

Another concern about premotor theory is that there appear to be other explanations for its primary supporting evidence, the meridian effect. For example, there is some question about whether the meridian effect can be obtained with direct cues (Reuter-Lorenz & Fendrich, 1992; Umiltà et al., 1991). If the cost of direction recalibration does not apply to stimulus-driven attention shifts to direct cues, then there is little grounds for arguing that stimulus-driven attention shifts are the product of the oculomotor system, and this means Rizzolatti et al.'s proposal is less convincing. Also, an experiment indicating that the meridian effect may be associated with hand movements appears to suggest that the effect is not specifically tied to oculomotor preparation (Eimer et al., 2005). In addition, the meridian effect has been replicated with *auditory* stimuli (Ferlazzo et al., 2002), which raises doubts about the effect arising from oculomotor preparation. In chapter 7, after describing the physiology of orienting in more detail, we revisit premotor theory and discuss additional concerns.

Interdependent Systems Proposal

An alternative to the independent systems proposal and to the common system proposal is the idea that attention shifts and saccades may be mediated by partially independent systems that share some common mechanisms. Posner is sympathetic to this idea and suggested that, while the neural systems mediating attention and eye movements partly overlap, there are important differences (Gazzaniga, 1996, p. 43). That is, (a) not all attention shifts may involve activation of the superior colliculus (i.e., when attention is shifted between targets that are close together) and (b) attention and saccade mechanisms may be different because eye movements are always made to a peripheral target, whereas attention shifts can also occur from the visual periphery to the foveated region. In the next section, we discuss ideas about the relationship between attention shifts and saccade preparation.

Saccade Preparation and Attention

One of the first empirical demonstrations of a link between eye-movement preparation and attention shifts was a finding by Crovitz and Davies (1962). Subjects in their experiment performed a target-identification task involving

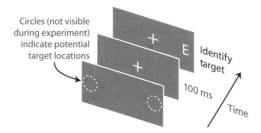

Circles (not visible during experiment) indicate potential target locations

Identify target

100 ms

Time

Figure 6.15 Example of the type of stimulus display in Crovitz and Davies' (1962) experiment. Each trial began with a blank field, followed by a central fixation point for 100 ms, and then the presentation of a target to be identified.

a manual response in which, 100 ms after a central fixation point onset, the target appeared with equal probability to the left or right of center (see Figure 6.15). Unlike the covert orienting experiments discussed in previous chapters, eye movements were not restricted. Given that normal saccade latency is about 220 ms, however, the 100-ms interval between fixation point onset and target onset was not long enough for the subject to program a saccade from the center of the display to the target location after fixation point onset. In other words, the target would already be visible before an eye movement could be made. The most interesting finding was a correlation between response accuracy and the direction of subjects' first eye movement on each trial. Accuracy was greater when the first eye movement was in the direction of the (already visible) target than when it was in the direction of a nontarget location. It was suggested that, during the 100 ms between central fixation point onset and target onset, saccade *preparation* to the target location may have facilitated responses when the target appeared at the intended saccade destination. This was one of the first indications that a potential target location may be processed during the preparation (but prior to the execution) of a saccade.

One of the first experiments to use location cueing to study the effect of saccade preparation on target detection was conducted in Posner's laboratory by M.J. Nissen, Posner, and C.R.R. Snyder (1978; described in Posner, 1980, p. 14). The stimulus display was similar to those used in covert orienting experiments discussed in previous chapters (see, e.g., Figure 2.4). In particular, a direct cue (outline box) was presented on either the left or the right side of the central fixation point and then, 0–500 ms later, the target was presented. On most trials (80%), the target appeared at the cued location. On the remaining trials, the target appeared at the uncued location on the opposite side of the display or at the central location. Unlike the covert orienting experiments discussed previously, subjects were also required to make a saccade to the cued location on each trial. The most interesting result involved the CTOA manipulation. That is, when the CTOA was 50 and 100 ms, targets were detected faster when they appeared at cued locations than when they appeared at the central location (even though 50–100 ms is not sufficient time for the saccade to have occurred to the cued location before the target appeared). This result was also replicated with a low-validity location cue (20% probability of target appearing there). It was concluded that saccade preparation to cued locations may have facilitated detection of targets appearing there.

Another early study was conducted to determine whether stimulus-driven and goal-driven saccade preparation would have similar effects on target detection (Remington, 1980). As was the case in Nissen et al.'s experiment, subjects were required to make saccades from the central fixation point to a cued location to the left or right of center. In this experiment, however, the location was indicated by a direct cue (brightening of an outline box) in the stimulus-driven saccade condition, and by a symbolic cue (central arrow pointing to one of the two outline boxes) in the goal-driven condition (see Figure 6.16). On all trials, making a saccade to the cued location was the primary task. In addition, on 50% of (randomly selected) trials, a

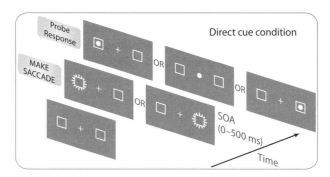

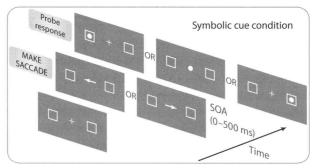

Figure 6.16 Example of the type of displays in Remington's (1980) experiment. Subjects made a saccade to the location indicated by a direct cue or a symbolic cue. Also, on 50% of trials, subjects detected the onset of a target (probe dot) at cued or uncued locations.

target appeared with equal probability at the cued, the center, or the uncued location on the opposite side of center. Target detection with a manual response (button press) was the secondary task. One interesting result was an interaction between cue type and CTOA. In particular, on direct cue trials, target-detection response times were facilitated at shorter CTOAs before the saccade was executed and also at longer CTOAs after the saccade was made. On symbolic-cue trials, however, target-detection response times were facilitated only at longer CTOAs after the saccade was made. These results were interpreted as indicating that saccade preparation initiated by symbolic location cueing did not have the same facilitative effect on target detection as saccade preparation initiated by direct location cueing. This study is often cited as evidence that while attentional focus may precede ocular focus to locations indicated by direct cues, it does not precede ocular focus to locations indicated by symbolic cues.

In both the Nissen et al. and Remington experiments, facilitation of target-detection response times by direct cues at short CTOAs (50–100 ms) was claimed to be caused by saccade preparation. There is another explanation, however, that is consistent with the ideas outlined in chapter 4 about direct cue effects arising, in part, from sensory facilitation. To elaborate, in both experiments, both direct location cue onsets and target onsets may have triggered the formation of transient sensory activity distributions at their locations. When targets appeared at direct cue locations within 100 ms of cue onset, residual cue-triggered activation may have combined with target-triggered activation to produce an activity distribution of greater magnitude than could be produced by a target appearing at an uncued location (see Figure 4.2). This would cause a channel of attention to open there more quickly than would be the case if the activity distribution was of a lesser magnitude. In other words, facilitation of responses by direct cues at short CTOAs in these experiments may have resulted from sensory processing triggered by cue and target onsets rather than saccade preparation.

More recently, it has been suggested that attention functions as a slave to the eye-movement system by playing a role in saccade programming (e.g., Deubel & Schneider, 1996; Kowler et al., 1995; see also, Hoffman & Subramaniam, 1995; Peterson et al., 2004). In an earlier work, we referred to this preview role for attention in saccade programming as the *advance scout* hypothesis (Wright & Ward, 1998, p. 169; see Figure 6.17). The idea appears to originate from a reading model that involved the use of an "attentional pointer" for guiding the eyes to words in passages of text (Morrison, 1984). It is also consistent with a number of findings suggesting that attention is directed to a saccade destination prior to the eye movement. In one experiment, for example, an increase in the speed of processing of peripheral

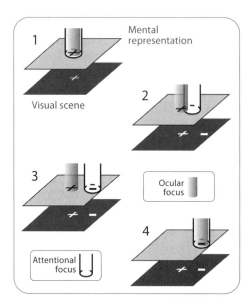

Figure 6.17 Depiction of the advance scout hypothesis about the relationship between attentional and ocular focus. The attentional focal point is said to be oriented to the saccade destination prior to saccade execution in order to facilitate eye-movement programming.

objects occurred if these objects were also targets of saccades that were about to be executed (Henderson et al., 1989). On the basis of this type of finding, it is tempting to conclude that attention and eye-movement mechanisms are closely coupled, and that saccades are guided by covert attention.

Does attentional focus always precede ocular focus to locations indicated by cues? Several studies have been conducted to answer this question. In one dual-task experiment, subjects were required to make a goal-driven saccade to a symbolically cued location while performing a letter identification task (Kowler et al., 1995). As seen in Figure 6.18, following a 500-ms mask field (letters were randomly chosen; personal communication Eileen Kowler, May 2007), the saccade target was indicated by a central arrow that pointed to one of the letters in a circular array. The letters were visible for only 200 ms and then were replaced with another mask field (also randomly chosen letters). In one condition, following the mask field, the letter "Q" appeared randomly at one of the display positions to indicate the position of the letter to be identified (i.e., the letter at this position within the display at the time that the symbolic saccade cue was presented). Identification accuracy was best when the symbolically cued destination for the primary-task saccade and the secondary-task letter target were at the same location. On this basis, the experimenters concluded that attention must have been shifted to the location that the saccade was prepared to. In addition, they made

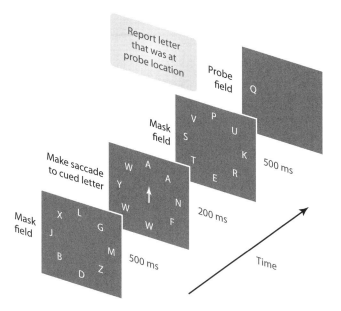

Figure 6.18 Example of the type of display used in Kowler et al.'s (1995) experiment. The primary task required subjects to make a saccade to a letter indicated by a symbolic arrow cue. The secondary task required subjects to identify the letter that was at the position indicated by a postmask probe symbol (i.e., the letter Q). Secondary-task response accuracy was highest when the letter to be identified was also the letter that subjects made a saccade to when performing the primary task.

the stronger claim that focused attention must precede saccades to their common destination to contribute to saccade programming.

The Kowler et al. (1995) claim has been challenged by other researchers. Godjin and Pratt (2002, pp. 84–85) pointed out, for example, the potential problems with the dual-task paradigm that was used. One is that it is difficult to know whether subjects delayed making a saccade to concentrate on the secondary target-identification task. Another potential problem is that simultaneous execution of an attention-demanding task and a saccade-execution task could have resulted in a strategic bias to attend to the stimuli at the cued location first, thereby increasing identification accuracy there. Godjin and Pratt concluded that a dual-task paradigm is not the best choice for studying the eye-movement/attention relationship.

A different approach to studying this relationship involves temporal-order judgments (TOJs). When a TOJ task is performed, two objects appear at different locations in the visual periphery and subjects are required to judge which one appeared first. Previous research demonstrated that TOJs are sensitive to attentional allocation (e.g., Jaskowski, 1993; McDonald et al., 2005; Stelmach & Herdman, 1991). That is, if attention is directed to one of the objects, there is a greater probability that it will be judged to have

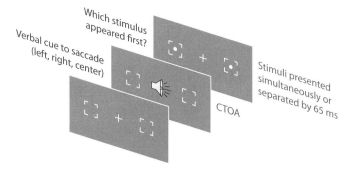

Figure 6.19 Example of the type of display used in Stelmach et al.'s (1997) experiment. A verbal cue instructed subjects to make a saccade and then, a short time later, two stimuli were presented. Subjects were required to judge which appeared first.

appeared first. Therefore, if attention is allocated to a saccade destination *prior* to the saccade, then an object appearing at that location immediately afterwards should also be attended to and seem to appear first when a TOJ task is performed. This prediction was tested in an experiment with a stimulus display like that shown in Figure 6.19 (Stelmach et al., 1997). Following an auditory symbolic cue to make a saccade to an outline box on the left or the right side of the central fixation point (or to make no saccade), two stimuli appeared within the boxes. When subjects made TOJs shortly after cue presentation, no advantage was found for stimuli appearing at the destinations that the saccades were prepared to. In other words, following a symbolic cue, attention did not appear to be directed to the saccade destination prior to its execution.

Another challenge to the advance scout proposal is a growing body of data indicating that more than one saccade can be prepared at the same time. In one visual search study, when two saccades occurred in quick succession, neurons in the deep layers of the monkey superior colliculus associated with the second saccade destination became active before the first saccade was executed (McPeek & Keller, 2002; see also McPeek et al., 2000). In other words, two saccade destinations were encoded simultaneously. This suggests that the advance scout proposal is valid only if it is also assumed that the attentional focal point can be split into multiple attentional foci whenever there is more than one simultaneously planned saccade destination (Findlay & Gilchrist, 2003, p. 43). As discussed in chapter 7, saccades can also be made under conditions that preclude attention shifts to their destinations (which also raises questions about the necessity of an attentional advance scout role for saccade programming; cf., Baldauf et al., 2006).

In summary, there is a general consensus that when attention is shifted to the same location to which a saccade is made, the attention shift will be completed first. Perhaps this is not surprising, given that saccades have a longer latency (220 ms) that is due, in part, to motor programming. A stronger claim is that attentional focus precedes ocular focus to their common destination in order to contribute to saccade preparation (e.g., Duebel & Schneider, 1996; Kowler et al., 1995). This contribution may be some form of spatial coordinate information required to calibrate the direction and amplitude of the saccade movement vector. Not all researchers, however, are willing to accede to a claim that there is a causal relationship between attention shifts and saccades (e.g., Klein et al., 1992; Remington, 1980). They suggest, instead, that while both types of orienting may have a common destination and a common goal of facilitating identification of the object there, they may have some degree of functional independence. If so, then attentional focus might simply arrive at the common destination before ocular focus and start attentional analysis at that location before the eyes reach it.

Saccade Destination Encoding and IOR

Clues about the processes involved in saccade destination encoding might be found by examining the relationship between eye movements and inhibition of return (IOR). The results of one such experiment indicated that IOR occurs, even when subjects merely *prepare* saccades to symbolically cued locations but do not execute them (Rafal et al., 1989). This is particularly interesting given that IOR does not normally occur following the presentation of symbolic cues unless the attention shift is also accompanied by an eye movement (Posner et al., 1985; Vaughan, 1984; cf., Chica et al., 2006). Figure 6.20 shows an example of trials in which subjects either made a saccade to a symbolically cued location, or prepared but "cancelled" the saccade before executing it. In both cases, IOR occurred at the saccade destination. This indicates that, while shifting attention to a symbolically cued location is not sufficient to produce IOR, a saccade to that location is sufficient, even if it is only prepared but not executed. Given that IOR may be mediated by spatial indexing, this raises the intriguing possibility that preparation of a saccade vector involves allocation of an index to the saccade destination.

Another indication that saccade destinations may be spatially indexed during saccade preparation is the result of an IOR experiment with infants who were unable to make these eye movements. The experiment was conducted to compare 3-month-old and 6-month-old infants' performance of a target-detection task (Harman et al., 1994). Location cues were presented in succession as is typically the case in IOR experiments. The first of two cues was presented peripherally at an eccentricity of 10° or 30°. While 6-month olds are able to make single 30° saccades, 3-month olds cannot. Instead, they

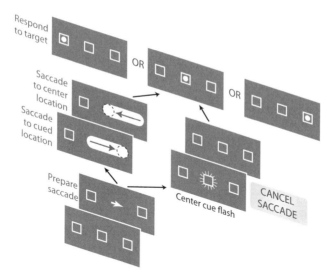

Figure 6.20 Example of two conditions in Rafal et al.'s (1989) experiment. In one condition, subjects moved their eyes to a symbolically cued location and then back to the central location. In the other condition, the subjects prepared to move their eyes to the cued location, but then canceled the saccade. Inhibition of return (IOR) at this cued location occurred in both conditions, indicating that saccade preparation alone is sufficient for producing IOR.

make a series of hypometric saccades to foveate objects at this eccentricity (see Figure 6.4). Both 6-month olds and 3-month olds are able to make single 10° saccades, however. The main finding was that while 6-month olds showed IOR with cues at both eccentricities, 3-month olds did not show IOR with cues at the 30° eccentricity. They only showed IOR with cues at the 10° eccentricity (see Figure 6.21). Thus, when the eccentricity of cues is outside infants' saccadic range, it is also beyond their capacity for showing IOR there. This suggests that only those locations that can be spatially indexed during saccade preparation produce the IOR effect. It also suggests that saccade preparation involves allocation of a spatial index to the saccade

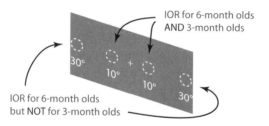

Figure 6.21 The eccentricities of direct location cues in Harman et al.'s (1994) experiment with 3-month-old and 6-month-old subjects.

destination. A number of other studies of the relationship between IOR and eye movements have been conducted (e.g., Danziger et al., 1997; Dorris et al., 1999; Godijn & Theeuwes, 2002, 2004; Hunt & Kingstone, 2003; Ro et al., 2000) and the results indicate that this research may hold promise as a source of new insights about the linkage between eye movements and attention shifts. Given that IOR appears to be mediated by spatial indexing, this research may provide more information about the role of indexing in the programming of saccadic eye movements.

Summary

The organization of the retina requires us to move our eyes frequently to process fine details of the visual scene because only the foveal receptors provide high-acuity analysis. The two types of eye movements we make most often are saccades and smooth pursuit movements. Saccades are fast and impressively accurate but, before each saccade, there is a refractory period that usually lasts about 150–350 ms. Pursuits are considerably slower than saccades, and occur when we visually track moving objects. To prevent a blurring effect, visual analysis is suppressed during the 10–100-ms period in which the saccade is initiated and the eye is in motion. As a result, information about the visual scene is not updated until the saccade is completed, even though our experience is a "seamless comprehension" of the visual world with no awareness of visual suppression. In this sense, saccadic eye movements are discrete because, like discrete attention shifts, processing focus is "turned off" while the eyes are in motion.

When studying our ability to shift attention independently of eye movements, researchers often require that subjects' eyes remain stationary throughout experimental trials. Many different techniques for monitoring eye position have been used over the past 100 years including those based on photography, contact lens movements, EOG, and corneal reflection. While the EOG method was widely used in the 1970s, the most common contemporary method of eye tracking involves video-based image processing of changes in infrared light reflected off the cornea as the eyes change position. This point-of-regard measurement uses two points of reference (usually the pupil and the iris/scleral boundary) to disambiguate head movement from eye movement. Real-time eye-monitoring techniques enable experimenters to detect movements during the course of data collection, and to eliminate and re-present trials contaminated by saccades.

The relationship between eye movements and attention shifts is controversial and there are several proposals about how tightly linked these two types of orienting are. The *independent systems proposal* holds that saccade and attention shift mechanisms are entirely different, and part of separate systems. But the results of neuroimaging, single-cell, and lesion studies indicate that there is significant overlap in the neural structures mediating saccades and attention shifts (particularly in the IPS and the FEF), and that attention shifting and saccade mechanisms are not physiologically independent. The *common system proposal* holds that saccades and attention shifts may be mediated by the same mechanism. On the basis of a result called the meridian effect, some advocates of this proposal have argued that covert orienting is a by-product of the motor system responsible for generating saccades (e.g., Rizzolatti et al., 1987). For a number of reasons outlined in this chapter and the next, not all researchers agree with this interpretation. Finally, the *interdependent systems proposal* holds that saccade and attention shift mechanisms are not mediated by a common system but do share resources or computations at some stages of processing. It has also been proposed that attention shifts are made to eye-movement destinations prior to saccade initiation to facilitate saccade programming (e.g., Deubel & Schneider, 1996; Kowler et al., 1995). There is a general consensus among researchers that when attention is shifted to the same location that a saccade is made to, the attention shift will be completed first. But studying the relationship between attention shifts and eye movements is challenging, in part because of limitations of dual-task experimentation. For this reason, the possibility that attentional focus may *not* be a slave to the oculomotor system, and may simply arrive at a common destination before ocular focus and then initiate attentional analysis before the eyes reach that location, has not been conclusively ruled out.

The relationship between eye movements and attention shifts will become clearer as we gain a better understanding of the physiological mechanisms that mediate orienting. In the next chapter, we discuss research on the brain's attention orienting network and recent findings that provide clues about the physiological instantiation of eye-movement programming and attention shifting.

7

Physiology of Attention Shifts

A number of ideas have been proposed about the physiology of attention. Until the past few decades, however, they often involved localization within a single brain area. In the late 1800s, a popular idea was that the attention mechanism is located in the frontal cortex. In the mid-1900s, as mentioned in chapter 1, there was considerable support for the idea that the reticular activating system (RAS) is the brain's primary attention center. It is now clear that attentional processing and covert orienting are mediated not only by the RAS, but also by a functional network of several other subcortical and cortical areas.

There is a strong correlation between the performance of target-detection tasks by humans and monkeys (Figure 7.1). And it could be argued that we first began to appreciate the extent to which attention mechanisms are distributed throughout the brain when researchers started to study orienting in monkeys in the 1970s (e.g., Goldberg & Wurtz, 1972; Mohler & Wurtz, 1976). They used single-cell recording techniques to measure neural activity in brain areas thought to be associated with eye movements (e.g., superior colliculus, frontal eye fields [FEF], posterior parietal cortex), and found neurons that showed enhanced activation before and during saccades. But, in each of these areas, they also found neurons that showed enhanced activation

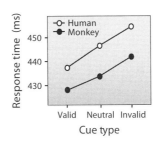

Figure 7.1 Although monkey overall response times are slightly faster than those of humans, they show the same response time pattern for target-detection tasks involving direct location cueing (data from Davidson et al., 1994).

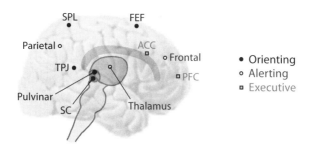

Figure 7.2 Brain areas associated with the three attention networks proposed by Posner and colleagues. SPL is superior parietal lobule, FEF is frontal eye fields, TPJ is temporoparietal junction, SC is superior colliculus, ACC is anterior cingulate cortex, and PFC is prefrontal cortex.

when monkeys shifted attention *without* an accompanying saccade. The development of functional neuroimaging techniques in the 1980s (positron emission tomography [PET]) and 1990s (fMRI) allowed others to confirm that these areas mediate shifts of attention in humans as well.

On the basis of these findings, several ideas about the nature of the brain's attention networks were proposed (e.g., Fernandez-Duque & Posner, 2001; Mesulam, 1999; Posner & Fan, in press; Posner & Petersen, 1990; Posner & Rothbart, 2007; Raz & Buhle, 2006). Posner and Petersen (1990), for example, suggested that there are three different networks: one for alerting, one for executive control, and one for attention orienting. Figure 7.2 shows some of the brain areas said by Posner and Rothbart (2007) to be associated with these networks.

Our focus here is mostly on the orienting network. Six of the brain areas involved in attention orienting to visual stimuli are the RAS, superior colliculus, pulvinar, occipital lobe, parietal lobe, and frontal lobe. The cortical areas (particularly parietal and frontal lobes) play a greater role in mediating goal-driven attention shifts, and the subcortical areas (particularly the superior colliculus) play a significant role in mediating stimulus-driven shifts. In this chapter, we discuss research on the physiology of attention shifts and what it indicates about the nature of the orienting network. Note that when we use the term monkey to describe experimental subjects, we are referring to the rhesus monkey (also commonly referred to in the literature as macaque).

Subcortical Attention Mechanisms

Several subcortical areas play a role in attention orienting. One of them, the RAS, is located in the brainstem below the superior colliculus (see Figure 7.3). Its neurons receive inputs from the cranial nerves and its outputs project diffusely to many regions of the brain. Another area, the superior colliculus, is located on the roof of the brain stem above the RAS. It receives inputs from the retinae, the oculomotor generating centers in the brain

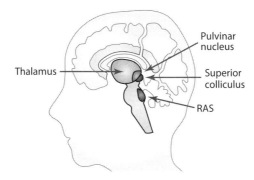

Figure 7.3 Mid-sagittal schematic view of the brain showing subcortical structures involved in shifts of attention.

stem, and cortical areas. The inferior colliculus is immediately below the superior colliculus and also receives inputs from several brain areas including the auditory cortex. The functions of these areas differ with respect to the mediation of attention shifts. In particular, the RAS is critically involved in the control of overall arousal and attention. The superior colliculus, on the other hand, plays a role in the localization of visual stimuli, and the control of saccades and stimulus-driven attention shifts. Similarly, the inferior colliculus plays a role in sound localization and perhaps stimulus-driven attention shifts to these sounds.

The RAS is the brain area that many theorists in the mid-20th century believed was in control of attentional processing. This was primarily because of its critical role in the regulation of arousal. RAS neurons are characterized by the neurotransmitter they are associated with (neurotransmitters are chemicals that take a nerve signal across the synaptic gap between a sending and a receiving neuron). Several neurotransmitter systems play a role in mediating shifts of attention, and this is particularly true of the cholinergic system (acetylcholine) and the noradrenergic system (norepinephrine). Acetylcholine appears to be specifically involved in reorienting attention from the location of an invalid cue to that of the target, while norepinephrine appears to be involved in alerting (Posner & Fan, in press). In one study, after being injected with a norepinephrine-blocking drug, monkeys performed a target-detection task involving direct location cueing (Witte & Marrocco, 1997). Reduction of norepinephrine levels significantly decreased the alerting effect of stimuli. That is, warning signals that normally reduced target-detection response times no longer did so after administration of the drug. On the other hand, reduction of norepinephrine did not influence the effect of cue validity on response times. This indicates that norepinephrine is involved in maintaining sensory readiness to external stimuli, but not in shifting the attentional focal point. Dopamine and serotonin are two other neurotransmitters involved in attentional processing. Dopamine appears to play a critical role in regulating areas of the frontal lobe associated with voluntary control of attention. Serotonin is involved in arousal and alerting but, unlike norepinephrine, serotonin production appears to decrease when attention is shifted to new objects. Thus, each of these neurotransmitters plays a different but complementary role in the mediation of attention shifts.

Superior Colliculus

Whereas a number of brain areas, including the frontal and parietal cortex, are active when we make saccades, the superior colliculus is the subcortical area that plays the most important role in programming and executing these eye movements. Visual analysis carried out by the superior colliculus is not sufficient for making the fine discriminations required to identify objects (its neurons, e.g., are not sensitive to color or to shape). Instead, the primary purpose of this analysis is to determine the *locations* of objects. Its neurons are particularly suited for this because, unlike any known cortical neurons, they exhibit a pan-directional sensitivity to motion contrast (Davidson & Bender, 1991). More specifically, they respond best when the motion in their receptive-field center and surround is in different directions, which makes them ideal for detecting the locations of movements. This movement and abrupt-onset location information can then be used to guide the fovea (eye movement) and the attentional focal point (covert orienting) to a particular object of interest.

As seen in Figure 7.4, the superior colliculus is composed of left and right colliculi. Location information represented in each colliculus corresponds to the opposite (contralateral) half of the visual field. This is the case because the superior colliculus is part of a phylogenetically older visual system. Most of the optic nerve fibers that project from the retinae to each colliculus cross over so that colliculi receive inputs from retinal receptors sensitive to the contralateral hemifield. Figure 7.4 depicts this crossover from retinae to superior colliculi. Notice that each retina is divided into two hemiretinae. The lateral hemiretina of each eye is physically closest to the temple and the medial hemiretina is physically closest to the nose. The lateral hemiretina of the left eye and the medial hemiretina of the right eye are therefore sensitive to the right hemifield. Conversely, the lateral hemiretina of the right eye and the medial hemiretina of the left eye are sensitive to the left hemifield. Thus, information in the left visual field is projected primarily to the right superior colliculus, and vice versa. There are also a smaller number of optic nerve fibers projecting from the retinae to the superior colliculus that do not cross over (i.e., from the lateral hemiretina of the ipsilateral eye), but most do. This makes the superior colliculus largely monocular. While the asymmetry ratio of crossed and uncrossed fibers in humans is not known precisely (Berger & Henik, 2000), it is 80/20 in cats (Sherman, 1974).

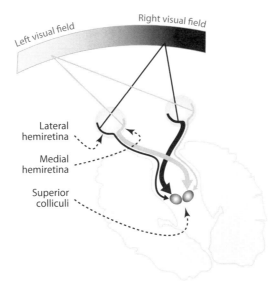

Figure 7.4 Visual pathways from retinae to superior colliculi are dominated by crossed optic nerve fibers. More specifically, each colliculus is innervated primarily by fibers from the medial hemiretina of the contralateral eye, and to a lesser extent by fibers from the lateral hemiretina of the ipsilateral eye. As a result, the left colliculus is innervated primarily by inputs from the right visual field, and the right colliculus is innervated primarily by inputs from the left visual field.

As mentioned in chapter 6, the superior colliculus has multiple layers that are stacked like the pages of a book. Each layer contains maps of visual and oculomotor space, and some neurons in these layers have both visual and oculomotor responsiveness (e.g., Robinson, 1972; Schiller & Koerner, 1971). The superficial (upper) layers receive direct inputs from the retina, and the results of their processing are relayed to topographically organized maps in a part of the thalamus called the pulvinar nucleus (see Figure 7.3). The intermediate and deep (lower) layers receive cortical inputs primarily from visual areas in the frontal and parietal lobes, and there is also evidence that many of these neurons are multimodal (responding to vision, audition, and touch; e.g., Meredith & Stein, 1983, 1986; Stein & Meredith, 1993). Neurons in the intermediate and deep layers are involved in the selection of attention shift and saccade destinations and the calibration of saccade vectors (e.g., Kustov & Robinson, 1996). The results of this processing are then relayed to the saccade generation centers (e.g., Sparks & Mays, 1990).

Not much research on *human* superior collicular involvement in attention shifts has been conducted, in part, because this area is too deep within the brain to be studied effectively with electrophysiological methods (e.g., event-related potential [ERP], magnetoencephalography [MEG]), or transcranial magnetic stimulation (TMS). The superior colliculus is also difficult to study with fMRI because of its small size, deep location, and proximity to pulsating vascular structures (although a recent study indicates that fMRI research on this area is possible; Schneider & Kastner, 2005). For these reasons, most of the data on the attentional function of the superior colliculus have been obtained through the study of neural activation when monkeys perform orienting tasks. As described in this section, some experiments involved single-cell recording, others involved microstimulation, and still others involved lesion work.

The results of single-cell recording studies indicate that neurons in the superficial layers of the superior colliculus respond to transient and moving visual stimuli (e.g., Cynader & Berman, 1972; Goldberg & Wurtz, 1972; Marraco & Li, 1977; Schiller & Koerner, 1971; Schiller & Stryker, 1972). They also appear to be involved in mediating shifts of attention. This was demonstrated in experiments in which monkeys were trained to make saccades to peripheral visual targets and also to shift their attention to the targets without making an accompanying eye movement (Goldberg & Wurtz, 1972; Mohler & Wurtz, 1976). While the task was being performed, the experimenters measured the activity of superficial layer neurons. It was found that some were very active prior to and during saccades and attention shifts to the targets. In addition, the activity of some of these neurons also increased when attention was shifted to targets in the absence of saccades. It has been suggested that the activity of these superficial layer neurons only increases when attention is shifted in a stimulus-driven manner, and that it is not influenced by goal-driven attention shifts (e.g., Robinson & Kertzman, 1995).

There are at least three distinct types of neurons in the intermediate and deep layers of the superior colliculus. Visual neurons code the locations of visual stimuli, motor neurons code the destinations of impending eye movements, and visuomotor neurons are driven by a combination of visual and motor influences. When a motor or visuomotor neuron is electrically stimulated, this can trigger the generation of a saccade (e.g., Robinson, 1972; Schiller & Koerner, 1971; Sparks & Mays, 1983). The receptive fields of neurons in the intermediate and deep layers are laid out topographically; and the size and direction of an electrically evoked saccade depends on the stimulated neuron's location within an oculomotor map (Robinson, 1972). Stimulation of anterior neurons, for example, produces small amplitude saccades, and stimulation of posterior neurons produces larger amplitude saccades.

The relationship between neurons that mediate attention shifts and those that mediate saccades has also been studied with electrical stimulation. In one study, monkeys performed a target-detection task involving direct and symbolic location cueing (Kustov & Robinson, 1996). Shortly after cue presentation (and presumably after the initiation of an attention shift to the cued location), superior colliculus neurons were stimulated to trigger a saccade. The results indicated that both direct and symbolic cues influenced the trajectories of electrically evoked saccades, although in qualitatively different ways. Direct cues caused a strong and stable modification of the evoked movement whereas symbolic cues had a modifying effect that was more gradual. The experimenters concluded that direct cues had an immediate effect on intermediate-layer build-up cells. As discussed in chapter 6, the activity of these cells begins to increase well before the movement, and it reaches a peak as the saccade is initiated (e.g., Fuchs et al., 1985). The effect of symbolic cues on these cells, however, was said to be more gradual because the meaning of such cues must be analyzed (perhaps by frontoparietal cortical areas) before build-up cell activity is affected.

The electrically evoked saccade technique has also been used to demonstrate that visuomotor collicular neurons are modulated by attention, but motor neurons are not. Monkeys were trained to shift their attention in one direction in response to a location cue and, at the same time, an electrically evoked saccade was induced in the opposite direction (Ignashchenkova et al., 2004). As the task was performed, visuomotor neurons (but not visual or motor neurons) were active at the time monkeys shifted attention to a new destination. These neurons were also active during attention shifts in the complete absence of a motor response (saccade). In addition, visuomotor neuron activation only occurred in response to direct location cueing and not in response to symbolic location cueing. Thus, electrical stimulation has proven useful for identifying the types of collicular neurons that are active during attention shifts.

The results of another study indicated that when monkeys performed a visual motion discrimination task, microstimulation of intermediate-layer neurons below the threshold required to evoke a saccade still induced shifts of attention—and the destinations of these shifts corresponded to the receptive fields of the stimulated neurons (Müller et al., 2005). The experimenters concluded that the microstimulation improved performance by causing attention to be focused on a specific region in visual space without an accompanying saccade. A related finding is that sub-saccade-threshold microstimulation of monkey intermediate-layer neurons increased visual sensitivity and improved the ability to detect changes in visual scenes (Cavanaugh & Wurtz, 2004). These findings further evidence that the superior colliculus mediates shifts of attention.

The results of lesion studies also indicate that this area plays a role in attention shifting. Some early findings suggested that collicular lesions disrupt the ability to locate targets (MacKinnon et al., 1976; Schneider, 1969). This was supported by a later finding that when superior colliculus function was impaired by injection of gamma-aminobutyric acid (GABA—a chemical that temporarily depresses neural activity in the region of the injection), attentional filtering was disrupted (Desimone et al., 1990). That is, after the GABA injection, monkeys had difficulty making target-discrimination responses when more than one item was present in the visual field. In a related study, when the function of one colliculus was impaired by injection of muscimol (a chemical that potentiates GABA effects and thus also depresses neural activity), responses to contralesional targets were slowed but responses to ipsilesional targets (by the unimpaired colliculus) were not (Robinson & Kertzman, 1995). A similar study was conducted with impairment of collicular function by muscimol and lidocaine (a chemical that blocks neural action potentials) injections (McPeek & Keller, 2004). When monkeys searched for targets in the inactivated visual field, saccades were often misdirected to distractors. The severity of the deficit also depended on the difficulty of discriminating the target from surrounding distractor items (see Figure 7.5). This study clearly shows that superior colliculus inactivation caused a target-localization deficit rather than a motor (saccade) deficit. More generally, these lesion studies indicate that when shifting attention, the superior colliculus plays an important role in determining stimulus locations.

Superior colliculus lesions in humans also indicate that this area is involved in the mediation of covert orienting. For example, patients with progressive supranuclear palsy (PSP) have difficulty shifting their attention from one location to another. PSP is a relatively rare midbrain/collicular degenerative disease that affects superior colliculus neurons. During the early stages of the

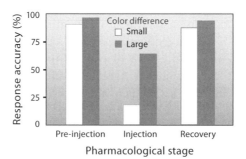

Figure 7.5 Results of experiment by McPeek and Keller (2004) on the effects of pharmacological inactivation of the superior colliculus on visual discrimination. Performance depended on the perceptual discriminability of the target. In the large-color-difference condition, isoluminant distractor items were less similar to the color of the target. In the small-color-difference condition, distractor items were more similar to the color of the target. Saccade accuracy was lowered by the injection and was particularly impaired in the small-color-difference condition.

disease's progression, PSP patients have difficulty making eye movements away from currently fixated positions (particularly in the vertical plane) much like the way animals with collicular lesions have difficulty making saccades (Rafal & Grimm, 1981; Schiller et al., 1987; Steele et al., 1964). When PSP patients in one study performed a location-cueing task, target-detection responses were slower when attention was shifted in the vertical than in the horizontal plane (Rafal et al., 1988). This suggests that PSP impairs attention shifts, and is further evidence that the superior colliculus is involved in covert orienting.

With reference to premotor theory (discussed in chapter 6), it is also worth noting that even when PSP progresses to the point at which patients are no longer able to make eye movements, they still retain some ability to covertly shift attention. This is not consistent with the claim that attention shifts are simply planned-but-not-executed saccades. In another study, subjects unable to program eye movements because of congenital blindness were still able to shift attention normally (Garg et al., 2007). More specifically, if attention shifts are inhibited saccades (premotor theory), then inability to make saccades presumably should result in an inability to covertly shift attention—which is not the case with PSP patients and the congenitally blind.

The superior colliculus also appears to play a critical role in the mediation of IOR. Although most of the evidence comes from research involving humans, IOR has been studied in monkeys as well (e.g., Bell et al., 2004; Dorris et al., 1999, 2002). In one experiment, for example, monkeys performed a task that elicited IOR and single-cell recordings of superior colliculus neurons indicated a reduction of sensory response to target stimuli (Dorris et al., 2002)—which indicates that this brain area is involved in target detection.

The superior colliculus is also implicated in IOR in humans. Subjects in one experiment performed an IOR task while viewing the stimulus display monocularly (i.e., with a patch over one eye; Rafal et al., 1991). As mentioned previously, the superior colliculus is essentially monocular. Each of the two colliculi is less sensitive to stimuli in their respective nasal visual hemifields than in their temporal hemifields (Figure 7.4). Thus, as seen in Figure 7.6, when one eye is patched so that the stimulus display is viewed monocularly, the medial (nasal) hemiretina of the unpatched eye projects significantly more fibers to the contralateral colliculus than the lateral (temporal) hemiretina projects to the ipsilateral colliculus. As a result, the temporal visual hemifield of the unpatched eye is more strongly represented in the superior colliculus than is the nasal hemifield. The findings of this experiment are shown in Figure 7.6. Even though monocular viewing does not appear to affect target detection in either hemifield (Rafal & Inhoff, 1986), the magnitude of the IOR effect was greater in the temporal hemifield

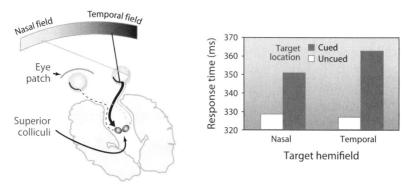

Figure 7.6 The essentially monocular function of the superior colliculus is the result of each colliculus being innervated primarily by fibers from the medial hemiretina of the contralateral eye, and to a lesser extent by fibers from the lateral hemiretina of the ipsilateral eye. As a result, when one eye is patched, the eye that is used to view the stimulus display is most sensitive to the temporal visual hemifield. In this figure, the unpatched right eye projects strong input to the superior colliculus from the medial hemiretina (temporal hemifield) and less input from the lateral hemiretina (nasal hemifield). The results of Rafal et al.'s (1991) study with normal subjects showed that IOR was stronger in the temporal hemifield than in the nasal hemifield of the unpatched eye.

than in the nasal hemifield. This indicates that IOR is mediated, at least in part, by a monocular structure; and it reinforces the claim that the superior colliculus plays a role in its occurrence.

Although the available data on humans with superior colliculus lesions are limited, there are some indications that patients with damage to this area do not show IOR. As mentioned previously, patients with PSP (associated with collicular degeneration) have difficulty shifting their attention from one location to another, and particularly in the vertical plane (Rafal et al., 1988). They also show a reduced capacity for IOR in the vertical plane (Posner et al., 1985; see Figure 7.7). In another study, a patient (SR)

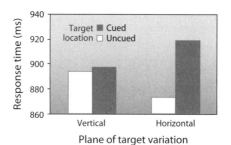

Figure 7.7 Results of Posner et al.'s (1985) study with PSP patients. In the early stages of this disease, these patients have an impaired capacity for eye movements, attention shifts and, as indicated by this graph, IOR in the vertical plane (although it still persists in the horizontal plane).

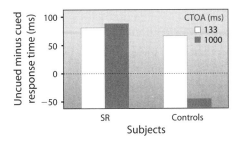

Figure 7.8 A comparison of mean response times (manual and saccadic) of patient SR in Sereno et al.'s (2006) study and healthy control subjects when a direct location-cueing task was performed. Control subjects showed IOR at the 1000 ms CTOA, but SR did not.

with midbrain/collicular dysfunction due to a thiamine deficiency did not show any IOR (Sereno et al., 2006). Figure 7.8 shows SR's reduced capacity for IOR relative to a group of elderly but healthy control subjects (data for the control group are from a study by Briand et al., 2001). Another patient (SG) with a unilateral (right) superior colliculus lesion did not show IOR when stimuli were presented in the region of the visual field affected by the lesion (Sapir et al., 1999). More specifically, when SG viewed the stimulus display monocularly, IOR did not occur when targets were presented in the temporal field of the left eye (with right eye patched) or the nasal field of the right eye (with left eye patched). It did, however, continue to occur when targets were presented in the region of the visual field that provided inputs to the intact colliculus (see Figure 7.9). These findings are compelling support

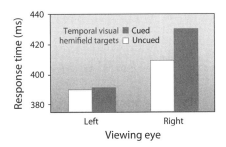

Figure 7.9 Results of Sapir et al.'s (1999) study of a patient with a unilateral lesion of the right superior colliculus. Data shown are for displays viewed monocularly by each eye, and a cue-target onset asynchrony (CTOA) of 1000 ms. The IOR effect was preserved when stimuli appeared in the temporal visual hemifield viewed by the right eye (intact left colliculus), but did not occur when stimuli appeared in the temporal visual hemifield viewed by the left eye (damaged right colliculus). This indicates that IOR will not occur when stimuli appear in the visual hemifield associated with the damaged side of the superior colliculus and, therefore, that this brain area is involved in the mediation of IOR.

for the claim that the superior colliculus plays a critical role in the mediation of IOR. As discussed in chapter 5, this may involve tagging locations so that they can be referred back to at some point in the future.

Whereas the claim that the superior colliculus plays a role in the mediation of IOR is well-supported, it is not the only brain area involved. To elaborate, (a) the occurrence of object-based IOR associated with moving cues (e.g., Tipper et al., 1991) implicates cortical areas sensitive to visual motion; (b) the demonstration that IOR is cognitively penetrable (i.e., depends on the observers' beliefs) as reported by Jefferies et al. (2005) implicates higher level (perhaps frontal) cortical areas; and (c) the discovery that frontal-cortex TMS disrupts IOR (Ro et al., 2003) also implicates this cortical area. Thus, there is a good deal of converging evidence that IOR is mediated by a network of brain areas—not just by the superior colliculus.

Frontocollicular Circuit. Like the superior colliculus, the frontal eye fields (FEF) of the frontal cortex also appear to mediate attention shifts (e.g., Bruce et al., 1985; Thompson et al., 1997) and saccades (e.g., Bizzi, 1968; Bruce & Goldberg, 1984, 1985; Bruce et al., 1985). Unlike the superior colliculus, however, FEF activity appears to be associated primarily with goal-driven eye movements (Paus, 1996), and its neurons show little response to stimulus-driven feature selectivity (Bichot et al., 1996). Other areas of the frontal cortex (orbital and medial regions) appear to be involved in inhibiting or overriding stimulus-driven eye movements initiated and controlled by the superior colliculus (Paus et al., 1991; as discussed in chapter 6, to preserve consistency with our attention shift terminology, we refer to saccades initiated by sensory events as stimulus-driven, and saccades initiated on the basis of an observer's goals and intentions as goal-driven). The FEF may also have an inhibiting effect on superior colliculus function. In one study, for example, monkey FEF appeared to facilitate superior colliculus neurons involved in moving the eyes in the same direction as the planned saccade while inhibiting superior colliculus neurons associated with movements in other directions (Schlag-Rey et al., 1992). It appears that conflict between the two areas does not occur because the FEF has precedence and a strong influence over the superior colliculus.

If the FEF is damaged, it is difficult to suppress stimulus-driven eye movements to objects that appear in the visual periphery, presumably because this area can no longer inhibit responses by the superior colliculus (Paus et al., 1991). The results of an eye-movement study involving patients with FEF lesions support this (Henik et al., 1994). In particular, latency of saccades to the contralesional field was disrupted to a greater extent when patients made goal-driven saccades to symbolically cued targets as opposed to stimulus-driven saccades to direct-cued targets (see Figure 7.10). In fact, FEF lesions made stimulus-driven saccade latencies *shorter*. This suggests

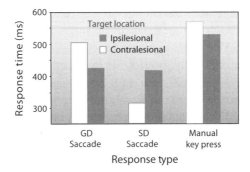

Figure 7.10 Results of a study by Henik et al. (1994) with FEF lesion patients showed that while this damage slowed goal-driven (GD) saccades, it had the opposite effect on stimulus-driven (SD) saccades. This indicates that the FEF has an inhibitory effect on collicular function that was disinhibited by the lesion. Given that this did not occur with key press responses, the disinhibition appears to be specific to oculomotor function.

that the FEF has two separate effects on eye movements. (a) It is involved in generating goal-driven saccades and (b) it has inhibitory connections to the midbrain collicular area that, when disrupted by lesions, results in disinhibition of these subcortical areas and faster stimulus-driven saccades. Key press responses to direct-cued targets did not show this disinhibition, which indicates that it is an oculomotor phenomenon (Figure 7.10). A related finding is that frontal lobe damage disrupts the ability to suppress pro-saccades when an anti-saccade task is performed (Walker et al., 1998; the anti-saccade paradigm is described in chapter 6). The experimenters suggested that before an anti-saccade can be programmed, the frontal system must send a signal to the superior colliculus to inhibit the natural, reflexive (pro) saccade.

If the superior colliculus is damaged, goal-driven saccadic eye movements still can be made because the FEF and superior colliculus have a common output pathway to the brainstem centers that direct eye movements. In one study, for example, the superior colliculus of a monkey was removed but electrical microstimulation of the FEF still triggered eye movements (Schiller et al., 1980). Results like this provide converging evidence that there is a frontocollicular network with the superior colliculus in control of stimulus-driven saccades and attention shifts, and the FEF and other frontal cortical areas in control of goal-driven saccades and attention shifts.

In summary, the research described in this section indicates that when attention shifts occur, a primary role of the superior colliculus is to select locations of abrupt-onset stimuli and visual transients. The involvement of the superior colliculus in IOR suggests that it may also maintain this location information so that it can be referred back to later. Lesions to this area disrupt attention shifts (cause a general slowing of responses), which may be due to a reduced capacity to localize stimuli. The superior colliculus is involved primarily in stimulus-driven attention shifts and may work in tandem with cortical areas like the FEF that appear to mediate goal-driven shifts. The FEF, for example, may exert executive control over the superior colliculus and override reflexive orienting. A reciprocal relationship between the FEF and superior colliculus could also explain why IOR, which is closely associated with collicular function, can be disrupted by impaired FEF function (Ro et al., 2003). That is, the superior colliculus could mark locations and the frontal cortex could determine whether sensitivity to these marked locations is to be enhanced or inhibited (see chapter 5 for a discussion of the idea that attention to marked locations can be facilitated or inhibited). A reciprocal relationship between the FEF and superior colliculus also makes sense from an evolutionary perspective. Subcortical orienting mechanisms are part of a phylogenetically older visual system that is likely to play a greater role in mediating stimulus-driven attention shifts. The more recently evolved cortical orienting mechanisms, on the other hand, are likely to play a greater role in goal-driven attention shifts and the inhibitory control of stimulus-driven shifts.

Pulvinar Nucleus

The thalamus is an egg-shaped structure at the rostral end of the brainstem (see Figure 7.3). Like the superior colliculus and the cortex, it contains maps of visual space. It is also innervated by projections from the brainstem and midbrain, and has reciprocal connections with all cortical regions. This high degree of interconnectivity with other brain areas makes the thalamus uniquely suited for (a) serving as a gateway that relays (stimulus-driven) sensory inputs to the cortex for further analysis and (b) receiving cortical inputs required to coordinate this process (some of which are goal-driven).

Several areas of the thalamus appear to be involved in attentional processing. The medial, dorsal, and intralaminar subregions, for example, receive input from the RAS, which indicates that the thalamus plays a role in the control of arousal. Its location between peripheral sensory structures and their associated cortical areas also suggests that the thalamus may act as an attentional filter that selects a subset of sensory input to be relayed to the cortex (e.g., Crick, 1984; LaBerge, 1990, 1995a). For example, the mediodorsal nucleus has prominent reciprocal connections with the prefrontal cortex (PFC; e.g., Giguere & Goldman-Rakic, 1988) and it may play a critical "selective engagement" role in the analysis of semantic properties of language (Crosson, 1999). The lateral geniculate nucleus also appears to be involved in selective attention (e.g., O'Connor et al., 2002; Schneider et al., 2004). It receives visual inputs, is retinotopically organized, and appears to be sensitive to visual features (e.g., edge orientations) and their combinations (e.g., convexity; Pasupathy & Connor, 1999). In addition, it has been suggested that the reticular nucleus may play an important role in attentional gating (e.g., Guillery et al., 1998; McAlonan et al., 2000; Purpura & Schiff, 1997; Weese et al., 1999; Yingling & Skinner, 1976, 1977). We focus our discussion on the pulvinar nucleus, however, because this area appears to be centrally involved in the mediation of attention shifts.

The pulvinar is located at the posterior of the thalamus, contains several retinotopic maps, and the majority of its neurons are involved in visual processing (e.g., Robinson & Cowie, 1997). It appears to be so named (pulvinar is a synonym of "cushion") because, anatomically, it covers much of the superior colliculus and its axonal tract (see Figure 7.3). Like other regions of the thalamus, the pulvinar has reciprocal connections with subcortical and cortical areas (e.g., Ungerleider et al., 1983). Inputs from superficial and intermediate layers of the superior colliculus, for example, project to the parietal lobe and other cortical areas via the pulvinar.

While it has been suggested that the pulvinar's role in attentional processing is still poorly understood (e.g., Michael & Buron, 2005, p. 1353), there is a growing body of data indicating that it may be involved in covert orienting and attentional filtering. The results of a single-cell recording study, for example, suggested that neurons in several areas of the monkey pulvinar and particularly the dorsomedial portion of the lateral region (Pdm) play a role in selective attention (Petersen et al., 1985). More specifically, neural responses of Pdm neurons were enhanced when attention shift and saccade targets were presented in their receptive fields, which indicates that the pulvinar plays a role in attentional selection of visual stimuli.

The results of neuroimaging studies involving healthy human subjects also indicate that the pulvinar is involved in attentional selection. Subjects in one study identified small targets surrounded by small flanking distractors (as seen in Figure 7.11) or large targets without flanking distractors (LaBerge & Buchsbaum, 1990). PET imaging indicated that there was

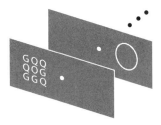

Figure 7.11 Stimuli used in LaBerge and Buchsbaum's (1990) PET study and Buchsbaum et al.'s (2006) fMRI study. The general finding was greater activation of the pulvinar when subjects identified small targets surrounded by small distractors as opposed to large targets presented without distractors.

stronger pulvinar activation when targets were flanked by distractors. The experimenters concluded that the pulvinar is involved in the mediation of attentional filtering (see also LaBerge, 1990). Although the filtering account of this finding has since been challenged by the results of another study involving thalamic lesion patients (Michael & Desmedt, 2004; see also, Danziger et al., 2004), the original PET finding has since been replicated with fMRI imaging (Buchsbaum et al., 2006). Again, the pulvinar was more active [as indicated by a larger blood oxygenation level-dependent (BOLD) signal] when subjects identified small targets flanked by distractors than when they identified large targets without distractors. Thus, neuroimaging and neural recording data are consistent with the proposal that the pulvinar plays a role in attentional selection.

This is also supported by data from several pulvinar lesion studies. One involved pharmacological deactivation of the monkey pulvinar (Petersen et al., 1987). In particular, monkeys performed a target-detection task after either muscimol (a GABA agonist that enhances GABA-induced inhibition of neural activity) or bicuculline (a GABA antagonist that prevents normal GABA-caused inhibition of neural activity) was injected into Pdm neurons in one of the pulvinars. The general finding was that muscimol appeared to disrupt attentional processing in the visual field contralateral to the injection. To elaborate, when a direct cue and target were both presented in the ipsilateral field (valid-cue trial), neither drug affected target-detection response times (see Figure 7.12). On the other hand, when the cue and

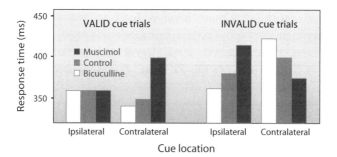

Figure 7.12 Results of Petersen et al.'s (1987) study involving pharmacological inhibition or facilitation of Pdm neurons in monkey pulvinar. Data shown are from the 450 ms CTOA condition. On valid-cue trials with stimuli in the contralateral visual field, muscimol injections inhibited detection response times and bicuculline facilitated them. The same pattern of results occurred on invalid-cue trials when the cue was presented in the ipsilateral field and the target was presented in the contralateral field. But when the cue was presented in the contralateral field and the target appeared in the ipsilateral field, the opposite pattern occurred. Muscimol facilitated response times relative to the control condition and bicuculline inhibited them. The interaction of cue validity and drug effects on response times indicates that the pulvinar plays a role in covert orienting.

target were both presented in the contralateral field (also a valid-cue trial), muscimol increased response times relative to a control (no-drug) condition. Bicuculline had the opposite effect on response times (a slight decrease). The experimenters suggested that muscimol slowed attention shifts to the contralateral stimuli, and that bicuculline speeded shifts to these stimuli. Perhaps most interesting, however, were the invalid-cue trials. When the cue was presented in the ipsilateral field and the target appeared in the contralateral field, muscimol increased response times and bicuculline decreased them. Conversely, when the cue was presented in the contralateral field and the target appeared in the ipsilateral field, the drugs had the opposite effects—muscimol decreased response times and bicuculline increased them. The experimenters suggested that when the invalid cue was in the contralateral field, muscimol would impair its selection and, thereby, facilitate detection of the target when it appeared in the opposite field. On the other hand, bicuculline would enhance the selection of the invalid cue and, thereby, inhibit detection of the target when it appeared in the opposite field. These results are not readily explained in terms of sensory processing or motor responding because the effects of the drugs on response times depended on location-cue validity (unlike, e.g., the inhibitory effect of muscimol on superior colliculus function regardless of cue validity—e.g., Robinson & Petersen, 1992). They indicate, instead, that the pulvinar plays a role in covert orienting.

Pulvinar lesions also appear to disrupt attentional processing in humans. One report of this involved patients with unilateral lesions described simply as "thalamic" (as opposed to restricted to the pulvinar; Rafal & Posner, 1987). When these patients performed a target-detection task involving direct location cues, responses were faster when the target was in the ipsilesional field (even on invalid-cue trials when the cue was in the contralesional field). Responses were slower when the target was in the contralesional field, and particularly on invalid-cue trials when the cue was in the ipsilesional field (Figure 7.13). Also of note was that slower responses on invalid-cue trials occurred only while the cue was still present. This could indicate that the thalamic lesion patients had difficulty engaging their attention on the contralesional target while the cue in the ipsilesional field was still visible—but once it was removed, their attention was more easily engaged at the target location. This result has since been replicated with pulvinar lesion patients (Sapir et al., 2002). In both studies, subjects were slower to detect targets in the contralesional field than in the ipsilesional field, and showed a larger cue validity effect in the contralesional field. The replication with pulvinar lesion patients is a further indication that this area plays a role in covert orienting.

The results of another study indicate that, in some cases, the impaired attentional selection caused by damage to the pulvinar may be caused by a

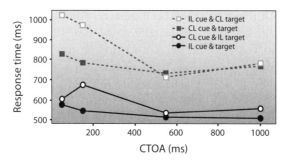

Figure 7.13 Results of Rafal and Posner's (1987) study with thalamic lesion patients indicated that they were slower to detect targets in the contralesional (CL) field, and particularly when the cue was first presented in the ipsilesional (IL) field. This cue validity effect is consistent with their claim that the thalamus plays a role in covert orienting.

stimulus localization deficit (R. Ward et al., 2002). A pulvinar lesion patient performed a variant of a target-identification task known to produce illusory conjunction errors. These are said to occur when a disruption of attentional analysis causes features of objects in a visual scene to be miscombined (e.g., Treisman & Schmidt, 1982). Illusory conjunctions are, therefore, different from erroneous reports of any number of different possible features that were not originally present in the visual scene. When illusory conjunction errors occur, the features themselves are processed, but attentional disruption while performing the task is thought to reduce the accuracy with which features are bound together to form a perceptual object. In the current study, the patient with the unilateral pulvinar lesion made more illusory conjunction errors when stimuli were presented in the contralesional field than when they were presented in the ipsilesional field. On this basis, the experimenters concluded that pulvinar damage can impair stimulus localization.

Other data indicate that the pulvinar, like the superior colliculus, has a nasal-temporal input asymmetry. In one study, unilateral pulvinar lesion patients performed an attention-orienting task while viewing the stimulus display monocularly (Sapir et al., 2002). When the display was viewed with the contralesional eye (ipsilesional eye patched), targets in the nasal visual field were detected faster than those in the temporal field. Conversely, when the display was viewed with the ipsilesional eye (contralesional eye patched), targets in the temporal field were detected faster than those in the nasal field (see Figure 7.14). This indicates that tectothalamic fibers arising from the superficial layers of the superior colliculus project to the pulvinar ipsilaterally as in Figure 7.15. This finding is also consistent with another report (Michael & Buron, 2005) that, when viewed monocularly by healthy observers, the capacity of task-irrelevant motion onsets to capture attention and distract from performance of the primary visual task is greater

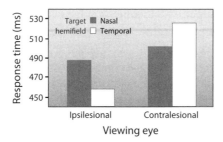

Figure 7.14 Results of Sapir et al.'s (2002) study with unilateral pulvinar lesion patients showed that with monocular viewing with the ipsilesional eye (contralesional eye patched), targets were detected faster in the temporal than in the nasal field. Conversely, with monocular viewing with the contralesional eye, targets were detected faster in the nasal than the temporal field. This indicates that the pulvinar is asymmetrically innervated by the retinae. Data shown are for displays with a 1000 ms CTOA.

when these onsets are in the temporal hemifield than in the nasal hemifield (although, as the superior colliculus exhibits the same nasal-temporal asymmetry of retinal inputs and is also extremely sensitive to motion onsets, this finding is perhaps more indicative of collicular than thalamic function). Another interesting aspect of the Sapir et al. (2002) study is that, despite patients having unilateral pulvinar lesions, IOR still occurred. This refutes

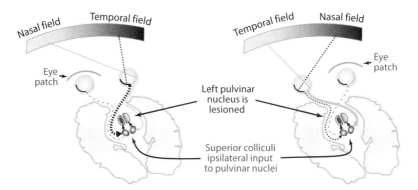

Figure 7.15 Each superior colliculus is innervated primarily by fibers from the medial hemiretina of the contralateral eye, and to a lesser extent by fibers from the lateral hemiretina of the ipsilateral eye. This monocularity is preserved in the pulvinar with inputs from the superior colliculi to the ipsilateral pulvinar nuclei. In this figure, there is a lesion in the left pulvinar. When the left eye is patched and the right (contralesional) eye views the display, inputs from the temporal field are disrupted (as indicated by the dashed line) relative to those from the nasal hemifield. When the right eye is patched and the left (ipsilesional) eye views the display, inputs from the nasal field are disrupted (as indicated by the dashed line) relative to those from the temporal hemifield. Given the asymmetric innervation of the pulvinar, it would be expected that response times would be fastest when viewing temporal field stimuli with the ipsilesional eye (as found by Sapir et al., 2002).

the suggestion that superior colliculus damage may eliminate IOR primarily because the lesions prevent the superior colliculus from sending inputs further along the visual pathway to the pulvinar. Instead, it demonstrates that a functioning pulvinar is not necessary for the occurrence of IOR, and that this inhibitory effect is mediated to a greater degree by other areas such as the superior colliculus.

The pulvinar is uniquely located between subcortical structures involved in stimulus-driven attention shifts (e.g., superior colliculus) and cortical structures involved in goal-driven attention shifts (e.g., parietal and frontal cortex). For this reason, it has been suggested that the primary spatial map in the ventral pulvinar may function as a *salience map* that is used to coordinate stimulus-driven and goal-driven attention shift signals (e.g., Bundesen et al., 2005; Shipp, 2004). The concept of a salience map was developed by Koch and Ullman (1985) as a representation of visual space containing salient stimuli that compete for the attentional focal point in a winner-take-all manner. The essential feature of a *master* salience map, according to Shipp (2004), is that it pools the outputs of visuospatial salience maps in other brain areas. Note that the pulvinar is not the only candidate for this type of representation. Others have proposed that it could be located in a number of different areas including the FEF, parietal cortex, and visual cortex (e.g., Bundesen et al., 2005, p. 300; Gottlieb, 2007; Treue, 2003; cf., Fecteau & Munoz, 2006). It has also been suggested that assumptions about a single "master" salience map located in one particular brain area may be incorrect because attention has a modulating effect to some degree or another at every level of the visual system past the retina (Serences & Yantis, 2006). While more research must be done before proposals about structures like a master salience map can be refined, the idea that the ventral pulvinar is involved in the coordination of stimulus-driven and goal-driven attention shift signals is a compelling one.

In summary, subcortical structures play important roles in the orienting of attention. The neurotransmitter systems of the RAS are involved in the innervation of brain areas that mediate covert orienting. The superior colliculus contains neurons that play a role in stimulus localization and calibration of vectors of stimulus-driven attention shifts. More specifically, (a) these neurons show enhanced activation when attention is shifted to locations corresponding to their receptive fields, (b) subthreshold microstimulation of these neurons elicits attention shifts in the absence of eye movements, and (c) damage to these neurons disrupts attention shifts and IOR. The superior colliculus projects neural output to the dorsal pulvinar, which is then relayed to cortical areas and to a visuospatial map in the ventral pulvinar. The pulvinar contains neurons (particularly in the Pdm) that show enhanced activation when attention is shifted to locations corresponding to their receptive fields, and when attentional filtering tasks are performed (as indicated by PET and fMRI data). Pulvinar lesions, however, disrupt attentional selection of stimuli. The pulvinar's unique anatomical location has prompted many researchers to suggest that it serves an attentional gateway (filtering) function. It has even been suggested that stimulus-driven shifts of attention could be mediated subcortically by a colliculo-thalamic circuit independent of inputs from the frontal and parietal cortices (e.g., Shipp, 2004, p. 227). In the sections that follow, we discuss cortical attention mechanisms and their integration with subcortical areas to form an attention-orienting network.

Cortical Attention Mechanisms

Cortical structures also play important roles in the orienting of attention. The human cerebral cortex is composed of a thin sheet of neural tissue that is divided into left and right hemispheres. Cortical tissue has extensive convolutions made up of bulges (gyri) and fissures (sulci) that allow its large surface area to fit within a restricted cranial volume. The total surface area of the cortex in both hemispheres is estimated to be 1570 cm^2, 70% of which is buried in sulci (Van Essen & Drury, 1997). As seen in Figure 7.16, the larger sulci form the boundaries between the four major lobes. The central sulcus divides the parietal and frontal lobes; the lateral (Sylvian) fissure divides the temporal lobe from the overlying frontal and parietal lobes; and the parietooccipital sulcus divides the occipital and parietal lobes. The frontal lobe makes up an estimated 35% of the human cortex; and the parietal, temporal, and occipital lobes each make up roughly 20% (Van Essen & Drury, 1997). The remaining 5% is occupied by the limbic lobe (not visible in Figure 7.16, but seen in sagittal views of the brain).

Two cortical areas involved in covert orienting are the parietal and frontal lobes. The parietal lobe is located at the intersection of visual, auditory, and tactile cortices. The posterior parietal cortex (portion of the parietal

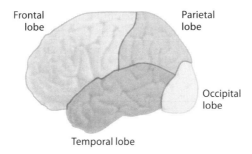

Figure 7.16 The four main lobes of the human neocortex.

lobe that does not include the somatosensory cortex) contains spatial maps that are used for (a) determining the locations of objects and (b) integrating information about location with body movements (limbs or eyes) so that they can be directed with precision to a particular position in space. The frontal lobe is thought to be involved in goal-driven control of attention; and also the selection, initiation, and inhibition of motor responses (e.g., saccades) associated with attentional processing. The PFC makes up about half of the frontal lobe (does not include the motor cortex, FEF, Broca's area, or posterior cingulate cortex) and is considered to be the main source of goal-driven signals to other cortical areas (e.g., Miller & Cohen, 2001). The FEF is dorsal to the PFC, and has a more specialized role in orienting. It has been suggested that the parietal and frontal lobes work together as a frontoparietal network that mediates attentional disengagement and goal-driven shifts of attention (e.g., Corbetta & Shulman, 2002).

Whereas neurons in the visual cortex also play a role in attentional selection of inputs, they are not considered to be part of the purely attentional mechanism that mediates covert orienting. Serences and Yantis (2006) described this distinction as one between the source of attention control (e.g., frontoparietal covert orienting network) and the target of attention control signals (e.g., visual cortical processing). It could also be thought of as the distinction between *mechanisms* of attention shifting and *consequences* of these shifts (LaBerge, 1995a). One of the first reports of visual cortex neurons mediating attentional selection involved recordings of neurons in area V4 of the monkey (Moran & Desimone, 1985). It was found that attended visual stimuli within the receptive fields of these neurons increased response rates, while unattended stimuli within these receptive fields decreased response rates. Neuroimaging research also demonstrated that the visual cortex plays a role in attentional selection. The results of a study involving PET imaging, for example, indicated that selectively attending to stimulus features like color, form, and movement led to the activation of distinct and largely nonoverlapping areas of the extrastriate visual cortex (Corbetta et al., 1991). In another study involving fMRI imaging, selective attention to different aspects of visual displays also resulted in increased activation in different visual cortical areas including V1 (Tootell et al., 1998). Figure 7.17 is based on Silver et al.'s (2005) comparison of fMRI response amplitudes across different visual areas during passive viewing and during a task that involved focused attention (see also, Serences & Yantis, 2006). It shows the relative extent to which attentional modulation may occur in different visual cortical areas (as indicated by fMRI), and that whereas this modulation also occurs in early visual areas, it is less pronounced there. Note that the locations of the visual cortical areas in Figure 7.17 are approximations, and that some of these areas are buried in sulci or best seen

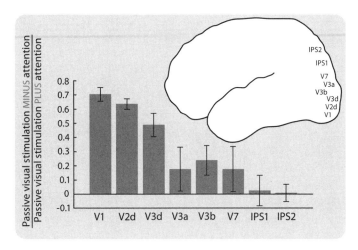

Figure 7.17 Silver et al.'s (2005) comparison of relative BOLD response amplitudes during passive visual stimulation and during top-down attentional deployments (comparison is based on the difference between passive viewing and attention amplitudes divided by their sum). The graded decrease across visual areas indicates that the relative influence of sensory stimulation is large in early visual areas (e.g., V1), whereas in later areas (e.g., IPS1 and IPS2), sensory stimulation and deployments of attention have a relatively comparable modulatory effect. Error bars = SE. Based on Silver et al. (2005) Figure 7. We thank Michael Silver for providing a re-plotted graph of the original data.

from a mid-sagittal view (for more precise location information, see Larsson & Heeger, 2006; Wandell et al., 2005).

Attentional processing in the human visual cortex has also been studied with electrophysiological techniques. One of these, *electroencephalography* (EEG), involves measuring minute electrical fluctuations associated with brain activity. To elaborate, when populations of neurons are active, they generate ionic currents that produce fluctuating electrical fields. Electrodes on the surface of the scalp can measure these changes with millisecond precision. An EEG recording of neural activity is a time series of waves of varying field strength and polarity.

Stimulation by an external event (e.g., a visual stimulus) can trigger changes in brain activity, and the waveform associated with this stimulation is called an *event-related potential* (ERP). Relative to those of typical EEG waves, the amplitudes of ERP wave components are so small (on the order of 1–2 μV) that they can be difficult to discern. For this reason, during an ERP experiment, the evoking stimulus is repeated many times so that potentially unrelated events can be averaged out. The result is a cleaner wave form with characteristic peaks and troughs representing the most positive and negative voltage polarities (see Figure 7.18). Visual P1, for example, is a common positive peak that occurs approximately 100 ms or more after the onset of a

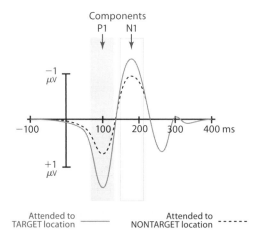

Figure 7.18 Idealized ERP data. Visual P1 and N1 components are enhanced when eliciting target stimulus is attended to. As is the convention in the electrophysiology literature, positive voltages are plotted below the abscissa and negative voltages above it.

visual stimulus. The label P1 refers to it being the first positive peak in the wave form. N1 is the first negative peak in the wave form, P2 is the second positive peak, and so on. ERP components are also identified by their latency (although many researchers avoid this; see e.g., Luck, 2005, p. 11). N100, for example, refers to the negative peak occurring roughly 100 ms or more after the evoking stimulus.

Eason and Harter and colleagues were among the first to measure ERPs while subjects performed tasks involving attention to visual stimuli (e.g., Eason, 1981; Eason et al., 1969; Harter & Aine, 1984; Harter et al., 1982). They found that attended stimuli elicited enlarged ERP components over the 100–400 ms latency range. Another common finding is that, relative to visual stimuli at unattended locations, stimuli at attended locations typically evoke larger P1 (80–150 ms) and N1 (150–200 ms) components (e.g., Anllo-Vento, 1995; Eimer, 1994; Harter et al., 1989; Hillyard et al., 1994; Mangun & Hillyard, 1991; Mangun et al., 1993). Visual P1 and N1 differ, however, in the way they are modulated by attention. In one experiment, for example, N1 was larger for valid-cue targets (relative to invalid-cue targets), but only for discrimination responses and not for detection responses (Mangun & Hillyard, 1991). P1, on the other hand, was enhanced by attention for either discrimination or detection responses. The results of a similar experiment also showed N1 enhancement for discrimination responses but not by detection responses (whereas P1 was enhanced by both types of responses; Vogel & Luck, 2000). In another experiment, ERPs elicited by valid-cue and invalid-cue targets were compared to those elicited by neutral-cue targets (Luck et al., 1994b). Only N1 was modulated

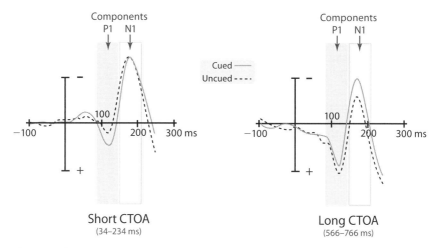

Figure 7.19 Approximate reproduction of ERP data from Hopfinger and Mangun's (1998) experiment. On short CTOA trials (34–234 ms) with a valid cue, P1 was enhanced. On long CTOA trials (566–766 ms) with a valid cue, the P1 effect was reversed (targets at cued locations elicited significantly smaller responses than targets at uncued locations) and N1 was enhanced.

(enhanced) on valid-cue trials, and only P1 was modulated (attenuated) on invalid-cue trials. The researchers concluded that costs (P1 attenuation) and benefits (N1 enhancement) of location cueing may arise from qualitatively different mechanisms. Luck (1995) refined this idea by proposing that the P1 effect reflects attention to sensory inputs whereas the N1 effect reflects limited-capacity processing at attended locations.

Visual P1 and N1 components also appear to be affected differently by CTOA manipulations. In particular, when subjects in one experiment performed a direct location-cueing task (Hopfinger & Mangun, 1998), the P1 elicited by valid-cue targets (when compared to P1 elicited by invalid-cue targets) was larger at short CTOAs (34–234 ms) and smaller at long CTOAs (566–766 ms; see Figure 7.19). On the other hand, the N1 elicited by valid-cue targets was unaffected at short CTOAs and (unlike P1) enhanced at long CTOAs (see also, Prime & Ward, 2006). The association of P1 modulation with short CTOAs and N1 modulation with long CTOAs is consistent with Hopfinger and Mangun's (1998, 2001) claim that P1 is associated with reflexive processing but N1 is not.

Topographical scalp voltage distributions in Figure 7.20 show that when the visual target is attended to, P1 (110–120 ms latency range) is maximal at a location in the right visual cortex contralateral to the target in the left visual hemifield. On the other hand, when attention is directed to the non-target location, the magnitude of P1 in the right visual cortex is smaller. Several studies have indicated that, as shown in Figure 7.20, visual P1 is

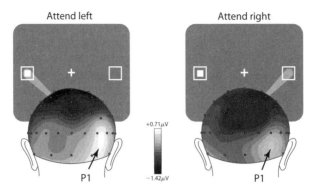

Figure 7.20 When subjects attend to a target location (attend left in this figure), P1 component enhancement is greater than when subjects attend to a nontarget location (attend right in this figure). The topographic voltage maps of occipital scalp sites show the effects of attention at the peak of the P1 component (110–120 ms latency range; scalp maps adapted from Hopfinger and Mangun, 1998).

largest over occipital regions contralateral to the attended visual hemifield, and that the probable source of this ERP is a population of neurons in the extrastriate visual cortex (e.g., Clark et al., 1996; Gomez et al., 1994; Heinze et al., 1994b; Hugdahl, 1995).

The spatial precision of scalp voltage maps like those shown in Figure 7.20 is limited because scalp-recorded ERPs only indicate locations of active neural populations *indirectly*. Occasionally, however, researchers use a combination of ERP and hemodynamic (sensitive to changes in cerebral blood flow) neuroimaging techniques in the same experiment to obtain both temporally and spatially precise data. Subjects in one such experiment attended to stimuli in the left or right visual hemifields while ERPs were measured in one session and PET data were collected in another (Heinze et al., 1994b). The ERP results revealed an enhanced P1 (80–140 ms latency range) in the ventral extrastriate visual cortex contralateral to the attended hemifield. The PET results indicated that there was a significant increase in blood flow in this region of the visual cortex (and also in the pulvinar). On this basis, the researchers concluded that the extrastriate visual cortex is the source of visual P1. A combination of electrophysiology and hemodynamic neuroimaging has also been used to determine the source of visual N1 (e.g., Hopf et al., 2002). As discussed later in the chapter, hemodynamic techniques like fMRI can be used to determine which brain areas are part of an attention orienting network, but electrophysiological analysis is better suited for determining the temporal dynamics of this network.

Parietal Cortex
Unlike the visual cortex, neurons in the parietal cortex are not particularly sensitive to color or to form, or to items positioned in central (foveal) vision.

Human	**Monkey**
Intraparietal sulcus (IPS)	Lateral intraparietal area (LIP)
Superior parietal lobule (SPL)	Inferior parietal lobule (IPL)
Temporoparietal junction (TPJ)	Area 7a

Table 7.1 Possible Homologous Parietal Areas in Human and Macaque Monkey

This indicates that they are not well-suited for object recognition. Like the superior colliculus, parietal cortical processing is much more sensitive to *where* objects are (particularly in the visual periphery) than to *what* they are.

A good deal of progress has been made in mapping the functional areas in monkey parietal cortex, but less is known about human parietal cortex. Table 7.1 lists some of the human and monkey parietal areas thought to be homologous (Culham & Kanwisher, 2001; Milner, 1996; Muri et al., 1996; Van Essen et al., 2001). Some of the parietal subregions related to attentional processing are shown in Figure 7.21. The intraparietal sulcus (IPS) serves as the boundary between the superior parietal lobule (SPL) and inferior parietal lobule (IPL). Each of these areas appears to play different roles in the mediation of attention shifts. The IPL also contains the parietal portion of the temporoparietal junction (TPJ). This portion is part of the supramarginal gyrus (SMG). The temporal lobe portion of the TPJ is part of the superior temporal gyrus (STG). As seen in Table 7.1, the functional areas of monkey parietal cortex are arranged differently than the homologous human functional areas. Note the potential for confusion, for example, when discussing neural activation in the IPL or SPL without specifying whether

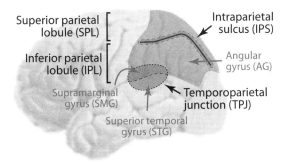

Figure 7.21 Subregions of the human posterior parietal cortex. The intraparietal sulcus (IPS) is the boundary between the superior and inferior parietal lobules. It is also, along with the temporoparietal junction (TPJ), centrally involved in attention shifting.

this refers to monkey or to human cortex. To minimize this, we have adopted the following naming convention in this chapter and the next: when we mention a brain area without a species-related prefix (e.g., IPS), we refer only to the human brain. References to nonhuman brain areas will always include a prefix (e.g., monkey lateral intraparietal [LIP] area), and references to human brain areas will sometimes include a species-related prefix (for clarity or emphasis).

Human IPS/Monkey LIP. The results of several studies indicate that human IPS and monkey LIP may play a similar role in attention orienting. In particular, a number of single-cell recording studies showed that activation of monkey LIP neurons was enhanced when attention was directed to locations associated with their receptive fields (e.g., Bisley & Goldberg, 2003; Bushnell et al., 1981; Colby et al., 1996; Gottlieb et al., 1998, 2005; Snyder et al., 1997). This appears to be the case regardless of whether attention was directed to auditory or to visual information, which indicates that the attentional processing carried out by this area is not specific to the visual sensory modality. Microstimulation of monkey LIP neurons also appears to evoke shifts of attention (as indicated by reduced target-detection times in an experiment involving direct location cueing; Cutrell & Marrocco, 2002). Thus, monkey LIP neurons appear to play a role in orienting attention.

Other studies demonstrated that monkey LIP neurons show a rapid response to abrupt-onset stimuli and visual transients (e.g., Bisley et al., 2004; Colby et al., 1996; Gottlieb et al., 1998, 2005). In one experiment, abrupt-onset stimuli triggered monkey LIP neuron on-responses that peaked at about 40–60 ms poststimulus, and then were followed by a gradual ramping up of activity that reached a peak at about 200 ms poststimulus (Gottlieb et al., 2005). Although faster (which is typically the case when comparing monkey and human response times; see Figure 7.1), this roughly mirrors the time course of direct and symbolic location cue effectiveness in humans (i.e., in humans, direct-cue effectiveness peaks rapidly at about 100-ms poststimulus, whereas symbolic-cue effectiveness shows a gradual ramping up that peaks at about 300 ms poststimulus; see Figure 2.9B). Another indication that monkey LIP may be involved in the mediation of stimulus-driven covert orienting is that it appears to have the capacity to simultaneously encode multiple stimulus onsets (Gottlieb et al., 2005). More specifically, in addition to their involvement in goal-driven orienting, monkey LIP neurons appear to play a role in the sensory processing associated with the initial stages of stimulus-driven attention shifts.

The results of several studies indicate that human IPS shows a pattern of activation similar to monkey LIP. For example, experiments involving neuroimaging with PET and fMRI showed sustained activation of IPS when observers voluntarily paid attention to peripheral stimuli, with or without concurrent eye movements (e.g., Corbetta et al., 1993, 1998; Gitelman et al., 1996; Nobre et al., 1997; Vandenberghe et al., 1996). Furthermore, IPS is activated during voluntary orienting toward a spatial location before the presentation of the target to be detected, and it has been suggested that this may reflect a shift toward and maintenance of attention at the cued location throughout the cue period (Corbetta et al., 2000). Cue-related activity in IPS might also be associated with a signal that "marks" a location of interest. In addition, it appears that voluntary attention shifts result in IPS activation that is predominantly lateralized (i.e., attending to the left visual field results in activation of the right hemisphere IPS, and vice versa), and dissociated from visual or motor control responses (i.e., attentional rather than sensory or motor-related; e.g., Corbetta et al., 2000). These neuroimaging results are supported by findings that when human parietal lesions are centered in the IPS (e.g., Friedrich et al., 1998), and when TMS is directed to the IPS (e.g., Koch et al., 2005), voluntary attention shifts can be impaired.

Human TPJ/Monkey Area 7a. Neurons in the TPJ are activated during the performance of location-cueing tasks. The pattern of this activation, however, indicates that it plays a different role in the mediation of covert orienting than does the IPS. The results of neuroimaging studies indicate that, unlike the IPS, when subjects perform a target-detection task involving location cueing, TPJ activation is not enhanced during the period between cue and target presentation—instead, its activation is delayed until the target is detected (e.g., Arrington et al., 2000; Corbetta et al., 2000). In addition, this activation is lateralized to the right hemisphere. Other studies indicated that when attention-orienting tasks are performed, TPJ activation is more likely to occur when (a) the target is at an unattended, unexpected location (e.g., invalid-cue trial) and (b) when it is relevant to the task (see e.g., Corbetta & Shulman, 2002; Serences et al., 2005; Shulman et al., 2003). This is consistent with the finding that TPJ damage (but not damage to other regions such as the frontal lobe) reduces the amplitude of an ERP (P300) associated with the detection of infrequent (unexpected) targets (Knight & Scabini, 1998; Knight et al., 1989). It is also consistent with the results of a monkey visual search study in which area 7a neurons showed spatially specific enhanced responses to unattended stimuli (Constantinidis & Steinmetz, 2001). Thus, TPJ activation appears to play a greater role in the processing of targets after their onset than in shifting attention to their expected locations prior to onset.

The results of studies involving patients with parietal lesions also suggest that the TPJ is involved in attentional reorienting. For example, parietal lesion patients in one experiment (Posner et al., 1984b) were able to detect

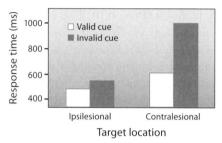

Figure 7.22 Results of an experiment by Posner et al. (1984b) indicated that parietal lesion patients were slower to detect targets in the contralesional field following an invalid cue in the ipsilesional (unimpaired) field. They concluded that parietal damage can disrupt the function of an attentional disengagement mechanism.

targets in the contralesional visual field when they were correctly cued (i.e., on valid-cue trials with targets appearing at the same location as the cue). As illustrated by Figure 7.22, however, they were slower to detect targets in the contralesional field when the cues that preceded them were presented in the ipsilesional (unimpaired) field. The experimenters concluded that this was evidence of an attentional disengagement deficit. To elaborate, they suggested that when attention is directed to a cued location and then must be reoriented to a different (target) location, it must be disengaged at the cued location before this reorienting can occur. If the disengagement mechanism is damaged, then reorienting to the target and the subsequent detection response will be slowed. Note that Posner et al.'s (1984b) lesion data seemed to indicate that the dorsal parietal cortex was the most likely brain area to mediate attentional disengagement. With the development of neuroimaging techniques over the past 20 years, however, it became clear that the deficit also may be associated with ventral parietal (TPJ) function (e.g., Friedrich et al., 1998). And recent work with spatial neglect patients indicates that attentional disengagement deficit may be due to a breakdown in functional connectivity between ventral (TPJ) and dorsal (IPS) parietal areas (He et al., 2007). In other words, given this linkage, damage to *either* area may cause an attentional disengagement deficit. Other studies showed that the deficit is more severe with right parietal lesions than with left parietal lesions (Morrow & Ratcliff, 1988). In addition, when normal subjects performed a similar task during event-related fMRI recording, there was enhanced TPJ activation on invalid-cue trials, as would be expected if the attentional disengagement occurred and was mediated by this brain area (Corbetta et al., 2000). These findings are consistent with the proposal that the TPJ may play a critical role in reorienting attentional focus toward visual stimuli appearing at unattended locations.

Frontoparietal Orienting Network. There is growing consensus among attention researchers (particularly those involved in human neuroimaging) that frontal and parietal cortical areas work in tandem to mediate shifts of attention from one location to another. This idea is nicely summarized by Corbetta and Shulman (2002). They proposed that the human brain has two partially segregated networks of brain areas that mediate attention orienting. The IPS and FEF (bilateral dorsal network) play a primary role in voluntary, goal-driven attention shifts. The TPJ and ventral areas of the frontal cortex (right-lateralized ventral network) play a primary role in reorienting attention to unattended, unexpected stimuli.

The dorsal network operates in both hemispheres and shows enhanced activation after the presentation of location cues indicating where attention is to be voluntarily shifted. As seen in Figure 7.23, input from the FEF is said to provide a control signal to the IPS which, in turn, directs processing in the visual cortex. This is consistent with results of a number of detection and discrimination experiments indicating that voluntary, goal-driven attentional processing occurs most consistently in dorsal areas of the frontal and parietal cortex (e.g., Culham et al., 1998; Nobre et al., 1997; Wojciulik & Kanwisher, 1999). The IPS and FEF also appear to be active during the performance of other attention-related tasks including visual search (Shulman et al., 2001), change detection (Beck et al., 2001; Huettel et al., 2001), multiple-object tracking (Beauchamp et al., 2001), and execution of both pro- and anti-saccades (Connolly et al., 2002; Corbetta et al., 1998). Several researchers have suggested that the dorsal network mediates "pure" voluntary attention control (Corbetta et al., 2000; Hopfinger et al., 2000; Liu et al., 2003; Serences et al., 2004; Vandenberghe et al., 2001; Yantis et al., 2002).

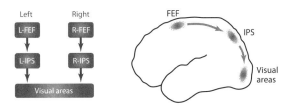

Figure 7.23 The dorsal component of the frontoparietal attention network proposed by Corbetta and Shulman (2002). Bilateral activity in the frontal eye fields (FEF) is said to mediate goal-driven processing by sending an attention control signal to the intraparietal sulci (IPS) in each hemisphere. This IPS activity, in turn, is said to direct attentional processing in the visual cortical areas. This proposal is supported by findings that the FEF and IPS show enhanced activation during the performance of tasks associated with voluntary attention control.

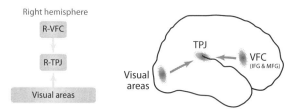

Figure 7.24 The ventral component of the frontoparietal attention network proposed by Corbetta and Shulman (2002). Visual cortical areas are said to signal the right temporoparietal junction (TPJ) about the presence of new stimuli, and right-lateralized activity in the ventral frontal cortex (VFC; particularly in the inferior [IFG] and middle [MFG] frontal gyri) is said to send signals to the right TPJ about the novelty of these stimuli. The TPJ may, in turn, determine their behavioral relevance to the task at hand. This proposal is supported by findings that the right TPJ and right VFC show enhanced activation during and after the detection of targets, and particularly when these targets appear at unattended and unexpected locations.

In contrast to the bilateral organization of the dorsal network, the ventral network is strongly lateralized to the right hemisphere. It is composed of the right TPJ and the right ventral frontal cortex (VFC; e.g., Arrington et al., 2000; Corbetta et al., 2000; Corbetta & Shulman, 2002). The critical regions of the TPJ in this network are centered on the right SMG and the right STG; and as seen in Figure 7.24, the critical regions of the VFC are centered on the inferior frontal gyrus (IFG) and middle frontal gyrus (MFG). This network shows enhanced activation after the detection of targets, and particularly when these targets appear at unattended and unexpected locations (e.g., when the subject must reorient attention from an invalidly cued location to the actual target location; e.g., Arrington et al., 2000; Corbetta et al., 2000). Unlike the dorsal network, the ventral network does not show enhanced activation after the presentation of cues that carry advance information about forthcoming stimuli. It has been suggested that the VFC may evaluate the novelty of stimuli and the TPJ may be more involved in detecting their behavioral relevance to the task at hand (Corbetta & Shulman, 2002).

Corbetta and Shulman (2002) also proposed that one role of the ventral network is to function in a bottom-up manner as a "circuit breaker" for the dorsal network. In particular, when the ventral network detects a task-relevant stimulus outside the current focus of processing, it may interrupt the ongoing activity of the dorsal network with a signal that enables attention to be disengaged and redirected to this new stimulus. As seen in Figure 7.25, the TPJ of the ventral network sends this signal to the IPS of the dorsal network. The dorsal network, on the other hand, may "filter" bottom-up interrupt signals from the ventral network to select which stimuli to attend to (and which to ignore). The dorsal network is also thought to contain

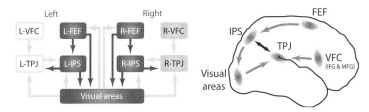

Figure 7.25 The frontoparietal attention network proposed by Corbetta and Shulman (2002). They suggested that if the right-lateralized ventral (TPJ–VFC) network detects a task-relevant stimulus that is outside the current focus of the goal-driven attentional processing being carried out by the dorsal (IPS–FEF) network, the ventral network may interrupt the dorsal network in order to direct attention to the new stimulus. In this sense, the ventral network may function as a "circuit breaker" for the dorsal network. They also suggested that the dorsal network may "filter" stimulus-driven signals it receives from the ventral network in order to determine which stimuli to attend to and which stimuli to ignore (behavioral valence). The critical information exchange between the ventral and dorsal networks occurs via the TPJ and IPS.

higher resolution maps of space than does the ventral network. Thus, while the ventral network may be sensitive to salient new stimuli and may play a role in the initiation of stimulus-driven attention shifts toward them, the dorsal network may be required to precisely locate these stimuli. Again, as seen in Figure 7.25, the exchange of inputs between the networks is said to occur between the right TPJ and right IPS (and perhaps the PFC; see Fox et al., 2006, p. 10050).

The suggestion that the dorsal network mediates voluntary attention control appears to extend to eye movements as well. In one fMRI study, subjects made goal-driven, voluntary saccades to symbolically cued locations (indicated by arrow cues) and more "reflexive" saccades to locations of abrupt-onset stimuli (Mort et al., 2003). Voluntary saccades were associated with greater IPS and FEF activation than were reflexive saccades. And whereas increased IPS and FEF activation associated with voluntary saccades was bilateral, increased activation associated with reflexive (stimulus-driven) saccades was more right-lateralized in a ventral parietal area called the angular gyrus (see Figure 7.21). Deactivation of the right angular gyrus with TMS also disrupts stimulus-driven attention shifts (Rushworth et al., 2001). These findings are a further indication that a bilateral dorsal network is involved in the voluntary control of orienting, and that right ventral parietal areas may mediate more reflexive orienting.

Other evidence that the dorsal parietal cortex is involved in goal-driven control of attention is that the SPL is activated (briefly) when attention is voluntarily shifted during the performance of rapid serial visual presentation (RSVP) tasks. To elaborate, in one event-related fMRI study, subjects attended to one of two continuous RSVP streams of letters in the left and right visual field (Yantis et al., 2002). Occasionally, a digit target appearing

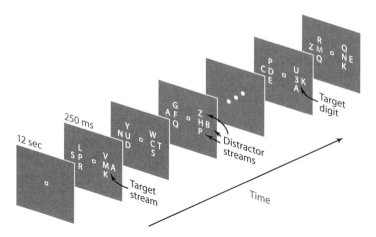

Figure 7.26 Depiction of the RSVP stimulus display used by Yantis et al. (2002). Subjects attended to the center (target) stream in either the left or right visual field in order to detect "hold" or "switch" targets. The target shown in this figure is the digit "3." Hold targets instructed subjects to continue attending to the current target stream. Switch targets instructed subjects to begin attending to the target stream in the opposite visual field. Event-related fMRI indicated that attending to the left visual stream produced enhanced activation in the right visual cortex, and vice versa. Also, when subjects switched their attention from one target stream to the other, there was transient activation of a region in the right superior parietal lobule (SPL) regardless of the direction of the switch. They concluded that transient SPL activation may be associated with control signals time-locked to voluntary attention shifts.

in the currently attended stream would instruct them to either maintain their attention on that stream (a "hold" target), or to shift attention to the other (currently ignored) stream (a "switch" target; see Figure 7.26). The fMRI data indicated enhanced activation in visual cortical regions when attention was shifted to the stream in the contralateral visual field. In addition, they indicated a transient activation in the SPL (particularly in the right hemisphere) whenever attention was shifted between locations, regardless of the direction of the shift. The experimenters concluded that this SPL activation is associated with a transient attention control signal that is time-locked to voluntary attention shifts evoked by interpreted cues. Yantis and colleagues also found similar transient SPL activation in other experiments in which attention was shifted between motion and color (Liu et al., 2003), between spatially superimposed objects (Serences et al., 2004), between spatial and nonspatial tasks (Shomstein & Yantis, 2006), and (as discussed in chapter 8) between sensory modalities (Shomstein & Yantis, 2004). This is a further indication that the dorsal parietal cortex plays a role in goal-driven control of attention.

Reports of a right-lateralized ventral attention network are consistent with the proposal that there is a hemispheric asymmetry associated

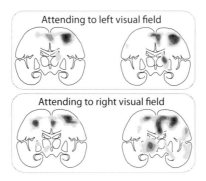

Figure 7.27 An approximate depiction of Corbetta et al.'s (1993) PET results indicating that when subjects attended to stimuli in their left visual field, enhanced parietal activation was strongly right-lateralized. On the other hand, when they attended to stimuli in their right visual field, enhanced parietal activation was more bilateral. This is consistent with the idea that there is a right hemisphere dominance for attention control.

with the control of attention. Some researchers have suggested that the right hemisphere appears to be dominant for spatial attention and the maintenance of spatial representations (e.g., Weintraub & Mesulam, 1987). This dominance view holds that the right hemisphere has neural mechanisms for attending to both visual fields whereas the left hemisphere has mechanisms for attending primarily to the right visual field. This is supported by the results of a PET experiment in which asymmetric activation was found when attention was shifted (Corbetta et al., 1993; Figure 7.27). It is also consistent with the results of studies indicating that there is a right hemisphere dominance for spatial memory (e.g., Jonides et al., 1993; Pigott & Milner, 1994; Smith et al., 1996; Smith & Milner, 1981, 1984). In addition, the right dominance proposal is consistent with the finding that spatial neglect is more pronounced after right hemisphere damage than after left hemisphere damage (e.g., Weintraub & Mesulam, 1987). Neglect is a complex syndrome characterized by a failure to attend to, look at, and respond to stimuli located on the contralesional side of space or of the body (e.g., Halligan & Marshall, 1994; Mesulam, 1999). Instead, neglect patients appear to be forcefully attracted to stimuli on their ipsilesional side, as if attention was "stickier" on this side of space. In over 90% of cases, neglect is left-sided. As seen in Figure 7.28, some believe that the predominance of left-side neglect is due to a right hemisphere dominance of attention control; perhaps because the right hemisphere may play a larger role in arousal and sustaining overall attention (e.g., Cohen et al., 1988).

Another idea is that the predominance of left-side spatial neglect is caused by a dynamic hemispheric imbalance. Corbetta et al. (2005) proposed that such an imbalance may be due to dysfunction of the frontoparietal network.

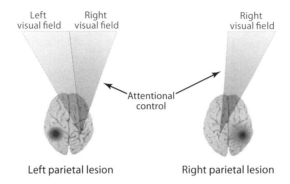

Figure 7.28 One account of the predominance of left-side spatial neglect is that while the right parietal cortex mediates attentional processing of both the left and right visual fields, the left parietal cortex mediates attentional processing of only the right field. Proponents of this view argue that left parietal damage may not disrupt attentional processing of the right visual field because the right parietal function is still intact and can compensate. As seen in the figure, however, right parietal damage is said to result in disrupted attentional processing of the left visual field because the intact left parietal cortex cannot compensate and is able to mediate this processing only for the right field.

Although several brain regions are involved in spatial neglect (see Figure 7.29), the most frequently reported is the right TPJ (e.g., Vallar & Perani, 1987). According to Corbetta et al. (2005), frontoparietal network dysfunction could produce neglect, in part, because a stroke in the ventral cortex (either frontal or parietal) should interfere with attentional reorienting. In addition, if the ventral (TPJ) portion of the network plays a "circuit breaking" role with regard to target detection, then damage to this right-lateralized component

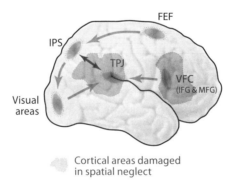

Figure 7.29 Corbetta et al. (2005) noted that spatial neglect is most frequently the result of damage to the right-lateralized ventral areas (TPJ and VFC) that are part of their proposed frontoparietal attention network. They suggested, on this basis, that attention deficits associated with spatial neglect may be due to network dysfunction. More specfically, damage to the right TPJ and/or right VFC could cause a relative deactivation of the right dorsal parietal cortex (IPS). The resulting hemispheric imbalance of dorsal parietal activation could produce the rightward spatial bias characteristic of neglect.

should result in a relative deactivation of the ipsilateral (right) dorsal parietal cortex. They suggest that this would, in turn, lead to a hemispheric imbalance that could produce a rightward spatial bias in visual processing characteristic of neglect. More specifically, the resulting dynamic imbalance would be manifested as a relative hyperactivation of the dorsal parietal cortex on the left and a relative deactivation on the right (see also, He et al., 2007). This idea is supported by a finding that when TMS is applied to the left IPS of neglect patients (with the goal of reducing its hyperactivation), neglect is attenuated (Brighina et al., 2003).

Recall that Yantis and colleagues found transient activation in the right SPL when subjects in their studies switched attention from one RSVP stream to another (Figure 7.26). They concluded that this activation may be associated with an attention control signal. A similar study, however, indicated that perhaps not all forms of attention control associated with this transient activation of the SPL are mediated predominantly by the right hemisphere. That is, performance of an RSVP task that required subjects to switch attention within or between objects led to enhanced left parietal (SPL) activity (as indicated by fMRI) for within-object attention shifts (Shomstein & Behrmann, 2006). Thus, while the right hemisphere may dominate control of space-based attention, the left hemisphere may play a critical role in object-based attention.

Integrating Cortical and Subcortical Networks. Earlier in the book, we described Posner et al.'s (1988) proposal that shifts of attention are mediated by a functional network of brain areas that includes the posterior parietal cortex, the superior colliculus, and the pulvinar (see chapter 3). They suggested (as in Figure 7.30) that the parietal cortex mediates attentional disengagement, the superior colliculus is involved in shifting the attentional focal point to a new location, and the pulvinar plays a role in focusing/engaging attention on the object of interest at the attention shift destination (see also Figures 3.4 and 3.5). This general framework has stood the test

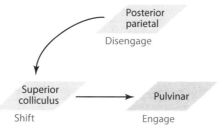

Figure 7.30 Posner et al. (1988) proposed that the brain areas involved in attentional disengagement, attention shifting, and attentional re-engagement are the posterior parietal cortex, superior colliculus, and pulvinar respectively.

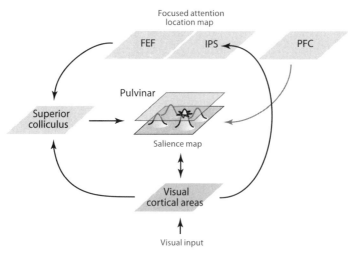

Figure 7.31 A simplified depiction of Shipp's (2004) model of attention shifting. The key to the model is a salience map in the pulvinar that is involved in coordinating stimulus-driven and goal-driven inputs from the superior colliculus, visual cortical areas, and frontoparietal areas in order to direct the attentional focal point.

of time, and has been expanded by several theorists. LaBerge (1995b), for example, proposed that information about locations to be attended to is relayed to visual cortical areas through the pulvinar by a frontoparietal attention control network. Shipp's (2004) model also incorporates extensive interactions between the visual areas and the pulvinar. Figure 7.31 is a simplified version of the Shipp model (with the addition of LaBergian activity distributions). Note that it also includes goal-driven control by the PFC, and input from the visual areas to the frontoparietal network (IPS and FEF) about locations of salient stimuli.

In Shipp's model, a visually topographic map in the ventral pulvinar is said to pool spatial information from several other brain areas to coordinate stimulus-driven and goal-driven attention shift signals. As mentioned earlier in the chapter, the pulvinar is particularly suited for this role because of its unique location between subcortical structures that mediate stimulus-driven shifts and cortical structures that mediate goal-driven shifts. A focal state of attention within the pulvinar map is said to emerge when all of the salience values are summed and neural activity peaks at the most salient location (we convey this with an activity distribution surpassing a criterion threshold). This results in a signal to the visual cortical areas that is relayed, in turn, to the frontoparietal components and used to determine the location of the attentional focal point. Frontoparietal signals about the attentional focal point's location are said to be relayed back to the pulvinar salience map via the superior colliculus. Thus, the pulvinar plays a key

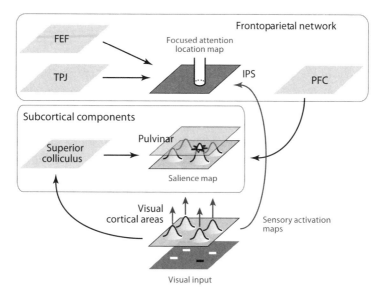

Figure 7.32 A speculative account of the physiological instantiation of the activity distribution model discussed in chapter 4 with reference to the multiple location cueing. For simplicity's sake, not all connections between brain areas are shown. Sensory activity distributions may be triggered in visual cortical areas, intermediate-level activity distributions may be triggered in a salience map in the ventral pulvinar as proposed by Shipp (2004), and the attentional focal point may be directed within a representation in the parietal cortex (IPS) through the actions of a frontoparietal network as proposed by Corbetta and Shulman (2002).

role in Shipp's model because it is said to combine stimulus-driven and goal-driven inputs, in Shipp's terms, within a single theater of salience computation (cf., Gottlieb, 2007).

The framework of Shipp's model can also be used as a guide when speculating about the physiological instantiation of the LaBergian activity distribution model discussed in chapter 4. A simplified version of this is depicted in Figure 7.32. The maps containing sensory activity distributions correspond to Shipp's maps in the visual cortical areas. The map containing intermediate-level activity distributions (one of which may exceed threshold and cause a channel of attention to open) may be in the ventral pulvinar (i.e., in the manner of a salience map as suggested by Shipp, 2004). The map within which a channel of attention is opened may be in IPS. Not all projections between brain areas are shown in Figure 7.32 for the sake of simplicity. And clearly this is not intended to be anything more than specu-lation about the physiology of the type of model we discussed in chapter 4. It does, however, integrate the frontoparietal attention network described by Corbetta and Shulman (2002) and the subcortical attentional components discussed earlier in this chapter.

Stimulus-Driven and Goal-Driven Attention Shifts

As mentioned previously, the superior colliculus appears to be involved in mediating stimulus-driven attention shifts, and higher level cortical areas are thought to be involved in mediating goal-driven attention shifts. In the section on subcortical attention mechanisms, we described a target-detection study performed by patients with PSP (associated with degeneration of superior colliculus function; Rafal et al., 1988). The main finding was that PSP impaired their capacity to shift attention. A similar study was conducted with parietal lesion patients (see Rafal, 1996, pp. 147–149). Figure 7.33 is a comparison of the results. While the PSP patients showed a greater performance impairment with direct location cueing (stimulus-driven shifts), the parietal patients showed a greater impairment with symbolic cueing (goal-driven shifts). In addition, the parietal patients showed a greater impairment on invalid-cue trials, which is consistent with claims about this region's involvement in reorienting. This is further evidence that the midbrain superior colliculus region is involved more in shifting attention in a stimulus-driven manner, and the parietal cortex plays a greater role in attentional disengagement and shifting attention in a goal-driven manner.

Different patterns of cortical activity are associated with stimulus-driven and goal-driven attention shifts, and cortical activation (particularly in parietal and frontal areas) appears to be significantly greater during goal-driven shifts (as indicated by event-related fMRI; Mayer et al., 2004). This is further evidence that goal-driven shifts are mediated to a greater degree by cortical mechanisms than are stimulus-driven shifts. And it is consistent with Corbetta et al.'s (2000) proposal that the dorsal (IPS-FEF) component of the frontoparietal network may be primarily responsible for voluntary, goal-driven shifts.

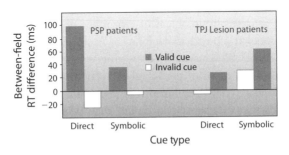

Figure 7.33 Results of experiments involving patients with progressive supranuclear palsy (PSP) and those with parietal lesions. The results are depicted as the difference in detection response times between the more affected and the more normal visual fields. A greater difference in a given condition indicates a greater impairment in orienting in that condition. Response time differences are shown for valid and invalid direct and symbolic location cueing. PSP patients showed greater impairment on valid-cue trials, and especially with direct location cues. Parietal patients showed greater impairment on invalid-cue trials, and especially with symbolic location cues.

Note that it can be challenging to use fMRI (a relatively slow imaging procedure) to study the physiological instantiation of stimulus-driven cue effects because they occur only when the delay between location cue and target is quite brief. More specifically, whereas the hemodynamic response measured by fMRI can take several seconds to reach its peak (e.g., Huettel et al., 2004), the effectiveness of the direct cues that trigger stimulus-driven shifts is maximal when the CTOA is just 100 ms, as seen in Figure 2.9B, and declines with further CTOA increases (e.g., Sheperd & Müller, 1989). A 100-ms delay between cue and target was used in the Mayer et al. (2004) experiment mentioned in the previous paragraph, but not in several other fMRI experiments conducted with the goal of studying stimulus-driven attention shifts. Hahn et al. (2006), for example, proposed that several brain areas are associated with stimulus-driven covert orienting on the basis of an experiment involving symbolic location cueing (which is associated with goal-driven rather than stimulus-driven shifts) and CTOAs ranging from 400 to 1300 ms (significantly longer than the critical 100-ms interval required for stimulus-driven shifts). These design parameters are not suitable for studying stimulus-driven attention shifts to cued locations (for a more detailed discussion of this issue, see chapter 2). Most of the experiments in the current fMRI literature on covert orienting involve long delays between location cue and target (e.g., CTOAs of 2000 ms or more are commonly used), presumably because fMRI is relatively slow. Unless experiments are designed so that attention shifts triggered by cues are indeed stimulus-driven and the analysis of related neural activation has sufficient temporal precision, the conclusions to be drawn from such studies are pertinent only to goal-driven processing.

While there is a good deal of supporting evidence for a frontoparietal network, little is known about the timing and sequence of activations of network components. This is due, in part, to the limited temporal precision of fMRI measures (which cannot be used to delineate the relative timing of activations), and the limited spatial precision of techniques like ERP and TMS that are more sensitive to timing (but cannot be used to pinpoint the locations of activations). An important part of future research may involve combining spatially and temporally precise measures to study the dynamics of attention networks. One recent attempt to do so involved a combination of event-related fMRI and ERP measures (Grent-'t-Jong & Woldorff, 2007). Subjects performed a symbolic-cueing task and, as seen in Figure 7.34, fMRI indicated that the frontal and parietal regions were activated. In addition, ERP measures indicated a prolonged response to cues that began initially in the frontal areas (400-ms latency) and then extended to the parietal areas (700-ms latency). FEF activation also appeared to precede IPS activation in a TMS study in which subjects shifted attention in a goal-driven manner to symbolically cued locations (Chambers & Mattingley,

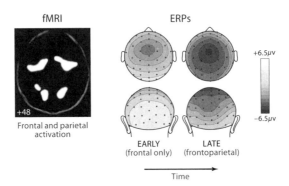

Figure 7.34 Approximation of fMRI and scalp voltage maps from Grent-'t-Jong and Woldorff's (2007) study. The results suggest that within the frontoparietal network (indicated by fMRI), the frontal areas were active earlier than the parietal areas (indicated by ERPs).

2005). These findings suggest that when attention shifts are goal-driven, the initial stages of frontoparietal network activation may involve the FEF without parietal activation, followed several hundred milliseconds later by joint activation of the FEF and IPS (which is consistent with Corbetta & Shulman's (2002) description of the dorsal network).

But questions about the temporal dynamics of the orienting network are far from answered. An earlier finding, for example, indicated that parietal activation may *precede* rather than follow frontal activation (Hopf & Mangun, 2000). The results of another study indicated that the activation sequence may depend on whether task performance involves goal-driven or stimulus-driven attentional processing (Buschman & Miller, 2007). Multiple electrodes simultaneously inserted into monkey FEF and LIP indicated that when visual search was effortful and required focused attention, frontal activation preceded parietal activation. When visual search involved targets that popped out, however, parietal activation preceded frontal activation. Visual search tasks may produce a different pattern of frontoparietal network activation than (simpler) location-cueing tasks, but this result is intriguing and suggests that the relative timings of activations depend on whether attention shifts are goal-driven or stimulus-driven.

Another as yet unanswered question about the cortical and subcortical networks subserving attention orienting is how they are functionally integrated in such a way that they can shift attention to various perceptual objects rapidly and accurately under the control of memory, emotion, and stimulus input. One tentative answer is that the functional integration is provided by local and long-distance synchronization of the activity in the various brain areas in particular frequency bands (e.g., Varela et al., 2001; Ward, 2003). In one study, goal-driven attention shifts to the location of visual targets resulted in coordinated, lateralized changes in synchronous oscillations in the alpha (8–14 Hz) and gamma (30–60 Hz) bands over occipital cortices, and in lateralized increases in long-distance synchronization between the occipital areas cued to respond to the target and other, widespread cortical areas (Doesburg et al., 2007c). These changes in synchronized activity were supposed to coordinate elements of the dorsolateral attention network to prepare the appropriate visual cortical areas for the target. Furthermore, attention appeared to be maintained at the appropriate location in visual space by prolonged synchronization between the appropriate cortical and parietal areas in the alpha band of frequencies (Doesburg & Ward, 2007; Doesburg et al., 2007b).

Premotor Theory Revisited

According to premotor theory, covert orienting is mediated by the motor system responsible for generating saccades, although the actual eye movements are withheld (Rizzolatti et al., 1987). In other words, attention shifts are said to be planned but not-executed saccades. As described in chapter 6, the original motivation for premotor theory was to account for the meridian effect. Subsequent research has raised questions about the extent to which the meridian effect supports premotor theory. For example, there are some questions about whether the effect occurs when direct cues are used (e.g., Reuter-Lorenz & Fendrich, 1992). Therefore, the meridian effect does not indicate a tight link between eye movements and stimulus-driven attention shifts. Moreover, the occurrence of the meridian effect following the presentation of auditory stimuli (Ferlazzo et al., 2002) and with hand movement responses (Eimer et al., 2005) indicates that the effect is not specifically tied to oculomotor preparation. Whereas the great degree of overlap between brain areas that appear to mediate both attention shifts and eye movements is consistent with premotor theory, it is not conclusive because the overlap is only partial and there are, for example, parietal and frontal cortical areas that are uniquely active when either attention shifts or saccades occur (e.g., Corbetta & Shulman, 1998, p. 1357). Moreover, as Corbetta et al. (1998, p. 768) pointed out, even when there is physiological overlap (indicated by neuroimaging), separate populations of neurons can be driven by different signals within the same cortical region which allows for the possibility that attention shift and saccade processes may be using entirely different neuronal mechanisms within the same area. Thus, the evidence supporting premotor theory is not as strong as it might at first appear.

There are other reasons for believing that the premotor theory is not well-supported. Microstimulation of monkey FEF neurons that was below the threshold required to evoke a saccade was found to induce shifts of attention to the locations corresponding to the stimulated neurons' receptive fields (Moore & Fallah, 2004). As mentioned previously, a similar effect of subthreshold microstimulation was found with superior colliculus neurons as well (Müller et al., 2005). This indicates that attention shifts are dissociable from saccadic eye movements, which is not consistent with the claim that attention shifts are planned-but-not-executed saccades. In another study in which monkeys were trained to make prosaccades or antisaccades depending on the orientation of a target, microstimulation of FEF neurons elicited saccades to different destinations than their accompanying attention shifts (Juan et al., 2004; see also Murthy et al., 2001; Sato & Schall, 2003; Thompson et al., 2005). To elaborate, on a given trial, microstimulation elicited a saccade in the prosaccade direction while attention was shifted in the antisaccade direction, or vice versa. This indicates that not only are attention shifts and saccades dissociable, but also their destinations need not be the same. This result is not consistent with premotor theory and also raises questions about the advance scout hypothesis discussed in chapter 6.

If attention shifts are unexecuted saccades, then presumably damage to areas that mediate attention shifts (e.g., monkey FEF and LIP) should also disrupt eye movements. A number of studies indicate, however, that while inactivation of these areas impaired ability to selectively attend to targets, it did not impair saccades (McPeek & Keller, 2004; Schiller & Tehovnik, 2005; Wardak et al., 2004). This is further evidence that the two types of orienting are dissociable. The human equivalent is the finding that neglect patients unable to make leftward attention shifts are still able to make leftward saccades (i.e., without a corresponding attention shift; Ladavas et al., 1997). These findings are also not consistent with the advance scout hypothesis that a shift of attention must precede a saccade to its destination as part of the saccade preparation process.

In the next chapter, we discuss shifts of attention involving other sensory modalities (auditory and tactile). It could be argued that our capacity for covert orienting to stimuli of modalities other than vision is not consistent with the claim that attention shifts are unexecuted saccades that involve the oculomotor centers. There is little evidence, for example, that oculomotor preparation would be needed to shift attention between, say, a location on our forearm and another on our back. Thus, a strong version of premotor theory such as that advocated by Rizzolatti et al. (1987) may be an overstatement of the relationship between attention shifts and eye movements.

Summary

Three important subcortical areas for mediating attention shifts are the RAS, superior colliculus, and pulvinar. The neurotransmitter systems of the RAS are involved in the innervation of structures that mediate covert orienting. The superior colliculus is centrally involved in stimulus localization and calibration of stimulus-driven attention shift vectors. The pulvinar shows enhanced activation during covert orienting, and particularly when the target of interest is surrounded by irrelevant, distractor items. This finding led to the proposal that the pulvinar may play a role in attentional filtering and engagement. The superior colliculus and pulvinar (particularly the ventral pulvinar region that contains spatial maps) may work in tandem to initiate stimulus-driven attention shifts.

The two cortical areas most involved in covert orienting are the parietal and frontal lobes. Monkey LIP and human IPS (thought to be homologous areas) appear to play an important role in voluntary, goal-driven attention shifts. The TPJ does not appear to be active when attention is shifted to a cued location (unlike the IPS), but does appear to be involved in the process of reorienting attention from an invalid-cue location to the actual target location. There is a growing consensus that the parietal and frontal areas work in tandem to mediate attention shifts. That is, a bilateral dorsal network that includes the IPS and FEF is said to mediate goal-driven shifts; and a right-lateralized ventral network that includes the TPJ and VFC areas is said to mediate reorienting. Corbetta and Shulman (2002) also proposed that the TPJ (ventral network) might function as a "circuit breaker" that interrupts processing of the IPS (dorsal network) when attention is to be disengaged and directed to a new stimulus. In addition, the SPL shows transient activation during goal-driven attention shifts and may be involved in planning and control. Thus, parietal and frontal cortical areas appear to play a primary role in the mediation of goal-driven attention shifts.

The thalamus appears to act as a gateway between peripheral sensory structures and their associated cortical areas. Its function is therefore not specific to the visual sensory modality. Some attention-orienting components of the parietal lobe also appear to be largely modality nonspecific (as would be expected, given its location at the intersection of the visual, auditory, and tactile cortices). In particular, monkey LIP (possible homologue of human IPS) shows enhanced activation regardless of whether attention is directed to visual or auditory stimuli; human IPS also responds in a modality nonspecific manner; and the transient activation of SPL (thought to be associated with control of goal-driven attention shifts) will occur even when attention is shifted from visual to auditory stimuli, or vice versa. This raises several questions regarding attention shifts to stimuli of other sensory modalities. For example, to what extent do the functional networks outlined in this chapter mediate shifts of attention to locations indicated by auditory cues? Does this mediation also occur in a crossmodal manner, such as when visual cues are used to indicate locations of auditory targets? We address these issues in the next chapter and discuss the physiology of an attention network that could mediate crossmodal covert orienting.

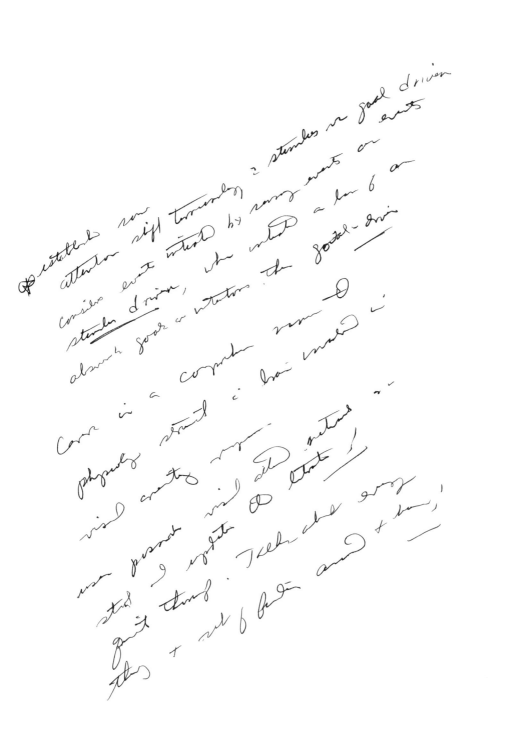

8

Crossmodal Attention Shifts

What we see may dominate our perceptual world, but objects are seldom only visual. Most environments in which we find ourselves are filled with sounds, smells, touches, and tastes as well as sights. Important environmental events such as the approach of a hungry lion generate information in several modalities. It could be slow visual movement, the sound of rustling tall grass, and perhaps a faint scent of musk; or fast visual movement, a loud roar, and the smell of rotting meat on the breath of the attacking (and too close!) cat.

As these aspects of the event are initially processed in separate sensory and perceptual systems, how do we perceive the big cat's attack in a unitary way as a single, terrifying event? Does attention bind together features of an environmental event across sensory systems (Figure 8.1) the way it is thought to within the visual system? If attention plays an important role in crossmodal integration, then studying it could help us to understand how events that influence one sensory modality can cause attention shifts that

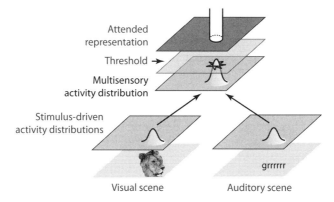

Figure 8.1 A representation of how attention could bind features of an auditory scene to features of a visual scene to create a unitary perceptual object.

affect processing of stimuli in other modalities. In particular, as human vision seems to dominate the other distance senses, we might expect that shifts of attention to locations of visual stimuli would affect the way stimuli in other sensory modalities (particularly hearing and touch) are processed and responded to (and vice versa). This is the essence of what is referred to as crossmodal attention shifting.

In the sections that follow, we (a) review some early studies of crossmodal attention shifting; (b) examine some of the work completed so far on crossmodal inhibition of return (IOR); and (c) discuss research on the neurophysiological basis of crossmodal attention shifting. A central theme of this chapter is whether there are qualitatively different types of modality-specific attention orienting (e.g., visual attention orienting, auditory attention orienting) or, instead, attention orienting is a supramodal process. Also, whereas our emphasis is on spatial orienting, we refer, in places, to other types of attention orienting. This is necessary because of the unique properties of the sensory systems. For example, attention can be oriented to sound frequency as well as to sound location. Studies of this ability may yield insight into properties of attention orienting specific to the auditory system, as well as to properties that are more general. And it is possible that the specifics of stimulus coding within a modality could interact with the ability of a stimulus to cause crossmodal attention shifts. When these matters are relevant we will discuss them, but we will maintain our emphasis on spatial orienting.

Lights, Sounds, and Touches Can Cause Attention Shifts

One early use of crossmodal location cueing was in a study of the storage capacity of very short-term (iconic) visual memory (Sperling, 1960; see chapter 2). As shown in Figure 2.1, subjects saw a briefly presented visual array of letters that was followed by a blank visual field. A short time after the offset of the letters (e.g., 50 ms), an auditory cue (low, medium, or high pitched tone) was presented. This cue indicated the location to which subjects were to direct their attention within the display (which continued to persist in visual memory). In other words, a location cue in one sensory modality (audition) was used to guide an attention shift to stimuli in another modality (vision). Typically, crossmodal attention shifting is studied with a variant of the covert orienting task (described in chapter 2) in which the cue comes before the target, and most experiments discussed in this chapter are based on this paradigm.

Early Research on Crossmodal Attention Shifting

Research has been conducted since the 1950s on listeners' ability to voluntarily orient their attention to auditory stimuli at particular spatial locations (e.g., Broadbent, 1958). Thus, it was surprising that one of the first direct examinations of crossmodal location cueing indicated that visual cues had no effect on the time required simply to detect sounds or touches (Posner et al., 1976). These cues did, however, facilitate response times for sounds and touches when the task involved discrimination rather than detection. Posner (1978, p. 210) suggested that the discrepancy between the detection and discrimination task results might reflect fundamental differences in the way attention mechanisms are activated in the different sensory modalities. We wonder, instead, if crossmodal location cueing is more likely to have an effect when target stimuli must be localized in space for a response to occur (as is the case for discrimination tasks but not necessarily for detection tasks). This requirement may not have been met by the simple reaction-time tasks, but was probably met by the discrimination tasks in Posner et al.'s (1976) pioneering study.

Since Posner et al. (1976) conducted this research, it has become apparent that studying stimulus-driven crossmodal shifts is more challenging than studying goal-driven shifts. There is little debate that shifts of goal-driven attention can be informed by any stimulus that carries information about where in space a particular target is likely to occur. Once a cue has been decoded into spatial information, the sensory modality in which the cue was delivered is no longer relevant to the initiation of a goal-driven attention shift. Location information alone is important. Thus, it is not surprising that a centrally presented visual symbolic cue (e.g., an arrow) pointing to a speaker can facilitate responses to target sounds occurring at the speaker location shortly after cue presentation (Figure 8.2).

Several studies have demonstrated reliable goal-driven cue effects in crossmodal cue-target experiments (e.g., Bedard et al., 1993; Buchtel & Butter,

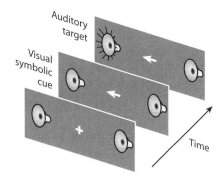

Figure 8.2 Example of an experimental trial involving the presentation of a symbolic visual cue and a peripheral auditory target.

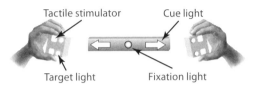

Tactile stimulator   Cue light

Target light   Fixation light

Figure 8.3 Depiction of the stimulus-response apparatus in Spence et al.'s (2000b) experiment. Goal-driven attention shifts were initiated by symbolic visual cues (arrows) to locations of expected tactile targets (produced by stimulators in left and right hands). On noncrossmodal trials, visual cues also preceded visual targets (lights in each hand-held box).

1988; Butter et al., 1989; Scharf et al., 1987; Spence & Driver, 1996; Spence et al., 1998, 2000b; for reviews, see Spence & McDonald, 2004; Spence et al., 2004). Figure 8.3 shows the apparatus used in one study involving symbolic visual cues (central arrows) and tactile targets (stimulators held in left and right hands; Spence et al., 2000b). It also appears that crossmodal attentional processing can be object-based as well as location-based (Turatto et al., 2005; see chapter 5 for a description of object- and location-based attention). And it is now apparent that goal-driven crossmodal attention shifts occur with each of the possible visual, auditory, and touch cue-target pairings.

Determining whether stimulus-driven attention shifts occur in a crossmodal fashion was initially more difficult. One early attempt indicated that while uninformative auditory direct cues facilitated detection-response times to visual targets, visual direct cues did not do the same for auditory targets (Klein et al., 1987). This finding was partially replicated in a later study involving patients with right-hemisphere parietal lesions (Farah et al., 1989). Note, however, that effects of auditory cues were reported only for targets in the left visual field, which is the one that was served by the patients' lesioned right parietal lobe. Moreover, while a facilitative effect of location cueing was found with cue-target onset asynchronies (CTOAs) as short as 0 ms in one of these experiments (Klein et al., 1987), it was also found for CTOAs as long as 1000 ms in the other experiment (Farah et al., 1989). Both are outside the range of CTOAs in which stimulus-driven shifts are thought to occur (50–200 ms), casting doubt on whether these researchers were actually studying purely stimulus-driven effects.

Perhaps the first systematic study of the stimulus-driven effects of cross-modal cue-target presentation was conducted using a target-localization task (Ward, 1994). This has proven to be a more appropriate way to study these effects than using simple reaction-time tasks. The stimulus setup in this study, similar to that used by most previous researchers, is shown in

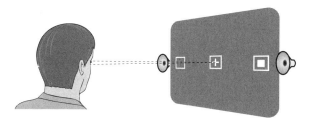

Figure 8.4 Stimulus display like that used in Ward's (1994) study. Sounds from one of the speakers were localized at or near the closest peripheral box, and simultaneous sounds from both speakers were localized at the central box.

Figure 8.4. In one experiment, subjects had to indicate with a button press whether a target sound came from the left or right speaker. In another experiment, subjects had to indicate whether a visual target appeared in the left or right marker box. Targets were preceded by either a visual cue (a flash of one of the marker boxes), an auditory cue (a tone presented from one of the speakers), both, or neither. One of the main findings was that, at a CTOA of 100 ms, visual cues facilitated responses to both visual and auditory targets whereas auditory cues facilitated responses only to auditory targets. Thus, along with within-modality visual and auditory cue effects, stimulus-driven crossmodal cue effects occurred in this study, but only in one direction.

Another pair of studies (Spence & Driver, 1994, 1997) yielded results exactly opposite to those of Ward's (1994) study, and led to some confusion about the nature of crossmodal stimulus-driven cueing effects. As seen in Figure 8.5, visual and auditory targets in one of these studies appeared at one of four possible locations (Spence & Driver, 1994). Visual cues and targets were flashes of light-emitting diodes (LEDs) positioned on the fronts of the speakers. Auditory cues were pure tones played from only the middle speaker on each side, whereas auditory targets were bursts of white noise

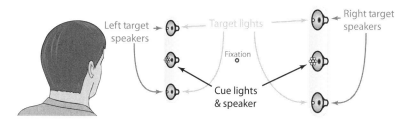

Figure 8.5 Stimulus display like that used by Spence and Driver (1994) to implement the orthogonal cueing paradigm. Auditory or visual cues occurred at either the left or right middle location. Auditory or visual targets occurred at either the top or bottom location on either the cued or uncued side. Fixation was at the central light.

presented from one of the four speakers above or below the middle speakers. In the first experiment, an auditory cue was presented on either the left or right side of the display. Following this, either an auditory or visual target appeared at the top or bottom location on the cued side (a valid cue trial) or on the uncued side (an invalid-cue trial). Subjects had to indicate by a button press whether the target was above or below the horizontal meridian (see Figure 8.6). In other experiments, all cues were visual. The net effect of this procedure was that while both cues and targets varied in spatial location, the dimension of cue variation (horizontal) was orthogonal to that on which the targets had to be discriminated (vertical). To restate, when performing this *orthogonal cueing task*, the elevation discriminations (above–below) of the targets were spatially orthogonal to the azimuthal (left–right) variation of the cues. This procedure eliminated response biases like the Simon effect (e.g., Simon et al., 1970) that result from cues and targets varying on the same spatial dimension.

It was found that auditory cues facilitated both auditory and visual elevation judgments, whereas visual cues facilitated only visual elevation judgments and not auditory ones. On the basis of these results, the experimenters claimed that visual stimuli are unable to trigger stimulus-driven shifts of attention in auditory space. They accounted for this with the suggestion that there may be a "missing link" in the physiology of crossmodal processing; in particular, in the operation of the superior colliculus. Because of this hypothesized missing link, it was implied that there is more than one type of attention (i.e., each sensory modality was said to have its own attention subsystem).

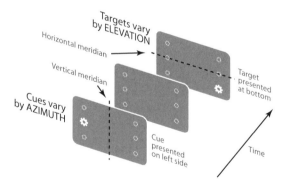

Figure 8.6 Example of the orthogonal cueing paradigm used by Spence and Driver (1994). On this trial, a cue is presented to the left of the vertical meridian and then, after a brief delay, a target is presented on the opposite side of the display. Subjects must state whether the target is above or below the horizontal meridian. Thus, the spatial position of the cue varies in terms of azimuth (left–right) whereas the target response varies in terms of elevation (top–bottom).

One possible reason why the results of Ward's (1994) study and Spence and Driver's (1994, 1997) studies differed is that subjects performed different tasks. More specifically, in Spence and Driver's study, visual cues and auditory targets varied on orthogonal spatial dimensions. This difference is important because the physiological mechanisms that mediate auditory spatial localization are different from those that mediate visual localization. Auditory localization is subserved by separate mechanisms for azimuth and elevation. Visual localization, on the other hand, preserves both dimensions in a common cortical map. Figure 8.7 shows how performance of an elevation discrimination task involving an auditory target would not be facilitated by a visual location cue that varied as a function of azimuth because visual azimuth information would not project to the auditory elevation mechanism. On the other hand, auditory azimuth cues would facilitate elevation responses to visual targets because auditory azimuth information would project to the visual mechanism that codes azimuth and elevation in a common map. This difference in the physiology of spatial localization could mean that visual location cues can facilitate responses to auditory targets, but only if these targets vary in the same dimension (azimuth or elevation) as the cues that precede them.

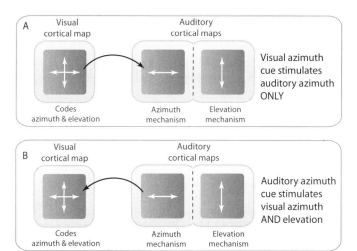

Figure 8.7 Whereas the visual system encodes azimuth and elevation in the same representation, the auditory system encodes them with separate mechanisms. For this reason, when the orthogonal cueing paradigm is used, a visual azimuth cue may have no effect on judgments about the elevation of auditory targets. An auditory azimuth cue, on the other hand, may affect judgments about the elevation of visual targets because both azimuth and elevation are encoded by the same visual mechanism. This could explain why Spence and Driver (1994, 1997) found no effect of visual orthogonal cueing on auditory targets, but a significant effect of auditory orthogonal cueing on visual targets.

A series of experiments was conducted to test this idea (Prime et al., 2006). A cue-target display like that shown in Figure 8.5 was used, and there were two types of tasks: one was the orthogonal cueing task and the other an *implicit spatial discrimination* task. As seen in Figure 8.8, the latter involves responding to a target only when it appears at particular locations in the display, and not when it appears at other locations (see McDonald & Ward, 1999). Implicit spatial discrimination eliminates response biases while fulfilling the requirement that auditory cueing involve spatial localization. When orthogonal cueing was used, several manipulations did not yield a significant visual cue effect on auditory target responses. Among them were (a) presenting cues at all possible target locations on the cued side, (b) requiring a target azimuth discrimination before the elevation discrimination, and (c) rotating the entire stimulus display so that the cue varied in elevation and targets had to be discriminated horizontally (i.e., an azimuth response). In contrast, when implicit spatial discrimination was used with the same cue-target display, large and reliable visual cue effects on auditory target responses occurred. Thus, in this study at least, it was the *orthogonal variation* of visual cues and auditory targets that appeared to be responsible for the absence of visual cue effects on responses to auditory targets.

Another possible reason why visual cues sometimes do not facilitate responses to auditory targets is that whereas the spatial location of visual stimuli is, in general, available with high precision, there is a large zone of location

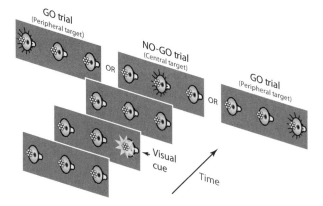

Figure 8.8 Implicit spatial discrimination task developed by McDonald and Ward (1999). Subjects maintain ocular fixation on the central location throughout each trial. Following presentation of a nonpredictive cue (visual in this example), a target appears at one of the three locations. Subjects respond when the target is at a peripheral location (GO trial), but not when the target is at the central location (NO–GO trial). Response is usually a discrimination (e.g., high vs. low sound frequency). The implicit spatial discrimination task does not cause response biases and, unlike the orthogonal cueing task, is not confounded with modality-specific location encoding physiology.

uncertainty associated with auditory stimuli, and particularly in the vertical dimension. It is therefore possible that, because of this difference, visual cues only facilitate responses to nearby auditory stimuli, whereas auditory cues, being less localizable, facilitate responses to stimuli across a wider range of locations (see Figure 8.9). In Ward's (1994) experiments, locations of auditory and visual cues and targets were relatively close together. In Spence and Driver's (1994) experiments, on the other hand, the cues were separated from the targets by about 15° vertically. Perhaps this cue-to-target distance was too large to allow the visual cues to affect far away auditory targets, but not too large to allow auditory cues to affect far away visual targets. And the relative effectiveness of these cues would also be exacerbated by the differences in the physiology of auditory and visual localization mechanisms mentioned above.

This "narrow zone" hypothesis was tested in another study that involved both orthogonal cueing and implicit spatial discrimination experiments (Prime et al., in press). All cues were visual and the cue-target display was similar to that depicted in Figure 8.5. In the orthogonal cueing experiment, all auditory targets appeared 14° from the cue. Subjects made elevation responses (i.e., above or below the horizontal meridian). As was the case in the Spence and Driver (1994, 1997) studies, visual cues did not facilitate auditory target responses. In the implicit spatial discrimination experiment, the same configuration of visual cues and auditory targets was used with the exception that targets also appeared at the same physical location as cues on some trials. In addition, subjects discriminated target intensity (rather

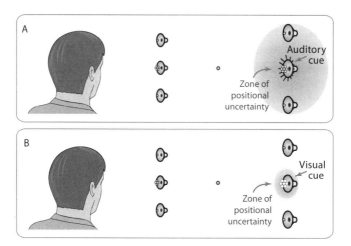

Figure 8.9 Positional uncertainty associated with auditory location cueing (A) is greater than with visual cueing (B) because the spatial locations of auditory stimuli are determined with far less precision (particularly in the vertical dimension). As a result, facilitative effects of visual cues on target responses may occur within a much smaller spatial zone than facilitative effects of auditory cues on target responses.

than elevation). In this experiment, there was a large visual cueing effect on responses to auditory targets if targets were presented at cued locations, but not if they were presented far from the cued locations. This finding supports the hypothesis that visual direct cues have a restricted "zone of influence" regardless of the experimental paradigm (orthogonal cueing or implicit spatial discrimination) in which they are used.

The results of a number of other experiments also showed that visual cues can facilitate responses to auditory targets (e.g., Ward, 1993; Ward et al., 1998). In one implicit spatial discrimination experiment, crossmodal audio-visual cue effects were studied in the simplest possible manner by varying all cues and targets only in terms of azimuth (McDonald & Ward, 2005). At a 100-ms CTOA (associated with stimulus-driven attention shifts), both auditory and visual cues facilitated responses to targets of the other modality. This was also the case in another study involving the implicit spatial discrimination task, but with a more complicated display that was similar to that of Spence and Driver's (1994, 1997) experiments (Ward et al., 2000). This is a further indication that the disparate results of Ward's (1994) study and Spence and Driver's (1994, 1997) studies are attributable, in part, to the nature of the cue and target environments that were used. Despite initial claims to the contrary, it is now clear that visual cues can facilitate responses to auditory targets (and vice versa). In one electrophysiological study, subjects performed a direct cueing task while event-related potentials (ERPs) were measured (McDonald et al., 2001a). As discussed in chapter 7, the initial negative peak of a visual ERP is typically larger for stimuli at attended locations than for those at unattended locations (see Figure 7.18). Similarly, sounds at attended locations typically elicit a larger negativity than those at unattended locations (e.g., Hillyard et al., 1973; Näätänen, 1992; Tata et al., 2001). The experimenters found that ERPs elicited by the auditory targets were more negative on valid visual cue trials than on invalid visual cue trials. The resulting negative difference wave (i.e., valid-cue ERP minus invalid-cue ERP) had an initial negative peak (Nd1) in the 120–150 ms latency range. The scalp voltage map depicted in Figure 8.10 indicates that Nd1 was largest over the parietal cortex. These results show unequivocally that visual cueing can facilitate auditory target responses, and they refute the suggestion that there is a missing (visual to auditory) link in the physiology of crossmodal processing.

It is also worth noting that, in addition to visual and auditory space, attention can also be shifted in auditory *frequency* space. In particular, sounds at an unexpected frequency are more difficult to detect than those at an expected frequency (e.g., Greenberg & Larkin, 1968; Tanner & Norman, 1954). Informative cues about which frequency to expect therefore improve sound detection (e.g., Johnson & Hafter, 1980; Scharf et al., 1987) and sound

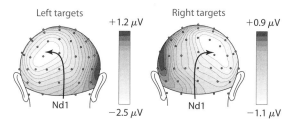

Figure 8.10 Approximation of event-related potential (ERP) data in McDonald et al.'s (2001a) experiment involving visual cueing of auditory targets. Topographic scalp voltage maps show the effects of attention at the peak of the NI component (120–150 ms latency range). Nd1 is the mean valid-cue minus invalid-cue difference wave, and it was largest over parietal areas.

intensity discrimination (Ward, 1997; Ward & Mori, 1996). But do effects of auditory frequency cues and location cues interact? Some researchers suggested that such an interaction occurs in an obligatory way (e.g., Mondor et al., 1998). Others have argued that an interaction between auditory frequency and location cues will occur only if both are relevant to the task being performed, and that separate processing of spatial and nonspatial aspects of auditory stimuli is the norm (e.g., McDonald & Ward, 1999). One way of conceptualizing this is that attention may be shifted somewhat independently within the "what" and "where" neural systems in audition (see e.g., Alain et al., 2001; Rauschecker & Tian, 2000; Tata & Ward, 2005). The question is intriguing, but more research is required before a definitive statement can be made about the relationship between location cueing and frequency cueing.

Supramodal or Separate-but-Linked Attention Mechanisms?

Are crossmodal attention shifts mediated by an attention mechanism within a common multisensory representation of space? If so, then the mechanism is supramodal. Figure 8.11 is a simplified account of how this could occur. A cue-triggered activity distribution within a representation associated with one sensory modality causes the formation of another activity distribution in a common, multisensory map of space around and on the body. This alone may be sufficient to cause a channel of attention to open at that location. If, a short time later (e.g., 100 ms), a subsequent target stimulus of another modality occurs at the corresponding location within its representation, this also contributes to the formation of an activity distribution in the multisensory representation. That target stimulus could undergo immediate attentive processing if the channel of attention is already open at that location. Or, if the attention channel is not yet open there, the target stimulus could increase the magnitude of the common activity distribution in the multisensory representation sufficiently to cause the attention channel to open at that location. In both cases, this would result in faster and more accurate processing

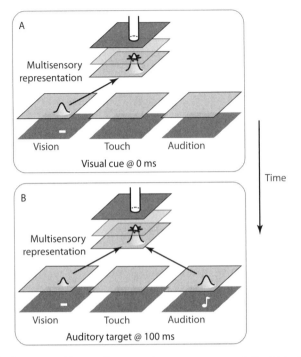

Figure 8.11 One view of how a direct cue in one sensory modality (vision) could cause a stimulus-driven shift of attention that would affect the response to a target occurring at that location 100 ms later in another modality (audition). This is a supramodal framework with a single, nonmodality-specific attentional focal point.

of the target stimulus in one modality than would be the case if the cue in the other modality had not occurred (e.g., McDonald et al., 2000).

It has also been suggested that crossmodal attention shifts are mediated instead by a system composed of separate attention mechanisms for each sensory modality that can, under some circumstances, affect each other (as depicted in Figure 8.12). The initial wide acceptance of Spence and Driver's (1997) claim that visual cues do not facilitate responses to auditory targets led many researchers to favor the separate mechanisms hypothesis and the idea that there are different (modality-specific) types of attention (e.g., Driver & Spence, 1998). More recently, however, there is little doubt that visual cues can affect processing of auditory targets, and that Spence and Driver's (1997) report to the contrary was an artifact of their orthogonal cueing task. As a result, the hypothesis that crossmodal attention shifts are mediated by separate mechanisms that could, but do not have to, be linked is no longer as preeminent.

At this time, there is little behavioral evidence that can be used to choose between the two hypotheses. Both make similar predictions about

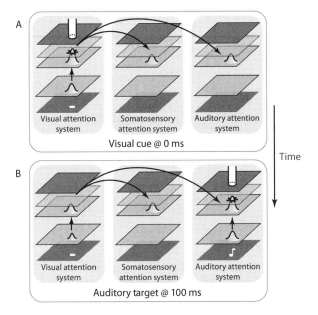

Figure 8.12 Simplified example of how separate-but-linked attention mechanisms could operate. A cue in one sensory system could, via a sensory link, cause activity distributions to arise in the spatial maps of other sensory systems, thereby facilitating responses to targets occurring in those systems.

crossmodal attention shifts. And the peculiarities of the different sensory systems in the way in which they map space (in particular, the auditory system's two independent mechanisms) make it difficult to design critical experiments. Moreover, failures to find cue effects when a particular paradigm is used do not necessarily disconfirm the existence of a supramodal mechanism, although they may indicate limits to the conditions under which it could operate. In a sense, the positions converge because a supramodal mechanism with significant limitations is not that much different from a set of separate mechanisms that can be linked, but only under certain circumstances. As evidence about the neural bases of crossmodal attention shifting accumulates, however, it may become possible to differentiate between the supramodal and the separate-but-linked hypotheses.

Crossmodal Inhibition of Return

In keeping with the explanatory framework we used in chapter 5, orienting to a particular cued location in space and then away from there, may result in a tag being allocated to that location. This tag may then inhibit reorienting of attention to that position (IOR). Figure 8.13 is an example of how a mechanism that utilizes tagging could mediate IOR when the cue and target stimuli are of different sensory modalities. A cue in one modality (vision

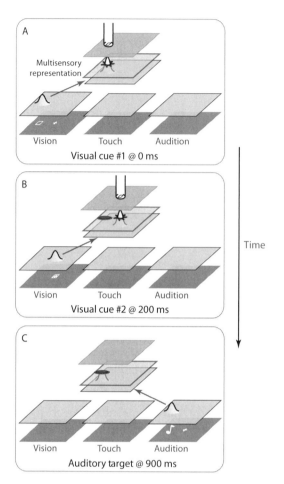

Figure 8.13 A representation of how crossmodal inhibition of return (IOR) could occur with spatial indexing.

in the figure) results in an inhibitory tag being allocated to its corresponding location in a multimodal spatial map. Then, if a target of a different modality (audition in the figure) should occur at that location, the tag within the multimodal spatial map will inhibit reorienting of attention there, and slow target-related responses.

It was initially difficult for researchers to obtain crossmodal IOR. Several, for example, failed to find it using discrimination tasks (e.g., Spence & Driver, 1997; Vroomen et al., 2001; Ward et al., 2000). This led to the inference that crossmodal IOR occurs only under some, possibly biased, circumstances. When detection tasks were used, it seemed possible that, rather than IOR occurring, subjects simply required more evidence of the target's presence at cued locations before responding (termed a criterion difference in the language of signal detection theory). Other researchers found that, even with a simple detection task involving auditory cues and visual targets, they still needed to provide subjects with an audio-visual reorienting event to obtain evidence of IOR (Spence & Driver, 1998). This is a point of concern because reorienting events are not required to obtain IOR with tasks involving simple detection of visual stimuli (e.g., Pratt & Fischer, 2002), although they do appear to be necessary for more complicated discrimination tasks (Prime et al., 2006). There have been, however, some reports of success in obtaining crossmodal IOR (e.g., Reuter-Lorenz et al., 1996; Spence & Driver, 1998; Spence et al., 2000a; Tassinari & Campara, 1996). And crossmodal IOR has been found in both detection and discrimination experiments using an implicit spatial discrimination task (McDonald & Ward, 2005). Crossmodal IOR also has been studied with a target–target paradigm. Unlike the cue-target sequence discussed in previous chapters, only targets are presented and subjects are required to respond to each one. This paradigm was invented to refute the idea that, with the typical cue-target presentation commonly used in visual experiments, IOR arises from the tendency to inhibit responding to the cue (Tassinari et al., 2002). A limitation of the target–target paradigm, however, is that when stimuli and/or responses are repeated, subjects may quickly repeat their previous response, and this "bypass strategy" may prevent IOR from occurring (e.g., Pratt & Abrams, 1999; Tanaka & Shimojo, 1996). It is important to control for use of this strategy. As shown in Figure 8.14, one study that did this involved an auditory task (sound frequency discrimination) and a visual task (color/orientation discrimination; Roggeveen et al., 2005). Trials on which stimulus or response repetition occurred were analyzed separately from those on which no such repetition occurred. Both

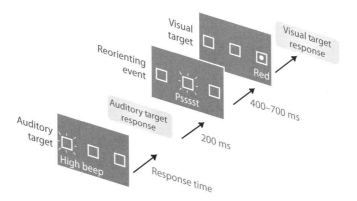

Figure 8.14 The paradigm used by Roggeveen et al. (2005) to establish crossmodal inhibition of return (IOR) in an audio-visual, target–target, discrimination task. The figure depicts an auditory-visual trial. A visual target follows the response to an auditory target and an audio-visual reorienting event.

within and across modalities, response facilitation occurred on all stimulus or response repetition trials, but strong IOR occurred on all no-repetition trials. This indicates that IOR can occur across auditory and visual modalities in a discrimination task when not "swamped" by other effects.

To our knowledge, there is currently no evidence that IOR occurs in discrimination tasks in a crossmodal fashion with visual-touch or auditory-touch pairs of modalities. But, given that IOR occurs with the more difficult auditory-visual pairing, we are confident that such evidence will be forthcoming. It appears that we can safely assume that crossmodal IOR is real and common and closely resembles visual IOR.

Multisensory Integration and Attention

Can activation of one sensory system enhance processing in another sensory system? One indication that this occurs is a finding that activation of the touch-system-enhanced responses to simultaneously appearing visual targets (Macaluso et al., 2000). A number of ideas have been proposed about the physiological instantiation of multisensory integration. One is that when activity in two sensory systems reach their maximum at the same time, certain neurons that respond to stimuli of both sensory modalities have a higher-than-normal level of activation that is superadditive (e.g., Stein & Meredith, 1993). These neurons have been discovered in several attention-related areas including the superior colliculus and the posterior parietal cortex. It is tempting, therefore, to suggest that multisensory integration may play a role in crossmodal attentional processing (cf., McDonald et al., 2001b).

One example of multisensory integration is the ventriloquist illusion. In a typical ventriloquism show, the ventriloquist will attempt to make the audience believe that his or her voice is emerging from a dummy's mouth as in Figure 8.15. This is clearly not the case, but the illusion is compelling because the locations of sounds are somewhat ambiguous. As mentioned previously, sound localization mechanisms are not nearly as accurate as visual localization mechanisms. As a result, even when the locations of simultaneous visual

Figure 8.15 A typical ventriloquism situation. The ventriloquist makes the dummy's mouth move while saying words without moving his own mouth.

and auditory stimuli differ, the visual stimulus can "capture" the auditory stimulus. Thus, when the ventriloquist illusion occurs, the speaker's voice is visually captured at the location of the dummy's moving mouth (rather than at the speaker's carefully unmoving mouth).

Before the modern era of digital surround sound, visual capture was used to make movie sound seem realistic. And even when there was only a single audio speaker behind the middle of the screen, the sound source always seemed to be at the location of whoever was talking. Visual capture of sounds can occur as long as the locations of the two stimuli are within about 30° of visual angle (e.g., Bertelson, 1999; Jack & Thurlow, 1973). Note that it is also possible for sounds to capture the location of visual stimuli if the latter are difficult to localize (e.g., a single luminous point in complete darkness; Radeau & Bertelson, 1976). In either case, capture of one modality by another is the result of multisensory integration.

Some have proposed that attention plays a central role in multisensory integration. The ventriloquist illusion, for example, was thought to be the result of the perceiver making a deliberate, conscious effort to compensate for poor auditory localization by matching it to the location of a visual stimulus that could reasonably be the sound source. Thurlow and Jack (1973, p. 1171) argued that when this occurred, "attentional variables appeared to be critical." More recently, however, the consensus is that attention is not required for the ventriloquist illusion. In particular, it occurs even when we are not consciously aware that there is a discrepancy between locations of the auditory and visual stimuli. Also, it can induce aftereffects that are not commonly associated with the manipulation of attention. Furthermore, even when observers keep their attention focused on a particular location in visual space, the location of sounds can be biased in the opposite direction by other synchronous visual stimuli (Bertelson et al., 2000, 2003). Thus, it seems that ventriloquism is a multisensory integration phenomenon that is mediated by a mechanism that pairs crossmodal stimuli preattentively (Bertelson, 1999).

Ventriloquism is not the only audio-visual conflict situation with possible relevance to attention. Usually when people talk, they move their mouths appropriately for the sounds they are generating. But what if a speaker's mouth movements do not coincide with the sounds they are making? For example, a listener might be asked to say what he or she hears when the lips of a speaker make movements that would usually produce a "bah" sound, but the sound is actually "gah." In this case, the typical listener would say they heard a "dah" sound, which is a compromise between the conflicting phonemes indicated by sound and sight (Figure 8.16). This is called the *McGurk effect* (McGurk & McDonald, 1976). Although visual information is not crucial to understanding speech (otherwise we would not understand the radio or someone talking out of sight in another room), it does help. For

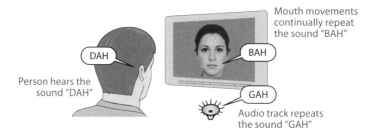

Figure 8.16 The McGurk effect occurs when the subject sees the lips of a speaker appear to make one sound while a different sound is presented. The sound that is heard is often a compromise between the conflicting phonemes presented visually and auditorily.

example, understanding what a conversational partner is saying at a noisy party is much easier if you can see their lips moving (Massaro, 1987). Again, we could ask whether this multisensory integration involves attention or, instead, takes place automatically or preattentively. In one study, auditory adaptation effects for McGurk stimuli depended on the sound that was presented ("gah" in the example above)—not on the sound that was heard ("dah") or the sound indicated by the lip movements ("bah"; Roberts & Summerfield, 1981). Although this indicates that the McGurk effect arises from a low-level auditory sensory process and is probably not influenced by attentional processing, more recent results indicate that crossmodal speech integration is subject to attentional demands (Alsius et al., 2005).

Whereas the ventriloquist illusion does not appear to be mediated by attentional processes, one study did demonstrate that it can influence selective attention (Driver, 1996). Visual lip-movement information was presented on a video monitor while subjects heard a pair of simultaneously presented audio streams of nonsense words (see Figure 8.17). The lip movements were congruent with one audio stream and incongruent with the other. Subjects were required to shadow one of the streams of words (repeat them as quickly as possible) while visually fixating on the video monitor. The shadowing task was close to impossible when just listening to the sounds because they were completely mixed together. It was also close to impossible when just looking at the monitor because the lip movements were not informative enough to allow subjects to distinguish words in the target stream from those in the distractor stream. In one experiment, however, the two audio streams either came from a speaker located below the monitor showing the lip movements (Figure 8.17A) or from another speaker located below a blank monitor some distance away from the active monitor (Figure 8.17B). The accuracy of subjects' performance was about 58% correct when sounds came from the speaker below the active video monitor, but about 77% correct when sounds came from the other speaker to one side of the active video monitor. Subjects

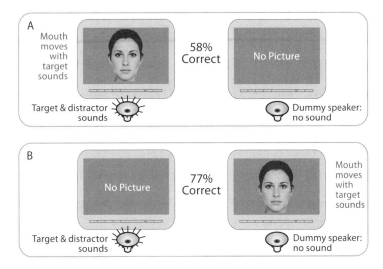

Figure 8.17 A situation in which the ventriloquist effect helps separate distractor sounds from target sounds. (A) The moving lips of the speaker, although aligned with the target sounds, do not help because both sets of sounds seem to come from the speaker below. (B) The moving lips of the speaker seen on the video monitor make the target sounds appear to come from the dummy speaker, separating them from the distractor sounds.

said they experienced a powerful ventriloquist effect in the latter situation. That is, target words seemed to come from the dummy speaker below the active monitor, and distractor words seemed to come from the active speaker below the inactive monitor. This indicates that the ventriloquist effect can enhance our ability to separate multiple audio streams.

The results of this study also indicate that attentional selection of auditory stimuli occurred after word streams were segregated by visual capture of the apparent source of the target stream. Subsequent experiments showed that the same manipulation could be used to pull initially spatially separated target and distractor streams closer together, thus impairing subjects' ability to shadow the target stream (Driver, 1996). Whereas attention mechanisms were not responsible for this effect (or any of the compelling multisensory integration effects described in this section), attentional operations (focusing, shifting) do appear to benefit from the operation of crossmodal integration mechanisms.

Neural Mechanisms of Crossmodal Attention Shifts

When discussing the physiological bases of crossmodal attention shifts, a distinction should be made between the *mechanisms* of attention shifting and the *consequences* of these shifts (cf., LaBerge, 1995a). The previous chapter on the physiology of covert orienting emphasized the mechanisms and it was implied that the consequences of attention shifts to visual stimuli would be reflected by increased activation in the visual cortex. In the case

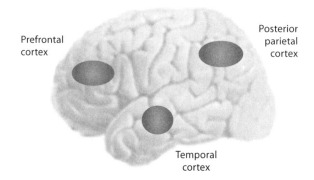

Figure 8.18 Some cortical areas of the brain where multimodal neurons are found.

of multimodal attention, however, the consequences of attention shifting are associated with different modality-specific cortical mechanisms (visual, auditory, and somatosensory). Within these systems, processing of attended perceptual objects appears to be enhanced either by suppressing neural activity associated with distractors and noise, or by enhancing neural activity associated with the attended object. It is also very likely that sensory modalities differ in the way in which such consequences of attention shifts are manifested.

Ignoring for the moment the relatively nonspatial modalities of taste and smell, what evidence is there for neural attention mechanisms that are common to the various sensory modalities? And what evidence is there for modality-specific, spatial processing systems in the human brain? Although these have not been easy questions to answer, it is now clear that neurons in several brain areas receive inputs from at least the three spatial sensory systems. These include the deep layers of the superior colliculus and the superior temporal sulcus at the confluence of the inferior parietal, temporal, and rostral occipital cortices (e.g., Stein & Meredith, 1993; see Figure 8.18), as well as several thalamic nuclei and even the sensory cortices themselves (e.g., Schroeder & Foxe, 2005). Some of these areas are candidate sites for a supramodal, stimulus-driven attention mechanism or for the loci of linkages between separate systems. There are also indications that separate, modality-specific spatial attention mechanisms appear to converge near, among other places, the temporoparietal junction (TPJ; e.g., Coren et al., 2004; see Figure 8.19). This suggests that some kind of multimodal spatial representation in this brain area could coordinate neural activity arising from spatial maps in the various sensory modalities. In this section, we examine recent research on the neurophysiology of crossmodal attention shifting, and on the existence of both common and modality-specific attention areas.

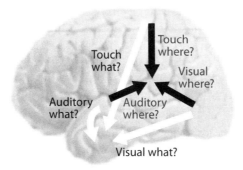

Figure 8.19 Convergence of "where" pathways in the superior temporal sulcus near the temporoparietal junction (TPJ) and "what" pathways in the ventral temporal lobe.

Goal-Driven Crossmodal Attention Shifts

There are a number of indications that goal-driven crossmodal attention shifts are mediated by a supramodal mechanism. One is that neural inputs from each of the sensory modalities are integrated by the prefrontal cortex (e.g., Fuster, 1997; Fuster et al., 2000; see Figure 8.20). This area is the center of goal-driven processing in the brain, and carries out activities related to planning, decision making, and goal-setting.

There is also considerable ERP and functional magnetic resonance imaging (fMRI) evidence for a supramodal goal-driven attention system. One study showed that, even when target modality varied randomly within a block of trials, attention-related ERP modulations were the same as those for visual-target-only blocks and for auditory-target-only blocks (Martín-Loeches et al., 1997). In other words, ERPs were not affected by mixing target modalities. Also of interest was that ERP effects began in the

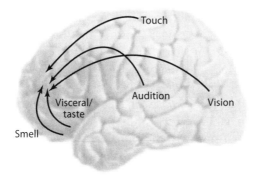

Figure 8.20 Convergence of sensory pathways in the prefrontal cortex (after Pico, 2002; cf., Fuster et al., 2000).

frontal cortex 240 ms after the target appeared, and continued 40 ms later in the parietal cortex. This is consistent with claims that the frontoparietal attention orienting network (discussed in chapter 7) is not restricted to the visual modality (e.g., Foxe & Simpson, 2005; Foxe et al., 2005). Other ERP studies also indicated that goal-driven attention shifts to targets of different modalities cause activation in similar brain areas. In one experiment, whereas some attentional modulations of ERPs occurred in modality-specific areas of the brain, others for visual and auditory targets occurred in common midline areas and were highly similar (Eimer & Schröger, 1998). In another experiment, modulations of early (<200 ms post target onset) ERPs were obtained when attended visual and auditory targets occurred at the same location but not when they occurred at different locations (Eimer, 1999). This implies that goal-driven attention cannot be directed simultaneously to different modality-specific locations (as might be predicted if there were separate attention systems). Anterior and posterior attention-directing ERP modulations have also been found with both visual and touch targets (Eimer et al., 2003). This was the case even when subjects could not see where the visual and touch targets would occur. In other words, the similar ERP modulations to both modalities did not arise because visual information was guiding the attention shifts. Thus, several findings involving goal-driven attention shifts favor the supramodal hypothesis.

As revealing as these ERP studies are, however, they do not precisely indicate *where* the relevant neural modulations arose. In the preceding discussion, it was assumed that neural activity occurred in brain areas close to the electroencephalogram (EEG) electrode locations. These inferences, however, are not always justified because EEG activity can travel for some distance from its origin to recording electrodes near other brain areas. For this reason (even though it is temporally less precise than EEG or magneto-encephalography [MEG]), fMRI has become the gold standard for localization of neural activity associated with perceptual and cognitive processes.

In one fMRI study, auditory symbolic cues (80% valid) were followed by either visual or touch targets (Macaluso et al., 2002). Regardless of target modality, the ventral frontal cortex (VFC) and the TPJ were more active on invalid-cue trials than on valid-cue trials. As discussed in chapter 7, these areas (part of the ventral frontoparietal network) also show enhanced activation on trials involving invalid *visual* cue-target pairings. The experimenters also found that the frontal eye field (FEF) regions of the superior frontal cortex and the intraparietal sulcus (IPS) were activated regardless of cue validity. These areas (part of the dorsal frontoparietal network) are also involved in goal-driven shifts of attention to *visual* stimuli. Association of crossmodal covert orienting (to touch and visual targets) with frontoparietal activation is another indication that it is mediated by supramodal attentional processing.

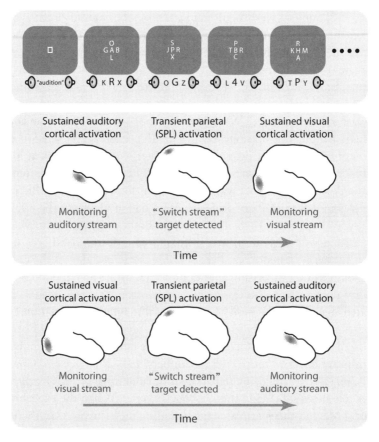

Figure 8.21 Rapid serial visual presentation (RSVP) audio-visual stimulus streams used by Shomstein and Yantis (2004) to study attention shifts between vision and audition. Subjects viewed a visual display containing five RSVP streams of letters appearing in the center of the computer screen. At the same time, they listened via headphones to three streams of letters spoken at the same rate as the visual streams. They monitored either the central visual stream or the central auditory stream for targets. Depending on the identity of these targets, subjects either continued to monitor the current stream, or switched to monitoring the stream of the other sensory modality. The visual cortex was more active when monitoring visual stimuli, the auditory cortex was more active when monitoring auditory stimuli, and the right superior parietal lobule (SPL) showed brief activation. Although the temporal dynamics of these activations cannot be precisely determined with functional magnetic resonance imaging (fMRI), future electrophysiological research may indicate that when this type of task is performed, SPL activation occurs at the time that the "switch stream" target is detected and prior to the attention switch between the two modalities (as conveyed in this figure).

In another fMRI study, simultaneous streams of visual and auditory stimuli were presented as in Figure 8.21 (Shomstein & Yantis, 2004). The rapid serial visual presentation (RSVP) stimulus displays were similar to those involving visual stimuli in studies by Yantis and colleagues discussed in chapter 7 (e.g., Liu et al., 2003; Serences et al., 2004; Yantis et al., 2002;

Figure 7.22). Subjects were required to attend to the centrally located stimuli in either the visual or auditory stream. When they detected a target within that stream, it would indicate whether they were to shift their attention to the stream of stimuli in the other modality or maintain their attention in the current stimulus stream. When subjects shifted their attention from visual to auditory stimuli, activity in the auditory cortex increased and activity in the visual cortex decreased. When they shifted their attention from auditory to visual stimuli, the opposite occurred. This reflects the sensory consequences of attention shifting. In addition, there was also a transient increase in activity in the superior parietal lobule (SPL). Although the temporal resolution of the fMRI data was not sufficient to indicate that SPL activity *preceded* goal-driven shifts of attention from one modality to the other, this may be what happened. Thus, like the results of the previous study (Macaluso et al., 2002), when attention was shifted, a common parietal area (in this case, SPL) was activated, regardless of the sensory modality of the targets.

It should not be surprising that not all regions of the parietal cortex are modality nonspecific. The results of one crossmodal study (visual–tactile) indicated that the application of transcranial magnetic stimulation (TMS) to a portion of the supramarginal gyrus (SMG) region of the inferior parietal lobule (see Figure 7.17) reduced the facilitative effects of visual cues but had no significant effect on touch cues (Chambers et al., 2004; see also Chambers et al., 2007). This indicates that the stimulated area in SMG may play a greater role in visual cueing than in touch cueing. When the experimenters applied TMS to other parietal areas including TPJ (involved in the ventral frontoparietal orienting network), however, there was no significant difference across modalities. In other words, this result does not appear to conflict with evidence that the IPS-FEF (dorsal) and TPJ-VFC (ventral) networks are modality nonspecific.

Figure 8.22 shows a version of the visual orienting network proposed by Corbetta and Shulman (2002; described in chapter 7) and also a modified network that incorporates auditory and somatosensory attentional processing. In the multimodal version of the network, the visual, auditory, and somatosensory cortices all send input to TPJ and all receive input from IPS. Also in the modified version, the FEFs are referred to more generally as the frontal orienting fields (FOF) to reflect their modality nonspecific role in guiding attention to auditory and tactile stimuli as well as to visual stimuli. Multimodal processing in homologous areas has been studied in other species. For example, the arcopallial gaze field (AGF) of the barn owl (considered to be homologous to FEF in primates) controls gaze direction and contains neurons that, when exposed to subthreshold microstimulation, show enhanced responses to auditory stimuli presented within their receptive fields (Cohen & Knudsen, 1999; Winkowski & Knudsen, 2006). This

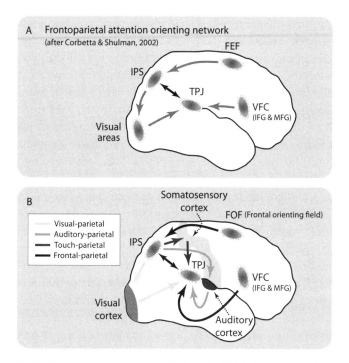

Figure 8.22 (A) Version of Corbetta and Shulman's (2002) frontoparietal attention network outlined in chapter 7. (B) A multimodal version of Corbetta and Shulman's frontoparietal orienting network. In addition to visual inputs, the temporoparietal junction (TPJ) also receives auditory and somatosensory inputs. The intraparietal sulcus (IPS) sends inputs not only to the visual areas, but also to the auditory and somatosensory cortex as well. The frontal eye field (FEF) is relabeled the frontal orienting field (FOF) to reflect its *multimodal* role in initiating attention shifts.

suggests that activation of an area homologous to human FEF can produce a spatial attention-like bias in auditory sensory processing. The modified version of the frontoparietal network in Figure 8.22 is also consistent with findings that the IPS is activated by attending to visual and tactile targets (Grefkes et al., 2002; Macaluso et al., 2003), and that right TPJ and VFC are activated by changes in visual, auditory, and tactile stimuli (Downar et al., 2000, 2002).

Stimulus-Driven Crossmodal Attention Shifts

Determining whether stimulus-driven crossmodal attention shifts are mediated by a supramodal mechanism has proven to be more difficult than doing so with goal-driven shifts. There are, however, close intersensory links between vision, audition, and touch. For example, prism goggles that change the spatial topography of stimuli in vision also affect auditory localization (Zwiers et al., 2003). This auditory recalibration, however, occurs only with azimuth and not elevation (even though prism goggles affect both dimensions of visual space). This shows that even when close intersensory links are demonstrated, modality-specific effects can still be expected because not all modalities encode space in the same manner. And it indicates the difficulty of choosing between a supramodal and a separate-but-linked attention systems model.

A popular approach to studying this issue has been to determine whether attention interacts with multisensory integration. In one ERP study, subjects performed an audio-visual integration task with a stimulus display similar to that in Figure 8.4 (Talsma et al., 2007). A very early component of the ERP to the audio-visual stimulus stream (P50) was enhanced by attending to both modalities, but not by attending to either modality alone. In another study with a similar setup, an enhanced gamma-band (30–50 Hz oscillations in the EEG) response was found around 50 ms after the presentation of *multimodal* audio-visual stimuli that subjects attended to (Senkowski et al., 2005; see also Doesburg et al., 2007a). It did not occur, however, after the presentation of attended unimodal auditory or visual stimuli (cf., Fries et al., 2001; Talsma & Woldorff, 2005). Thus, it seems that attending to two modalities simultaneously helps to integrate stimuli in those modalities into a multimodal perceptual object. It also seems that attention affects the integration of multimodal stimuli at very early processing stages (e.g., by increasing phase locking of responses in the gamma band).

This is consistent with the results of an fMRI study in which brain responses to visual stimuli were enhanced by a simultaneous touch delivered to the hand where the light was, relative to when no touch occurred (Macaluso et al., 2000). The enhancement occurred in the left lingual gyrus (a visual processing area in the occipital cortex). Of note is that when the light occurred simultaneously with a touch, the connections were said to be stronger between this brain area and the right SMG, and a couple of other parietal and occipital areas. The experimenters suggested that this was evidence that reciprocal connections between modality-specific and multimodal brain areas were responsible for stimulus-driven, crossmodal attention orienting effects.

Although this finding is intriguing and possibly reveals something about how the brain accomplishes stimulus-driven orienting across modalities, it is not definitive. One concern is that the response task involved simple detection. Subjects pressed a button with a finger on their left hand whenever they detected a visual stimulus (a flickering LED). On no-touch trials, responses were 9 ms faster for the left-side visual stimulus, presumably because of stimulus-response compatibility. On touch trials, this difference decreased to 2 ms and was not statistically reliable. This is clearly not strong evidence for attentional facilitation. Furthermore, because the visual and touch stimuli occurred simultaneously, it is possible that the enhancement of the brain response reflected the superadditive effect that many multimodal neurons display when stimulated by two or more of their sensitive modalities within a time frame that allows the stimulation to reach them at roughly the same time (e.g., Stein & Meredith, 1993). Moreover, there are many multimodal integration effects that do not involve attention directly (e.g., visual capture as described in an earlier section of the chapter). To demonstrate that attention is shifted independently of such effects, it would be necessary to have a time frame in which the observed effects could not easily arise from sensory interactions independently of attention shifts (McDonald et al., 2001b).

Other studies conducted to determine whether stimulus-driven crossmodal attention shifts are mediated by a supramodal mechanism showed that both auditory and visual (unpredictive) cues affect ERPs to targets of the opposite modality. In one study, an auditory cue effect on visual targets occurred around 200–300 ms post-target-onset, and was expressed in the occipital cortex (McDonald & Ward, 2000). In another experiment, as mentioned in the previous section (see Figure 8.10), a visual cue effect on auditory targets was expressed in the same time frame but in the auditory cortex (McDonald et al., 2001a; cf., Widmann & Schröger, 1999). There is also evidence that touch cues can affect ERPs to subsequent visual targets in a stimulus-driven manner (Kennett et al., 2001), and that visual temporal order judgments are affected by nonpredictive auditory cues (McDonald et al., 2005; see chapter 6 for a description of the temporal order judgment task). Each of these findings is consistent with the hypothesis that stimulus-driven crossmodal attention shifts are mediated by a supramodal mechanism.

It has been suggested on the basis of other data that, during the 100–300 ms post-target-onset interval, stimulus-driven attention shifts to visual stimuli can suppress the brain's response to auditory stimuli (Oray et al., 2002). One concern about the design of this experiment is that the locations of auditory and visual stimuli were never the same on a given trial. Thus, the inhibition of responses said to be caused by auditory suppression could have arisen instead from subjects shifting attention away from auditory stimuli when orienting toward visual stimuli.

Stimulus-driven attention shifts are also mediated, in part, by subcortical processing. As discussed in chapter 7, Shipp (2004) proposed a model of stimulus-driven shifts that involved collicular and thalamic mechanisms. In Figure 8.23, we modify this model to incorporate multimodal stimuli. More specifically, information from the various sensory systems (visual, auditory, tactile) all affect activation in the ventral pulvinar salience map. Coding within sensory systems, however, is modality specific. To elaborate, horizontal and vertical locations in the visual field are coded in a common two-dimensional map based on retinal location that is eventually referred to a gaze-centered reference frame. In audition, however, as we discussed

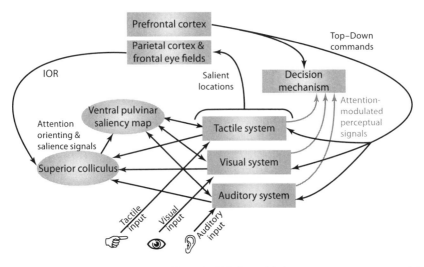

Figure 8.23 A modified version of Shipp's (2004) model that incorporates crossmodal attention shifting.

earlier, horizontal and vertical location are inferred via separate mechanisms (time or intensity disparities and spectral characteristics, respectively) and are referred to a head-centered reference frame (e.g., Ferlazzo et al., 2002). Tactile locations clearly refer only to body space, and are coded in dermatomes (large receptive fields in the somatosensory cortex). Under different conditions, these various maps will overlap or conflict, leading to complex expressions in different experimental paradigms (e.g., Zwierset al., 2003).

The framework outlined in Figure 8.23 could also be modified to conform with the separate-but-linked hypothesis. Note, however, that positing separate attention systems for each sensory modality requires linkages via pathways that are as yet unknown (although presumably they could take advantage of multimodal neurons in the sensory cortical areas; e.g., Schroeder & Foxe, 2005).

To recap, like the results of studies of attention shifts to visual stimuli, those of crossmodal shifts (e.g., Grefkes et al., 2002; Macaluso et al., 2002, 2003) indicate that this orienting is mediated by a multimodal frontoparietal network. Most of the support for this claim is based on the results of goal-driven attention shift experiments. Although there are fewer results from stimulus-driven experiments, they are also consistent with the multimodal frontoparietal network proposal, perhaps like that outlined in Figure 8.22.

Summary

There is now convincing behavioral evidence that crossmodal attention shifts can occur between all possible pairs of the visual, auditory, and tactile sensory modalities. In particular, goal-directed shifts of attention can be triggered by spatially predictive cues to targets in any of the modalities, completely analogous to how such shifts are triggered in vision. Like visual covert orienting, crossmodal attention shifts can also be object based or location based. Although researchers had some difficulty establishing it initially, it is also now clear that stimulus-driven shifts of attention can occur between all possible cue-target pairings of the three major spatial sensory systems. One reason why there was some early disagreement about research on stimulus-driven crossmodal shifts is the modality-specific properties of the space-encoding systems. For example, elevation and azimuth are encoded by different subsystems in audition, but in the same maps in vision and touch. Another finding (also initially difficult to establish) is that IOR occurs across modalities in the same way that it occurs in vision.

There are two competing hypotheses about the mechanisms that mediate crossmodal attention shifts. One is that a single multimodal type of attention is oriented within a supramodal network. Another is that different types of attention are oriented by modality-specific systems that are linked under some circumstances. It could be argued that most neurophysiological evidence accumulated to date indicates that a supramodal attention system is responsible for crossmodal shifts. This seems particularly true of goal-driven shifts. Note, however, that constraints are placed on the operation of a supramodal mechanism by modality-specific encoding (e.g., attention is shifted independently within the elevation- and azimuth-encoding auditory subsystems). This makes it difficult to differentiate between the two hypotheses without additional information about the neurophysiology of crossmodal attention.

The mechanisms that mediate goal-driven crossmodal shifts appear to be associated with frontal and parietal cortical areas, but the role of subcortical areas is less clear. Neuroimaging studies conducted to date have not implicated any of these of areas, and the EEG method cannot "see" activity in subcortical areas directly, so this remains an open question. Although less is known about the mechanisms that mediate stimulus-driven crossmodal shifts, there is some evidence that they are associated with the areas of the posterior parietal cortex that are involved in goal-driven shifts. Thus, it seems plausible that both goal-driven and stimulus-driven crossmodal attention shifts are mediated by a supramodal frontoparietal mechanism.

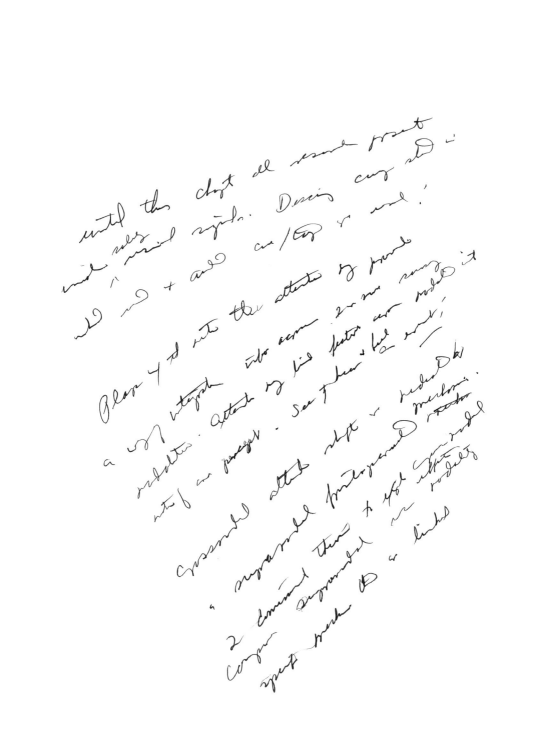

9

Epilogue

Helmholtz's 19th-century foundational demonstration that attention can be shifted independently of ocular gaze influenced, to a great degree, the contemporary study of attention shifts now known as covert orienting. Posner is credited with developing the location-cueing task best suited for studying it, and so many researchers have used a variant of this method that it is often referred to simply as the "Posner task." Its simplicity and flexibility preserve links with neuroscience research because it can be performed by animals and by brain-injured patients. The task has also been used to show that attention can be shifted crossmodally between all possible cue-target pairings of visual, auditory, and tactile stimuli.

The development and application of the Posner task confirmed early speculation about the nature of covert orienting (e.g., James, 1890) and contributed significantly to our understanding of attention control. It can be used to elicit stimulus-driven attention shifts in response to direct cues that produce their effect by virtue of being physically close to target locations. Or it can be used to elicit goal-driven attention shifts in response to symbolic cues that are meaningfully associated with a particular location and therefore must be interpreted by an observer to produce an effect.

Early use of the location-cueing task entrenched the spotlight as a metaphor for movement of the attentional focal point. After some debate about whether this movement is analog or discrete, it now seems clear that it can be both, depending on the task being performed. Speculation by 18th- and 19th-century thinkers about how the attentional focal point might vary in its spatial extent was also tested with variants of the location-cueing task. Several results were consistent with the idea that there is a reciprocal relationship between the spatial extent and the concentration of attention. In special cases, it also appears that attention can be simultaneously divided across discrete locations, particularly when performing feature-based tasks (e.g., dividing attention between regions on the basis of a unique feature like color). The evidence that attention can be divided in this way while performing space-based tasks involving location cueing, however, is equivocal.

The results of location-cueing experiments usually implicate some form of attentional processing of the target that is initiated by cue presentation. Less has been said about the potential contribution to location-cue effects of *sensory* processing initiated by cue presentation. The initial stages of all visual analysis, however, are necessarily sensory and encode, in at least a crude manner, the locations of new objects (including those of direct cues). The LaBergian activity distribution model (e.g., LaBerge, 1995a, 1998; LaBerge & Brown, 1989) holds that sensory analysis contributes to the direction of attention through the formation of neural activity distributions at object locations within a sensory representation of space. This model may provide clues about the relationship between sensory and attentional processing when covert orienting occurs while performing location-cueing tasks. A critical assumption is that neural activity triggered by a direct cue will persist for a short period of time. If it is still present when a target appears at its location, cue-triggered sensory activation can facilitate target detection if it combines with target-triggered activation. The result is a location-cueing effect that arises, in part, from sensory operations. The multiple simultaneous direct cueing task described in chapter 4 is particularly suited for distinguishing between sensory and attentional contributions to these effects.

Location-cueing tasks have also been used to study the relationship between attention shifts and eye movements. One hypothesis is that the two types of orienting are mediated by separate systems. A good deal of research, however, indicates that there is significant physiological overlap of attention shift and saccade mechanisms, which is not consistent with the idea that the systems are completely independent. Another hypothesis is that the two types of orienting are mediated by the same system (premotor theory). Recent physiological data, however, indicate that this claim may be overstated. An intermediate position is that attention shifts and saccades are not mediated by a common system, but they do share resources and computations at some stages of processing. There is also a general consensus that when attention is shifted to the same location to which a saccade is made, the attention shift will be completed first. Some researchers believe shifting attention to the planned saccade's destination is an integral part of saccade preparation (e.g., Deubel & Schneider, 1996; Kowler et al., 1995). Others believe that whereas attentions shifts precede eye movements to their destination, saccade preparation is functionally independent of attention (e.g., Kingstone & Klein, 1993; Klein & Taylor, 1994). In other words, attentional focus is not an advance scout for the oculomotor system, and may simply arrive at a common destination before ocular focus. This issue is controversial and perhaps will be resolved only as we learn more about the physiology of orienting.

The use of the location-cueing paradigm in conjunction with neuroimaging, single-cell recording, and other techniques has led to a better understanding of the functional network of brain areas that mediates attention orienting. The subcortical areas of this network (particularly the superior colliculus) play a primary role in the mediation of stimulus-driven attention shifts, and the cortical areas play a primary role in the mediation of goal-driven shifts. The latter appear to constitute a frontoparietal network. One of its components may be a bilateral dorsal (intraparietal sulcus-frontal eye field [IPS-FEF]) network associated with voluntary, goal-driven processes, and another may be a right-lateralized ventral (temporal parietal junction-ventral frontal cortex [TPJ-VFC]) network that is controlled in part by stimulus-driven inputs (Corbetta & Shulman, 2002). A salience map in the ventral pulvinar nucleus may be the site at which stimulus-driven and goal-driven inputs are coordinated when attention orienting occurs.

Recent neurophysiological work also indicates that frontoparietal areas are deeply involved in attention orienting regardless of the sensory modality of cue and target stimuli. This is *not* consistent with the proposal that each sensory system has its own unique attention orienting mechanism (see Figure 9.1). Instead, orienting mechanisms appear to be supramodal, but with special relationships with the individual sensory systems. For example, locations of visual stimuli are coded directly on the retina and mapped in several early cortical areas, whereas locations of auditory stimuli are inferred from temporal, intensity, or spectral cues, and possibly not mapped at all in the auditory cortex. One ramification of a supramodal orienting network is that the use of the term "visual attention" may be misleading. It is becoming clearer that many (if not most) of the brain areas that subserve

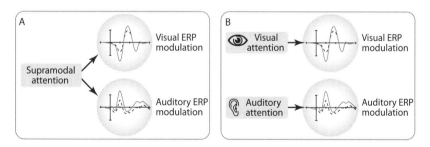

Figure 9.1 Two accounts of attentional modulation of ERP components elicited by visual and auditory stimuli. (A) The supramodal account holds that ERPs are modulated by a modality nonspecific type of attention that is allocated to all types of stimuli regardless of their sensory modality. (B) The modality-specific attention account holds that visual ERPs are modulated by a special "visual" attention and that auditory ERPs are modulated by a special "auditory" attention.

attention orienting to visual stimuli are involved in orienting to auditory and tactile stimuli as well (and perhaps even to odors). Moreover, the ability of stimuli in one modality to orient attention to targets in another modality, the ability of symbolic cues to orient attention to targets in any modality, and the similarities in the inferred mechanisms underlying these abilities, all indicate that attention orienting is very general, and not really a phenomenon of vision at all.

Highly Familiar Symbolic and Social Cues

In chapter 2, we mentioned that small but significant response-time benefits have been reported for targets appearing at locations indicated by uninformative symbolic (arrow) cues (e.g., Eimer, 1997; Shepard et al., 1986). This result has also been reported when the symbolic cue is a schematic face with eyes gazing laterally to the left or right to the cued location as in Figure 9.2 (e.g., Friesen & Kingstone, 1998). Symbolic cues like the faces in Figure 9.2 are often referred to as *gaze cues* because targets at gazed-at locations appear to be processed faster and more accurately than targets presented elsewhere. Similar results have been obtained with variations of this type of cue such as faces with a tongue extended laterally to the left or right (Downing et al., 2004). The discovery that unpredictive (e.g., Friesen & Kingstone, 1998) and low-validity (Driver et al., 1999) gaze cues still facilitate responses to targets led some researchers to conclude that gaze cue effects are reflexive (like direct cue effects).

This claim may be overstated in that there appear to be several differences between the processes mediating gaze cue effects and those mediating direct cue effects (we use the latter to exemplify reflexive effects). For example, gaze cue effects persist at longer cue-target onset asynchronies (CTOAs; e.g., up to 500 ms) than do direct cue effects (Friesen & Kingstone, 1998). Also, whereas direct cues can produce inhibition of return (IOR), gaze cues (like other types of symbolic cues) do not (Friesen & Kingstone, 1998). Moreover, IOR produced by a direct cue can co-occur with the facilitative effect of

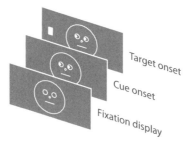

Figure 9.2 Stimulus display like those used by Friesen and Kingstone (1998) to cue locations with the direction of gaze of a schematic face.

gaze cueing, which is another indication that the mechanisms underlying the two effects are qualitatively different (Friesen & Kingstone, 2003). A study involving split-brain patients showed that unlike direct cue effects (which are associated with subcortical processes), gaze cue effects appear to be lateralized to one cortical hemisphere (Kingstone et al., 2000). Other evidence that gaze cue effects arise from cortical operations is the result of a study with a frontal-lobe damage patient whose initials are EVR (Vecera & Rizzo, 2004, 2006). Patients with damage to this area show difficulties using symbolic cues (e.g., arrows, words) to direct attention (Alivisatos & Milner, 1989; Koski et al., 1998). Although EVR's ability to shift attention in response to direct cues was intact, the ability to shift attention in response to symbolic cues, including gaze cues, was disrupted. This indicates that direct cue effects (known to be closely associated with subcortical superior collicular processes) are not dependent on frontal-lobe function, but that gaze cue effects do depend on this cortical area. The researchers concluded that gaze-cued attention shifts involve goal-driven processing rather than stimulus-driven processing. Another indication that gaze cue effects can be influenced in a goal-driven manner is the result of a study in which these effects only occurred if subjects *believed* that the cue stimulus was a face possessing eyes that gazed in a particular direction (Ristic & Kingstone, 2005). When subjects believed that the identical stimulus was an automobile, no cue effect occurred. In other words, gaze cueing in this experiment was cognitively penetrable (dependent on subjects' beliefs) rather than reflexive.

If gaze cue effects are not reflexive, then why are they rapid, like direct cue effects, and also produced by low-validity cues? One possibility suggested by Vecera and Rizzo (2006) is that although gaze cue effects are not reflexive, they may be very well-learned, or even overlearned to the point of automatization. Itier et al. (2007) pointed out that the human face is the most important social stimulus that we process, and its eyes bear a fundamental role in social cognition. Children develop the capacity to orient attention in the direction of another's eye gaze usually before the end of their first year, and presumably this behavior is so well-practiced that it is soon becomes automatic.

Note that whereas reflexive and automatic processes are both rapid, and automatic processes can have the appearance of being triggered reflexively, there are also critical differences between them. Unlike reflexive processes, for example, automatic processes are the product of learning and practice. Also, unlike reflexive processes, automatic processes tend to be task-dependent. For example, in one study, targets defined by a unique visual feature not shared with distractor objects were easy to find (i.e., they popped out); and the same was true for targets that were initially difficult to find but, with extensive practice, became easy to find (Treisman et al., 1992). In other words, once their processing was automatized, the latter popped out too.

The critical finding was that when the task was changed, unique-feature targets continued to pop out but automatized targets did not. That is, the pop-out effect for the latter was task dependent. Gaze cue effects have also been found to be task dependent (Itier et al., 2007), which indicates that they arise, in part, from learning.

There is also some physiological evidence that gaze cue effects arise from highly automatized processes. Several fMRI studies have shown that the extent and magnitude of task-relevant regional BOLD activation decreases as task performance becomes automatic with practice (e.g., Cheina & Schneider, 2005). When the performance of tasks involving symbolic arrow and gaze cues were compared in one fMRI study, there was significantly less BOLD activation for the gaze cues (Hietanen et al., 2006). This is consistent with the idea that these effects arise from automatized processes.

Rather than emphasizing the distinction between direct and symbolic cues, as has been done in most of the literature to date, it has been proposed that a new taxonomy should be adopted in which both direct and gaze cues are referred to as "deicitic" location cues (Gibson & Kingstone, 2006). This is motivated, in part, by the apparent reflexive nature of gaze cues that seems to be equivalent to that of direct cues. As argued here, however, these two types of cues are not equivalent in their reflexiveness nor in the extent to which they are mediated by stimulus-driven processing. Moreover, as discussed in chapter 7, recent research on the physiology of covert orienting has yielded many new findings about qualitative differences between subcortical and cortical attention processes that reinforce the stimulus-driven/goal-driven dichotomy when direct and symbolic cueing effects are compared. Thus, we believe that the direct versus symbolic cue distinction proposed by Posner and colleagues should be preserved.

If we can use someone else's direction of gaze to orient attention and facilitate our responses, is it also possible to use social cues to *inhibit* responses? Pairs of subjects in one experiment (Welsh et al., 2005) performed a finger-pointing task that involved rapid aiming movements to locations of target stimuli (illuminated buttons; see Figure 9.3). The critical aspect of the experiment was that subjects alternated responses to targets. It was found that even though an immediately previous response was made by one subject, it was able to produce IOR in the other subject. In other words, mere observation of another person's responses appears to be sufficient to produce IOR, and social cues can inhibit as well as facilitate responses. Perhaps this should not be surprising given that search-based tasks such as hunting, gathering, and predator evasion were likely carried out by groups of our ancestors in a manner that involved joint attention (Laughlin, 1968).

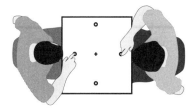

Figure 9.3 Depiction of the apparatus used in Welsh et al.'s (2005) study. A pair of subjects perform a finger-pointing task by alternating responses.

Evolution of Attention Orienting

Our discussion of gaze following and joint attention raises questions about how these capacities came to be present in humans and other animals. Although some ideas about the evolution of attention have been proposed (see e.g., Dukas, 1998; Johnston & Strayer, 2001), there is, as far as we know, no complete account of the evolution of attention orienting, or indeed of any other aspect of attention. We have, however, assembled a few preliminary indications of the direction that such an account might take.

It could be argued that attention orienting in modern humans had its origin at least as early as the Cambrian explosion of multicellular life forms a half-billion years ago. For many simple organisms, orienting may have been the result of sensory systems performing a drastic selection of species-relevant information from all that is available. Von Uexküll (1909/1985) called this sense-limited world the animal's *umvelt*. He proposed that anything outside the umvelt is not observed and does not directly affect the animal's behavior. On the other hand, relevant (sign) stimuli within the umvelt were said to reflexively evoke fixed action patterns. More specifically, a sign stimulus may trigger orienting toward it, even though other perceptible stimuli are available (but are in a sense filtered out). A herring gull chick, for example, will gape to the red spot on its mother's beak even though it can see other visual stimuli at the same time. Simple orienting mechanisms like this may have been precursors of the more sophisticated orienting we see in humans and other complex organisms.

One useful clue when tracing the development of orienting mechanisms across species is that many of the basic features of the vertebrate brain are highly conserved across taxa (e.g, reptiles, fish, amphibians, and mammals). One such conserved feature is the neural machinery required to integrate sensory input from the various modalities and to use that input to initiate stimulus-appropriate coherent behavior. These neural systems are concentrated in the mesodiencephalon, which is an area that in humans includes attention-related structures such as the superior colliculus and the thalamus

(Merker, 2007). Thus, the evolution of specialized orienting mechanisms in vertebrates may have begun with the development of this brain area.

As discussed in chapter 1, an orienting reflex can be produced in animals when stimulation of the reticular activating system activates other brain areas (see Figure 1.9). This may have been an antecessor of covert attention orienting in humans. To elaborate, the orienting reflex involves not only movements of the eyes, head, and body, but also changes in skin conductance, pupil dilation, heart rate decrease, breathing pause, and constriction of the peripheral blood vessels (e.g., Sokolov, 1975). The heart rate decrease component of the orienting reflex, or bradycardia, is highly similar to (but less dramatic) and mediated by the same neural circuitry as fear bradycardia. The latter is a dramatic lowering of heart rate and (usually) behavioral immobility or "freezing" in response to perceived threat (Campbell et al., 1997). Presumably fear bradycardia involves covert orienting of some sort because orienting to the threat must take place while the animal is immobile. The extension of this mechanism to novel, neutral stimuli by mammals sometime during their early evolutionary history (possibly involving additional cortical circuitry) would have made them successful in a wide variety of niches that required rapid adaptation to change. It is likely that all existing mammals exhibit the ability to orient attention covertly in a stimulus-driven manner (although of course not all have been tested carefully for this ability). For example, as seen in Figure 9.4, even the lowly rat can orient covertly to a light cue and respond faster to a target on the cued side of an apparatus than to a target on the uncued side (e.g., Phillips et al., 2000; Ward & Brown, 1996).

The ability to orient attention covertly in a goal-driven manner is more difficult to study in animals but we know that at least rhesus monkeys and chimpanzees can do so (e.g., Bowman et al., 1993; Emery, 2000; Tomasello et al., 2001; Tomonaga, 2007). It is possible that some of the apparatus of covert, stimulus-driven orienting was taken over for this purpose sometime during the evolution of primates, possibly in the service of social interaction. Primates living in groups spend much of their time paying attention to visual stimuli involving conspecifics (members of the same species). Observing these patterns can reveal what they know about social dynamics. Rhesus monkeys, for example, spend less time looking at higher ranking than at lower-ranking members of their dominance hierarchy. Nonhuman primates can also direct their attention to locations and objects toward which other individuals are gazing. This is thought to be one of the hallmarks of human (and other primate) social interaction and, although there is some controversy about the age at which it first occurs, human children develop the ability to follow another's gaze sometime during the first 3–18 months (Corkum & Moore, 1995). Its early development predicts early

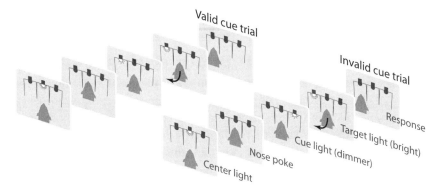

Figure 9.4 Depiction of the apparatus used by Ward and Brown (1996) to study covert orienting in rats. Each of the three holes contained a cue/target light. Responses were nose pokes into these holes. They were measured by photoelectric cells at the entrance of each hole that detected breaks in a beam of infrared light. Each trial began with illumination of the center light until a nose poke into the central hole occurred. Then a cue light was presented for 100 ms at one of the two peripheral locations, followed 100, 300, 500, or 700 ms later by a target light at either the cued location (valid-cue trial) or the uncued location on the opposite side of the display (invalid-cue trial) for 150 ms. Rats had to hold their nose in the central hole until 100 ms after target onset to eliminate movement during the cue-target interval. 80% of trials involved a valid cue and 20% involved an invalid cue, and response times were significantly greater on invalid-cue trials.

language development (e.g., Brooks & Meltzoff, 2005), whereas its delayed development is associated with autism (e.g., Baron-Cohen, 1995).

Some nonhuman primates can also follow the gaze of humans (e.g., Tomasello et al., 2001). In one study involving 11 species of new and old world monkeys, chimpanzees, and orangutans used gaze cues by human experimenters to respond correctly on at least 70% of trials (Ikatura, 1996). Nonape monkeys (e.g., rhesus monkeys) were unable to do so. Even nonape monkeys, however, appear capable of following the gaze of conspecifics (e.g., Lorincz et al., 1999; Tomasello et al., 1997). Whereas apes and monkeys can follow gaze cues, it is unclear whether or not they understand the intentions or the mental state of the individual providing these cues. This capacity is sometimes called *theory of mind* and one aspect of it is associated with manipulation of another's use of attention cues for the purpose of tactical deception (e.g., Whiten & Byrne, 1988, p. 212). This would seem to require not only the ability to orient attention in a goal-driven manner but also to understand something about the capacity of others to do so, so as to cause their attention to be misdirected to one's own benefit.

Some have argued that theory of mind is a human specialty (e.g., Heyes, 1998; Povinelli & Preuss, 1995) and that nonhuman primates do not understand the concept of attention sufficiently to allow them to use gaze for tactical deception, in spite of the fact that they routinely display gaze following during social interactions. The clear implication of early work in controlled laboratory conditions was that chimpanzees cannot use another individual's gaze cues to evaluate and predict their intentions. More recent research, however, indicates that they might understand more about the nature of other's gaze than previously thought. In one set of experiments, for example, a subordinate and a dominant chimpanzee were positioned on opposite sides of a cage that contained a highly valued piece of food (Hare et al., 2000). As seen in Figure 9.5, this food was plainly visible to both animals. On some trials, however, another piece of food was hidden behind a barrier so that only the subordinate could see it. In this case, the subordinate attempted to retrieve only the food that the dominant could not see (presumably to avoid a conflict situation). This suggests that the subordinate was sensitive to what the dominant could and could not see, and understood the dominant chimpanzee's intentions based on its gaze. There is also evidence that gaze following by chimpanzees is not reflexive. In a recent study, the magnitude of gaze cue effects was greater with high-validity than with low-validity cues, which suggests that, like humans, chimpanzees appreciate the relative informativeness of another individual's gaze as an attention-directing cue (Tomonaga, 2007).

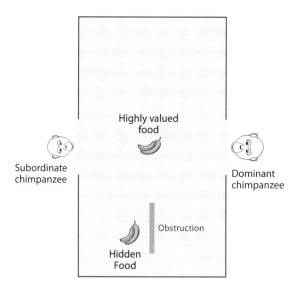

Figure 9.5 Depiction of apparatus used by Hare et al. (2000) to study the extent to which chimpanzees understand the intentions of a conspecific based on their gaze. In this experiment, a dominant and subordinate chimpanzee competed for a highly valued pieces of food and, on some trials, additional food was hidden so that only the subordinate could see it.

Although clearly more speculative than comparing orienting mechanisms of humans and animals, ideas have also been proposed about how these mechanisms may have changed as humans evolved. Archeological records indicate that modern humans are survivors of a radiation of human-like (hominid) species. Some 6 million years ago hominids diverged from apes (coinciding with bipedalism) and about 2.5 million years ago the genus *Homo* emerged. During this time, the hominid brain became enormously enlarged and structurally diversified. This involved encephalization of sensory functions in the cerebral cortex and a relative increase in the proportion of the prefrontal cortex and related connectional systems (e.g., Preuss, 2000). There was also a progressive increase in the degree of thalamic interconnectivity with areas thought to be part of the frontoparietal attention network (which would coincide with the evolution of more refined goal-driven control of covert orienting). One indication of this is that whereas a similar number of thalamic nuclei project to the primary visual and auditory cortex in humans and apes (gorillas, chimpanzees, orangutans), there are two to three times as many thalamic nuclei projecting to the frontal and parietal cortex in humans (Armstrong, 1982). Thus, it seems likely that as a result of hominid brain evolution over the last 4 million or so years, *Homo sapiens* would exhibit more refined covert orienting than *Homo ergaster*, who in turn would have exhibited more refined covert orienting than *Homo habilis*, and so on.

About 50,000 years ago there was a profound change in human evolution. The pace of behavioral and technological development increased significantly, and this has led many to speculate about a possible growth of cognitive abilities to account for it (see e.g., Allman, 1999). One provocative idea is that after a long period in which the mind became progressively more fragmented, it then became more "fluid" with the emergence of *Homo sapiens* (Mithen, 1996). Inspired by Fodor's (1983) modularity hypothesis, Mithen proposed that the minds of early hominids grew to be more modular over time to increase the speed and efficiency of mental processing (although at the price of mental flexibility). The Neanderthal mind, for example, was said to be more modular than that of early *Homo*, which in turn was said to be more modular than those of earlier hominids such as Australopithecus. The limited mental flexibility that is thought to be a consequence of increasing modularity may explain why primitive stone tools that first appeared about 2.6 million years ago were used for almost a million years with little modification. The cognitive "big bang" 50,000 years ago, according to Mithen, coincided with the collapse of this modularity. In comparison to the fragmented (highly modular) mind of the Neanderthals, the modern *Homo sapiens* mind was said to have far greater communication and interaction between brain areas. And this, he claimed, increased our capacity for invention, analogical thinking, and art. Mithen's proposal has been criticized on the grounds that any conclusions about brain physiology based strictly on behavioral artifactual evidence seems tenuous (e.g., Sarnecki & Sponheimer, 2002). The proposal is, however, consistent with evidence that interconnectivity of different subcortical and cortical areas has become more elaborate as the brain has evolved.

Mithen (1996) might argue that the Neanderthals, because their attentional processing (he claims) was carried out to a greater extent by informationally-encapsulated modules (see Fodor, 1983), would not be able to divide attention as efficiently as modern humans. A more fragmented Neanderthal brain, for example, would be less able to maintain a balance between focusing attention on the performance of a particular task while remaining vigilant for new and important external stimuli. As discussed in chapter 7, this balance may occur as a result of communication between areas in the frontal and parietal cortices (Corbetta & Shuman, 2002). That is, the temporoparietal junction (TPJ) might function as a "circuit breaker" that interrupts processing in the intraparietal sulcus (IPS) when attention is to be disengaged and directed to a new stimulus. The ventral frontal and prefrontal cortex also appear to modulate this exchange between the TPJ and IPS. Perhaps increased interconnectivity between brain areas during the course of evolution led to a more refined frontoparietal orienting network that is better able to filter out distracting stimuli during task performance while, at the same time, retaining the capacity for attentional disengagement when a new, unexpected, and important stimulus occurs.

Another brain area that has evolved considerably is the frontal cortex. Research described in chapter 7 indicates that it plays a significant role in goal-driven control of covert orienting and we would expect that some modification of this area would be associated with the development of executive control in primates. One type of cell associated with this development is the spindle or Von Economo neuron. These are located in the anterior cingulate and fronto-insular cortex and appear to play a role in the relay of fast, intuitive judgments to the frontal and temporal cortices, and in the executive attention network that mediates self-regulation (e.g., Posner, 2007). The executive attention network presumably influences goal-directed orienting in humans because the anterior cingulate is functionally connected to auditory or visual cortex depending on which modality is being monitored in a goal-driven attention task (Crottaz-Herbette & Menon, 2006) and also to other attention-related areas including the thalamus and parietal cortex (Amiez et al., 2005). Von Economo neurons appear only in the apes and humans, and are far more abundant in the latter. Monkeys do not possess Von Economo neurons, which may be one reason why their covert orienting to goal-related objects is less refined and efficient than human covert orienting.

It is also worth noting that these neurons, in both apes and humans, are more common in the right hemisphere of the frontal cortex. This is thought to be the dominant hemisphere for space-based attentional control. According to Corbetta and Shulman (2002), the right ventral frontal cortex also may play a critical role in evaluating the novelty of unattended and unexpected stimulus onsets, and thereby may contribute to attentional disengagement by the TPJ (see chapter 7). Thus, the evolution of frontal cortex orienting mechanisms may have coincided with the development of its connectional systems to other brain areas and, in particular, the proliferation of cells like Von Economo neurons.

There are still many mysteries associated with the evolution of human attention orienting and, more generally, with how the brain mediates attention shifts. The past 30 years of study of this phenomenon have consolidated methodologies and raised many theoretical questions about how the attentional focal point is controlled. Much of what will be revealed about covert orienting in the future will result from research on the neurophysiology of attention networks (orienting, alerting, executive attention). This should lead to a better understanding of how these networks are integrated, and how they work together to mediate attentional operations such as filtering, searching, and expecting. These discoveries, in turn, will inform the path the field will take in the coming years.

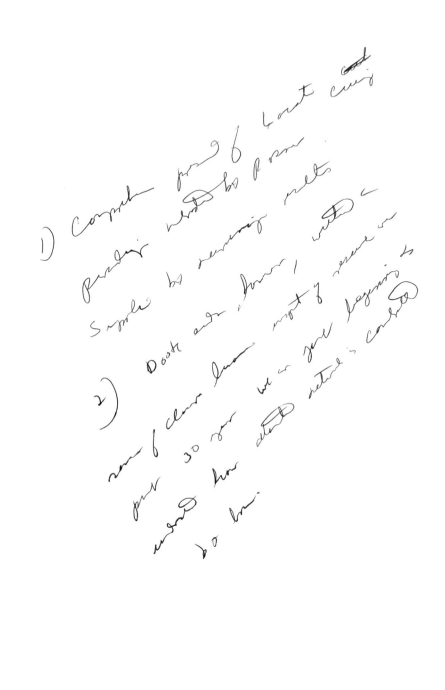

References

Abrams, R. A., & Dobkin, R. S. (1994). Inhibition of return: Effects of attentional cueing on eye movement latencies. *Journal of Experimental Psychology: Human Perception & Performance, 20*, 467–477.

Adam, J. J., Nieuwenstein, J. H., Huys, R., Paas, F. G., Kingma, H., Willems, P., et al. (2000). Control of rapid aimed hand movements: The one-target advantage. *Journal of Experimental Psychology: Human Perception & Performance, 26*, 295–312.

Alain, C., Arnott, S. R., Hevenor, S., Graham, S., & Grady, C. L. (2001). "What" and "where" in the human auditory system. *Proceedings of the National Academy of Sciences USA, 98*, 12301–12306.

Alivisatos, B., & Milner, B. (1989). Effects of frontal or temporal lobectomy on the use of advance information in a choice reaction time task. *Neuropsychologia, 27*, 495–503.

Allman, J. M. (1999). *Evolving brains.* New York: Scientific American Library.

Alsius, A., Navarra, J., Campbell, R., & Soto-Faraco, S. (2005). Audiovisual integration of speech falters under high attention demands. *Current Biology, 15*, 839–843.

Alvarez, G. A., Horowitz, T. S., Arsenio, H. C., DiMase, J. S., & Wolfe, J. M. (2005). Do multielement visual tracking and visual search draw continuously on the same visual attention resources? *Journal of Experimental Psychology: Human Perception & Performance, 31*, 643–667.

Amiez, C., Joseph, J.-P., & Procyk, E. (2005). Primate anterior cortex and adaptation of behavior. In S. Dehaene, J.-R. Duhamel, M. D. Hauser, & G. Rizzolatti (Eds.), *From monkey brain to human brain* (pp. 315–336). Cambridge, MA: MIT Press.

Andersen, R. A., Essick, G. K., & Seigel, R. M. (1985). Encoding of spatial location by posterior parietal neurons. *Science, 230*, 456–458.

Anllo-Vento, L. (1995). Shifting attention in visual space: The effects of peripheral cueing on brain cortical potentials. *International Journal of Neuroscience, 80*, 353–370.

Annan, V., & Pylyshyn, Z. (2002). Can indexes be voluntarily assigned in multiple-object tracking? *Journal of Vision, 2*, 243.

Armstrong, E. (1982). Mosaic evolution in the primate brain: Differences and similarities in the hominoid thalamus. In E. Armstrong & D. Falk (Eds.), *Primate brain evolution* (pp. 131–161). New York: Plenum Press.

Arrington, C. M., Carr, T. H., Mayer, A. R., & Rao, S. M. (2000). Neural mechanisms of visual attention: Object-based selection of a region in space. *Journal of Cognitive Neuroscience, 12,* 106–117.

Aslin, R. N. (1981). Development of smooth pursuit in human infants. In D. F. Fisher, R. A. Monty, & J. W. Senders (Eds.), *Eye movements: Cognition and visual perception* (pp. 31–51). Hillsdale, NJ: Erlbaum.

Aslin, R. N., & Salapatek, P. (1975). Saccadic localization of targets by the very young human infant. *Perception & Psychophysics, 17,* 293–302.

Averbach, E., & Coriell, A. S. (1961). Short-term memory in vision. *Bell System Technical Journal, 40,* 309–328.

Baldauf, D., Wolf, M., & Deubel, H. (2006). Deployment of visual attention before sequences of goal-directed hand movements. *Vision Research, 46,* 4355–4374.

Baldwin, J. M. (1889). *Handbook of psychology: Senses and intellect.* New York: Henry Holt.

Baron-Cohen, S. (1995). The eye direction detector (EDD) and the shared attention mechanism (SAM): Two cases for evolutionary psychology. In C. Moore & P. Dunham (Eds.), *Joint attention: Its origins and role in development* (pp. 41–59). Hillsdale, NJ: Erlbaum.

Beauchamp, M. S., Petit, L., Ellmore, T. M., Ingeholm, J., & Haxby, J. V. (2001). A parametric fMRI study of overt and covert shifts of visuospatial attention. *Neuroimage, 14,* 310–321.

Beck, D. M., Muggleton, N., Walsh, V., & Lavie, N. (2006). Right parietal cortex plays a critical role in change blindness. *Cerebral Cortex, 16,* 712–717.

Beck, D. M., Rees, G., Frith, C. D., & Lavie, N. (2001). Neural correlates of change detection and change blindness. *Nature Neuroscience, 4,* 645–650.

Bedard, M. A., El Massioui, F., Pillon, B., & Nandrino, J. L. (1993). Time for reorienting of attention: A premotor hypothesis of the underlying mechanism. *Neuropsychologia, 31,* 241–249.

Bell, A. H., Fecteau, J. H., & Munoz, D. P. (2004). Using auditory and visual stimuli to investigate the behavioral and neuronal consequences of reflexive covert orienting. *Journal of Neurophysiology, 91,* 2172–2184.

Bennett, P. J., & Pratt, J. (2001). The spatial distribution of inhibition of return. *Psychological Science, 12,* 76–80.

Berger, A., & Henik, A. (2000). The endogenous modulation of IOR is nasal-temporal asymmetric. *Journal of Cognitive Neuroscience, 12,* 421–428.

Bertelson, P. (1999). Ventriloquism: A case of crossmodal perceptual grouping. In G. Aschersleben, T. Bachmann, & J. Musseler (Eds.), *Cognitive contributions to the perception of spatial and temporal events* (pp. 347–363). Amsterdam: Elsevier.

Bertelson, P., Vroomen, J., De Gelder, B., & Driver, J. (2000). The ventriloquist effect does not depend on the direction of visual attention. *Perception & Psychophysics, 62,* 321–332.

Bertelson, P., Vroomen, J., & De Gelder, B., (2003). Visual recalibration of auditory speech identification: A McGurk aftereffect. *Psychological Science, 14*, 592–597.

Bichot, N., Cave, K., & Pashler, H. (1999). Visual selection mediated by location: Feature-based selection of non-contiguous locations. *Perception & Psychophysics, 61*, 403–423.

Bichot, N., Schall, J. D., & Thompson, K. G. (1996). Visual feature selectivity in frontal eye fields induced by experience in mature macaques. *Nature, 381*, 697–699.

Bisley, J. W., & Goldberg, M. E. (2003). Neuronal activity in the lateral intraparietal area and spatial attention. *Science, 299*, 81–86.

Bisley, J. W., Krishna, B. S., & Goldberg, M. E. (2004). A rapid and precise on-response in posterior parietal cortex. *Journal of Neuroscience, 24*, 1833–1838.

Bizzi, E. (1968). Discharge of frontal eye field neurons during saccadic and following eye movements in unanesthetized monkeys. *Experimental Brain Research, 6*, 69–80.

Bonnel, A. M., Possamai, C., & Schmitt, M. (1987). Early modulation of visual input: A study of attentional strategies. *Quarterly Journal of Experimental Psychology, 39*, 757–776.

Bowman, E. M., Brown, V. J., Kertzman, C., Schwarz, U., & Robinson, D. L. (1993). Covert orienting of attention in Macaques I. Effect of behavioral context. *Journal of Neurophysiology, 70*, 431–443.

Braun, J. (1999). On the detection of salient contours. *Spatial Vision, 12*, 211–225.

Braunschweiger, D. (1899). *Die Lehre von der Aufmerksamkeit in der Psychologie des 18. Jahrhundert*. Leipzig: Haacke.

Breitmeyer, B. (1980). Unmasking visual masking: A look at the 'why' behind the veil of the 'how.' *Psychological Review, 83*, 1–36.

Breitmeyer, B. G., & Ganz, L. (1976). Implications of sustained and transient channels for theories of visual pattern masking, saccadic suppression, and information processing. *Psychological Review, 83*, 1–36.

Briand, K., Hening, W., Poizner, H., & Sereno, A. B. (2001). Automatic orienting of visuospatial attention in Parkinson's disease. *Neuropsychologia, 39*, 1240–1249.

Brighina, F., Bisiach, E., Oliveri, M., Piazza, A., La Bua, V., Daniele, O., et al. (2003). 1 Hz repetitive transcranial magnetic stimulation of the unaffected hemisphere ameliorates contralesional visuospatial neglect in humans. *Neuroscience Letters, 336*, 131–133.

Broadbent, D. E. (1954). The role of auditory localization and attention in memory spans. *Journal of Experimental Psychology, 47*, 191–196.

Broadbent, D. E. (1958). *Perception and communication*. New York: Pergamon Press.

Brooks, R., & Meltzoff, A. N. (2005). The development of gaze following and its relation to language. *Developmental Science, 8*, 535–543.

Bruce, C. J., & Goldberg, M. E. (1984). Physiology of the frontal eye fields. *Trends in Neuroscience Research, 7*, 436–441.

Bruce, C. J., & Goldberg, M. E. (1985). Primate frontal eye fields. I. Single neurons discharging before saccades. *Journal of Neurophysiology, 53*, 603–635.

Bruce, C. J., Goldberg, M. E., Bushnell, M. C., & Stanton, G. B. (1985). Primate frontal eye fields. II. Physiological and anatomical correlates of electrically evoked eye movements. *Journal of Neurophysiology, 54*, 714–734.

Buchsbaum, M. S., Buchsbaum, B. R., Chokron, S., Tang, C., Wei, T. C., & Byne, W. (2006). Thalamocortical circuits: fMRI assessment of the pulvinar and medial dorsal nucleus in normal volunteers. *Neuroscience Letters, 404*, 282–287.

Buchtel, H. A., & Butter, C. M. (1988). Spatial attentional shifts: Implications for the role of polysensory mechanisms. *Neuropsychologia, 26*, 499–509.

Bundesen, C., Habekost, T., & Kyllingsbæk, S. (2005). A neural theory of visual attention: Bridging cognition and neurophysiology. *Psychological Review, 112*, 291–328.

Burr, D. C., Morrone, M. C., & Ross, J. (1994). Selective suppression of the magnocellular visual pathways during saccadic eye movements. *Nature, 371*, 511–513.

Buschman, T. J., & Miller, E. K. (2007). Top-down versus bottom-up control of attention in the prefrontal and posterior parietal cortices. *Science, 315*, 1860–1862.

Bushnell, M. C., Goldberg, M. E., & Robinson, D. L. (1981). Behavioral enhancement of visual responses in monkey cerebral cortex. I. Modulation in posterior parietal cortex related to selective visual attention. *Journal of Neurophysiology, 46*, 755–772.

Buswell, G. T. (1935). *How people look at pictures.* Chicago: University of Chicago Press.

Butter, C. M., Buchtel, H. A., & Santucci, R. (1989). Spatial attentional shifts: Further evidence for the role of polysensory mechanisms using visual and tactile stimuli. *Neuropsychologia, 27*, 1231–1240.

Campbell, B. A., Wood, G., & McBride, T. (1997). Origins of orienting and defensive responses: An evolutionary perspective. In P. J. Lang, R. F. Simons, & M. Balaban (Eds.), *Attention and orienting: Sensory and motivational processes* (pp. 41–67). Mahwah, NJ: Erlbaum.

Carrasco, M., & Frieder, K. S. (1997). Cortical magnification neutralizes the eccentricity effect in visual search. *Vision Research, 37*, 63–82.

Carrasco, M., & Yeshurun, Y. (1998). The contribution of covert attention to the set-size and eccentricity effects in visual search. *Journal of Experimental Psychology: Human Perception & Performance, 24*, 673–692.

Castel, A. D., Pratt, J., & Craik, F. I. M. (2003). The role of spatial working memory in inhibition of return: Evidence from divided attention tasks. *Perception & Psychophysics, 65*, 970–981.

Castiello, U., & Umiltà, C. (1992). Splitting focal attention. *Journal of Experimental Psychology: Human Perception & Performance, 18*, 837–848.

Cavanagh, P. (2004). Attention routines and the architecture of selection. In M. I. Posner (Ed.), *Cognitive neuroscience of attention* (pp. 13–28). New York: Guilford Press.

Cavanagh, P., & Alvarez, G. A. (2005). Tracking multiple targets with multifocal attention. *Trends in Cognitive Sciences, 9*, 349–354.

Cavanaugh, J., & Wurtz, R. H. (2004). Subcortical modulation of attention counters change blindness. *Journal of Neuroscience, 24*, 11236–11243.

Chambers, C. D., & Mattingley, J. B. (2005). Neurodisruption of selective attention: Insights and implications. *Trends in Cognitive Sciences, 9*, 542–550.

Chambers, C. D., Payne, J. M., & Mattingley, J. B. (2007). Parietal disruption impairs reflexive spatial attention within and between sensory modalities. *Neuropsychologia, 45*, 1715–1724.

Chambers, C. D., Stokes, M. G., & Mattingley, J. B. (2004). Modality-specific control of strategic spatial attention in parietal cortex. *Neuron, 44*, 925–930.

Cheal, M., Chastain, G., & Lyon, D. R. (1998). Inhibition of return in vision identification tasks. *Visual Cognition, 5*, 365–388.

Cheal, M., & Lyon, D. R. (1991). Central and peripheral precueing of forced-choice discrimination. *Quarterly Journal of Experimental Psychology, 43A*, 859–880.

Cheina, J. M., & Schneider, W. (2005). Neuroimaging studies of practice-related change: fMRI and meta-analytic evidence of a domain-general control network for learning. *Cognitive Brain Research, 25*, 607–623.

Cherry, E. C. (1953). Some experiments on the recognition of speech with one and two ears. *Journal of the Acoustical Society of America, 25*, 975–979.

Chica, A. B., Lupiañez, J., & Bartolomeo, P. (2006). Dissociating IOR from endogenous orienting of spatial attention: Evidence from detection and discrimination tasks. *Cognitive Neuropsychology, 23*, 1015–1024.

Clark, V., Fan, S., & Hillyard, S. A. (1996). Identification of early visual evoked potential generators by retinotopic and topographic analyses. *Human Brain Mapping, 2*, 170–187.

Clohessy, A. B., Posner, M. I., Rothbart, M. K., & Vecera, S. P. (1991). The development of inhibition of return in early infancy. *Journal of Cognitive Neuroscience, 3/4*, 345–350.

Cohen, R. M., Semple, W. E., Gross, M., Holcomb, H. J., Dowling, S. M., & Nordahl, T. E. (1988). Functional localization of sustained attention. *Neuropsychiatry, Neuropsychology & Behavioral Neurology, 1*, 3–20.

Cohen, Y. E., & Knudsen, E. I. (1999). Maps versus clusters: Different representations of auditory space in the midbrain and forebrain. *Trends in Neurosciences, 22*, 128–135.

Colby, C. L., Duhamel, J. R., & Goldberg, M. E. (1996). Visual, presaccadic, and cognitive activation of single neurons in monkey lateral intraparietal area. *Journal of Neurophysiology, 76*, 2841–2852.

Colegate, R., Hoffman, J. E., & Eriksen, C. W. (1973). Selective encoding from multielement visual displays. *Perception & Psychophysics, 14*, 217–224.

Collewijn, H. J. (1998). Eye movement recording. In R. H. S. Carpenter & G. J. Robson (Eds.), *Vision research: A practical guide to laboratory methods* (pp. 245–285). New York: Oxford University Press.

Connolly, J. D., Goodale, M. A., Menon, R. S., & Munoz, D. P. (2002). Human fMRI evidence for the neural correlates of preparatory set. *Nature Neuroscience, 5*, 1345–1352.

Constantinidis, C., & Steinmetz, M. A. (2001). Neuronal responses in area 7a to multiple-stimulus displays. I. Neurons encode the location of the salient stimulus. *Cerebral Cortex, 11*, 581–591.

Corbetta, M. (1998). Frontoparietal cortical networks for directing attention and the eye to visual locations: Identical, independent, or overlapping systems? *Proceedings of the National Academy of Science USA, 95*, 831–838.

Corbetta, M., Akbudak, E., Conturo, T. E., Snyder, A. Z., Ollinger, J. M., Drury, H. A., et al. (1998). A common network of functional areas for attention and eye movements. *Neuron, 21*, 761–773.

Corbetta, M., Kincade, M. J., Lewis, C., Snyder, A. Z., & Sapir, A. (2005). Neural basis of recovery and spatial attention deficits in spatial neglect. *Nature Neuroscience, 11*, 1603–1610.

Corbetta, M., Kincade, J. M., Ollinger, J. M., McAvoy, M. P., & Shulman, G. L. (2000). Voluntary orienting is dissociated from target detection in human posterior parietal cortex. *Nature Neuroscience, 3*, 292–297.

Corbetta, M., Miezin, F., Dobmeyer, S., Shulman, G., & Petersen, S. (1991). Selective and divided attention during visual discrimination of shape, color, and speed: Functional anatomy by positron emission tomography. *Journal of Neuroscience, 11*, 2383–2402.

Corbetta, M., Miezin, F. M., Shulman, G. L., & Petersen, S. E. (1993). A PET study of visuospatial attention. *Journal of Neuroscience, 13*, 1202–1226.

Corbetta, M., & Shulman, G. L. (1998). Human cortical mechanisms of visual attention during orienting and search. *Philosophical Transactions of the Royal Society of London Series B, 353*, 1353–1362.

Corbetta, M., & Shulman, G. L. (2002). Control of goal-directed and stimulus-driven attention in the brain. *Nature Reviews Neuroscience, 3*, 201–215.

Coren, S., Ward, L. M., & Enns, J. T. (2004). *Sensation and perception 6e.* New York: Wiley.

Corkum, V., & Moore, C. (1995). The development of joint attention in infants. In C. Moore & P. J. Dunham (Eds.), *Joint attention: Its origins and role in development* (pp. 61–83). Hillsdale, NJ: Erlbaum.

Crane, H. D. (1994). The Purkinje image eyetracker, image stabilization, and related forms of stimulus manipulation. In D. H. Kelly (Ed.), *Visual science and engineering: Models and applications* (pp. 13–89). New York: Marcel Dekker, Inc.

Crawford, T. J., & Müller, H. J. (1993). Spatial and temporal effects of spatial attention on human saccadic eye movements. *Vision Research, 32*, 293–304.

Crick, F. (1984). Function of the thalamic reticular complex: The searchlight hypothesis. *Proceedings of the National Academy of Sciences USA, 81*, 4586–4590.

Crosson, B. (1999). Subcortical mechanisms in language. *Brain & Cognition, 40*, 414–438.

Crottaz-Herbette, S., & Menon, V. (2006). Where and when the anterior cingulate cortex modulates attentional response: Combined fMRI and ERP evidence. *Journal of Cognitive Neuroscience, 18*, 766–780.

Crovitz, H. F., & Davies, W. (1962). Tendencies to eye movements and perceptual accuracy. *Journal of Experimental Psychology, 63*, 495–498.

Culham, J. C., Brandt, S. A., Cavanagh, P., Kanwisher, N. G., Dale, A. M., & Tootell, R. B. H. (1998). Cortical fMRI activation produced by attentive tracking of moving targets. *Journal of Neurophysiology, 80*, 2657–2670.

Culham, J. C., & Kanwisher, N. G. (2001). Neuroimaging of cognitive functions in human parietal cortex. *Current Opinion in Neurobiology, 11*, 157–163.

Cutrell, E. B., & Marrocco, R. T. (2002). Electrical microstimulation of primate posterior parietal cortex initiates orienting and alerting components of covert attention. *Experimental Brain Research, 144*, 103–113.

Cynader, M., & Berman, N. (1972). Receptive-field organization of monkey superior colliculus. *Journal of Neurophysiology, 35*, 187–201.

Danziger S., Fendrich R., & Rafal R. D. (1997). Inhibitory tagging of locations in the blind field of hemianopic patients. *Consciousness & Cognition, 6*, 291–307.

Danziger, S., Kingstone, A., & Snyder, J. J. (1998). Inhibition of return to successively stimulated locations in a sequential visual search paradigm. *Journal of Experimental Psychology: Human Perception & Performance, 24*, 1467–1475.

Danziger, S., Ward, R., Owen, V. & Rafal, R. (2004). Contributions of the human pulvinar to linking vision and action. *Cognitive, Affective, & Behavioral Neuroscience, 4*, 89–99.

Davidson, M. C., Villareal, M., & Marrocco, R. T. (1994). Pharmacological manipulation of noradrenaline activity influences covert orienting in rhesus monkey. *Neuroscience Abstracts, 21*, 829.

Davidson, M. L., Fox, M. J., & Dick, A. O. (1973). Effects of eye movements on backward masking and perceived location. *Perception & Psychophysics, 14*, 110–116.

Davidson, R. M., & Bender, D. B. (1991). Selectivity for relative motion in the monkey superior colliculus. *Journal of Neurophysiology, 65*, 1115–1133.

DeRenzi, E., (1982). *Disorders of space: Exploration and cognition.* New York: Wiley.

Descartes, R. (1649). "Les Passions de l'àme." Le Gras, Paris.

Desimone, R., Wessinger, M., Thomas, L., & Schneider, W. (1990). Attentional control of visual perception: Cortical and subcortical mechanisms. *Cold Spring Harbor Symposia on Quantitative Biology, 55*, 963–971.

Deubel, H., & Schneider, W. X. (1996). Saccade target selection and object recognition: Evidence for a common attentional mechanism. *Vision Research, 36*, 1827–1837.

De Valois, R. L., & De Valois, K. K. (1988). *Spatial vision.* New York: Oxford University Press.

Doallo, S., Lorenzo-López, L., Vizoso, C., Rodríguez-Holguín, S., Amenedo, E., Bará, S., et al. (2004). The time course of the effects of central and peripheral cues on visual processing: An event-related potentials study. *Clinical Neurophysiology, 115*, 199–210.

Dodd, M. D., Castel, A. D., & Pratt, J. (2003). Inhibition of return with rapid serial shifts of attention: Implications for memory and visual search. *Perception & Psychophysics, 65*, 1126–1135.

Dodge, R. (1907). An experimental study of visual fixation. *Psychological Monographs, 8*(4), 1–95.

Doesburg, S. M., Emberson, L., Rahi, A., Cameron, D., & Ward, L. M. (2007a). Asynchrony from synchrony: Gamma-band neural synchrony and perception of audiovisual speech asynchrony. *Experimental Brain Research*, DOI: 10.1007/s00221–007–1127–5.

Doesburg, S. M., Herdman, A., & Ward, L. M. (2007b). *MEG reveals synchronized neural network for visuospatial attention*. Poster presentation at the May, 2007 Meeting of the Cognitive Neuroscience Society, New York.

Doesburg, S. M., Roggeveen, A. B., Kitajo, K., & Ward, L. M. (2007c). Large-scale gamma-band phase synchronization and selective attention. *Cerebral Cortex*, DOI: 10.1093/cercor/bhm073.

Doesburg, S. M., & Ward, L. M. (2007). Long-distance alpha-band MEG synchronization maintains selective attention. In D. Cheyne, B. Ross, G. Stroink, & H. Weinberg (Eds.), *New frontiers in biomagnetism: Proceedings of the 15th international conference on biomagnetism (BIOMAG 2006)* (pp. 551–554). Burlington, MA: Elsevier B.V.

Dorris, M. C., Klein, R. M., Everling, S., & Munoz, D. P. (2002). Contribution of the primate superior colliculus to inhibition of return. *Journal of Cognitive Neuroscience, 14*, 1256–1263.

Dorris, M. C., & Munoz, D. P. (1995). A neural correlate for the gap effect on saccadic reaction time. *Journal of Neurophysiology, 73*, 2558–2562.

Dorris, M. C., & Munoz, D. P. (1998). Saccadic probability influences motor preparation signals and time to saccadic initiation. *Journal of Neuroscience, 18*, 7015–7026.

Dorris, M. C., Pare, M., & Munoz, D. P. (1997). Neuronal activity in monkey superior colliculus related to the initiation of saccadic eye movements. *Journal of Neuroscience, 17*, 8566–8579.

Dorris, M. C., Taylor, T. L., Klein, R. M., & Munoz, D. P. (1999). Influence of previous visual stimulus or saccade on saccadic reaction times in monkey. *Journal of Neurophysiology, 81*, 2429–2436.

Downar, J., Crawley, A. P., Mikulis, D. J., & Davis, K. D. (2000). A multimodal cortical network for detecting changes in the sensory environment. *Nature Neuroscience, 3*, 277–283.

Downar, J., Crawley, A. P., Mikulis, D. J., & Davis, K. D. (2002). A cortical network sensitive to stimulus salience in a neutral behavioral context across multiple sensory modalities. *Journal of Neurophysiology, 87*, 615–620.

Downing, C. J. (1988). Expectancy and visual-spatial attention: Effects on perceptual quality. *Journal of Experimental Psychology: Human Perception & Performance, 14*, 188–202.

Downing, C. J., & Pinker, S. (1985). The spatial structure of visual attention. In M. I. Posner & O. S. M. Marin (Eds.), *Attention & Performance* (Vol. 11, pp. 171–188). Hillsdale, NJ: Erlbaum.

Downing, P. E., Dodds, C. M., & Bray, D. (2004). Why does the gaze of others direct attention? *Visual Cognition, 11*, 71–79.

Driver, J. (1996). Enhancement of selective listening by illusory mislocation of speech sounds due to lip-reading. *Nature, 381*, 66–68.

Driver, J., Davis, G., Ricciardelli, P., Kidd, P., Maxwell, E., & Baron-Cohen, S. (1999). Gaze perception triggers visuospatial orienting by adults in a reflexive manner. *Visual Cognition, 6*, 509–540.

Driver, J., & Spence, C. (1998). Attention and the crossmodal construction of space. *Trends in Cognitive Sciences, 2*, 254–262.

Duchowski, A. T. (2003). *Eye tracking methodology.* New York: Springer.

Dukas, R. (1998). Constraints on information processing and their effects on behavior. In R. Dukas (Ed.), *Cognitive ecology: The evolutionary ecology of information processing and decision making* (pp. 89–127). Chicago: University of Chicago Press.

Eason, R. (1981). Visual evoked potential correlates of early neural filtering during selective attention. *Bulletin of the Psychonomic Society, 18*, 203–206.

Eason, R., Harter, M., & White, C. (1969). Effects of attention and arousal on evoked cortical potentials and reaction time in man. *Physiology & Behavior, 4*, 283–289.

Edelman, J. A., & Keller, E. L. (1996). Activity of visuomotor neurons in the superior colliculus accompanying express saccades. *Journal of Neurophysiology, 76*, 908–926.

Eimer, M. (1994). Sensory gating as a mechanism for visual spatial orienting: Electrophysiological evidence from trial-by-trial cueing experiments. *Perception & Psychophysics, 55*, 667–675.

Eimer, M. (1997). Uninformative symbolic cues may bias visual-spatial attention: Behavioral and electrophysiological evidence. *Biological Psychology, 46*, 67–71.

Eimer, M. (1999). Can attention be directed to opposite locations in different modalities? An ERP study. *Clinical Neurophysiology, 110*, 1252–1259.

Eimer, M., Forster, B., Van Velzen, J., & Prabhu, G. (2005). Covert manual response preparation triggers attentional shifts: ERP evidence for the premotor theory of attention. *Neuropsychologia, 43*, 957–966.

Eimer, M., & Schröger, E. (1998). ERP effects of intermodal attention and cross-modal links in spatial attention. *Psychophysiology, 35*, 313–327.

Eimer, M., Van Velzen, J., Forster, B., & Driver, J. (2003). Shifts of attention in light and in darkness: An ERP study of supramodal attentional control and crossmodal links in spatial attention. *Cognitive Brain Research, 15*, 308–323.

Emery, N. J. (2000). The eyes have it: The neuroethology, function and evolution of social gaze. *Neuroscience & Biobehavioral Reviews, 24*, 581–604.

Engel, F. L. (1971). Visual conspicuity, directed attention and retinal locus. *Vision Research, 11*, 563–576.

Enns, J. T., & Cameron, S. (1987). Selective attention in young children: The relations between visual search, filtering, and priming. *Journal of Experimental Child Psychology, 44*, 38–63.

Eriksen, C. W. (1990). Attentional search of the visual field. In D. Brogan (Ed.), *Visual search* (pp. 3–19). London: Taylor & Francis.

Eriksen, C. W., & Hoffman, J. E. (1972a). Some characteristics of selective attention in visual perception determined by vocal reaction time. *Perception & Psychophysics*, *11*, 169–171.

Eriksen, C. W., & Hoffman, J. E. (1972b). Temporal and spatial characteristics of selective encoding from visual displays. *Perception & Psychophysics*, *12*, 201–204.

Eriksen, C. W., & Murphy, T. D. (1987). Movement of attentional focus across the visual field: A critical look at the evidence. *Perception & Psychophysics*, *42*, 299–305.

Eriksen, C. W., & St. James, J. D. (1986). Visual attention within and around the field of focal attention: A zoom lens model. *Perception & Psychophysics*, *40*, 225–240.

Eriksen, C. W., & Yeh, Y. (1985). Allocation of attention in the visual field. *Journal of Experimental Psychology: Human Perception & Performance*, *11*, 583–597.

Everling, S., Dorris, M. C., Klein, R. M., & Munoz, D. P. (1999). Role of the primate superior colliculus in preparation and execution of anti-saccades and prosaccades. *Journal of Neuroscience*, *19*, 2740–2754.

Everling, S., Pare, M., Dorris, M. C., & Munoz, D. P. (1998). Comparison of the discharge characteristics of brain stem omnipause neurons and superior colliculus fixation neurons in monkey: Implications for control of fixation and saccade behavior. *Journal of Neurophysiology*, *79*, 511–528.

Farah, M. I., Wong, A. B., Monheit, M. A., & Morrow, L. A. (1989). Parietal lobe mechanisms of spatial attention: Modality specific or supramodal? *Neuropsychologia*, *27*, 461–470.

Fecteau, J. H., & Munoz, D. P. (2006). Salience, relevance, and firing: A priority map for target selection. *Trends in Cognitive Sciences*, *10*, 382–390.

Ferlazzo, F., Couyoumdjian, A., Padovani, T., & Belardinelli, M. O. (2002). Head-centred meridian effect on auditory spatial attention orienting. *Quarterly Journal of Experimental Psychology*, *55A*, 937–963.

Fernandez-Duque, D., & Posner, M. I. (2001). Brain imaging of attentional networks in normal and pathological states. *Journal of Clinical & Experimental Neuropsychology*, *23*, 74–93.

Findlay, J. M., & Gilchrist, I. D. (2003). *Active vision*. New York: Oxford University Press.

Fischer, B. (1998). Attention in saccades. In R. D. Wright (Ed.), *Visual attention* (pp. 289–305). New York, NY: Oxford University Press.

Fischer, B., & Breitmeyer, B. (1987). Mechanisms of visual attention revealed by saccadic eye movements. *Neuropsychologia*, *25*, 73–83.

Fischer, B., & Ramsperger, E. (1984). Human express saccades: Extremely short reaction times of goal directed eye movements. *Experimental Brain Research*, *57*, 191–195.

Fischer, B., & Ramsperger, E. (1986). Human express saccades: Effects of randomization and daily practice. *Experimental Brain Research*, *64*, 569–578.

Fischer, B., & Weber, H. (1992). Characteristics of "anti" saccades in man. *Experimental Brain Research*, *89*, 415–424.

Fischer, B., & Weber, H. (1993). Express saccades and visual attention. *Behavioral & Brain Sciences, 16*, 553–610.

Fitts, P. M. (1954). The information capacity of the human motor system in controlling the amplitude of movement. *Journal of Experimental Psychology, 47*, 381–391.

Fodor, J. A. (1983). *The modularity of mind*. Cambridge, MA: MIT Press.

Folk, C. L., & Remington, R. W. (1999). Can new objects override attentional control settings? *Perception & Psychophysics, 61*, 727–739.

Folk, C. L., Remington, R. W., & Johnston, J. C. (1992). Involuntary covert orienting is contingent on attentional control settings. *Journal of Experimental Psychology: Human Perception & Performance, 18*, 1030–1044.

Fox, M. D., Corbetta, M., Snyder, A. Z., Vincent, J. L., & Raichle, M. E. (2006). Spontaneous neuronal activity distinguishes human dorsal and ventral systems. *Proceedings of the National Academy of Sciences USA, 103*, 10046–10051.

Foxe, J. J., & Simpson, G. V. (2005). Biasing the brain's attentional set: II. Effects of intersensory attentional deployment on subsequent sensory processing. *Experimental Brain Research, 166*, 393–401.

Foxe, J. J., Simpson, G. V., Ahlfors, S. P., & Saron, C. D. (2005). Biasing the brain's attentional set: I. Cue driven deployments of intersensory selective attention. *Experimental Brain Research, 166*, 370–392.

Francis, L., & Milliken, B. (2003). Inhibition of return for the length of a line? *Perception & Psychophysics, 65*, 1208–1221.

Friedrich, F. J., Egly, R., Rafal, R. D., & Beck, D. (1998). Spatial attention deficits in humans: A comparison of superior parietal and temporal-parietal junction lesions. *Neuropsychology, 12*, 193–207.

Fries, P., Reynolds, J. H., Rorie, A. E., & Desimone, R. (2001). Modulation of oscillatory neuronal synchronization by selective visual attention. *Science, 291*, 1560–1563.

Friesen, C. K., & Kingstone, A. (1998). The eyes have it! Reflexive orienting is triggered by nonpredictive gaze. *Psychonomic Bulletin & Review, 5*, 490–495.

Friesen, C. K., & Kingstone, A. (2003). Abrupt onsets and gaze direction cues trigger independent reflexive attention effects. *Cognition, 87*, B1–B10.

Fu, S., Caggiano, D. M., Greenwood, P. M., & Parasuraman, R. (2005). Event-related potentials reveal dissociable mechanisms for orienting and focusing visuospatial attention. *Cognitive Brain Research, 23*, 341–353.

Fuchs, A. F., Kaneko, C. R. S., & Scudder, C. A. (1985). Brainstem control of saccadic eye movements. *Annual Review of Neuroscience, 8*, 307–337.

Fuster, J. M. (1997). *The prefrontal cortex*. New York: Oxford University Press.

Fuster, J. M, Bodner, M., & Kroger, J. (2000). Cross-modal and cross-temporal associations in neurons of frontal cortex. *Nature, 405*, 347–351.

Garg, A., Schwartz, D., & Stevens, A. A. (2007). Orienting auditory spatial attention engages frontal eye fields and medial occipital cortex in congenitally blind humans. *Neuropsychologia, 45*, 2307–2321.

Gazzaniga, M. (1996). *Conversations in the cognitive neurosciences*. Cambridge, MA: MIT Press.

Gibson, B. S. (1996). Visual quality and attentional capture: A challenge to the special role of abrupt onsets. *Journal of Experimental Psychology: Human Perception & Performance, 22*, 1496–1504.

Gibson, B. S., & Kingstone, A. (2006). Visual attention and the semantics of space. *Psychological Science, 17*, 622–627.

Giguere, M., & Goldman-Rakic, P. S. (1988). Mediodorsal nucleus: Areal, laminar, and tangential distribution of afferents and efferents in the frontal lobe of rhesus monkeys. *Journal of Comparative Neurology, 277*, 195–213.

Gilchrist, I. D., Brown, V., & Findlay, J. M. (1997). Saccades without eye movements. *Nature, 390*, 130–131.

Gitelman, D. R., Alpert, N. M., Kosslyn, S., Daffner, K., Scinto, L., Thompson, W., et al. (1996). Functional imaging of human right hemispheric activation for exploratory movements. *Annals of Neurology, 39*, 174–179.

Gobell, J. L., Tseng, C. H., & Sperling, G. (2004). The spatial distribution of visual attention. *Vision Research, 44*, 1273–1296.

Godijn, R., & Pratt, J. (2002). Endogenous saccades are preceded by shifts of visual attention: Evidence from cross-saccadic priming effects. *Acta Psychologica, 110*, 83–102.

Godijn, R., & Theeuwes, J. (2002). Oculomotor capture and inhibition of return: Evidence for an oculomotor suppression account of IOR. *Psychological Research, 66*, 234–246.

Godijn, R., & Theeuwes, J. (2004). The relationship between inhibition of return and saccade trajectory deviations. *Journal of Experimental Psychology: Human Perception & Performance, 30*, 538–554.

Goldberg, M. E., & Wurtz, R. H. (1972). Activity of superior colliculus cells in behaving monkey. I. Visual receptive fields of single neurons. *Journal of Neurophysiology, 35*, 542–559.

Gomez, C., Clark, V., Luck, S. J., Fan, S., & Hillyard, S. A. (1994). Sources of attention-sensitive visual event-related potentials. *Brain Topography, 7*, 41–51.

Gottlieb, J. (2007). From thought to action: The parietal cortex as a bridge between perception, action, and cognition. *Neuron, 53*, 9–16.

Gottlieb, J., Kusunoki, M., & Goldberg, M. E. (1998). The representation of visual salience in monkey parietal cortex. *Nature, 391*, 481–484.

Gottlieb, J., Kusunoki, M., & Goldberg, M. E. (2005). Simultaneous representation of saccade targets and visual onsets in monkey lateral intraparietal area. *Cerebral Cortex, 15*, 1198–1206.

Gottlob, L. R., Cheal, M., & Lyon, D. R. (1999). Attention operating characteristics in a location cuing task. *Journal of General Psychology, 126*, 271–287.

Greenberg, G. Z., & Larkin, W. D. (1968). Frequency-response characteristic of auditory observers detecting signals of a single frequency in noise: The probe-signal method. *Journal of the Acoustical Society of America, 44*, 1513–1523.

Grefkes, C., Weiss, P. H., Zilles, K., & Fink, G. R. (2002). Crossmodal processing of object features in human anterior intraparietal cortex: An fMRI study implies equivalencies between humans and monkeys. *Neuron, 35*, 173–184.

Gregory, R. L. (1990). *Eye and brain*. Princeton, NJ: Princeton University Press.

Grent-'t-Jong, T., & Woldorff, M. G. (2007). Timing and sequence of brain activity in top-down control of visual-spatial attention. *PLoS Biology*, 5, e12.

Grimes, J. (1996). On the failure to detect changes in scenes across saccades. In K. Akins (Ed.), *Perception* (pp. 89–110). New York: Oxford University Press.

Grindley, C. G., & Townsend, V. (1968). Voluntary attention in peripheral vision and its effects on acuity and differential thresholds. *Quarterly Journal of Experimental Psychology*, 20, 11–19.

Grosbras, M. H., Laird, A. R., & Paus, T. (2005). Cortical regions involved in eye movements, shifts of attention, and gaze perception. *Human Brain Mapping*, 25, 140–154.

Gross, C. G. (1998). *Brain, vision, and memory*. Cambridge, MA: MIT Press.

Guillery, R. W., Feig, S. L., & Lozsadi, D. A. (1998). Paying attention to the thalamic reticular nucleus. *Trends in Neurosciences*, 21, 28–32.

Hahn, B., Ross, T. J., & Stein, E. A. (2006). Neuroanatomical dissociation between bottom-up and top-down processes of visuospatial selective attention. *NeuroImage*, 32, 842–853.

Hahn, S., & Kramer, A. F. (1998). Further evidence for the division of attention among non-contiguous locations. *Visual Cognition*, 5, 217–256.

Hainline, L. (1998). The development of basic visual abilities. In A. Slater (Ed.), *Perceptual development: Visual, auditory, and speech perception in infancy* (pp. 5–50). Hove: Psychology Press.

Halligan, P. W., & Marshall, J. C. (1994). Toward a principled explanation of unilateral neglect. *Cognitive Neuropsychology*, 11, 167–206.

Hare, B., Call, J., Agnetta, B., & Tomasello, M. (2000). Chimpanzees know what conspecifics do and do not see. *Animal Behavior*, 59, 771–785.

Harman, C., Posner, M. I., Rothbart, M. K., & Thomas-Thrapp, L. (1994). Development of orienting to objects and locations in human infants. *Canadian Journal of Experimental Psychology*, 48, 301–318.

Harter, M., & Aine, C. (1984). Brain mechanisms of visual selective attention. In R. Parasuraman & D. R. Davies (Eds.), *Varieties of attention* (pp. 293–321). San Diego, CA: Academic Press.

Harter, M., Aine, C., & Schroeder, C. (1982). Hemispheric differences in the neural processing of stimulus location and type: Effects of selective attention on visual evoked potentials. *Neuropsychologia*, 20, 421–438.

Harter, M., Miller, S. L., Price, N. J., LaLonde, M. E., & Keyes, A. L. (1989). Neural processes involved in directing attention. *Journal of Cognitive Neuroscience*, 1, 223–237.

Hatfield, G. (1998). Attention in early scientific psychology. In R. D. Wright (Ed.), *Visual attention* (pp. 3–25). New York: Oxford University Press.

He, B. J., Snyder, A. Z., Vincent, J. L., Epstein, A., Shulman, G. L., & Corbetta, M. (2007). Breakdown of functional connectivity in frontoparietal networks underlies behavioral deficits in spatial neglect. *Neuron*, 53, 905–918.

Heinze, H. J., Luck, S., Munte, T., Gos, A., Mangun, G., & Hillyard, S. (1994a). Attention to adjacent and separate positions in space: An electrophysiological analysis. *Perception & Psychophysics*, 56, 42–52.

Heinze, H. J., Mangun, G. R., Burchert, W., Hinrichs, H., Scholz, M., Münte, T. F., et al. (1994b). Combined spatial and temporal imaging of brain activity during visual selective attention in humans. *Nature, 372*, 543–546.

Helmholtz, H. von (1867/1925). *Treatise on physiological optics* (translated from the 3rd German edition). New York: Dover.

Helmholtz, H. von (1871). Über die Zeit, welche nötig ist, damit ein Gesichtseindruck zum Bewusstsein kommt. *Berliner Monatsberichte, Juni*, 333–337.

Henderson, J. M. (1997). Transsaccadic memory and integration during real-world object perception. *Psychological Science, 8*, 51–55.

Henderson, J. M., & Hollingworth, A. (1999). The role of fixation position in detecting scene changes across saccades. *Psychological Science, 10*, 438–443.

Henderson, J. M., Pollatsek, A., & Rayner, K. (1989). Covert visual attention and extrafoveal information use during object identification. *Perception & Psychophysics, 45*, 196–208.

Henik, A., Rafal, R., & Rhodes, D. (1994). Endogenously generated and visually guided saccades after lesions of the human frontal eye fields. *Journal of Cognitive Neuroscience, 6*, 400–411.

Hernández-Peón, R. (1964). Psychiatric implications of neuropsychological research. *Bulletin of the Menninger Clinic, 24*, 165–185.

Heyes, C. (1998). Theory of mind in nonhuman primates. *Behavioral & Brain Sciences, 21*, 101–134.

Hickey, C., McDonald, J. J., & Theeuwes, J. (2006). Electrophysiological evidence of the capture of visual attention. *Journal of Cognitive Neuroscience, 18*, 604–613.

Hietanen, J. K., Nummenmaa, L., Nyman, M. J., Parkkola, R., & Hämäläinen, H. (2006). Automatic attention orienting by social and symbolic cues activates different neural networks: An fMRI study. *NeuroImage, 33*, 406–413.

Hillyard, S. A., Hink, R. F., Schwent, V. L., & Picton, T. W. (1973). Electrical signs of selective attention in the human brain. *Science, 182*, 177–180.

Hillyard, S. A., Luck, S. J., & Mangun, G. R. (1994). The cueing of attention to visual field locations: Analysis with ERP recordings. In H. J. Heinze, T. F. Munte, & G. R. Mangun (Eds.), *Cognitive electrophysiology: Event-related brain potentials in basic and clinical research* (pp. 1–25). Boston: Birkhausen.

Hirsch, J., & Curcio, C. A. (1989). The spatial resolution capacity of human foveal retina. *Vision Research, 29*, 1095–1101.

Hobbes, T. (1655). *Elementorum Philosophie Sectio Prima de Corpore*. Crook, London.

Hoffman, J. E., & Subramaniam, B. (1995). The role of visual attention in saccadic eye movements. *Perception & Psychophysics, 57*, 787–795.

Holtzman, J. D., Sidtis, J. J., Volpe, B. T., Wilson, D. H., & Gazzaniga, M. (1981). Dissociation of spatial information for stimulus localization and the control of attention. *Brain, 104*, 861–871.

Holzman, P. S. (1985). Eye movement dysfunctions and psychoses. *International Review of Neurobiology, 27*, 179–205.

Holzman, P. S., Proctor, L. R., & Hughes, D. N. (1973). Eye tracking patterns in schizophrenia. *Science, 181,* 179–181.

Hooge, I. T. C., Over, E. A. B., van Wezel, R. J. A., & Frens, M. A. (2005). Inhibition of return is not a foraging facilitator in saccadic search and free viewing. *Vision Research, 45,* 1901–1908.

Hopf, J. M., & Mangun, G. R. (2000). Shifting visual attention in space: An electrophysiological analysis using high spatial resolution mapping. *Clinical Neurophysiology, 111,* 1241–1257.

Hopf, J. M., Vogel, E., Woodman, G., Heinze, H. J., & Luck, S. J. (2002). Localizing visual discrimination processes in time and space. *Journal of Neurophysiology, 88,* 2088–2095.

Hopfinger, J. B., Buonocore, M. H., & Mangun, G. R. (2000). The neural mechanisms of top-down attentional control. *Nature Neuroscience, 3,* 284–291.

Hopfinger, J. B., & Mangun, G. R. (1998). Reflexive attention modulates processing of visual stimuli in human extrastriate visual cortex. *Psychological Science, 9,* 441–447.

Hopfinger, J. B., & Mangun, G. R. (2001). Tracking the influence of reflexive attention on sensory and cognitive processing. *Cognitive, Affective, & Behavioral Neuroscience, 1,* 56–65.

Horowitz, T. S., & Wolfe, J. M. (1998). Visual search has no memory. *Nature, 394,* 575–577.

Huettel, S. A., Güzeldere, G., & McCarthy, G. (2001). Dissociating the neural mechanisms of visual attention in change detection using functional MRI. *Journal of Cognitive Neuroscience, 13,* 1006–1018.

Huettel, S. A., Song, A. W., & McCarthy, G. (2004). *Functional magnetic resonance imaging.* Sunderland, MA: Sinauer.

Hugdahl, K. (1995). *Psychophysiology: The mind-body perspective.* Cambridge, MA: Harvard University Press.

Hughes, H. C. (1984). Effects of flash luminance and positional expectancies on visual response latency. *Perception & Psychophysics, 36,* 177–184.

Hughes, H. C., & Zimba, L. D. (1985). Spatial maps of directed visual attention. *Journal of Experimental Psychology: Human Perception & Performance, 11,* 409–430.

Humphreys, G. W. (1981). On varying the span of visual attention: Evidence for two modes of spatial attention. *Quarterly Journal of Experimental Psychology, 33A,* 17–30.

Hunt, A. R., & Kingstone, A. (2003). Inhibition of return: Dissociating attentional and oculomotor components. *Journal of Experimental Psychology: Human Perception & Performance, 29,* 1068–1074.

Iacono, W. G., & Lykken, D. T. (1979). Electrooculographic recording and scoring of smooth pursuit and saccadic eye tracking: A parametric study using monozygotic twins. *Psychophysiology, 16,* 94–107.

Ignashchenkova, A., Dicke, P. W., Haarmeier, T., & Thier, P. (2004). Neuron-specific contribution of the superior colliculus to overt and covert shifts of attention. *Nature Neuroscience, 7,* 56–64.

Ikatura, S. (1996). An exploratory study of gaze monitoring in non-human primates. *Japanese Psychological Research, 38*, 174–180.

Irwin, D. E. (1991). Information integration across saccadic eye movements. *Cognitive Psychology, 23*, 420–456.

Irwin, D. E. (1992). Visual memory within and across fixations. In K. Rayner (Ed.), *Eye movements and visual cognition: Scene perception and reading* (pp. 146–165). New York: Springer-Verlag.

Itier, R. J., Villate, C., & Ryan, J. D. (2007). Eyes always attract attention but gaze orienting is task-dependent: Evidence from eye movement monitoring. *Neuropsychologia, 45*, 1019–1028.

Jack, C. E., & Thurlow, W. R. (1973). Effects of degree of visual association and angle of displacement on the "ventriloquism" effect. *Perceptual & Motor Skills, 37*, 967–979.

James, W. (1890). *Principles of psychology* (Vols. 1–2). New York: Dover (reprinted in 1950).

Jaskowski, P. (1993). Selective attention and temporal-order judgment. *Perception, 22*, 681–689.

Javal, E. (1878, 1879). Essai sur la physiologie de la lecture (in several parts). *Annales d'Oculistique, 79*, 97, 240; *80*, 135; *81*, 61; *82*, 72, 159, 242.

Jefferies, L. N., Wright, R. D., & Di Lollo, V. (2005). Inhibition of return to an occluded object depends on expectation. *Journal of Experimental Psychology: Human Perception & Performance, 31*, 1224–1233.

Johnson, D. M., & Hafter, E. R. (1980). Uncertain-frequency detection: Cuing and condition of observation. *Perception & Psychophysics, 28*, 143–149.

Johnston, W. A., & Strayer, D. L. (2001). A dynamic, evolutionary perspective on attention capture. In C. Folk & B. Gibson (Eds.), *Attraction, distraction, and action: Multiple perspectives on attentional capture* (pp. 375–397). New York: Elsevier.

Jonides, J. (1980). Towards a model of the mind's eye's movement. *Canadian Journal of Psychology, 34*, 103–112.

Jonides, J. (1981). Voluntary versus automatic control over the mind's eye's movement. In J. B. Long & A. D. Baddeley (Eds.), *Attention & Performance* (Vol. 9, pp. 187–203). Hillsdale, NJ: Erlbaum.

Jonides, J. (1983). Further towards a model of the mind's eye's movement. *Bulletin of the Psychonomic Society, 21*, 247–250.

Jonides, J., & Mack, R. (1984). On the cost and benefit of cost and benefit. *Psychological Bulletin, 96*, 29–44.

Jonides, J., Smith, E. E., Koeppe, R. A., Awh, E., Minoshima, S., & Mintun, M. A. (1993). Spatial working memory in humans as revealed by PET. *Nature, 363*, 623–625.

Jonides, J., & Yantis, S. (1988). Uniqueness of abrupt onset in capturing attention. *Perception & Psychophysics, 43*, 346–354.

Jordan, H., & Tipper, S. P. (1998). Object-based inhibition of return in static displays. *Psychonomic Bulletin & Review, 5*, 504–509.

Jovicich, J., Peters, R. J., Koch, C., Braun, J., Chang, L., & Ernst, T. (2001). Brain areas specific for attentional load in a motion-tracking task. *Journal of Cognitive Neuroscience, 13*, 1048–1058.

Juan, C. H., Shorter-Jacobi, S. M., & Schall, J. D. (2004). Dissociation of spatial attention and saccade preparation. *Proceedings of the National Academy of Sciences USA, 101*, 15541–15544.

Kahneman, D. (1973). *Attention and effort*. Englewood Cliffs, NJ: Prentice Hall.

Kahneman, D., Treisman, A., & Gibbs, B. J. (1992). The reviewing of object files: Object specific integration of information. *Cognitive Psychology, 24*, 175–219.

Kennett, S., Eimer, M., Spence, C., & Driver, J. (2001). Tactile-visual links in exogenous spatial attention under different postures: Convergent evidence from psychophysics and ERPs. *Journal of Cognitive Neuroscience, 4*, 462–478.

Kiefer, R. J., & Siple, P. (1987). Spatial constraints on the voluntary control of attention across visual space. *Canadian Journal of Psychology, 41*, 474–489.

Kingstone, A., Friesen, C. K., & Gazzaniga, M. S. (2000). Reflexive joint attention depends on lateralized cortical connections. *Psychological Science, 11*, 159–165.

Kingstone, A., & Klein, R. M. (1993). Visual offsets facilitate saccade latency: Does pre-disengagement of visuo-spatial attention mediate this gap effect? *Journal of Experimental Psychology: Human Perception & Performance, 19*, 1251–1265.

Kingstone, A., & Pratt, J. (1999). Inhibition of return is composed of attentional and oculomotor processes. *Perception & Psychophysics, 61*, 1046–1054.

Klein, R. (1980). Does oculomotor readiness mediate cognitive control of visual attention? In R. S. Nickerson (Ed.), *Attention & Performance* (Vol. 8, pp. 259–276). Hillsdale, NJ: Erlbaum.

Klein, R. (1988). Inhibitory tagging system facilitates visual search. *Nature, 334*, 430–431.

Klein, R., Brennan, M., & Gilani, A. (1987). *Covert cross-modality orienting of attention in space*. Paper presented at the annual meeting of the Psychonomic Society, Seattle, Washington.

Klein, R., Kingstone, A., & Pontefract, A. (1992). Orienting of visual attention. In K. Rayner (Ed.), *Eye movements and visual cognition: Scene perception and reading* (pp. 46–65). New York: Springer-Verlag.

Klein, R., & MacInnes, W. J. (1999). Inhibition of return is a foraging facilitator in visual search. *Psychological Science, 10*, 346–352.

Klein, R., & McCormick, P. A. (1989). Covert visual orienting: Hemifield activation can be mimicked by zoom lens and midlocation placement strategies. *Acta Psychologica, 70*, 235–250.

Klein, R., & Pontefract, A. (1994). Does oculomotor capture readiness mediate cognitive control of visual attention? Revisited! In C. Umiltà & M. Moscovitch (Eds.), *Attention & Performance* (Vol. 15, pp. 333–350). Cambridge, MA: MIT Press.

Klein, R. M., & Taylor, T. L. (1994). Categories of cognitive inhibition with reference to attention. In D. Dagenbach & T. Carr (Eds.), *Inhibitory processes in attention, memory, and language* (pp. 113–150). Orlando, FL: Academic Press.

Knight, R. T., & Scabini, D. (1998). Anatomic bases of event-related potentials and their relationship to novelty detection in humans. *Journal of Clinical Neurophysiology, 15*, 3–13.

Knight, R. T., Scabini, D., Woods, D. L., & Clayworth, C. C. (1989). Contribution of temporal-parietal junction to the human auditory P3. *Brain Research, 502*, 109–116.

Koch, C., & Ullman, S. (1985). Shifts in selective visual attention: Towards the underlying neural circuitry. *Human Neurobiology, 4*, 219–227.

Koch, G., Oliveri, M., Torriero, S., & Caltagirone, C. (2005). Modulation of excitatory and inhibitory circuits for visual awareness in the human right parietal cortex. *Experimental Brain Research, 160*, 510–516.

Koffka, K. (1935). *Principles of gestalt psychology.* London: Lund Humphries.

Köhler, W. (1947). *Gestalt psychology: An introduction to new concepts in modern psychology.* New York: Liveright Publications.

Koski, L. M., Paus, T., & Petrides, M. (1998). Directed attention after unilateral frontal excisions in humans. *Neuropsychologia, 36*, 1363–1371.

Kowler, E. (1989). Cognitive expectations, not habits, control anticipatory smooth oculomotor pursuit. *Vision Research, 29*, 1049–1057.

Kowler, E., Anderson, E., Dosher, B., & Blaser, E. (1995). The role of attention in the programming of saccades. *Vision Research, 35*, 1897–1916.

Kowler, E., & Martins, A. J. (1982). Eye movements of preschool children. *Science, 215*, 997–999.

Kramer, A. F., & Hahn, S. (1995). Splitting the beam: Distributions of attention over noncontiguous regions of the visual field. *Psychological Science, 6*, 381–385.

Kröse, B. J. A., & Julesz, B. (1989). The control and speed of shifts of attention. *Vision Research, 29*, 1607–1619.

Kustov, A., & Robinson, D. L. (1996). Shared neural control of attentional shifts and eye movements. *Nature, 384*, 74–77.

Kwak, H., Dagenbach, D., & Egeth, H. (1991). Further evidence for a time-independent shift of the focus of attention. *Perception & Psychophysics, 49*, 473–480.

LaBerge, D. (1983). The spatial extent of attention to letters and words. *Journal of Experimental Psychology: Human Perception & Performance, 9*, 371–379.

LaBerge, D. (1990). Thalamic and cortical mechanisms of attention suggested by recent positron emission tomographic experiments. *Journal of Cognitive Neuroscience, 2*, 358–372.

LaBerge, D. (1995a). *Attentional processing: The brain's art of mindfulness.* Cambridge, MA: Harvard University Press.

LaBerge, D. (1995b). Computational and anatomical models of selective attention in object identification. In M. Gazzaniga (Ed.), *The cognitive neurosciences* (pp. 649–664). Cambridge, MA: MIT Press.

LaBerge, D. (1998). Attentional emphasis in visual orienting and resolving. In R. D. Wright (Ed.), *Visual attention* (pp. 417–454). New York: Oxford University Press.

LaBerge, D., & Brown, V. (1989). Theory of attentional operations in shape identification. *Psychological Review, 96,* 101–124.

LaBerge, D., & Buchsbaum, M. S. (1990). Positron emission tomographic measurements of pulvinar activity during an attention task. *Journal of Neuroscience, 10,* 613–619.

Ladavas, E., Zeloni, G., Zaccara, G., & Gangemi, P. (1997). Eye movements and orienting of attention in patients with visual neglect. *Journal of Cognitive Neuroscience, 9,* 67–74.

Lambert, A., Spencer, E., & Mohindra, N. (1987). Automaticity and the capture of attention by a peripheral display change. *Current Psychological Research & Reviews, 6,* 136–147.

Lamy, D., & Tsal, Y. (1999). A salient distractor does not disrupt conjunction search. *Psychonomic Bulletin & Review, 6,* 93–98.

Land, M. F., Mennie, N., & Rusted, J. (1999). The roles of vision and eye movements in the control of activities of everyday living. *Perception, 28,* 1311–1328.

Larsson, J., & Heeger, D. J. (2006). Two retinotopic visual areas in human lateral occipital cortex. *Journal of Neuroscience, 26,* 13128–13142.

Laughlin, W. S. (1968). Hunting: An integrating biobehavior system and its evolutionary importance. In R. B. Lee & I. DeVore (Eds.), *Man the hunter* (pp. 304–320). Chicago: Aldine Publishing.

Lee, D., & Quessy, S. (2003). Visual search is facilitated by scene and sequence familiarity in rhesus monkeys. *Vision Research, 43,* 1455–1463.

Lee, D. K., Itti, L., Koch, C., & Braun, J. (1999). Attention activates winner-take-all competition among visual filters. *Nature Neuroscience, 2,* 375–381.

Leek, E. C., Reppa, I., & Tipper, S. P. (2003). Inhibition of return for objects and locations in static displays. *Perception & Psychophysics, 65,* 388–395.

Levin, S., Lipton, R. B., & Holzman, P. S. (1981). Pursuit eye movements in psychopathology: Effects of target characteristics. *Biological Psychiatry, 16,* 255–267.

Liu, G., Austen, E. L., Booth, K. S., Fisher, B. D., Argue, R., Rempel, M. I., et al. (2005). Multiple-object tracking is based on scene, not retinal, coordinates. *Journal of Experimental Psychology: Human Perception & Performance, 31,* 235–247.

Liu, T., Slotnick, S. D., Serences, J. T., & Yantis, S. (2003). Cortical mechanisms of feature-based attentional control. *Cerebral Cortex, 13,* 1334–1343.

Lorincz, E. N., Baker, C. I., & Perrett, D. I. (1999). Visual cues for attention following in rhesus monkeys. *Cahiers de Psychologie Cognitive, 18,* 973–1003.

Luck, S. J. (1995). Multiple mechanisms of visual-spatial attention: Recent evidence from human electrophysiology. *Behavioral Brain Research, 71,* 113–123.

Luck, S. J. (2005). *An introduction to the event-related potential technique.* Cambridge, MA: MIT Press.

Luck, S. J., Hillyard, S. A., Mangun, G. R., & Gazzaniga, M. S. (1989). Independent hemispheric attentional systems mediate visual search in split-brain patients. *Nature, 342*, 544–545.

Luck, S. J., Hillyard, S. A., Mangun, G. R., & Gazzaniga, M. S. (1994a). Independent attentional scanning in the separated hemispheres of split-brain patients. *Journal of Cognitive Neuroscience, 6*, 84–91.

Luck, S. J., Hillyard, S. A., Mouloua, M., Woldorff, M. G., Clark, V. P., & Hawkins, H. L. (1994b). Effects of spatial cueing on luminance detectability: Psychophysical and electrophysiological evidence for early selection. *Journal of Experimental Psychology: Human Perception & Performance, 20*, 887–904.

Luck, S. J., Woodman, G. F., & Vofel, E. K. (2000). Event-related potential studies of attention. *Trends in Cognitive Sciences, 4*, 432–440.

Ludwig, C. J. H., & Gilchrist, I. D. (2002). Stimulus-driven and goal-driven control over visual selection. *Journal of Experimental Psychology: Human Perception & Performance, 28*, 902–912.

Lupiáñez, J., Milan, E. G., Tornay, F. J., Madrid, E., & Tudela, P. (1997). Does IOR occur in discrimination tasks? Yes, it does, but later. *Perception & Psychophysics, 59*, 1241–1254.

Lupiáñez, J., Weaver, B., Tipper, S. P., & Madrid, E. (2001). The effects of practice on cueing in detection and discrimination tasks. *Psicológica, 22*, 1–23.

Luria, A. R. (1973). *The working brain*. New York: Penguin.

Macaluso, E., Eimer, M., Frith, C. D., & Driver, J. (2003). Preparatory states in crossmodal spatial attention: Spatial specificity and possible control mechanisms. *Experimental Brain Research, 149*, 62–74.

Macaluso, E., Frith, C. D., & Driver, J. (2000). Modulation of human visual cortex by crossmodal spatial attention. *Science, 289*, 1206–1208.

Macaluso, E., Frith, C. D., & Driver, J. (2002). Supramodal effects of covert spatial orienting triggered by visual or tactile events. *Journal of Cognitive Neuroscience, 14*, 389–401.

Mack, A., & Rock, I. (1998). *Inattentional blindness*. Cambridge, MA: MIT Press.

Mackeben, M., & Nakayama, K. (1993). Express attentional shifts. *Vision Research, 33*, 85–90.

MacKinnon, D. A., Gross, C. G., & Bender, D. B. (1976). A visual deficit after superior colliculus lesions in monkeys. *Acta Neurobiologiae Experimentalis, 36*, 169–180.

Malinowski, P., Fuchs, S., & Müller, M. M. (2007). Sustained division of spatial attention to multiple locations within one hemifield. *Neuroscience Letters, 414*, 65–70.

Mangun, G. R., & Hillyard, S. A. (1991). Modulations of sensory-evoked brain potentials indicate changes in perceptual processing during visual-spatial priming. *Journal of Experimental Psychology: Human Perception & Performance, 17*, 1057–1074.

Mangun, G. R., Hillyard, S. A., & Luck, S. J. (1993). Electrocortical substrates of visual selective attention. In D. Meyer & S. Kornblum (Eds.), *Attention & Performance* (Vol. 14, pp. 219–243). Cambridge, MA: MIT Press.

Marrocco, R. T., & Li, R. H. (1977). Monkey superior colliculus: Properties of single cells and their afferent inputs. *Journal of Neurophysiology, 40,* 844–860.

Massaro, D. W. (1987). *Speech perception by ear and eye: A paradigm for psychological inquiry.* Hillsdale, NJ: Erlbaum.

Martín-Loeches, M., Barceló, F., & Rubia, F. J. (1997). Sources and topography of supramodal effects of spatial attention in ERP. *Brain Topography, 10,* 9–22.

Martinez-Conde, S., Macknik, S. L., & Hubel, D. H. (2004). The role of fixational eye movements in visual perception. *Nature Reviews Neuroscience, 5,* 229–240.

Matin, L. (1972). Eye movements and perceived visual direction. In D. Jameson & L. M. Hurvich (Eds.), *Handbook of sensory physiology: Volume 7/4 Visual psychophysics* (pp. 331–380). Berlin: Springer-Verlag.

Maurer, D., & Lewis, T. L. (1998). Overt orienting toward peripheral stimuli: Normal development and underlying mechanisms. In J. E. Richards (Ed.), *Cognitive neuroscience of attention: A developmental perspective* (pp. 51–102). Mahwah, NJ: Erlbaum.

Mayer, A. R., Dorflinger, J. M., Rao, S. M., & Seidenberg, M. (2004). Neural networks underlying endogenous and exogenous visual-spatial orienting. *Neuroimage, 23,* 534–541.

Mayfrank, L., Mobashery, M., Kimmig, H., & Fischer, B. (1986). The role of fixation and visual attention on the occurrence of express saccades in man. *European Journal of Psychiatry & Neurological Science, 235,* 269–275.

Maylor, E. A. (1985). Facilitatory and inhibitory components of orienting in visual space. In M. I. Posner & O. S. M. Marin (Eds.), *Attention & Performance* (Vol. 11, pp. 189–204). Hillsdale, NJ: Erlbaum.

Maylor, E. A., & Hockey, R. (1985). Inhibitory component of externally controlled covert orienting in space. *Journal of Experimental Psychology: Human Perception & Performance, 11,* 777–787.

Maylor, E. A., & Hockey, R. (1987). Effects of repetition on the facilitatory and inhibitory components of orienting in visual space. *Neuropsychologia, 25,* 41–54.

McAlonan, K., Brown, V. J., & Bowman, E. M. (2000). Thalamic reticular nucleus activation reflects attentional gating during classical conditioning. *Journal of Neuroscience, 20,* 8897–8901.

McCormick, P. A. (1997). Orienting attention with awareness. *Journal of Experimental Psychology: Human Perception & Performance, 23,* 168–180.

McCormick, P. A., & Klein, R. (1990). The spatial distribution of attention during covert visual orienting. *Acta Psychologica, 75,* 225–242.

McCormick, P. A, Klein, R. M., & Johnston, S. (1998). Splitting versus sharing focal attention: Comment on Castiello and Umiltà (1992). *Journal of Experimental Psychology: Human Perception & Performance, 24,* 350–357.

McDonald, J. J., Teder-Sälejärvi, W. A., Di Russo, F., & Hillyard, S. A. (2005). Neural basis of auditory-induced shifts in visual time-order perception. *Nature Neuroscience, 8,* 1197–1202.

McDonald, J. J., Teder-Sälejärvi, W. A., Heraldez, D., & Hillyard, S. A. (2001a). Electrophysiological evidence for the "missing link" in crossmodal attention. *Canadian Journal of Experimental Psychology, 55,* 141–149.

McDonald, J. J., Teder-Sälejärvi, W. A., & Hillyard, S. A. (2000). Involuntary orienting to sound improves visual perception. *Nature, 407,* 906–908.

McDonald, J. J., Teder-Sälejärvi, W. A., & Ward, L. M. (2001b). Multisensory integration and crossmodal attention effects in the human brain. *Science, 292,* 1791.

McDonald, J. J., & Ward, L. M. (1999). Spatial relevance determines facilitatory and inhibitory effects of auditory covert spatial orienting. *Journal of Experimental Psychology: Human Perception & Performance, 25,* 1234–1252.

McDonald, J. J., & Ward, L. M. (2000). Involuntary listening aids seeing: Evidence from human electrophysiology. *Psychological Science, 11,* 167–171.

McDonald, J. J., & Ward, L. M. (2005). *Crossmodal attention modulates detection and discrimination.* Unpublished manuscript, University of British Columbia.

McGurk, H., & MacDonald, J. (1976). Hearing lips and seeing voices. *Nature, 264,* 746–748.

McMains, S. A., & Somers, D. C. (2004). Multiple spotlights of attentional selection in human visual cortex. *Neuron, 42,* 677–686.

McMains, S. A., & Somers, D. C. (2005). Processing efficiency of divided spatial attention mechanisms in human visual cortex. *Journal of Neuroscience, 25,* 9444–9448.

McPeek, R. M., & Keller, E. L. (2002). Superior colliculus activity related to concurrent processing of saccade goals in a visual search task. *Journal of Neurophysiology, 87,* 1805–1815.

McPeek, R. M., & Keller, E. L. (2004). Deficits in saccade target selection after inactivation of superior colliculus. *Nature Neuroscience, 7,* 757–763.

McPeek, R. M., Skavenski, A. A., & Nakayama, K. (2000). Concurrent processing of saccades. *Vision Research, 40,* 2499–2516.

Meredith, M. A., & Stein, B. E. (1983). Interactions among converging sensory inputs in the superior colliculus. *Science, 221,* 389–391.

Meredith, M. A., & Stein, B. E. (1986). Visual, auditory, and somatosensory convergence on cells in superior colliculus results in multisensory integration. *Journal of Neurophysiology, 56,* 640–662.

Merker, B. (2007). Consciousness without a cerebral cortex: A challenge for neuroscience and medicine. *Behavioral & Brain Sciences, 30,* 63–124.

Mertens, J. J. (1956). Influence of knowledge of target location upon the probability of observations of peripherally observable test flashes. *Journal of the Optical Society of America, 46,* 1069–1070.

Mesulam, M. M. (1981). A cortical network for directed attention and unilateral neglect. *Annals of Neurology, 10,* 309–315.

Mesulam, M. M. (1999). Spatial attention and neglect: Parietal, frontal, and cingulate contributions to the mental representation and attentional targeting of salient extrapersonal events. *Philosophical Transactions of the Royal Society of London, B354,* 1325–1346.

Michael, G. A., & Buron, V. (2005). The human pulvinar and stimulus-driven attentional control. *Behavioral Neuroscience, 119*, 1353–1367.

Michael, G. A., & Desmedt, S. (2004). The human pulvinar and attentional processing of visual distractors. *Neuroscience Letters, 362*, 176–181.

Miller, E. K., & Cohen, J. D. (2001). An integrative theory of prefrontal cortex function. *Annual Review of Neuroscience, 24*, 167–202.

Milner, A. D. (1996). Neglect, extinction, and the cortical streams of visual processing. In H. P. Thier & H. O. Karnath (Eds.), *Parietal lobe contributions to orientation in 3D space* (pp. 3–22). Heidelberg: Springer.

Milner, P. (1974). A model for visual shape recognition. *Psychological Review, 81*, 521–535.

Mithen, S. (1996). *The prehistory of the mind*. New York: Thames & Hudson.

Mitroff, S. R., Scholl, B. J., & Wynn, K. (2004). Divide and conquer: How object files adapt when a persisting object splits into two. *Psychological Science, 15*, 420–425.

Mohler, C. W., & Wurtz, R. H. (1976). Organization of monkey superior colliculus: Intermediate layer cells discharging before eye movements. *Journal of Neurophysiology, 39*, 722–744.

Moore, T., & Fallah, M. (2004). Microstimulation of the frontal eye field and its effects on covert spatial attention. *Journal of Neurophysiology, 91*, 152–162.

Mondor, T. A., Zatorre, R. J., & Terrio, N. A. (1998). Constraints on the selection of auditory information. *Journal of Experimental Psychology: Human Perception & Performance, 24*, 66–79.

Moran, J., & Desimone, R. (1985). Selective attention gates visual processing in extrastriate cortex. *Science, 229*, 782–784.

Morrison, R. E. (1984). Manipulation of stimulus onset delay in reading: Evidence for parallel programming of saccades. *Journal of Experimental Psychology: Human Perception & Performance, 5*, 667–682.

Morrow, L. A., & Ratcliff, G. (1988). The disengagement of covert attention and the neglect syndrome. *Psychobiology, 16*, 261–269.

Mort, D. J., Perry, R. J., Mannan, S. K., Hodgson, T. L., Anderson, E., Quest, R., et al. (2003). Differential cortical activation during voluntary and reflexive saccades in man. *NeuroImage, 18*, 231–246.

Moruzzi, G., & Magoun, H. W. (1949). Brain stem reticular formation and activation of the EEG. *Electroencephalography & Clinical Neurology, 1*, 455–473.

Mountcastle, V. B. (1978). Brain mechanisms for directed attention. *Journal of the Royal Society of Medicine, 71*, 14–28.

Mowrer, O. H. (1941). Preparatory set (expectancy)—further evidence for its "central" locus. *Journal of Experimental Psychology, 28*, 116–133.

Müller, H. J. (1994). Qualitative differences in response bias from spatial cueing. *Canadian Journal of Experimental Psychology, 48*, 218–241.

Müller, H. J., & Findlay, J. M. (1988). The effect of visual attention on peripheral discrimination thresholds in single and multiple element displays. *Acta Psychologica, 69*, 129–155.

Müller, H. J., & Humphreys, G. W. (1991). Luminance-increment detection: Capacity-limited or not? *Journal of Experimental Psychology: Human Perception & Performance, 17*, 107–124.

Müller, H. J., & Rabbitt, P. M. A. (1989). Reflexive and voluntary orienting of visual attention: Time course of activation and resistance to interruption. *Journal of Experimental Psychology: Human Perception & Performance, 15*, 315–330.

Müller, H. J., & Von Mühlenen, A. (1996). Attentive tracking and inhibition of return in dynamic displays. *Perception & Psychophysics, 58*, 224–249.

Müller, H. J., & Von Mühlenen, A. (2000). Probing distractor inhibition in visual search: Inhibition of return. *Journal of Experimental Psychology: Human Perception & Performance, 26*, 1591–1605.

Müller, J. R., Philiastides, M. G., & Newsome, W. T. (2005). Microstimulation of the superior colliculus focuses attention without moving the eyes. *Proceedings of the National Academy of Sciences USA, 102*, 524–529.

Müller, M. M., Malinowski, P., Gruber, T., & Hillyard, S. A. (2003). Sustained division of the attentional spotlight. *Nature, 424*, 309–312.

Muri, R. M., Iba-Zizen, M. T., Derosier, C., Cabanis, E. A., & Pierrot-Deseiligny, C. (1996). Location of the human posterior eye fields with functional magnetic resonance imaging. *Journal of Neurology, Neurosurgery, & Psychiatry, 60*, 445–448.

Murphy, B. J. (1978). Pattern thresholds for moving and stationary gratings during smooth eye movement. *Vision Research, 18*, 521–530.

Murthy, A., Thompson, K. G., & Schall, J. D. (2001). Dynamic dissociation of visual selection from saccade programming in frontal eye field. *Journal of Neurophysiology, 86*, 2634–2637.

Nakayama, K., & Mackeben, M. (1989). Sustained and transient components of focal visual attention. *Vision Research, 11*, 1631–1647.

Näätänen, R. (1992). *Attention and brain function.* Hillsdale, NJ: Erlbaum.

Navon, D. (1977). Forest before the trees: The precedence of global features in visual perception. *Cognitive Psychology, 9*, 353–383.

Nissen, M. J., Posner, M. I., & Snyder, C. R. R. (1978). *Relationship between attention shifts and saccadic eye movements.* Paper presented at the annual meeting of the Psychonomic Society.

Nobre, A. C., Sebestyen, G. N., Gitelman, D. R., Mesulam, M. M., Frackowiak, R. S., & Frith, C. D. (1997). Functional localization of the system for visuospatial attention using positron emission tomography. *Brain, 120*, 515–533.

Norman, D. A. (1968). Towards a theory of memory and attention. *Psychological Review, 75*, 522–536.

Noton, D., & Stark, L. (1971). Scanpaths in saccadic eye movements while viewing and recognizing patterns. *Vision Research, 11*, 929–942.

O'Connor, D. H., Fukui, M. M., Pinsk, M. A., & Kastner, S. (2002). Attention modulates responses in the human lateral geniculate nucleus. *Nature Neuroscience, 5*, 1203–1209.

Ogawa, H., Takeda, Y., & Yagi, A. (2002). Inhibitory tagging on randomly moving objects. *Psychological Science, 13*, 125–129.

Oksama, L., & Hyönä, J. (2004). Is multiple object tracking carried out automatically by an early vision mechanism independent of higher-order cognition? An individual difference approach. *Visual Cognition*, *11*, 631–671.

Oonk, H. M., & Abrams, R. A. (1998). New perceptual objects that capture attention produce inhibition of return. *Psychonomic Bulletin & Review*, *5*, 510–515.

Oray, S., Lu, Z. L., & Dawson, M. E. (2002). Modification of sudden onset auditory ERP by involuntary attention to visual stimuli. *International Journal of Psychophysiology*, *43*, 213–224.

O'Regan, J. K., Deubel, H., Clark, J. J., & Rensink, R. (2000). Picture changes during blinks: Looking without seeing and seeing without looking. *Visual Cognition*, *7*, 191–211.

Palmer, J. (1990). Attentional limits on the perception and memory of visual information. *Journal of Experimental Psychology: Human Perception & Performance*, *16*, 332–350.

Pasupathy, A., & Connor, C. E. (1999). Responses to contour features in macaque area V4. *Journal of Neurophysiology*, *82*, 2490–2502.

Paul, M. A., & Tipper, S. P. (2003). Object-based representations facilitate memory for inhibitory processes. *Experiment Brain Research*, *148*, 283–289.

Paus, T. (1996). Location and function of the human frontal eye-field: A selective review. *Neuropsychologia*, *34*, 475–483.

Paus, T., Kalina, M., Patockova, L., Angerova, Y., Cerny, R., Mecir, P., et al. (1991). Medial versus lateral frontal lobe lesions and differential impairment of central-gaze fixation in man. *Brain*, *114*, 2051–2067.

Pavlov, I. P. (1927). *Conditioned reflexes*. London: Oxford University Press.

Perry, R. J., & Zeki. S. (2000). The neurology of saccades and covert shifts in spatial attention: An event-related fMRI study. *Brain*, *123*, 2273–2288.

Petersen, S. E., Robinson, D. L., & Keys, W. (1985). Pulvinar nuclei of the behaving rhesus monkey: Visual responses and their modulation. *Journal of Neurophysiology*, *54*, 867–886.

Petersen, S. E., Robinson, D. L., & Morris, J. D. (1987). Contributions of the pulvinar to visual spatial attention. *Neuropsychologia*, *25*, 97–105.

Peterson, M. S., Kramer, A. F., & Irwin, D. E. (2004). Covert shifts of attention precede involuntary eye movements. *Perception & Psychophysics*, *66*, 398–405.

Phillips, J. M., McAlonan, K., Robb, W. G. K., & Brown, V. J. (2000). Cholinergic neurotransmission influences covert orientation of visuospatial attention in the rat. *Psychopharmacology*, *150*, 112–116.

Pico, R. M. (2002). *Consciousness in four dimensions*. New York: McGraw-Hill.

Pigott, S., & Milner, B. (1994). Capacity of visual short-term memory after unilateral frontal or anterior temporal-lobe resection. *Neuropsychologia*, *32*, 969–981.

Pollatsek, A., & Rayner, K. (1999). Is covert attention really unnecessary? *Behavioral & Brain Sciences*, *22*, 695–696.

Posner, M. I. (1978). *Chronometric explorations of mind*. Hillsdale, NJ: Erlbaum.

Posner, M. I. (1980). Orienting of attention. *Quarterly Journal of Experimental Psychology*, *32*, 3–25.

Posner, M. I. (2004). *Cognitive neuroscience of attention*. New York: Guilford.

Posner, M. I. (2007). *Evolution and development of self-regulation*. The 77th James Arthur Lecture, American Museum of Natural History, New York.

Posner, M. I., & Boies, S. J. (1971). Components of attention. *Psychological Review*, *78*, 391–408.

Posner, M. I., & Cohen, Y. (1984). Components of visual attention. In H. Bouma & D. G. Bouhuis (Eds.), *Attention & Performance* (Vol. 10, pp. 531–556). Hillsdale, NJ: Erlbaum.

Posner, M. I., Cohen, Y., Choate, L. S., Hockey, R., & Maylor, E. A. (1984a). Sustained concentration: Passive filtering or active orienting? In S. Kornblum & J. Requin (Eds.), *Preparatory states and processes* (pp. 49–65). Hillsdale, NJ: Erlbaum.

Posner, M. I., Davidson, B. J., & Nissen, M. J. (1976). The process of stimulus detection. Paper presented at the annual meeting of the Psychonomic Society, St. Louis. Cited in Posner, M. I. (1978). *Chronometric explorations of mind*. Hillsdale, NJ: Erlbaum.

Posner, M. I., & Fan, J. (in press). Attention as an organ system. In J. Pomerantz (Ed.), *Neurobiology of perception and communication: From synapse to society. The IVth De Lange conference*. Cambridge, UK: Cambridge University Press.

Posner, M. I., Nissen, M. J., & Ogden, W. C. (1978). Attended and unattended processing modes: The role of set for spatial location. In H. L. Pick & I. J. Saltzman (Eds.), *Modes of perceiving and processing information*. Hillsdale, NJ: Erlbaum.

Posner, M. I., & Petersen, S. E. (1990). The attention system of the human brain. *Annual Review of Neuroscience*, *13*, 25–42.

Posner, M. I., Petersen, S. E., Fox, P. T., & Raichle, M. E. (1988). Localization of cognitive operations in the human brain. *Science*, *240*, 1627–1631.

Posner, M. I., Rafal, R. D., Choate, L., & Vaughan, J. (1985). Inhibition of return: Neural basis and function. *Cognitive Neuropsychology*, *2*, 211–218.

Posner, M. I., & Rothbart, M. K. (2007). Research on attention networks as a model for the integration of psychological science. *Annual Review of Psychology*, *58*, 1–23.

Posner, M. I., Snyder, C. R. R., & Davidson, B. J. (1980). Attention and the detection of signals. *Journal of Experimental Psychology: General*, *109*, 160–174.

Posner, M. I., Walker, J. A., Friedrich, F. J., & Rafal, R. D. (1984b). Effects of parietal injury on covert orienting of attention. *Journal of Neuroscience*, *4*, 1863–1874.

Possamai, C. (1985). Relationship between inhibition and facilitation following a visual cue. *Acta Psychologica*, *61*, 243–258.

Possamai, C., & Bonnel, A. M. (1991). Early modulation of visual input: Constant versus varied cueing. *Bulletin of the Psychonomic Society*, *29*, 323–326.

Povinelli, D. J., & Preuss, T. M. (1995). Theory of mind: Evolutionary history of a cognitive specialization. *Trends in Neurosciences*, *18*, 418–424.

Pratt, J., & Abrams, R. A. (1999). Inhibition of return in discrimination tasks. *Journal of Experimental Psychology: Human Perception & Performance, 25,* 229–242.

Pratt, J., Adams, J. J., & McAuliffe, J. (1998). The spatial relationship between cues and targets mediates inhibition of return. *Canadian Journal of Experimental Psychology, 52,* 213–216.

Pratt, J., & Fischer, M. H. (2002). Examining the role of the fixation cue in inhibition of return. *Canadian Journal of Experimental Psychology, 56,* 294–301.

Pratt, J., Kingstone, A., & Khoe, W. (1997). Inhibition of return in location- and identity-based choice decision tasks. *Perception & Psychophysics, 59,* 964–971.

Pratt, J., & Nghiem, T. (2000). The role of the gap effect in the orienting of attention: Evidence for express attentional shifts. *Visual Cognition, 7,* 629–644.

Pratt, J., Spalek, T. M., & Bradshaw, F. (1999). The time to detect targets at inhibited and noninhibited locations: Preliminary evidence for attentional momentum. *Journal of Experimental Psychology: Human Perception & Performance, 25,* 730–746.

Preuss, T. M. (2000). What's human about the human brain. In M. S. Gazzaniga (Ed.), *The new cognitive neurosciences* (pp. 1219–1234). Cambridge, MA: MIT Press.

Prime, D. J., McDonald, J. J., Green, J. J., & Ward, L. M. (in press). When crossmodal attention fails: A controversy resolved? *Canadian Journal of Experimental Psychology.*

Prime, D. J., McDonald, J. J., & Ward, L. M. (2006). *When crossmodal attention fails: Narrow zone or dimension conflict?* Unpublished manuscript, University of British Columbia.

Prime, D. J., Visser, T., & Ward, L. M. (2006). Reorienting attention and inhibition of return. *Perception & Psychophysics, 68,* 1310–1323.

Prime, D. J., & Ward, L. M. (2006). Cortical expressions of inhibition of return. *Brain Research, 1072,* 161–174.

Purpura, K. P., & Schiff, N. D. (1997). The thalamic intralaminar nuclei: A role in visual awareness. *The Neuroscientist, 3,* 8–15.

Pye, M. F. (2003). *Evidence for a unitary focus of visual attention using an interference procedure.* Unpublished Thesis.

Pylyshyn, Z. (1984). *Computation and cognition.* Cambridge, MA: MIT Press.

Pylyshyn, Z. (1989). The role of location indexes in spatial perception: A sketch of the FINST spatial-index model. *Cognition, 32,* 65–97.

Pylyshyn, Z. (1998). Visual indexes in spatial vision and imagery. In R. D. Wright (Ed.), *Visual attention* (pp. 215–231). New York: Oxford University Press.

Pylyshyn, Z. (1999). Is vision continuous with cognition? The case for cognitive impenetrability of visual perception. *Behavioral & Brain Sciences, 22,* 341–423.

Pylyshyn, Z. (2001). Visual indexes, preconceptual objects, and situated vision. *Cognition, 80,* 127–158.

Pylyshyn, Z. (2003). *Seeing and visualizing.* Cambridge, MA: MIT Press.

Pylyshyn, Z. (2004). Some puzzling findings in multiple object tracking: I. Tracking without keeping track of object identities. *Visual Cognition, 11,* 801–822.

Pylyshyn, Z. (2007). *Things and places: How the mind connects with the world.* Cambridge, MA: MIT Press.

Pylyshyn, Z., & Storm, R. W. (1988). Tracking multiple independent targets: Evidence for a parallel tracking mechanism. *Spatial Vision, 3,* 179–197.

Radeau, M., & Bertelson, P. (1976). The effect of a textured visual field on modality dominance in a ventriloquism situation. *Perception & Psychophysics, 20,* 227–235.

Rafal, R. (1996). Visual attention: Converging operations from neurology and psychology. In A. F. Kramer & M. G. H. Coles (Eds.), *Converging operations in the study of visual selection* (pp. 139–192). Washington, DC: American Psychological Association.

Rafal, R., Calabresi, P. A., Brennan, C. W., & Sciolto, T. K. (1989). Saccade preparation inhibits reorienting to recently attended locations. *Journal of Experimental Psychology: Human Perception & Performance, 15,* 673–685.

Rafal, R., & Grimm, R. J. (1981). Progressive supranuclear palsy: Functional analysis of the response to methysergide and antiparkinsonian agents. *Neurology, 31,* 1507–1518.

Rafal, R., Henik, A., & Smith, J. (1991). Extrageniculate contributions to reflexive visual orienting in normal humans: A temporal hemifield advantage. *Journal of Cognitive Neuroscience, 3,* 323–329.

Rafal, R., & Inhoff, A. W. (1986). Midbrain mechanisms for orienting visual attention. *Proceedings of the 8th Annual Conference of the Cognitive Science Society.* Amherst, MA, USA.

Rafal, R., & Posner, M. I. (1987). Deficits in human visual spatial field following thalamic lesions. *Proceedings of the National Academy of Sciences USA, 84,* 7349–7353.

Rafal, R., Posner, M. I., Friedman, J. H., Inhoff, A. W., & Bernstein, E. (1988). Orienting of visual attention in progressive supranuclear palsy. *Brain, 111,* 267–280.

Rauschecker, J. P., & Tian, B. (2000). Mechanisms and streams for processing of "what" and "where" in auditory cortex. *Proceedings of the National Academy of Sciences USA, 97,* 11800–11806.

Rayner, K., & Pollatsek, A. (1983). Is visual information integrated across saccades? *Perception & Psychophysics, 34,* 39–48.

Raz, A., & Buhle, J. (2006). Typologies of attention networks. *Nature Reviews Neuroscience, 7,* 367–379.

Reddy, L., Quiroga, R. Q., Wilken, P., Koch, C., & Fried, I. (2006). A single-neuron correlate of change detection and change blindness in the human medial temporal lobe. *Current Biology, 16,* 2066–2072.

Remington, R. (1980). Attention and saccadic eye movements. *Journal of Experimental Psychology: Human Perception & Performance, 6,* 726–744.

Remington, R., Johnston, J. C., & Yantis, S. (1992). Involuntary attentional capture by abrupt onsets. *Perception & Psychophysics, 51,* 279–290.

Remington, R., & Pierce, L. (1984). Moving attention: Evidence for time-invariant shifts of visual selective attention. *Perception & Psychophysics, 35,* 393–399.

Rensink, R. A., O'Regan, J. K., & Clark, J. J., (1997). To see or not to see: The need for attention to perceive changes in scenes. *Psychological Science, 8,* 368–373.

Reuter-Lorenz, P. A., & Fendrich, R. (1992). Oculomotor readiness and covert orienting—differences between central and peripheral precues. *Perception & Psychophysics, 52,* 336–344.

Reuter-Lorenz, P. A., Hughes, H. C., & Fendrich, R. (1991). The reduction of saccadic latency by prior offset of the fixation point: An analysis of the gap effect. *Perception & Psychophysics, 49,* 167–175.

Reuter-Lorenz, P. A., Jha, A. P., & Rosenquist, J. N. (1996). What is inhibited in inhibition of return? *Journal of Experimental Psychology: Human Perception & Performance, 22,* 367–378.

Richard, C. M., Wright, R. D., & Ward, L. M. (2003). Goal-driven modulation of stimulus-driven attentional capture in multiple-cue displays. *Perception & Psychophysics, 65,* 939–955.

Ristic, J., & Kingstone, A. (2005). Taking control of reflexive social attention. *Cognition, 94,* B55–B65.

Ristic, J., & Kingstone, A. (2006). Attention to arrows: Pointing to a new direction. *Quarterly Journal of Experimental Psychology, 59,* 1921–1930.

Rizzolatti, G., Riggio, L., Dascola, I., & Umiltà, C. (1987). Reorienting attention across the horizontal and vertical meridians: Evidence in favor of a premotor theory of attention. *Neuropsychologia, 25,* 31–40.

Ro, T., Farnè, A., & Chang, E. (2003). Inhibition of return and the human frontal eye fields. *Experimental Brain Research, 150,* 290–296.

Ro, T., Pratt, J., & Rafal, R. D. (2000). Inhibition of return in saccadic eye movements. *Experimental Brain Research, 130,* 264–268.

Roberts, M., & Summerfield, Q. (1981). Audiovisual presentation demonstrates that selective adaptation in speech perception is purely auditory. *Perception & Psychophysics, 30,* 309–314.

Robinson, D. A. (1968). The oculomotor control system: A review. *Proceedings of the IEEE, 56,* 1032–1049.

Robinson, D. A. (1972). Eye movements evoked by collicular stimulation in the alert monkey. *Vision Research, 12,* 1795–1808.

Robinson, D. L., & Cowie, R. J. (1997). The primate pulvinar: Structural, functional, and behavioural components of visual salience. In M. Steriade, E. G. Jones, & D. A. McCormick (Eds.), *Thalamus* (Vol. 2, pp. 53–92). New York: Elsevier.

Robinson, D. L., Goldberg, M. E., & Stanton, G. B. (1978). Parietal association cortex in the primate: Sensory mechanisms and behavioral modulations. *Journal of Neurophysiology, 41,* 910–932.

Robinson, D. L., & Kertzman, C. (1995). Covert orienting of attention in macaques. III. Contributions of the superior colliculus. *Journal of Neurophysiology, 74*, 713–721.

Robinson, D. L., & Petersen, S. (1992). The pulvinar and visual salience. *Trends in Neuroscience, 15*, 127–132.

Roggeveen, A. B., Prime, D. J., & Ward, L. M. (2005). Inhibition of return and response repetition within and between modalities. *Experimental Brain Research, 167*, 86–94.

Roggeveen, A. B., & Ward, L. M. (2007a). *Anisotropy of covert endogenous orienting across the visual field.* Unpublished manuscript, University of British Columbia.

Roggeveen, A. B., & Ward, L. M. (2007b). *Effects of endogenous attentional distribution across the visual field: Alternative evidence for endogenous attentional anisotropy.* Unpublished manuscript, University of British Columbia.

Roggeveen, A. B., & Ward, L. M. (2007c). *The impact of paradigm parameters on the allocation of endogenous attention: The role of objects and likelihood.* Unpublished manuscript, University of British Columbia.

Ross, L. E., & Ross, S. M. (1980). Saccade latency and warning signals: Stimulus onset, offset, and change as warning events. *Perception & Psychophysics, 27*, 251–257.

Rushworth, M. F. S., Ellison, A., & Walsh, V. (2001). Complementary localization and lateralization of orienting and motor attention. *Nature Neuroscience, 4*, 656–661.

Ruz, M., & Lupiáñez, J. (2002). A review of attentional capture: On its automaticity and sensitivity to endogenous control. *Psicológica, 23*, 283–309.

Sachs, M. B., Nachmias, J., & Robson, J. G. (1971). Spatial-frequency channels in human vision. *Journal of the Optical Society of America A, 61*, 1176–1186.

Sagi, D., & Julesz, B. (1985). Fast noninertial shifts of attention. *Spatial Vision, 1*, 141–149.

Samuel, A. G., & Kat, D. (2003). Inhibition of return: A graphical meta-analysis of its time course and an empirical test of its temporal and spatial properties. *Psychonomic Bulletin & Review, 10*, 897–906.

Samuel, A. G., & Weiner, S. K. (2001). Attentional consequences of object appearance and disappearance. *Journal of Experimental Psychology: Human Perception & Performance, 27*, 1433–1451.

Sanders, A. E. (1963). *The selective process in the functional visual field.* Assen, Netherlands: Van Gorcum.

Sapir, A., Hayes, A., Henik, A., Danziger, S., & Rafal, R. (2004). Parietal lobe lesions disrupt saccadic remapping of inhibitory location tagging. *Journal of Cognitive Neuroscience, 16*, 503–509.

Sapir, A., Rafal, R., & Henik, A. (2002). Attending to the thalamus: Inhibition of return and nasal-temporal asymmetry in the pulvinar. *NeuroReport, 13*, 693–697.

Sapir, A., Soroker, N., Berger, A., & Henik, A. (1999). Inhibition of return in spatial attention: Direct evidence for collicular generation. *Nature Neuroscience, 2*, 1053–1054.

Sarnecki, J., & Sponheimer, M. (2002). Why Neanderthals hate poetry: A critical notice of Steven Mithen's *The prehistory of mind. Philosophical Psychology, 15*, 173–184.

Saslow, M. G. (1967). Effects of components of displacement-step stimuli upon latency of saccadic eye movement. *Journal of the Optical Society of America, 57*, 1024–1029.

Sato, T. R., & Schall, J. D. (2003). Effects of stimulus-response compatibility on neural selection in frontal eye field. *Neuron, 38*, 637–648.

Scharf, B., Quigley, S., Aoki, C., Peachey, N., & Reeves, A. (1987). Focused auditory attention and frequency selectivity. *Perception & Psychophysics, 42*, 215–223.

Schendel, K. L., Robertson, L. C., & Treisman, A. (2001). Objects and their locations in exogenous cueing. *Perception & Psychophysics, 63*, 577–594.

Schiller, P. H. (1998). Neural control of visually guided eye movements. In J. E. Richards (Ed.), *Cognitive neuroscience of attention: A developmental perspective* (pp. 3–50). Mahwah, NJ: Lawrence Erlbaum.

Schiller, P. H., & Koerner, F. (1971). Discharge characteristics of single units in superior colliculus of alert rhesus monkeys. *Journal of Neurophysiology, 34*, 920–936.

Schiller, P. H., Sandell, J. H., & Maunsell, J. H. R. (1987). The effect of frontal eye field and superior colliculus lesions on saccadic latencies in the rhesus monkey. *Journal of Neurophysiology, 57*, 1033–1049.

Schiller, P. H., & Stryker, M. (1972). Single-unit recording and stimulation in superior colliculus of the alert rhesus monkey. *Journal of Neurophysiology, 35*, 915–924.

Schiller, P. H., & Tehovnik, E. J. (2005). Neural mechanisms underlying target selection with saccadic eye movements. *Progress in Brain Research, 149*, 157–171.

Schiller, P. H., True, S. D., & Conway, J. L. (1980). Deficits in eye movements following frontal eye field and superior colliculus ablations. *Journal of Neurophysiology, 44*, 1175–1189.

Schlag-Rey, M., Schlag, J., & Dassonville, P. (1992). How the frontal eye field can impose a saccade goal on superior colliculus neurons. *Journal of Neurophysiology, 67*, 1003–1005.

Schneider, G. E. (1969). Two visual systems. *Science, 163*, 895–902.

Schneider, K. A., & Kastner, S. (2005). Visual responses of the superior colliculus: A high-resolution functional magnetic resonance imaging study. *Journal of Neurophysiology, 94*, 2491–2503.

Schneider, K. A., Richter, M. C., & Kastner, S. (2004). Retinotopic organization and functional subdivisions of the human lateral geniculate nucleus: A high-resolution functional magnetic resonance imaging study. *Journal of Neuroscience, 24*, 8975–8985.

Schneider, W., Dumais, S. T., & Shiffrin, R. M. (1984). Automatic and controlled processing and attention. In R. Parasuraman & D. R. Davies (Eds.), *Varieties of attention* (pp. 1–27). New York: Academic Press.

Scholl, B. J., & Pylyshyn, Z. (1999). Tracking multiple items through occlusion: Clues to visual objecthood. *Cognitive Psychology, 38*, 259–290.

Schroeder, C. E., & Foxe, J. J. (2005). Multisensory contributions to low-level, "unisensory" processing. *Current Opinion in Biology, 15*, 454–458.

Sears, C. R., & Pylyshyn, Z. (2000). Multiple object tracking and attentional processing. *Canadian Journal of Experimental Psychology, 54*, 1–14.

Senkowski, D., Talsma, D., Herrmann, C. S., & Woldorff, M. G. (2005). Multisensory processing and oscillatory gamma responses: Effects of spatial selective attention. *Experimental Brain Research, 166*, 411–426.

Serences, J. T., Schwarzbach, J., Courtney, S. M., Golay, X., & Yantis, S. (2004). Control of object-based attention in human cortex. *Cerebral Cortex, 14*, 1346–1357.

Serences, J. T., Shomstein, S., Leber, A. B., Golay, X., Egeth, H. E., & Yantis, S. (2005). Coordination of voluntary and stimulus-driven attentional control in human cortex. *Psychological Science, 16*, 114–122.

Serences, J. T., & Yantis, S. (2006). Selective visual attention and perceptual coherence. *Trends in Cognitive Sciences, 10*, 38–45.

Sereno, A. B., Briand, K. A., Amador, S. C., & Szapiel, S. V. (2006). Disruption of reflexive attention and eye movements in an individual with a collicular lesion. *Journal of Clinical and Experimental Neuropsychology, 28*, 145–166.

Shagass, C., Roemer, R., & Amadeo, M. (1976). Eye tracking performance and engagement of attention. *Archives of General Psychiatry, 33*, 121–125.

Shebilske, W. L., & Fisher, D. F. (1983). Understanding extended discourse through the eyes: How and why. In R. Groner, C. Menz, D. F. Fisher, & R. A. Monty (Eds.), *Eye movements and psychological functions: International views* (pp. 303–314). Hillsdale, NJ: Erlbaum.

Shepard, R. N. (1975). Form, formation, and transformations of internal representations. In R. L. Solso (Ed.), *Information processing and cognition: The Loyola symposium* (pp. 87–122). Hillsdale, NJ: Erlbaum.

Shepard, R. N., & Cooper, L. A. (1982). *Mental images and their transformations.* Cambridge, MA: MIT Press.

Shepard, M., Findlay, J. M., & Hockey, R. J. (1986). The relationship between eye movements and spatial attention. *Quarterly Journal of Experimental Psychology, 38*, 475–491.

Shepherd, M., & Müller, H. J. (1989). Movement versus focusing of visual attention. *Perception & Psychophysics, 46*, 146–154.

Sherman, S. M. (1974). Visual fields of cats with cortical and tectal lesions. *Science, 185*, 355–357.

Shipp, S. (2004). The brain circuitry of attention. *Trends in Cognitive Sciences, 8*, 223–230.

Shomstein, S., & Behrmann, M. (2006). Cortical systems mediating visual attention to both objects and spatial locations. *Proceedings of the National Academy of Sciences USA, 103*, 11387–11392.

Shomstein, S., & Yantis, S. (2002). Object-based attention: Sensory modulation or priority setting? *Perception & Psychophysics, 64,* 41–51.

Shomstein, S., & Yantis, S. (2004). Control of attention shifts between vision and audition in human cortex. *Journal of Neuroscience, 24*, 10702–10706.

Shomstein, S., & Yantis, S. (2006). Parietal cortex mediates voluntary control of spatial and nonspatial auditory attention. *Journal of Neuroscience, 26*, 435–439.

Shulman, G. L., McAvoy, M. P., Cowan, M. C., Astafiev, S. V., Tansy, A. P., d'Avossa, G., et al. (2003). Quantitative analysis of attention and detection signals during visual search. *Journal of Neurophysiology, 90*, 3384–3397.

Shulman, G. L., Ollinger, J. M., Linenweber, M., Petersen, S. E., & Corbetta, M. (2001). Multiple neural correlates of detection in the human brain. *Proceedings of the National Academy of Sciences USA, 98*, 313–318.

Shulman, G. L., Remington, R. W., & McLean, J. P. (1979). Moving attention through visual space. *Journal of Experimental Psychology: Human Perception & Performance, 5*, 522–526.

Shulman, G. L., Wilson, J., & Sheehy, J. B. (1985). Spatial determinants of the distribution of attention. *Perception & Psychophysics, 37*, 59–65.

Silver, M. A., Ress, D., & Heeger, D. J. (2005). Topographic maps of visual spatial attention in human parietal cortex. *Journal of Neurophysiology, 94*, 1358–1371.

Simon, J. R., Small, A. M., Jr., Ziglar, R. A., & Craft, J. L. (1970). Response interference in an information processing task: Sensory versus perceptual factors. *Journal of Experimental Psychology, 85*, 311–314.

Simons, D. J., & Ambinder, M. S. (2005). Change blindness: Theory and consequences. *Current Directions in Psychological Science, 14*, 44–48.

Simons, D. J., & Rensink, R. A. (2005). Change blindness: Past, present, and future. *Trends in Cognitive Sciences, 9*, 16–20.

Skelton, J. M., & Eriksen, C. W. (1976). Spatial characteristics of selective attention in letter matching. *Bulletin of the Psychonomic Society, 7*, 136–138.

Smith, E. E., Jonides, J., & Koeppe, R. A. (1996). Dissociating verbal and spatial working memory using PET. *Cerebral Cortex, 6*, 11–20.

Smith, M. L., & Milner, B. (1981). The role of the right hippocampus in the recall of spatial location. *Neuropsychologia, 19*, 781–793.

Smith, M. L., & Milner, B. (1984). Differential effects of frontal lobe lesions on cognitive estimation and spatial memory. *Neuropsychologia, 22*, 697–705.

Snyder, J., & Kingstone, A. (2001). Inhibition of return at multiple locations in visual search: When you see it and when you don't. *Quarterly Journal of Experimental Psychology, 54*, 1221–1237.

Snyder, J., Schmidt, W. C., & Kingstone, A. (2001). Attentional momentum does not underlie the inhibition of return effect. *Journal of Experimental Psychology: Human Perception & Performance, 27*, 1420–1432.

Snyder, L. H., Batista, A. P., & Andersen, R. A. (1997). Coding of intention in the posterior parietal cortex. *Nature, 386*, 167–170.

Sokolov, E. N. (1960). Neuronal models and the orienting reflex. In M. A. B. Brazier (Ed.), *The central nervous system and behaviour* (pp. 187–276). Madison, NJ: Madison Printing.

Sokolov, E. N. (1975). The neuronal mechanisms of the orienting reflex. In N. E. Sokolov & O. S. Vinogradova (Eds.), *Neuronal mechanisms of the orienting reflex* (pp. 217–238). New York: Wiley.

Somers, D. C., & McMains, S. A. (2005). Spatially-specific attentional modulation revealed by fMRI. In L. Itti, G. Rees, & J. K. Tsotsos (Eds.), *Neurobiology of attention* (pp. 377–382). San Diego: Elsevier.

Spalek, T. M., & Hammad, S. (2004). Supporting the attentional momentum view of IOR: Is attention biased to go right? *Perception & Psychophysics, 66,* 219–233.

Spalek, T. M., & Hammad, S. (2005). The left-to-right bias in inhibition of return is due to the direction of reading. *Psychological Science, 16,* 15–18.

Sparks, D. L., & Mays, L. E. (1983). Spatial localization of saccade targets: I. Compensation for stimulus-induced perturbations in eye position. *Journal of Neurophysiology, 49,* 45–63.

Sparks, D. L., & Mays, L. E. (1990). Signal transformations required for the generation of saccadic eye movements. *Annual Review of Neuroscience, 13,* 309–336.

Spence, C., & Driver, J. (1994). Covert spatial orienting in audition: Exogenous and endogenous mechanisms facilitate sound localization. *Journal of Experimental Psychology: Human Perception & Performance, 20,* 555–574.

Spence, C., & Driver, J. (1996). Audiovisual links in endogenous covert spatial attention. *Journal of Experimental Psychology: Human Perception & Performance, 22,* 1005–1030.

Spence, C., & Driver, J. (1997). Audiovisual links in exogenous covert spatial orienting. *Perception & Psychophysics, 59,* 1–22.

Spence, C., & Driver, J. (1998). Inhibition of return following an auditory cue: The role of central reorienting events. *Experimental Brain Research, 118,* 352–360.

Spence, C., Lloyd, D., McGlone, F., Nicholls, M. E. R., & Driver, J. (2000a). Inhibition of return is supramodal: A demonstration between all possible pairings of vision, touch, and audition. *Experimental Brain Research, 134,* 42–48.

Spence, C., & McDonald, J. J. (2004). The crossmodal consequences of the exogenous spatial orienting of attention. In G. Calvert, C. Spence, & B. Stein (Eds.). *The handbook of multisensory processes* (pp. 3–35). Cambridge, MA: MIT Press.

Spence, C., McDonald, J. J., & Driver, J. (2004). Exogenous spatial cuing studies of human crossmodal attention and multisensory integration. In C. Spence & J. Driver (Eds.), *Crossmodal space and crossmodal attention* (pp. 277–320). New York: Oxford University Press.

Spence, C., Nicholls, M. R., Gillespie, N., & Driver, J. (1998). Crossmodal links in exogenous covert spatial orienting between touch, audition, and vision. *Perception & Psychophysics, 60,* 544–557.

Spence, C., Pavani, F., Driver, J. (2000b). Crossmodal links between vision and touch in covert endogenous spatial attention. *Journal of Experimental Psychology: Human Perception & Performance, 26,* 1298–1319.

Sperling, G. (1960). The information available in brief visual presentations. *Psychology Monographs, 74,* Series 498.

Sperling, G., & Dosher, B. A. (1986). Strategy and optimization in human information processing. In K. Boff, L Kauffmann, & J. Thomas (Eds.), *Handbook of perception and human performance* (pp. 1–85). New York: John Wiley.

Steele, J. C., Richardson, J. C., & Olszewski, J. (1964). Progressive supranuclear palsy. *Archives of Neurology, 10,* 333–359.

Stein, B. E., & Meredith, M. A. (1993). *The merging of the senses.* Cambridge, MA: MIT Press.

Stelmach, L. B., Campsall, J. M., & Herdman, C. M. (1997). Attentional and ocular mechanisms. *Journal of Experimental Psychology: Human Perception & Performance, 23,* 823–844.

Stelmach, L. B., & Herdman, C. M. (1991). Directed attention and the perception of temporal order. *Journal of Experimental Psychology: Human Perception & Performance, 17,* 539–550.

Sternberg, S. (1966). High speed scanning in human memory. *Science, 153,* 652–654.

Sternberg, S. (1969). The discovery of processing stages. *Acta Psychologica, 30,* 34–78.

Takeda, Y., & Yagi, A. (2000). Inhibitory tagging in visual search can be found if search stimuli remain visible. *Perception & Psychophysics, 62,* 927–934.

Talsma, D., Doty, T. J., & Woldorff, M. G. (2007). Selective attention and audiovisual integration: Is attending to both modalities a prerequisite for early integration? *Cerebral Cortex, 17,* 679–690.

Talsma, D., & Woldorff, M. G. (2005). Selective attention and multisensory integration: Multiple phases of effects on the evoked brain activity. *Journal of Cognitive Neuroscience, 17,* 1098–1114.

Tanaka, Y., & Shimojo, S. (1996). Location vs. feature: Reaction time reveals dissociation between two visual functions. *Vision Research, 36,* 2125–2140.

Tanner, W., & Norman, R. (1954). The human use of information II: Signal detection for the case of an unknown signal parameter. *IEEE Transactions on Information Theory, 4,* 222–227.

Tassinari, G., Biscaldi, M., Marzi, C. A., & Berlucchi, G. (1989). Ipsilateral inhibition and contralateral facilitation of simple reaction time to non-foveal visual targets from non-informative visual cues. *Acta Psychologica, 70,* 267–291.

Tassinari, G., & Campara, D. (1996). Consequences of covert orienting to non-informative stimuli of different modalities: A unitary mechanism? *Neuropsychologia, 34,* 235–245.

Tassinari, G., Campara, D., Benedetti, C., & Berlucci, B. (2002). The contribution of general and specific motor inhibitory sets to the so-called auditory inhibition of return. *Experimental Brain Research, 146,* 523–530.

Tata, M. S., Prime, D. J., McDonald, J. J., & Ward, L. M. (2001). Transient spatial attention modulates distinct components of the auditory ERP. *Neuroreport, 12,* 3679–3682.

Tata, M. S., & Ward, L. M. (2005). Spatial attention modulates activity in a posterior "where" pathway. *Neuropsychologia*, *43*, 509–516.

Tatler, B. W., & Wade, N. J. (2003). On nystagmus, saccades, and fixations. *Perception*, *32*, 167–184.

Taylor, T. L., & Donnelly, M. P. W. (2002). Inhibition of return for target discriminations: The effect of repeating discriminated and irrelevant stimulus dimensions. *Perception & Psychophysics, 64*, 292–317.

Taylor, T. L., & Klein, R. M. (2000). Visual and motor effects in inhibition of return. *Journal of Experimental Psychology: Human Perception & Performance*, *26*, 1639–1656.

Theeuwes, J. (1991). Exogenous and endogenous control of attention: The effect of visual onsets and offsets. *Perception & Psychophysics*, *49*, 83–90.

Theeuwes, J. (1992). Perceptual selectivity for color and form. *Perception & Psychophysics*, *51*, 599–606.

Theeuwes, J. (1994). Endogenous and exogenous control of visual selection. *Perception*, *23*, 429–430.

Theeuwes, J. (1995). Abrupt luminance change pops out; abrupt color change does not. *Perception & Psychophysics*, *57*, 637–644.

Theeuwes, J., Kramer, A. F., Hahn, S., & Irwin, D. E. (1998). Our eyes do not always go where we want them to go: Capture of the eyes by new objects. *Psychological Science*, *9*, 379–385.

Theeuwes, J., Kramer, A. F., Hahn, S., Irwin, D. E., & Zelinsky, G. J. (1999). Influence of attentional capture on oculomotor control. *Journal of Experimental Psychology: Human Perception & Performance*, *25*, 1595–1608.

Thompson, K. G., Bichot, N. P., & Schall, J. D. (1997). Dissociation of visual discrimination from saccade programming in macaque frontal eye field. *Journal of Neurophysiology*, *77*, 1046–1050.

Thompson, K. G., Biscoe, K. L., & Sato, T. R. (2005). Neuronal basis of covert spatial attention in the frontal eye field. *Journal of Neuroscience*, *25*, 9479–9487.

Thurlow, W. R., & Jack, C. E. (1973). Certain determinants of the "ventriloquism effect." *Perceptual & Motor Skills*, *36*, 1171–1184.

Tipper, S. P., Driver, J., & Weaver, B. (1991). Object-centred inhibition of return of visual attention. *Quarterly Journal of Experiment Psychology*, *43A*, 289–298.

Tipper, S. P., Grison, S., & Kessler, K. (2003). Long-term inhibition of return of attention. *Psychological Science*, *14*, 19–25.

Tipper, S. P., Weaver, B., Jerreat, L. M., & Burak, A. L. (1994). Object-based and environment-based inhibition of return of visual attention. *Journal of Experimental Psychology: Human Perception & Performance*, *20*, 478–499.

Tipper, S. P., Weaver, B., & Watson, F. L. (1996). Inhibition of return to successively cued spatial locations: Commentary on Pratt and Abrams (1995). *Journal of Experimental Psychology: Human Perception & Performance, 22*, 1289–1293.

Titchener, E. B. (1908). *Lectures on the elementary psychology of feeling and attention.* New York: Macmillan.

Titchener, E. B. (1910). *A textbook of psychology.* New York: Macmillan.

Todd, J. T., & Van Gelder, P. (1979). Implications of a transient-sustained dichotomy for the measurement of human performance. *Journal of Experimental Psychology: Human Perception & Performance, 5,* 625–638.

Tomasello, M., Call, J., & Hare, B. (1997). Five primate species that follow the gaze of conspecifics. *Animal Behavior, 55,* 1063–1069.

Tomasello, M., Hare, B., & Fogelman, T. (2001). The ontogeny of gaze following in chimpanzees, *Pan troglodytes,* and rhesus macaques, *Macaca mulatta. Animal Behavior, 61,* 335–343.

Tomonaga, M. (2007). Is chimpanzee (*Pan troglodytes*) spatial attention reflexively triggered by gaze cue? *Journal of Comparative Psychology, 121,* 156–170.

Tootell, R. B., Hadjikhani, N., Hall, E. K., Marrett, S., Van Duffel, W., Vaughan J. T., et al. (1998). The retinotopy of visual spatial attention. *Neuron, 21,* 1409–1422.

Treisman, A. (1998). The perception of features and objects. In R. D. Wright (Ed.), *Visual attention* (pp. 26–54). New York: Oxford University Press.

Treisman, A., & Gelade, G. (1980). A feature integration theory of attention. *Cognitive Psychology, 12,* 242–248.

Treisman, A., & Sato, S. (1990). Conjunction search revisited. *Journal of Experimental Psychology: Human Perception & Performance, 16,* 459–478.

Treisman, A., & Schmidt, H. (1982). Illusory conjunctions in the perception of objects. *Cognitive Psychology, 14,* 107–141.

Treisman, A., & Souther, J. (1985). Search asymmetry: A diagnostic for preattentive processing of separable features. *Journal of Experimental Psychology: General, 114,* 285–310.

Treisman, A., Vieira, A., & Hayes, A. (1992). Automaticity and preattentive processing. *American Journal of Psychology, 105,* 341–362.

Treue, S. (2003). Visual attention: The where, what, how and why of saliency. *Current Opinion in Neurobiology, 13,* 428–432.

Tsal, Y. (1983). Movements of attention across the visual field. *Journal of Experimental Psychology: Human Perception & Performance, 9,* 523–530.

Tse, C. Y., Tien, K. R., & Penney, T. B. (2006). Event-related optical imaging reveals the temporal dynamics of right temporal and frontal cortex activation in pre-attentive change detection. *NeuroImage, 29,* 314–320.

Tsotsos, J. K., Itti, L., & Rees, G. (2005). A brief and selective history of attention. In L. Itti, G. Rees, & J. K. Tsotsos (Eds.), *Neurobiology of attention* (pp. xxiii–xxxii). San Diego, CA: Elsevier.

Turatto, M., Mazza, V., & Umiltà, C. (2005). Crossmodal object-based attention: Auditory objects affect visual processing. *Cognition, 96,* B55–B64.

Uexküll, J. von (1909/1985). Environment (Umwelt) and the inner world of animals (C. J. Mellor & D. Gove, Trans.). In G. M. Burghardt (Ed.), *The foundations of comparative ethology,* (pp. 222–245). New York, Van Nostrand Reinhold. (reprinted from Umwelt und Innenwelt der Tiere, 1909, Berlin: Jena).

Ullman, S. (1984). Visual routines. *Cognition*, *18*, 97–159.

Ullman, S. (1996). *High-level vision*. Cambridge, MA: MIT Press.

Umiltà, C., Riggio, L., Dascola, I., & Rizzolatti, G. (1991). Different aspects of central and peripheral cues on the reorienting of spatial attention. *European Journal of Cognitive Psychology*, *3*, 247–267.

Ungerleider, L. G., Galkin, T. W., & Mishkin, M. (1983). Visuotopic organization of projections from striate cortex to inferior and lateral pulvinar in rhesus monkey. *Journal of Comparative Neurology*, *217*, 137–157.

Vallar, G., & Perani, D. (1987). The anatomy of spatial neglect in humans. In M. Jeannerod (Ed.), *Neurophysiological and neuropsychological aspects of spatial neglect* (pp. 235–258). New York: Elsevier.

Vandenberghe, R., Dupont, P., De Bruyn, B., Bormans, G., Michiels, J., Mortelmans, L., et al. (1996). The influence of stimulus location on the brain activation pattern in detection and orientation discrimination: A PET study of visual attention. *Brain*, *119*, 1263–1276.

Vandenberghe, R., Gitelman, D. R., Parrish, T. B., & Mesulam, M. M. (2001). Functional specificity of superior parietal mediation of spatial shifting. *NeuroImage*, *14*, 661–673.

Van der Heijden, A. H. C. (1992). *Selective attention in vision*. New York, Routledge.

Van der Heijden, A. H. C., Wolters, G., & Enkeling, M. (1988). The effects of advance location cueing on latencies in a single-letter recognition task. *Psychological Research*, *50*, 94–102.

Van Essen, D. C., & Drury, H. A. (1997). Structural and functional analyses of human cerebral cortex using a surface-based atlas. *Journal of Neuroscience*, *17*, 7079–7102.

Van Essen, D. C., Lewis, J. W., Drury, H. A., Hadjikhani, N., Tootell, R. B. H., Bakircioglu, M., et al. (2001). Mapping visual cortex in monkeys and humans using surface-based atlases. *Vision Research*, *41*, 1359–1378.

Van Gelder, P., Anderson, S., Herman, E., Lebedev, S., & Tsui, W. H. (1990). Saccades in pursuit eye tracking reflect motor attention processes. *Comprehensive Psychiatry*, *31*, 253–260.

Van Gisbergen, J. A. M., Gielen, S., Cox, H., Bruijns, J., & Kleine Schaars, H. (1981). Relation between metrics of saccades and stimulus trajectory in visual target tracking: Implications for models of the saccade system. In A. F. Fuchs & W. Becker (Eds.), *Progress in oculomotor research* (pp. 17–27). Amsterdam: Elsevier.

Van Hoorn, W. (1972). *Ancient and modern theories of visual perception*. Amsterdam: University Press Amsterdam.

Varela, F., Lachaux, J. P., Rodriguez, E., & Martinerie, J. (2001). The brainweb: Phase synchronization and large-scale integration. *Nature Reviews Neuroscience*, *2*, 229–239.

Vaughan, J. (1984). Saccades directed at previously attended locations in space. In A. J. Gale & C. W. Johnson (Eds.), *Theoretical and applied aspects of eye movement research* (pp. 143–150). Amsterdam: North Holland.

Vecera, S. P., & Rizzo, M. (2004). What are you looking at? Impaired 'social attention' following frontal-lobe damage. *Neuropsychologia*, *42*, 1657–1665.

Vecera, S. P., & Rizzo, M. (2006). Eye gaze does not produce reflexive shifts of attention: Evidence from frontal-lobe damage. *Neuropsychologia*, *44*, 150–159.

Viswanathan, L., & Mingolla, E. (2002). Dynamics of attention in depth: Evidence from multi-element tracking. *Perception*, *31*, 1415–1437.

Vogel, E. K., & Luck, S. J. (2000). The visual N1 component as an index of a discrimination process. *Psychophysiology*, *37*, 190–203.

Vogel, E. K., & Luck, S. J. (2002). *Quartering the spotlight of attention*. Paper presented at the annual meeting of Cognitive Science Association for Interdisciplinary Learning, Hood River, Oregon, USA.

Vroomen, J., Bertelson, P., & De Gelder, B. (2001). The ventriloquist effect does not depend on the direction of automatic visual attention. *Perception & Psychophysics*, *63*, 651–659.

Wade, N. J. (2004). Philosophical instruments and toys: Optical devices extending the art of seeing. *Journal of the History of the Neurosciences*, *13*, 102–124.

Wade, N. J., & Heller, D. (1997). Scopes of perception: The experimental manipulation of space and time. *Psychological Research (Historical Archive)*, *60*, 227–237.

Wade, N. J., & Tatler, B. W. (2005). *The moving tablet of the eye: The origins of modern eye movement research*. New York: Oxford University Press.

Wade, N. J., Tatler, B. W., & Heller, D. (2003). Dodge-ing the issue: Dodge, Javal, Hering, and the measurement of saccades in eye-movement research. *Perception*, *32*, 793–804.

Walker, R., Husain, M., Hodgson, T. L., Harrison, J., & Kennard, C. (1998). Saccadic eye movement and working memory deficits following damage to human prefrontal cortex. *Neuropsychologia*, *36*, 1141–1159.

Wandell, B. S., Brewer, A. A., & Dougherty, R. F. (2005). Visual field map clusters in human cortex. *Philosophical Transactions of the Royal Society B*, *360*, 693–707.

Ward, L. M. (1982). Determinants of attention to local and global features of visual forms. *Journal of Experimental Psychology: Human Perception & Performance*, *8*, 562–581.

Ward, L. M. (1983). On processing dominance: Comment on Pomerantz. *Journal of Experimental Psychology: General*, *112*, 541–546.

Ward, L. M. (1985). Covert focussing of the attentional gaze. *Canadian Journal of Psychology*, *39*, 546–563.

Ward, L. M. (1993). *Visual/auditory capture of auditory/visual attention*. Paper presented at the annual meeting of the Psychonomic Society, Washington, DC.

Ward, L. M. (1994). Supramodal and modality-specific mechanisms for stimulus-driven shifts of auditory and visual attention. *Canadian Journal of Experimental Psychology*, *48*, 242–259.

Ward, L. M. (1997). Involuntary listening aids hearing. *Psychological Science*, *8*, 112–118.

Ward, L. M. (2003). Synchronous neural oscillations and cognitive processes. *Trends in Cognitive Sciences, 7,* 553–559.

Ward, L. M., McDonald, J. J., & Golestani, N. (1998). Crossmodal control of attention shifts. In R. D. Wright (Ed.), *Visual attention* (pp. 232–268). New York: Oxford University Press.

Ward, L. M., McDonald, J. J., & Lin, D. (2000). On asymmetries in crossmodal spatial attention orienting. *Perception & Psychophysics, 62,* 1258–1264.

Ward, L. M., & Mori, S. (1996). Attention cueing aids auditory intensity resolution. *Journal of the Acoustical Society of America, 100,* 1722–1727.

Ward, N. M., & Brown, V. J. (1996). Covert orienting of attention in the rat and the role of striatal dopamine. *Journal of Neuroscience, 16,* 3082–3088.

Ward, R., Danziger, S., Owen, V., & Rafal, R. (2002). Deficits in spatial coding and feature binding following damage to spatiotopic maps in human pulvinar. *Nature Neuroscience, 5,* 99–100.

Wardak, C., Olivier, E., & Duhamel, J. R. (2004). A deficit in covert attention after parietal cortex inactivation in the monkey. *Neuron, 42,* 501–508.

Warren, R. M., & Warren, R. P. (1968). *Helmholtz on perception: Its physiology and development.* New York: Wiley.

Watson, A. B., & Nachmias, J. (1980). Summation of asynchronous gratings. *Vision Research, 20,* 91–94.

Watson, D. G., & Humphreys, G. W. (1997). Visual marking: Prioritizing selection for new objects by top-down attentional inhibition of old objects. *Psychological Review, 104,* 90–122.

Watson, D. G., & Humphreys, G. W. (1998). Visual marking of moving objects: A role for top-down feature-based inhibition in selection. *Journal of Experimental Psychology: Human Perception & Performance, 24,* 946–962.

Watson, D. G., & Humphreys, G. W. (2000). Visual marking: Evidence for inhibition using a probe-dot paradigm. *Perception & Psychophysics, 62,* 471–481.

Weese, G. D., Phillips, J. M., & Brown, V. J. (1999). Attentional orienting is impaired by unilateral lesions of the thalamic reticular nucleus in the rat. *Journal of Neuroscience, 19,* 10135–10139.

Weichselgartner, E., & Sperling, G. (1987). Dynamics of automatic and controlled visual attention. *Science, 238,* 778–780.

Weintraub, S., & Mesulam, M. M. (1987). Right cerebral hemisphere dominance in spatial attention. *Archives of Neurology, 44,* 621–625.

Welsh, T. N., Elliott, D., Anson, J. G., Dhillon, V., Weeks, D. J., Lyons, J. L., et al. (2005). Does Joe influence Fred's actions? Inhibition of return across different nervous systems. *Neuroscience Letters, 385,* 99–104.

Wertheimer, M. (1923). Untersuchungen zur lehre von der Gestalt II. *Psycologische Forschung, 4,* 301–350 [translation published in Ellis, W. (1938). *A source book of Gestalt psychology* (pp. 71–88). London: Routledge & Kegan Paul].

Whiten, A., & Byrne, R. W. (1988). Tactical deception in primates. *Behavioral & Brain Sciences, 11,* 233–273.

Widmann, A., & Schröger, E. (1999). *Do lateralized visual stimuli exogenously orient auditory attention?* Poster presented at the annual meeting of the Society for Psychophysiological Research, Granada, Spain.

Winkowski, J., & Knudsen, E. I. (2006). Top-down gain control of the auditory space map by gaze control circuitry in the barn owl. *Nature, 439*, 336–339.

Witte, E. A., & Marrocco, R. T. (1997). Alteration of brain noradrenergic activity in rhesus monkeys affects the alerting component of covert orienting. *Psychopharmacology, 132*, 315–323.

Wojciulik, E., & Kanwisher, N. (1999). The generality of parietal involvement in visual attention. *Neuron, 23*, 747–764.

Wolfe, J. M. (1994). Guided Search 2.0: A revised model of visual search. *Psychonomic Bulletin & Review, 1*, 202–238.

Wolfe, J. M. (1998). What can 1 million trials tell us about visual search? *Psychological Science, 9*, 33–39.

Wolfe, J. M., & Pokorny, C. W. (1990). Inhibitory tagging in visual search: A failure to replicate. *Perception & Psychophysics, 48*, 357–362.

Wolff, C. (1738). *Psychologia empirica*. Frankfurt & Leipzig: Officina Libraria Rengeriana.

Wolff, C. (1740). *Psychologia rationalis*. Frankfurt & Leipzig: Officina Libraria Rengeriana.

Woodman, G. F., & Luck, S. J. (1999). Electrophysiological measurement of rapid shifts of attention during visual search. *Nature, 400*, 867–869.

Woodman, G. F., & Luck, S. J. (2003). Serial deployment of attention during visual search. *Journal of Experimental Psychology: Human Perception & Performance, 29*, 121–138.

Wright, R. D., & Richard, C. M. (1996). Inhibition-of-return at multiple locations in visual space. *Canadian Journal of Experimental Psychology, 50*, 324–327.

Wright, R. D., & Richard, C. M. (1998). Inhibition-of-return is not reflexive. In R. D. Wright (Ed.), *Visual attention* (pp. 330–347). New York: Oxford University Press.

Wright, R. D., & Richard, C. M. (2000). Location cue validity affects inhibition of return of visual processing. *Vision Research, 40*, 2351–2358.

Wright, R. D., & Richard, C. M. (2003). Sensory mediation of stimulus-driven attentional capture in multiple-cue displays. *Perception & Psychophysics, 65*, 925–938.

Wright, R. D., Richard, C. M., & McDonald, J. J. (1995). Neutral location cues and cost/benefit analysis of visual attention shifts. *Canadian Journal of Experimental Psychology, 49*, 540–548.

Wright, R. D., & Ward, L. M. (1994). Shifts of visual attention: An historical and methodological overview. *Canadian Journal of Experimental Psychology, 48*, 151–166.

Wright, R. D., & Ward, L. M. (1998). The control of visual attention. In R. D. Wright (Ed.), *Visual attention* (pp. 132–186). New York: Oxford University Press.

Wundt, W. (1912). *An introduction to psychology*. London: Allen & Unwin.

Wurtz, R. H., Goldberg, M. E., & Robinson, D. L. (1980). Behavioral modulation of visual responses in the monkey: Stimulus selection for attention and movement. *Progress in Psychobiology & Physiological Psychology, 9,* 43–83.

Yantis, S. (1988). On analog movements of visual attention. *Perception & Psychophysics, 43,* 203–206.

Yantis, S. (1992). Multielement visual tracking: Attention and perceptual organization. *Cognitive Psychology, 24,* 295–340.

Yantis, S. (1998). The control of visual attention. In H. Pashler (Ed.), *Attention* (pp. 223–256). East Sussex, UK: Psychology Press.

Yantis, S., & Egeth, H. E. (1999). On the distinction between visual salience and stimulus-driven attentional capture. *Journal of Experimental Psychology: Human Perception & Performance, 25,* 661–676.

Yantis, S., & Hillstrom, A. P. (1994). Stimulus-driven attentional capture: Evidence from equiluminant visual objects. *Journal of Experimental Psychology: Human Perception & Performance, 20,* 95–107.

Yantis, S., & Johnson, D. N. (1990). Mechanisms of attentional priority. *Journal of Experimental Psychology: Human Perception & Performance, 16,* 812–825.

Yantis, S., & Jones, E. (1991). Mechanisms of attentional selection: Temporally modulated priority tags. *Perception & Psychophysics, 50,* 166–178.

Yantis, S., & Jonides, J. (1984). Abrupt visual onsets and selective attention: Evidence from visual search. *Journal of Experimental Psychology: Human Perception & Performance, 10,* 601–621.

Yantis, S., & Jonides, J. (1990). Abrupt visual onsets and selective attention: Voluntary versus automatic allocation. *Journal Experimental Psychology: Human Perception & Performance, 16,* 121–134.

Yantis, S., & Jonides, J. (1996). Attentional capture by abrupt onsets: New perceptual objects or visual masking? *Journal Experimental Psychology: Human Perception & Performance, 22,* 1505–1513.

Yantis, S., Schwarzbach, J., Serences, J. T., Carlson, R. L., Steinmetz, M. A., Pekar, J. J., et al. (2002). Transient neural activity in human parietal cortex during spatial attention shifts. *Nature Neuroscience, 5,* 995–1002.

Yarbus, A. L. (1967). *Eye movements and vision.* New York: Plenum Press.

Yi, D. J., Kim, M. S., & Chun, M. M. (2003). Inhibition of return to occluded objects. *Perception & Psychophysics, 65,* 1222–1230.

Yingling, C. D., & Skinner, J. E. (1976). Selective regulation of thalamic sensory relay nuclei by nucleus reticularis thalami. *Electroencephalography & Clinical Neurophysiology, 41,* 476–482.

Yingling, C. D., & Skinner, J. E. (1977). Gating of thalamic input to cerebral cortex by nucleus reticularis thalami. In J. E. Desmedt (Ed.), *Attention, voluntary contraction and event-related cerebral potentials: Progress in clinical neurophysiology* (Vol. 1, pp. 70–96). Basel, Switzerland: Karger.

Young, L. R., & Sheena, D. (1975). Survey of eye movement recording methods. *Behavior Research Methods & Instrumentation, 7,* 397–429.

Zee, D. S., Optican, L. M., Cook, J. D., Robinson, D. A., & Engel, W. K. (1976). Slow saccades in spinocerebellar degeneration. *Archives of Neurology*, *33*, 243–251.

Zingale, C., & Kowler, E. (1987). Planning sequences of saccades. *Vision Research*, *27*, 1327–1341.

Zwiers, M. P., Van Opstal, A. J., & Paige, G. D. (2003). Plasticity in human sound localization induced by compressed spatial vision. *Nature Neuroscience*, *6*, 175–181.

Figure Credits

Figures 2.11, 3.10, 5.3, 5.14, 5.22, 6.3, and 7.33 © American Psychological Association.

Figures 2.14, 3.12, 5.16, 5.17, and 8.10 © Canadian Psychological Association.

Figures 2.12, 3.18, 3.25, 4.3, 4.8, 4.9, 4.13, 4.14, and 5.4 © Psychonomic Society.

Figure 6.13 © National Academy of Sciences USA.

Figure 7.34 © Public Library of Science.

Figures 1.1, 1.2, 1.3, 1.5, 2.7, 3.2, 3.16, 3.24, 3.26, 5.7, 5.8, 5.15, 5.18, 7.4, 7.6, and 7.15 © Arlene Surban / Viva Design.

Figures 4.5, 4.6, 4.7, 4.10, and 4.16 © Christian Richard.

Figure 8.15 © Hemera Images.

Index